高等学校英语专业系列教材
Textbook Series for Tertiary English Majors

高等学校英语专业系列教材 求知 STEM
Textbook Series for Tertiary English Majors

总 主 编 石 坚

副总主编 黄国文 陈建平 张绍杰 蒋洪新

编委单位（排名不分先后）

广东外语外贸大学	华南农业大学
广西大学	陕西师范大学
云南大学	武汉大学
中山大学	贵州大学
中南大学	贵州师范大学
四川大学	重庆大学
东北师范大学	重庆邮电大学
西安外国语大学	湖南师范大学
西安交通大学	……
华中师范大学	

策 划 张鸽盛 饶帮华 周小群

高等学校英语专业系列教材
Textbook Series for Tertiary English Majors

总 主 编: 石 坚
副总主编: 黄国文 陈建平 张绍杰 蒋洪新

美国文学选读
（第2版）

E

Selected Readings
of American Literature

张 强 编著

重庆大学出版社

内容提要

《美国文学选读》属于"求知高等学校英语专业系列教材",旨在为英语专业高年级学生、美国文学爱好者和研究者提供一片园地,用以学习和研究美国文学,提高文学素养,开拓视野,陶冶情操。本书是一本集历史、文本、批评理论于一书的文学选读教材。该书介绍了美国自殖民地时期到20世纪末的历史文化背景和各个时期的文艺思潮以及代表作家和他们的代表著作。本书按照美国文学的发展分九章,每章包括历史文化背景简介、作家作品选读、文学聚焦、阅读与欣赏和时代之声5个部分。精简而丰富的注释、引导自主性研究的思考题能有效帮助读者加深对所选作品的理解和鉴赏。

图书在版编目(CIP)数据

美国文学选读/张强编著. -- 2版. -- 重庆:重庆大学出版社,2020.9

求知高等学校英语专业系列教材

ISBN 978-7-5624-4382-7

Ⅰ.①美… Ⅱ.①张… Ⅲ.①英语—阅读教学—高等学校—教材 ②文学—作品—介绍—美国 Ⅳ.①H319.4:I

中国版本图书馆 CIP 数据核字(2012)第 262760 号

美国文学选读

(第2版)

张 强 编著

责任编辑:安 娜 版式设计:安 娜
责任校对:刘雯娜 责任印制:赵 晟

*

重庆大学出版社出版发行
出版人:饶帮华
社址:重庆市沙坪坝区大学城西路 21 号
邮编:401331
电话:(023)88617190 88617185(中小学)
传真:(023)88617186 88617166
网址:http://www.cqup.com.cn
邮箱:fxk@ cqup.com.cn(营销中心)
全国新华书店经销
重庆华林天美印务有限公司印刷

*

开本:787mm×1092mm 1/16 印张:19.75 字数:626 千
2008 年 4 月第 1 版 2020 年 9 月第 2 版 2020 年 9 月第 4 次印刷
ISBN 978-7-5624-4382-7 定价:59.00 元

总　序

　　进入 21 世纪，高等教育呈现快速扩展的趋势。我国高等教育从外延式发展过渡到内涵式发展后，"质量"已成为教育改革与发展的关键词。由国务院颁布的《国家中长期教育改革和发展规划纲要(2010—2020)》(以下简称《纲要》)明确要求狠抓本科教育人才培养存在的主要问题，厘清高等教育人才培养目标、理念、社会需求，制订本科教学培养模式、教学内容和方法、质量保障与评估机制，切实提高人才培养的质量。我国英语专业在过去的数十年中经过几代人的努力，取得了显著的成绩和长足的发展。特别是近年来随着经济社会的快速发展和对外交流活动的增多，"一带一路"倡议的提出和"讲好中国故事"的需要，英语专业的学科地位也随之大大提升，其规模目前发展得十分庞大。英语专业虽然经历了一个"跨越式""超常规"的发展历程，但规模化发展带来的培养质量下滑、专业建设和人才需求出现矛盾、毕业生就业面临巨大挑战等严峻的现实表明，英语专业的教育、教学与育人又到了一个不得不改的关键时刻。

　　《纲要》在强调狠抓培养质量的同时，也提出了培养"具有国际视野、通晓国际规则、能参与国际事务和国际竞争"人才的战略方针。基于这样的战略需求，外语专业教学指导委员会明确提出了人才"多元培养，分类卓越"的理念。基于这样的理念，即将颁布的《英语专业本科教学质量国家标准》(以下简称《国标》)对英语专业本科的现有课程设置提出新的改革思路：英语专业课程体系包括公共课程、专业核心课程、专业方向课程、实践环节和毕业论文(设计)五个部分；逐步压缩英语技能课程，用"内容依托式"课程替代传统的英语技能课程，系统建设语言学、文学、文化、国别研究等方面的专业课程。

　　自 2001 年开始，在重庆大学出版社的大力支持下，我们成立了由华中、华南、西南和西北以及东北地区的知名专家、学者和教学一线教师组成的"求知高等学校英语专业系列教材"编写组，以《高等学校英语专业英语教学大纲》为依据，将社会的需求与培养外语人才的全面发展紧密结合，注重英语作为一门专业的学科系统性和科学性，注重英语教学和习得的方法与规律，培养学生能力和育人并举，突出特色和系列教材的内在逻辑关系，反映了当时教学改革的新理念并具有前瞻性，建立了与英语专业课程配套的新教材体系。"求知高等学校英语专业系列教材"经历了 10 余年教学实践的锤炼，通过不断的修订来契合教学的发展变化，在教材的整体性和开放性、学生基本技能和实际应用能力的培养、学生的人文素质和跨文化意识的培养三方面有所突破。对于这套系列教材的开发建设工作，我们一直在探讨新的教学理念、模式，探索英语专业人才培养的新路子。今天，我们以《国标》为依据，回顾我们过去十多年在教学改革上所做的努力，我们欣慰地看到我们的方向是契合英语专业学科定位和发展的。随着《国标》指导思想的明确，为了适应英语专业学科课程设置的进一步调整，我们对"求知高等学校英语专业系列教材"进行了新一轮的建设工作。

全新的系列教材力求在以下方面有所创新：

第一，围绕听、说、读、写、译五种能力的培养来构建教材体系。在教材内容的总体设置上，颠覆以往"以课程定教材"的观念，不再让教材受制于刻板的课程设置体系，而是引入Program理念，根据《国标》中对学生的能力要求，针对某方面的具体能力编写对应的系列教材。读写和听说系列不再按照难度区分混合编排题材，而是依据文体或专业性质的自然划分，分门别类地专册呈现，便于教师在教学中根据实际需要搭配组合使用。例如，阅读教材分为小说类、散文类、新闻类等；口语教材分为基本表述、演讲、辩论等，并专题成册。

第二，将五种能力的提升融入人文素养的综合提升之中。坚持英语专业教育的人文本位，强调文化熏陶。在跨学科新专业不断涌现的背景下，盲目追求为每种新专业都专门编写一套教材，费时费力。最佳的做法是坚持英语专业核心教材的人文性，培养学生优秀的语言文化素养，并在此基础上依照专业要求填补相关知识上的空缺，形成新的教材配比模式和体系。

第三，以"3E"作为衡量教材质量的标准。教材的编写上，体现Engaging，Enabling，Enlightening的"3E"功能，强调教材的人文性与语言文化综合能力的培养，淡化技能解说。

第四，加入"微课""翻转课堂"等元素，便于课堂互动的开展。创新板块、活动的设计，相对减少灌输式的lecture，增加学生参与的seminar。

我们希望通过对这套系列教材的全新修订和建设，落实《国标》精神，继续推动高等学校英语专业教学改革，为提高英语专业人才的培养质量探索新的实践方法，为英语专业的学生拓展求知的新空间。

"求知高等学校英语专业系列教材"编委会
2017年6月

第 2 版序

一本教材能够出修订版，这对编者来说是件荣耀的事情，必须感谢使用者的厚爱。今后该书倘若能像《诺顿美国文学选集》那样一版再版，那就更美妙了。但是，作为《美国文学选读》的编者，我在修订完这本教程之后，却满怀愧疚之情，因为所谓的"修订"，包含了不少的错误订正，更包括少量拼写和语法错误的订正。另外我也颇为忐忑，因为即便在逐词逐句认真订正之后，也仍然不能保证教材中不再存在错误。因此，我诚挚地邀请读者与我一道在使用该教材的过程中认真审读，一旦发现问题不吝批评指正。

另外，修订的过程也是一个"瘦身"的过程。我根据教学过程中其他教师和学生以及自己的实际体会，对部分文学史知识的介绍和选读的章节加以删改，适当减少学生阅读文本的压力，以便他们将更多的时间和精力放在文学批评知识和方法的学习和运用上。与此同时，我也对文学批评概念和方法的介绍文字或删改，或调整，或添加，以期更有利于帮助使用者提高文学欣赏的素质和水平。

这本教材的第一版只选用了我初稿五分之二的内容，当时我有一种自己的孩子照相时被人遮住了眉眼的感觉。但当这本教材再次"瘦身"时，我已变得积极踊跃。只要这本教程保持了"集文史、文选和文学批评于一体"的特色，能够勾勒出美国文学的发展轮廓，激发读者对美国文学的欣赏情趣，帮助读者了解和掌握文学批评的基本概念和方法，这本为本科生准备的文学教程就很好地完成了自己的任务。

中国人学习语文往往从背记唐诗开始，英美的孩子也往往通过学习文学作品提高自己的文化水平。一个没听说过李白和杜甫的中国人谈不上有什么文化素质，而不了解马克·吐温、庞德和海明威等作家的英语专业学生也恐怕很难让人接受。文化交流缺少了文学的内容多半就不是一种"有文化档次"的交流，缺乏文学底蕴只怕连通俗艺术如音乐、电影和电视剧都难以充分欣赏。文学带给人们美的体验，但今天，我更希望有更多的人能跟我一道体验文学的美。

张　强

2019 年 6 月　写于武汉　剑桥铭邸

Preface

This course book of American literature has been written to meet the needs of English majors at the outset of their literary courses, primarily in the Mid-West of China. I hope, though, that it will also prove of interest to the general reader who feels that his reading would be enriched by a course book that puts the main outlines of American literature clearly before him and help him with the appreciation of American literature as well.

The very term American literature presupposes that there exists a work of literature that belongs to "America", many students thus, as I frequently meet in my classrooms, assume that a simple definition of literature and American literature would be given at the very beginning of the course. This is, of course, quite natural and necessary, but extremely difficult. For the term American literature, this course book will devote itself entirely to formulating *its* definition, and the concrete effort will begin with its very first chapter. As for the other term, though seemingly easier to be defined, it has been debated by writers, literary historians, and others for centuries without arriving at an uncontroversial definition. Some assume that literature is simply anything that is written, thereby declaring the pictographs like the *Walum Olum* ("Painted Record") by the Delaware (an Indian tribe) to be literary works along with *The Adventures of Huckleberry Finn* and *The Waste Land*. Derived from the Latin *liftera*, meaning "letter", the root meaning of the word *literature* refers primarily to the written word and seems to support this broad definition. Yet such a definition eliminates the important oral traditions upon which much of pre-colonial American literature is based. As we know, the traditional Indian mythologies, songs, and ritual chants were rarely written down. Most of these works of literature survived through oral tradition, each generation transmitting its literature to its young people by word of mouth.

To solve this problem, others choose to define *literature* as an art, thereby leaving open the question of its being written or oral. This definition further narrows its meaning, equating literature to works of the imagination or creative writing, that is, poetry, drama, fiction, and other imaginative writing. Although this narrowing of the definition seemingly simplifies what can and cannot be considered a literary work, the problem remains. This definition can be employed to explain why a textbook of American literature would include "Listen! Rain Approaches!", a ritual song of the Navaho (an Indian tribe) and "Calling One's Own", a song of the Ojibwa (another

Indian tribe) as literary pieces. Yet people may still feel confused why the compilers of the same book would not take in any of today's pop songs, say, "My Heart will Go On" (the theme song of the spectacular movie *Titanic*) though the song is as imaginative and creative a work as the Indian folklore. Specifying and narrowing the definition of literature to a "work of art" does not, then, immediately provide consistent rule about how to declare a text a "work of literature".

Whether one accepts the broad or narrow definition, he more than often agrees that a text must have certain peculiar qualities before it can be dubbed "literature". Those who hold this view believe that an artist's creation or secondary world often mirrors the author's primary world, the world in which the writer lives and moves and breathes. Because the primary world is highly structured, so must be the secondary world. To achieve this structure, the artist must create plot, character, setting, point of view, theme, symbols, and a host of other elements that work in a dynamic relationship to produce a literary work. Some would argue that it is the creation of these elements—how they are used and in what context—that determines whether a piece of writing is literature. It is in the hope of finding out the "literary" way of arranging these elements that this course book introduces and analyzes these elements in all its chapters and sections. The effort seems fruitless except that it becomes obvious that these elements are essential to a literary work: it seems that these elements can be used in any circumstance and in constantly changing ways.

Through this effort, however, we can see that it is generally accepted that American literature in the early period referred to the whole body of valued writing in society, whether factual or fictional: sermons, philosophy, history, speeches, essays and letters as well as poems and tales. But since 19th century, literature has meant the high skills of writing in the special context of high imagination. To give a shorter version, literature is an artistic form that is achieved through the use of language (The artistic use of other materials like pictures and musical components may work out other forms of art). In other words, literature can be defined as language artistically used to achieve identifiable literary qualities and to express significant messages. And literature is characterized with beauty of expression and form and with universality of intellectual and emotional appeal.

This definition of literature is still incomplete and debatable as what kind of language can be rendered as "artistically used" and who should make this judgment remain unsolved. Most critics, then, suggest that an examination of a text's total artistic situation would help us decide what constitutes literature. This total picture of the work involves such elements as the work itself (an examination of the secondary world created within the story), the artist, the primary world the work supposedly represents, and the audience or readers. Although readers and critics will emphasize one, two, or even three of these elements while de-emphasizing the others, such a consideration of a text's artistic situation immediately broadens the definition of literature from the concept that it is simply a written work that contains certain qualities to a definition that must include the dynamic interrelationship of the actual text and the readers. Perhaps, then, the literary competence of the readers themselves helps determine whether a work should be considered literature. If this is so, then a literary work may be more functional than ontological, its existence and therefore its value being determined by its readers and not by the work itself.

As the compiler of this course book, I am fully aware that the available space of this book does not allow me to take in all valued writings of American literature. Therefore, I have to select from a sea of American literary writings what I believe to be "great", "valuable", "timeless", and "universal"—what I think to have high artistic and literary values and therefore worthy of continued academic study. In other words, I am following the traditional practice of demonstrating the canon, or the core of American literature through my own choice. The canon has never been completely formalized, with particular writers being always either in or out (even Twain, Hemingway, and Eliot are not always "in" on American Literature courses). Of course, the range of what is counted as great remains restricted, and reliably reproduced, if only because teachers tend to teach what they are familiar with and publishers tend to publish what they know will sell. However, fashions always change, and the judgment of how a text might qualify for greatness, universality and value also changes with the age. In this case, I am fully confident that my choice will set up a canon that fits for today's English majors in China. I am a reader before I am a compiler. I share with the reader of this course book the right to determine the value of the work of American literature. For nearly twenty years, I have been studying and teaching English language and literature (American literature in particular), and I am now quite clear about the interest and preference of the teachers, publishers, and other professionals, abroad and at home. I trust myself in that I am among those who know both the distinguished scholar's requirements and the common reader's needs.

In writing a course book of this kind, with intention of an access to American literature as a whole, my main aim has been to acquaint the reader with the generally accepted view of the authors and periods under discussion as well as the history and the major works of American literature. Firstly, I have divided the history into nine periods to bring about a relatively clear outline of American literature. By far the greatest weight will fall on the 19th and the 20th century, where most of the reading of the beginning student and the general reader is likely to be. Secondly, many minor figures that would normally be expected to put in an appearance in a literary history are quietly forgotten, so that attention can be focused on the major figures. Thirdly, in treating these major writers, I have tried to concentrate on a few works, the ones that are most likely to be read, I hope, in this way, to increase the usefulness of the work to the student, but I hope, too, that this plan may give to the general reader a better grasp of the major writers through their most important works.

Of course, even teachers who choose to use this course book may occasionally hold different views. They may disagree on who are the major writers and what are the most important works. More than often they may interpret the selected texts differently. In this case, I suggest that the students should neither casually deny the insights of the teacher's views nor hastily doubt the value of the book. As has been mentioned, such thing as a formalized canon does not exist. Besides, the vitality of a literary work is attested to by the fact that it continues to provoke new explorations and new assessments, to provide new perspectives of meaning and invite new insights. While driving as hard as possible to make definitions, perform analyses, and sketch outlines, one should realize that absolute and total "truth" is certainly not possible in such matters and, if it were, perhaps not wholly desirable. I will never delude myself that this book is in any sense "definitive". Nor will I offer any precise prescription for its use. There are many ways to cut the cake. I have baked it; the teacher must cut it to suit himself. What I hope for is that what we have written will be regarded as a serious, thoughtful, and reasonably well-informed effort to make sense of a rich and various body of literature.

Zhang Qiang
Brighton & Hove, England
Autumn, 2017

How to Use This Course Book

Object and Objective

Selected Readings of American Literature is compiled primarily for the third-and fourth-year Chinese college students majoring in English language and literature, with the aim to give them a brief survey of American Literature from the colonial time to late 20th century. This is an attempt to introduce the basic concepts and methods of literary criticism as well as the history and the classical works of American Literature within a book, which mainly consists of two parts, namely, 1) introduction to the historical and cultural background, and 2) selected classical works. The compiler of this book hopes that the user will acquire the fundamental knowledge of literary criticism (mastering some basic concepts and methods of literary criticism) through the appreciation of the selected readings.

Academic Tasks and Hours

Selected Readings of American Literature involves American writers, selection of their masterpieces, the historical and cultural background of the age, and a few relevant concepts and methods of literary criticism. The teaching of this course book generally demands 36-40 academic hours. It is to be accomplished in one semester with 2 academic hours every week. To facilitate the further study and research of the English majors, the teaching of this course book should be carried out during the third academic year and the first semester of the fourth academic year. Providing the teacher maintains the clue of the development of American Literature, he may leave out some of the writers and their works in his teaching and ask the students to study the omitted parts after class.

Design

Selected Readings of American Literature consists of 9 chapters, thus dividing the history of American Literature into 9 periods. The chapters are all cut into the same basic pattern, which is made up of five sections:

1) **Introduction**: This is a summary overview of the historical and cultural background of the age. It focuses on the major literary thoughts and movements and compares the ideas and crafts of

the major writers of the period. This section will also mention the name of or even briefly introduce the life and career of some important or unique writers of the age concerned who will not be analyzed in the section of "Major Writers and Selected Readings".

2) **Major Writers and Selected Readings**: This section introduces the life and career of the major writers that belonged to the literary period and chooses excellent pieces from their writings for the students to read. Notes are provided to facilitate the understanding and questions are given for further discussion and thinking. The usual parts of this section are as follows.

  Life and Career: consisting of the profile, the major works, and the artistic features of the writer.

  Selected Readings: involving various literary styles such as poetry, essay, fiction, and drama, presenting the full text of relatively short works and excerptions of relatively long ones.

  Annotation: providing background knowledge of the selected readings, explanation of the key and difficult expressions, and definition and brief analysis of the relevant rhetorical devices.

  Questions: including questions for recalling, interpretation, comparison, and discussion.

3) **Literary Focus**: This section aims at helping the reader deepen his understanding and expand his horizons by introducing and exploring the relevant artistic thoughts and movements as well as a few popular literary theories.

4) **Reading for Appreciation**

This section is based on the assumption that "reading literature offers us an experience" and thus makes an attempt to offer a few methods of reading literature actively to make the words come alive and further the appreciation of the text.

5) **Voice of the Age**

This is a summary overview of the spirit of the age, supported by quotations from the selected readings.

Dec. 28,2019

《美国文学选读》使用说明

教学对象与目标

　　《美国文学选读》适用于英语语言文学专业三、四年级学生。本教程主要提供自殖民地时期至 20 世纪后期美国文学简要的历史文化背景和经典作品选读。编者希望读者能通过对相关选读材料的欣赏获取文学批评的基础知识,掌握一些文学批评的基本概念和方法。

教学任务及教学时数

　　《美国文学选读》前后共选录 35 位美国作家及其部分作品,同时涉及有关的文学史及文艺批评常识,共需 36～40 学时。以周学时 2 计,可一学期完成教学任务。开课时间宜安排在大三上学期至大四上学期之间,以有利于专业学生进一步的升学和深造。授课老师在不影响对美国文学发展的整体理解的前提下,可根据具体情况删减部分作家作品的讲授。

框架结构及主要内容

　　《美国文学选读》分 9 章,将美国文学划分成 9 个时期。每章都包括历史文化背景简介、作家作品选读、文学聚焦、阅读与欣赏和时代之声五个部分:

1) 历史文化背景简介:简要介绍该时期大致的社会文化背景、主要文艺思潮以及重要作家创作思想和技巧的异同等。对相关时期一些较为重要或有特色但未被收入"作家作品选读"部分的作家,该部分会对其生平和艺术特色加以简要介绍。

2) 作家作品选读:主要包括作家生平与创作、经典作品选读、注解和问题等部分。
   生平与创作:简要介绍作家生平、代表作、该作家创作的主要艺术特色等。
   经典作品选读:包括诗歌、散文、小说和戏剧等形式;较短的篇章完整的收录,较长的篇章则为选段。
   注解:对篇章的创作背景、关键词、疑难表达法、修辞与创作手法等加以注释,帮助理解。
   问题:包括理解、比较和探讨等类型的问题。

3) 文学聚焦:通过对相关艺术思潮、文艺运动和常见文艺理论的介绍,加深对作品的理解,拓展读者的批评视野。

4) 阅读与欣赏:基于"文学阅读为我们提供一种生活体验"的理解,尝试提供一些积极主动阅读文学作品的方法以促进对经典作品的分析和欣赏。

5) 时代之声:结合"作家作品选读"部分的文本材料分析介绍相关的时代精神。

2019 年 12 月 28 日

Contents

Chapter 1

EARLY AMERICA TO 1750

INTRODUCTION

American Beginnings

America has always been a land of beginnings. After Europeans "discovered" America in the 15th century, the mysterious New World became for many people a genuine hope of a new life, an escape from poverty and persecution, a chance to start again. We can say that, as a nation, America begins with that hope. When, however, does American *literature* begin?

American literature begins with American experiences. Long before the first colonists arrived, before Christopher Columbus, before the Northman who "found" America about the year 1,000, Native Americans lived here. Each tribe's literature was tightly woven into the fabric of daily life and reflected the unmistakably American experience of living with the land. Another kind of experience, one filled with fear and excitement, found its expression in the reports that Columbus and other explorers sent home in Spanish, French, and English. In addition, the journals of the people who lived and died in the New England wilderness told unforgettable tales of hard and sometimes heartbreaking experiences of those early years.

Experience, then, is the key to early American literature. The New World provided a great variety of experiences, and these experiences demanded a wide variety of expressions by an even wider variety of early American writers. These writers included John Smith, who spent only about two-and-one-half years on the American continent. They included Jonathan Edwards and William Byrd, who thought of themselves as British subjects, never suspecting a revolution that would create a United States of America with a literature of its own. American Indians, explorers, Pilgrims, Puritan ministers, frontier wives, plantation owners—they were all the creators of the first American literature.

American Indian Literature

When European explorers first set foot on the New World, they encountered people who had been native to the Americas for thousands of years. Because the Europeans thought they had landed in the "Indies", or the Far East, they called the natives Indians. No one name, however, would adequately describe the variety of cultures that flourished from one end of America to other.

Generation after generation these Native Americans had told stories, sung songs, and recited groups of tales that embodied their past and told of their close relationship with the natural world. Their mythologies, songs, and ritual chants were rarely written down. Most of the American Indian works of literature survived through oral tradition—the process of passing on literature by word of mouth. For an Indian group, as most other primitive tribes in the world, if a prayer or a history or a myth was important, someone in the group had to remember it. Otherwise, it would fade into oblivion. Its power and its pleasure would be lost. Traditionally, it was the tribal poet whose job it was to remember the tribe's history, its line of leaders, its victories, its gods and rituals. In a sense the first poets were memory banks, able to call up the treasure of the tribe's past whenever asked to do so. To make recitation surer, the poets used certain formulas and memory tricks. Generation after generation numerous poets transmitted the group's literature by word of mouth and improved the formulas and tricks. The result is a literature that is timeless, a literature created by no one author. It is a literature made by its people.

"Listen! Rain Approaches!" was among the ritual songs of the Navaho, a large and varied Indian group who settled in the American Southwest, where their culture still flourishes. In today's English, the song sings, "Truly in the East / The white bean / And the great corn plant / Are tied with the white lightning. / Listen! It approaches! / The voice of the bluebird is heard. // Truly in the East / The white bean / And the great squash / Are tied with the rainbow. / Listen! It approaches! / The voice of the bluebird is heard." An agricultural people, the Navaho composed such songs to celebrate the growth of crops and to control the coming of the vitally important rains. The repetition of words and lines (sometimes with variations) was characteristic of Native American ritual chants and songs. Imagine this song as part of a ceremony including dancing, music, and elaborate costumes.

"Calling One's Own" was a song of the Ojibwa, also known as the Chippewa, a group of American Indians who lived around the Great Lakes and throughout the Great Plains. It was a song that sounded much like the love songs of English-language poetry. The imagery of the song was drawn from the natural world, showing the close relationship between the Ojibwa and the landscape of waters, flowers, trees, and skies that surrounded them. In today's English, it reads, "Awake! Flower of the forest, sky treading bird of the prairie. // Awake! Awake! Wonderful fawn-eyed One. / When you look upon me I am satisfied, as flowers that drink dew. / The breath of your mouth is the fragrance of flowers in the morning, / Your breath is their fragrance at evening in the moon of fading-leaf. // Do not the red streams of my veins run toward you / As forest streams to the sun in the moon of bright nights? / When you are beside me my heart sings; a branch it is, dancing, / Dancing before the Wind spirit in the moon of strawberries. // When you frown upon me, beloved, my heart grows dark? / A shining river the shadows of clouds darken; / Then with your smiles comes the sun and makes to look like gold / Furrows the cold wind drew in the water's face. // Myself! Behold me! Blood of my beating heart. / Earth smiles—the waters smile—even the sky of clouds smiles—but I, / I lose the way of smiling when you are not near. / Awake! Awake! My beloved."

However, some tribes of the American Indians, such as the Delaware (a people who lived in the areas we now call New Jersey, Delaware, and parts of New York and Pennsylvania), did develop forms of writing (which was not based on a phonetic representation of sounds, as English is, but upon a kind of picture writing). The *Walum Olum* (*Painted Record*), for example, is a creation myth of the Delaware. It is a chronicle of the beginning of the world and the origins of the Delaware people in the far Northwest. Through this myth the Delaware kept in touch with their own past and placed themselves within a framework of history as they remembered it.

The Puritans

As a matter of fact, most course books on American literature begin with the Puritan writing. The term "Puritan" first began as a taunt or insult applied by traditional Anglicans to those who criticized or wished to "purify" the Church of England. A Puritan of the 16th and 17th century England was any person seeking "purity" of worship and doctrine, as well as personal and group piety. Although the word was often applied loosely, "Puritan" refers to two distinct groups: "separating" Puritans, such as the Plymouth colonists, who believed that the Church of England was corrupt and that true Christians must separate themselves from it; and non-separating Puritans, such as the colonists who settled the Massachusetts Bay Colony, who believed in reform but not separation.

Several beliefs differentiated Puritans from other Christians. First of all, The Puritans believed in an all-powerful God who freely granted to his "Saints" the gift of grace. Grace was a complicated matter for the Puritans, but it can be described as the spirit that would guarantee salvation—eternal happiness with God. In their daily lives the Puritans wanted to demonstrate at every moment that they possessed grace or that they were worthy of it.

For the Puritans everything was, ideally, aimed at personal salvation and the building of a new, God-centered society. They were willing to risk their lives for such a world. It would be a place where they would practice their religion freely and raise their children free from the frivolities and temptations of the Old World. As we listen to their language, which refers to the Bible easily and frequently, their passionate desire to establish a New Jerusalem is clear. In their dreams they would build the City of God on earth.

Puritans believed that belief in Jesus and participation in the sacraments could not alone result in one's salvation; one cannot choose salvation, for that is the privilege of God alone. All features of salvation are determined by God's sovereignty, including choosing those who will be saved and those who will receive God's irresistible grace. The Puritans distinguished between "justification", or the gift of God's grace given to the elect, and "sanctification", the holy behavior that supposedly resulted when an individual had been saved; according to *The English Literatures of America*, "Sanctification is evidence of salvation, but does not cause it."

Many Puritans immigrated to North America in the 1620s—1640s because they believed that the Church of England was beyond reform. However, most Puritans in both England and New England were non-separatists. They continued to profess their allegiance to the Church of England despite their dissent from Church leadership and practices.

Life for the average Puritan in the New World was essentially a life of work and prayer. In the pursuit of virtue, the Puritans passed laws against many activities that would distract good souls from their real task. Certain "delights" were forbidden, such as bowling, Maypole dancing, gambling, attending plays, and "unprofitable" hunting (For someone who was a bad shot, it was a sin to waste time and ammunition). Virtue was learned primarily at home, where the father had complete authority. The family was the center of activity; the aged were always cared for; young people were apprenticed to learn trades the community needed.

Yet the Puritan life was not a fanatically austere one. The Puritans worked long and hard under extremely difficult conditions so that their farms and trading enterprises would prosper. In fact, they believed prosperity was a sign of election, or God's special favor. Nevertheless, they did not turn away from eating and drinking, the pleasure of social gatherings, and the joys of a close family life. They simply kept reminding themselves that their souls were the constant battlegrounds of God and Satan and that every act and thought had to be judged according to whether or not it truly glorified God.

Some suggested that it is a "Puritan spirit" in the United States' political culture that creates a tendency to oppose things such as alcohol and open sexuality. Historically speaking, the Puritans were not opposed to drinking alcohol in moderation or to enjoying their sexuality within the bounds of marriage as a gift from God. In fact, spouses (in practice, only females) were disciplined if they did not perform their sexual marital duties, in accordance with Corinthians 7 and other biblical passages. Because of these beliefs, they did publicly punish drunkenness and sexual relations outside of marriage.

Writing was an important part of Puritan life; it was often an extension of religion. In fact, the first book published in America was the *Bay Psalm Book* (1640), a translation of the biblical Psalms. Many Puritans kept journals to help them carefully examine their spiritual lives. These journals and diaries, detailed and intense, were usually meant to be purely private writings. Even when they did write for a public, however, the Puritans wrote to instruct others or to testify to their experience of divine grace; they wrote spiritual autobiographies.

Puritan writings, in other words, were practical. The writers were not merely providing entertainment; they were deeply involved with their spiritual selves and attempts to improve them. They wrote no fiction, nor did they even approve of reading fiction, and they wrote no plays because they disapproved violently of the theater. Their writings consisted largely of journals, sermons, hymns, histories, and poems.

Just as the Puritans sought to purify their lives, so too they sought to purify their language. Everything they wrote avoided Ornate Style, the complicated and decorative style of their European contemporaries. They preferred to write in what they called Plain Style, even as they strove for plainness in their architecture, clothing, food, and household furnishings. Plain Style was meant simply to communicate ideas as clearly as possible. Writing was not a way of showing off cleverness or learning but a way of serving God and the community. The whole Puritan way of life is summed up in William Bradford's desire to tell the story of Plymouth Plantation in "a plain style, with singular regard unto the simple truth in all things."

Early Southern Literature

In its simplest form, early southern literature consists of writing about the life of American South, which, begun in 1607 with Jamestown, Virginia, developed quite differently from that in New England. Unlike the Puritans, who lived fairly closely together, much of the southern population lived on farms or plantations that were distant from one another. Often like little colonies of their own, these plantations were largely self-sufficient. The larger estates were owned and operated by wealthy and well-educated colonists who developed a more social and outgoing way of life than the Puritans.

Early southern literature reflects this experience. Though most writers were hardworking tradespeople, artisans, small farmers, indentured servants, and slaves, the sophisticated gentleman and lady dominated the sense of the early southern colonies. For the most part, these gentlemen and ladies carried on correspondence with friends who often lived at great distances from them, as well as with family and friends back in England. Many of the southern colonists belonged to the Church of England, the church that the Puritans had attempted to reform, and their ties with the Old World were stronger. As a result, they did not have the reasons the Puritans had to create a literature of their own.

Still, in their letters, journals, public reports, and "histories", southern writers recorded the details of their experience. During the 17th and 18th centuries, the southern English colonists produced a number of notable works. Two of the most famous were early memoirs of Virginia: the account of Captain John Smith (1580—1631) about the founding of Jamestown in the early decades of the 17th century, and the secret plantation diary of William Byrd Ⅱ (1674—1744) kept in the early 18th century. Both sets of recollections are critical documents in early southern history.

In addition to the geographical component of southern literature, certain themes have appeared because of the similar histories of the southern states. The conservative culture in the south has also produced a strong focus within southern literature on the significance of family, religion, community in one's personal and social life, the use of the southern dialect, and a strong sense of "place." The south's troubled history with racial issues also continually appears in its literature. As a result, one can hear at once, in the voice of a man like William Byrd, a strong contrast between the more worldly and witty southerners and the intense, self-examining Puritans. This contrast, too, is an important part of the American experience.

William Bradford (1590—1657)

William Bradford was a leader of the separatist settlers of the Plymouth Colony in Massachusetts, and was elected Governor of the Colony for 15 two-year terms. He was the second signer and primary architect of the Mayflower Compact in Provincetown Harbor. He also wrote another compact after the first one had been destroyed. Bradford is credited as the first to proclaim what popular American culture now views as the first Thanksgiving.

Unlike those "Reformers", Bradford and his Separatist group saw no compromise with the English church and suffered heavy persecution for their beliefs. They fled to Holland and later decided to establish their own colony in Virginia. Bradford and the Pilgrims sailed from Leyden in Holland in 1620, but because of storms they never reached Virginia. Instead, they landed their ship *Mayflower* at Plymouth on the coast of Massachusetts. In the Mayflower Compact, an agreement they signed before they left the ship, they decided to form a government and follow an elected leader. When their first governor, John Carver, died in April 1621, the people chose Bradford to take his place. In 1630 he began writing *Of Plymouth Plantation*, his history of these early Americans and their long geographical and spiritual pilgrimage.

Bradford's brilliant chronicle conveys not only facts but also feelings because the writer imaginatively projects himself and his readers into the experience of each moment. It makes a personal story out of the voyage, the settlement, and the grim realities of "the starving time". Through the chronicle, we share the struggle, the fears, and the victories over the elements, as well as the gradual changes that overtake the colony as people move away, as children grow up, as the original vision fades.

In the chronicle the writer always keeps sight of the signs of God's judgment and providence. He sees the signs everywhere, so that, for example, the Indian interpreter Squanto becomes "an instrument sent of God for their good." For the writer the Puritans' flight from Europe is guided by God in the same way as the Israelites' exodus from Egypt.

The chronicle is written in the Puritan plain style, almost without any metaphors or decorative expressions. Of course there is no reason for Bradford to decorate a chronicle of events so charged with excitement, danger, and emotion. Bradford's plain language reflects his belief that everything in the Puritan way of life should have the power of simplicity. To borrow from John Cotton (a great Puritan minister) , " God's altar needs no polishing. "

■ Selected Reading

from *Of Plymouth Plantation*

(Arrival)

… after long beating at sea they fell with that land which is called Cape Cod; the which being made and certainly known to be it, they were not a little joyful…

Being thus arrived in a good harbor, and brought safe to land, they fell upon their knees and blessed the God of Heaven who had brought them over the vast and furious ocean, and delivered them from all the perils and miseries thereof, again to set their feet on the firm and stable earth, their proper element…

But here I cannot but stay and make a pause, and stand half amazed at this poor people's present condition; and so I think—will the reader, too, when he well considers the same. Being thus passed the vast ocean, and a sea of troubles before in their preparation (as may be remembered by that which went before), they had now no friends to welcome them nor inns to entertain or refresh their weatherbeaten bodies; no houses or much less towns to repair to, to seek for succor. It is recorded in Scripture as a mercy to the Apostle and his shipwrecked company, that the barbarians showed them no small kindness in refreshing them, but these savage barbarians, when they met with them (as after will appear) were readier to fill their sides full of arrows than otherwise. And for the season it was winter, and they that know the winters of that country know them to be sharp and violent, and subject to cruel and fierce storms, dangerous to travel to known places, much more to search an unknown coast. Besides, what could they see but a hideous and desolate wilderness, full of wild beasts and wild men—and what multitudes there might be of them they knew not. Neither could they, as it were, go up to the top of Pisgah to view from this wilderness a more goodly country to feed their hopes; for which way soever they turned their eyes (save upward to the heavens) they could have little solace or content in respect of any outward objects. For summer being done, all things stand upon them with a weatherbeaten face, and the whole country, full of woods and thickets, represented a wild and savage hue. If they looked behind them, there was the mighty ocean which they had passed and was now as a main bar and gulf to separate them from all the civil parts of the world. If it be said they had a ship to succor them, it is true; but what heard they daily from the Master and company? But that with speed they should look out a place (with their shallop [1]) where they would be, at some near distance; for the season was such as he would not stir from thence till a safe harbor was discovered

---

1　**shallop**: small open boat with oars or sail.

by them, where they would be and he might go without danger; and that victuals consumed apace but he must and would keep sufficient for themselves and their return. Yea, it was muttered by some that if they got not a place in time, they would turn them and their goods ashore and leave them. Let it also be considered what weak hopes of supply and succor they left behind them that might bear up their minds in this sad condition and trials they were under; and they could not but be very small. It is true, indeed, the affections and love of their brethren at Leyden was cordial and entire towards them, but they had little power to help them or themselves.

What could now sustain them but the Spirit of God and His grace? May not and ought not the children of these fathers rightly say: "Our fathers were Englishmen which came over this great ocean, and were ready to perish in this wilderness; but they cried unto the Lord, and He heard their voice and looked on their adversity," etc. "Let them therefore praise the Lord, because He is good: and His mercies endure forever." "Yea, let them which have been redeemed of the Lord, show how He hath delivered them from the hand of the oppressor. When they wandered in the desert wilderness out of the way, and found no city to dwell in, both hungry and thirsty, their soul was overwhelmed in them. Let them confess before the Lord His lovingkindness and His wonderful works before the sons of men."

(The Starving Time)

But that which was most sad and lamentable was that in two or three months' time half of their company died, especially in January and February, being the depth of winter, and wanting houses and other comforts; being infected with the scurvy and other diseases which this long voyage and their inaccommodate condition had brought upon them. So as there died some times two or three of a day in the foresaid time, that of 100 and odd persons, scarce fifty remained. And of these, in the time of most distress, there was but six or seven sound persons who to their great commendations, be it spoken, spared no pains night nor day, but with abundance of toil and hazard of their own health, fetched them wood, made them fires, dressed them meat, made their beds, washed their loathsome clothes, clothed and unclothed them. In a word, did all the homely and necessary offices for them which dainty and queasy stomachs cannot endure to hear named; and all this willingly and cheerfully, without any grudging in the least, showing herein their true love unto their friends and brethren; a rare example and worthy to be remembered. Two of these seven were Mr. William Brewster, their reverend Elder, and Myles Standish, their Captain and military commander, unto whom myself and many others were much beholden in our low and sick condition. And yet the Lord so upheld these persons as in this general calamity they were not at all infected either with sickness or lameness. And what I have said of these I may say of many others who died in this general visitation, and others yet living; that whilst they had health, yea, or any strength continuing, they were not wanting to any that had need of them. And I doubt not but their recompense is with the Lord.

(Compact with the Indians)

All this while the Indians came skulking about them, and would sometimes show themselves aloof off, but when any approached near them, they would run away; and once they stole away their tools where they had been at work and were gone to dinner. But about the 16th of March, a certain Indian came boldly amongst them and spoke to them in broken English, which they could well understand but marveled at it. At length they understood by discourse with him that he was not of these parts, but belonged to the eastern parts where some English ships came to fish, with whom he was acquainted and could name sundry of them by their names, amongst whom he had got his language. He became profitable to them in acquainting them with many things concerning the state of the country in the east parts where he lived, which "was afterwards profitable unto them; as also of the people here, of their names, number and strength, of their situation and distance from this place, and who was chief amongst them. His name was Samoset. He told them also of another Indian whose name was Squanto, a native of this place, who had been in England and could speak better English than himself.

Being, after some time of entertainment and gifts, dismissed, a while after he came again, and five more with him, and they brought again all the tools that were stolen away before, and made way for the coming of their great Sachem, called Massasoit. Who, about four or five days after, came with the chief of his friends and other attendance, with the aforesaid Squanto. With whom, after friendly entertainment and some gifts given him, they made a peace with him (which hath now continued this twenty-four years) in these terms:

1. That neither he nor any of his should injure or do hurt to any of their people.

2. That if any of his did hurt to any of theirs, he should send the offender, that they might punish him.

3. That if anything were taken away from any of theirs, he should cause it to be restored; and they should do the like to his.

4. If any did unjustly war against him, they would aid him; if any did war against them, he should aid them.

5. He should send to his neighbors confederates to certify them of this, that they might not wrong them, but might be likewise comprised in the conditions of peace.

6. That when their men came to them, they should leave their bows and arrows behind them.

After these things he returned to his place called Sowams, some forty miles from this place, but Squanto continued with them and was their interpreter and was a special instrument sent of God for their good beyond their expectation. He directed them how to set their corn, where to take fish, and to procure other commodities, and was also their pilot to bring them to unknown places for their profit, and never left them till he died.

■ Study Questions

1. What was the Pilgrims' first action upon landing in the New World?

2. Identify four specific hardships that the Pilgrims faced in the New World, according to Paragraph 3. What sustained them, according to Paragraph 4?

3. What caused the starving time? How did the Pilgrims survive it?

4. How did the Indians act at first, according to Bradford? What did they do after "friendly entertainment and some gifts"? What information did Samoset and Squanto provide for the Pilgrims?

5. State two dominant characteristics of the *Mayflower* Pilgrims as they are pictured by Bradford during their first months of hardship in America.

6. What words and statements by Bradford create a picture of the Pilgrims as God's "chosen people"?

7. Describe Bradford's initial attitude towards the Indians and his attitude in the section "Compact with the Indians." How has Bradford changed? What seems to have caused the change?

8. Judging from Bradford's account, what qualities do you think would be necessary for a man or woman to survive for any length of time in the American wilderness? What attitudes brought from Europe had to be abandoned?

Anne Bradstreet (1612—1672)

Anne Dudley Bradstreet, one of the most important figures in the history of American Literature, was New England's first published poet. Her work met with a positive reception in both the Old World and the New World.

Born in Northampton, England, in 1612, Anne was the daughter of Thomas Dudley, the steward of the Earl of Lincoln estate. Anne lived in a time when the amount of education that a woman received was little to none. However, though she did not attend school, Anne was privileged enough to receive her education from eight tutors and from her father, who was always more than willing to teach her something new. Thanks to her father's position, she had unlimited access to the great library of the manor, where she became exposed to the writings of many well known authors. In 1628, she married Simon Bradstreet, her father's assistant.

Anne Bradstreet came to the Massachusetts Bay Colony with her husband and her parents in 1630. The Bradstreets settled in the frontier village of Andover, where Anne, under difficult conditions that tried her faith, maintained a household and raised 8 children. She had to defend her right to compose verses, for many Puritans, who did not disapprove of poetry itself, wondered if a woman should write it. Anne Bradstreet was bothered by the cultural bias in her time—that a woman's place was in the home attending to the family and her husband's needs. Women were often considered intellectual inferiors and for this reason, critics believed that Anne Bradstreet stole her ideas for her poems from men. Her poems were severely criticized, receiving rather different criticism than that of her male counterparts. When her first publication—also the first book written by a woman to be published in the United States—The Tenth Muse Lately Sprung Up in America was published in England in 1650, the idea that she was a virtuous women had to be stressed.

Bradstreet's finest poems as well as those collected in The Tenth Muse Lately Sprung Up in America are those closest to her personal experience as a Puritan wife and mother living on the edge of the wilderness. It is also a document of the struggles of a Puritan wife against the hardships of New England colonial life, and in some way a testament to the women's plight of the age. Like other Puritan works, Bradstreet's poems show similarities between the domestic details of daily life and the spiritual details of her religious life. For Bradstreet the everyday and the everlasting are simply two sides of the same experience.

In a poem called *Upon the Burning of Our House* Bradstreet records both her earthly sorrow and the faith that sustains her: "Thou hast a house on high erect, / Framed by that mighty Architect, / With glory richly furnished, / Stands permanent though this be fled. / ... / The world no longer let me love, / My hope and treasure lies above."

Similarly, in her tender poem *To My Dear and Loving Husband* Bradstreet places her earthly married life within the framework of eternity. Anne Bradstreet is not often accepted as an innovative poet, but her directness and her sincerity are moving.

■ Selected Reading

To My Dear and Loving Husband

If ever two were one, then surely we,

If ever man were loved by wife, then thee;

If ever wife was happy in a man,

Compare with me, ye women, if you can.

I prize thy love more than whole mines of gold

Or all the riches that the East doth hold.

My love is such that rivers cannot quench,

Nor ought but love from thee, give recompense.

Thy love is such I can no way repay.

The heavens reward thee manifold, I pray.

Then while we live, in love let's so perservere

That when we live no more, we may live ever.

■ Study Questions

1. What does the poet prize "more than whole mines of gold"? What is it that "rivers cannot quench"?

2. Which words tell us what will happen when she and her husband die if they persevere in love while they live?

3. What does Bradstreet actually mean by the seeming paradox in the last line about living "no more" yet living "ever"?

4. Besides declaring her human love for her husband during her earthly marriage, what other typical Puritan concern does this poem celebrate in Lines 9-10?

LITERARY FOCUS

Allusions: The Use of the Bible

For centuries English-speaking writers and their readers knew the Bible very well. After 1611 the version they knew best was the King James translation, which has had a powerful influence on English and American literature. Poets, storytellers, and orators referred to the Bible frequently, and phrases from the King James Version became part of everyone's vocabulary. The Puritans, especially, based their religion directly on a reading of the Bible, and their writers naturally made allusions to it.

An **allusion** is a short reference to a person, a place, an event, or another work of literature. When Bradford alludes to the "top of Pisgah", he knows his audience will understand that he is referring to the mountain from which Moses saw the Promised Land.

Writers use allusions to extend the meanings of their works. Sometimes they want to show that a particular experience is also a universal experience. Sometimes they want to remind us of connections that we might not have thought of ourselves.

■ Thinking About Allusions

• Find the two biblical allusions in Bradford's third paragraph. Why were these specific references appropriate to the experience of the Pilgrims?

READING FOR APPRECIATION

The Historical Imagination

Reading literature offers us an *experience*, but to have the experience, to make the words come alive, we must read actively. We must use our imaginations, participating with the writer in producing or reproducing the experience of the literature. That experience, which is never exactly the same for all readers, or for the same reader on all occasions, is only a potential until we ourselves release it.

One kind of imagination we must bring to literature is *historical*. After all, why should we limit ourselves to the experiences of the 20th century? In many ways, we share the same basic values and emotions that people had in Homer's Greece, Shakespeare's London, and Bradford's Plymouth. Yet at other times and in other places, people also had different ideas and feelings. As we learn to read literature with an active historical imagination, we release ourselves into those other times and places, illuminating our own time and our own place.

We certainly do not have to *agree* with the worldviews of other people, or with the opinions of any particular writer, in order to share imaginatively the experience of literature. We do not have to agree with the beliefs of William Bradford to feel the power and strength that the puritans picked up from the biblical allusions. We do not have to be a Puritan poet like Anne Bradstreet to know what it means to love someone. Yet the poet's expression of what it means to her helps us to see what it can mean to us. In just such a way, by using our historical imagination, we can make the past speak to us through literature.

Literature is not always an escape from our own time, nor should it be. It offers us the pleasure of learning about ourselves by learning about others. How are we different, say, from the Puritans of 17th-century New England? What do they still have to offer us in the way of wisdom? How can they, as people, expand our sense of the complexity and variety of human nature?

Reading the Puritan writers is not easy. They challenge even today's Americans to penetrate their time and place, their minds and hearts. The task is difficult not simply because the language has changed or because the Puritans did not share the modern ideas. The task is difficult because the past *is* the past. With the aid of the historical imagination, however, we can make the past live again.

VOICE OF THE AGE

Natural Paradise

The famous writers of this period have at least one thing in common: they all lived and wrote at a time when the New World was truly new. A place of possibility, America seemed to provide a second birth to anyone who desired to build a community, establish a church, gain fame and honor, or make a new life.

The initial awe and excitement of the early Americans, however, always seemed to focus on the land itself—an enormous garden, an untouched natural paradise. Words like the following, all examples of the American voices one might hear during this period, are a part of that myth of the American Eden:

Columbus: *During that time I walked among the trees which was the most beautiful thing which I had ever seen.*

Smith: *Here nature and liberty afford us that freely which in England we want...*

Edwards: *Hence the reason why almost all men, and those that seem to be very miserable, love life—because they cannot bear to lose sight of such a beautiful and lovely world.*

Columbus was writing of the Caribbean; Smith, New England; Edwards, the whole world. Yet they were all inspired by the American abundance before their eyes. They saw in America a dream coming true, a vision made real. As this book continues, we will hear other American writers voicing these same ideas and emotions. The abundant land is one American theme throughout her entire literary history.

Chapter 2

REASON AND REVOLUTION
1750—1800

INTRODUCTION

A New Nation

On April 19, 1775, a group of American Minutemen faced British redcoats across the little bridge outside the village of Concord, Massachusetts. Suddenly someone—no one knows who—fired a musket shot, "the shot heard round the world", and the American Revolution began. That shot was the climax of years of frustration, anger, and preparation among the colonists.

By 1763, Great Britain possessed a vast holding in North America. In addition to the 13 colonies, 16 smaller colonies were ruled directly by royal governors. In 1765, the colonists still considered themselves loyal subjects of the British Crown, with the same historic rights and obligations as subjects in Britain. The British government determined to tax its American possessions, primarily to help pay for its defense of North America from the French in the Seven Years War. The problem for many American colonists was not that taxes were high, but that the colonies were not consulted about the new taxes, as they had no representation in Parliament. The phrase "No Taxation without Representation" became popular in many American circles. London argued that the Americans were represented "virtually"; but most Americans rejected the theory that men in London, who knew nothing about their needs and conditions, could represent them.

As a matter of fact, by the mid-18th century colonial America was no longer a group of scattered, struggling settlements. It was a series of neighboring, flourishing colonies with rapidly expanding, mixed populations. The word "state", which suggests an independent government, was beginning to replace "colony" in the people's thinking—an important sign of the political trend. The people of these states were vigorous, the natural resources were rich and plentiful, and native industries were sprouting everywhere. Boston remained a major center of thought, but Philadelphia, New York, and the state of Virginia emerged as equal sources of political and literary talent.

The growth, particularly the industrial growth, led to intense strain with England. The British government did not want colonial industries competing with those in England and it wanted the colonies to remain politically and economically dependent on the mother country. It took a series of measures to insure this dependence. The Stamp Act in 1765 required that the colonists buy special stamps for newspapers, licenses, pamphlets, and many other documents. The Quartering Act in 1765 forced colonists to feed and house British soldiers in their own homes. The Townshend Acts in 1767 taxed tea, glass, lead, and paper. When some of the colonial assemblies refused to abide by the new laws, the British government declared those assemblies "dissolved". Violence was not far away: the Boston Massacre erupted in 1770 when British troops fired on a taunting mob. In 1773 the British Parliament insisted again on its right and power to tax Americans. The tax on tea became a symbol, and the famous Boston Tea Party became a symbol too—a symbol of American resistance—as colonists dressed as Indians dumped a shipment of British tea into Boston Harbor.

Britain replied with the Intolerable Acts of 1774, designed to punish Massachusetts for the Boston Tea Party. Many more rights that had been granted to the colonists in their charters were revoked. Then, when Paul Revere spotted the redcoats on their way to seize American arms at Concord, Americans responded with force.

Yet it was not until January 1776 that a widely heard public voice demanded complete separation from England. The voice was that of Thomas Paine, whose pamphlet *Common Sense*, with its heated language, increased the growing demand for separation. It pointed the way toward the Declaration of Independence in July. If ever writing affected public affairs, *Common Sense* did. We will not be surprised to find that most American literature in the 18th century was political. Through newspapers, magazines, pamphlets, broadsides, and letters, colonial leaders discussed their ideas of human nature and of government. They began forging a new sense of national identity. Battles had to be fought before the 13 colonies achieved independence. Nevertheless, for years before the first shot was fired, *language* was the source of growing American power. For those Americans it was language that connected reason and revolution. By the time the Revolutionary War was over in 1783, Americans were well on their way to establishing a literary heritage as extraordinary as their political one.

The Age of Reason

Thomas Jefferson once said that a rational society is one that "informs the mind, sweetens the temper, cheers our spirits, and promotes health." Jefferson's attitude—a firm belief in progress, common sense, and the pursuit of happiness—is typical of a period we now call the Age of Reason.

Some historians say we simplify the complex 18th century in suggesting it was a time when everyone was "reasonable". Of course everyone was not reasonable. The century was marked by fiery emotion as much as by cool logic. But it was a time when people believed in the *possibilities* of reason. It is that hope, that optimism, that gives the age its character.

Americans at this time were influenced by the European movement called the Enlightenment. Followers of Enlightenment ideas believed that people could discover truth by the light of reason alone. They shed light of reason on the dark of ignorance, superstition, social injustice, and political tyranny—all in a quest to build the perfect society. Through science and rational government as well as thought, order could be established in the world. Above followers of Enlightenment ideas stressed the importance of resisting arbitrary limitations on their own free thoughts.

Enlightened Americans, Europeans, came to trust in human potential. They began rely on the power of their own minds to shape their own destinies, and the power of their own *language* to express that destiny should be.

They thought, wrote, and spoke with a greater self-confidence than a young nation had ever done before. Jefferson once commented that one evening spent at Ben Franklin's house in Philadelphia in the company of musicians, lawyers, and politicians was worth a whole week in Paris.

Writing and Revolution

During the 1770s no one in America could claim to be a professional novelist, poet, or playwright. Yet a great number of Americans expressed themselves on the subjects of liberty, government, law, reason, and individual and national freedom. Throughout the land, weekly "Poet's Corners" in American newspapers never lacked locally written poems, songs, and satires. Americans filled pamphlets with anonymous poems on the issues of the day. They produced a great number of political broadsides—sheets of paper covered with anonymous poems, songs, and essays—that could be tacked up around the city, left on doorsteps, or even read to groups on street corners. This writing was not sophisticated, but it was the writing of people whose lives were touched by the events of a turbulent time.

The policies of Great Britain helped make writers—even poets—out of many colonials. Furor over the Stamp Act of 1765 brought out poems everywhere: in political pamphlets, in newspapers, nailed to trees, slipped under doors. When British soldiers killed several Boston citizens in 1770, a flurry of broadsides protested the senseless deaths. The awkward, naive verses—written by people who were not professional writers—suggest that the pain and shock of the events were intense enough to stir even in nonliterary people the need to express their feelings.

Gradually, negative protests turned into more positive expressions. Besides petitioning against "taxation without representation", more and more Americans started calling for more self-government. Paine's pamphlet *Common Sense* sold an extraordinary 100,000 copies in three months. The Declaration of Independence—the culmination of the writing of this period—carries the voice not of an individual but of a whole people. It is more than writing of the period; it defined the meaning of the Revolution.

Toward a National Literature

Americans of the 18th century produced a great variety of unusual forms of literature: ballads, skits, broadsides, newspaper poems, editorials, essays, private and public letters, satires, pamphlets—written by people of every social class and almost every degree of skill. The energy of the age did not express itself in the usual forms with great original poetry, fiction, drama, music, or art. Nevertheless, there were some writers, composers, and painters of note.

Joel Barlow, an urbane and sophisticated man, produced a mock-epic poem called "The Hasty Pudding". Phillis Wheatley, a former slave, produced highly praised religious and patriotic verses; in 1773 she published what was probably the first book by a black American. Philip Freneau wrote bitter satires and fiery political poems, earning the title "Poet of the American Revolution". The composer William Billings and the painter John Singleton Copley demonstrated that music and art could also flourish in America, even though these artists imitated the formal, balanced, restrained classical style of European artists.

It would be some time before America would learn to be itself artistically, but it did make a beginning. The new nation had the desire to be new in every way possible. Political independence brought with it a desire for literary and artistic independence. In 1783 Noah Webster, a literary nationalist, declared: "America must be as independent in literature as she is in politics, as famous for the arts as for arms."

What would make an *American* book? Many writers thought that the new nation possessed at least two unique subjects, two things no European had experienced: the natural wilderness and the Revolution. They believed that the majestic, awe-inspiring landscape provided a setting and even an antagonist that would be the basis of a great literature. They also believed the Revolution provided stories of great human experiences and the beginning of an American mythology. They began to see the possibility of typical American characters in literature: The first American comedy, Royall Tyler's *The Contrast* (1787), gave the public a homespun American who outsmarts more "sophisticated" characters. The Yankee hero was born.

If Columbus "discovered" America, then patriots such as Franklin, Paine, and Jefferson, in the words of one historian: "invented" it. That invention of an American self and society, an American *identity*, was greatest single imaginative creation of this period. The writing in this unit can give us an idea of the complexity and the excitement of trying to ask the question that was posed by Jean de Crevecoeur: "What then is the American, this new man?"

Benjamin Franklin (1706—1790)

Benjamin Franklin, one of the most critical Founding Fathers of the United States, was a leading author, political theorist, politician, printer, scientist, inventor, civic activist, and diplomat. As a scientist he was a major figure in the history of physics for his discoveries and theories regarding electricity. As a political writer and activist, he, more than anyone, invented the idea of an American nation. As a diplomat during the American Revolution, he secured the French alliance that helped to make independence possible. Franklin was an early proponent of colonial unity. Many historians hail him as the "First American".

Benjamin Franklin was born in Boston, the son of a poor craftsman. As his father could not afford to keep him long in school, the young Franklin educated himself by reading widely. However, success came early to Franklin. At the age of 17 he went to Philadelphia and began his career as a printer. Soon he published his first essay in his brother's newspaper. His weekly newspaper, the *Pennsylvania Gazette* (later the *Saturday Evening Post*) grew quickly to a circulation of 10,000—by far the leading publication in America at that time. Then he also established himself as a civic leader, became rich, and retired from business at the age of 42.

Such an outline of Franklin's life, however, does not do justice to his extraordinary range of accomplishments. While still a young man, he founded the Junto, a club for informal discussion of scientific, economic and political issues that led to quite a few practical civic improvements. In Philadelphia, Franklin also set up America's first circulating library and the college to become the University of Pennsylvania. After retiring from business, Franklin intended to devote the rest of his life to his deepest interest—science, an area in which his achievements, especially his many inventions such as the Franklin stove, bifocal lenses, a miniature printing press as well as the lightning rods, won international acclaim.

Nevertheless, it was public affairs that dominated the last half of his life. He developed and improved the postal system, making it run at a profit after years of losses. He spent many years in England and France. Before the Revolution he represented the colonies in London, trying in vain to talk the British government into policies that would let America grow and flourish in association with England. Then he turned to support the cause of independence, served in the Continental Congress, and joined at age 70 Thomas Jefferson, John Adams, and others on the committee that drafted the Declaration of Independence. Later he served as the American representative in Paris and helped negotiate the peace treaty with England. In his final years he was a delegate to the Constitutional Convention and worked for the ratification of the Constitution.

It is easy to forget, in the glory of his achievements, that Franklin with his gift for writing was the first major American writer. As an author he had power of expression, simplicity, and a subtle humor (which at times appeared sarcastic). Most of Franklin's writings can be found in his *Collected Works*, which contain writings from his periodical publications, odd essays and publications, together with his *Autobiography*. [2]

At the time of his death, no other American was better known or more respected in both the Old World and the New World. In one of his fellow American's words, "his shadow lies heavier than any other man's on this young nation."

■ Selected Reading

Poor Richard's Almanac [3] *was published every year for* 25 *years* (1733—1758), *giving the attitudes and observations of one " Richard Saunders". Franklin enlivened this almanac with Poor Richard's proverbs and aphorisms, short sayings memorable for their wit and wisdom, which he later collected into a book titled* **The Way to Wealth**. *A simple piece of writing,* **Poor Richard's Almanac** *appealed to the common man of colonial America and it is still well known and perhaps the most quoted of all the writings of Franklin.*

from *Poor Richard's Almanac*

God helps them that help themselves.

There are no ugly loves, nor handsome prisons.

Love your Neighbor; yet don't pull down your Hedge.

To err is human, to repent divine; to persist, devilish.

At the working man's house hunger looks in, but dares not enter.

You may be too cunning for One, but not for all.

Dost thou love Life? Then do not squander Time; for that's the Stuff Life is made of.

Beware of little Expenses: a small Leak will sink a great Ship.

For want of a Nail the Shoe is lost; for want of a Shoe the Horse is lost; for want of a Horse the Rider is lost.

Hide not your talents, they for use were made. What's a sun-dial in the shade?

He that would live in peace and at ease,

Fish and Visitors stink after three days.

Keep thy shop, and thy shop will keep thee.

The Cat in Gloves catches no Mice.

What you would seem to be, be really.

He that lives upon hope will die fasting.

You borrow today, you beg tomorrow.

He that falls in love with himself, will have no rivals.

No gains without pains.

If you would be wealthy, think of saving as well as getting.

He that is of the opinion money will do everything may well be suspected of doing everything for money.

A slip of the foot you may soon recover, but a slip of the tongue you may never get over.

---

[2] Franklin's *Autobiography*, generally believed to be his best writing, is still as popular as when it was written. Here we find a representative American, the clever, prudent, self-made man, the thrifty Yankee who works hard, who knows how to take advantage of an opportunity, and who "gets ahead".

[3] An almanac is an annual collection of statistics, weather forecasts, current events, and other useful or entertaining information.

must not speak all he knows nor judge all he sees.

■ Study Questions

1. According to the second aphorism, why do fish and visitors have a common characteristic? According to the third aphorism, why can little expenses be compared to a leak in a ship?

2. Why are there "no ugly loves, nor handsome prisons"?

3. Which of the aphorisms stress the importance of hard work? Of thrift? Of honesty? Of talents?

4. What recommendations and observations about human behavior do the other aphorisms make?

5. Which of these sayings do you find applicable today? Which do you think are amusing? Why?

Thomas Paine (1737—1809)

Thomas Paine was a pamphleteer, revolutionary, radical intellectual, and deist. His life was one of continual, unswerving fight for the rights of man. He wrote a number of works of such a revolutionary and inflammatory character that it is no exaggeration to state that he helped to spur and inspire two greatest revolutions that his age had witnessed. Born in Great Britain, he lived in America, having migrated to the American colonies just in time to take part in the American Revolution, mainly as the author of the powerful, widely-read pamphlet, *Common Sense*, advocating independence for the American Colonies from Great Britain. Paine had also great influence on the French Revolution. He wrote the *Rights of Man* as a guide to the ideas of the Enlightenment.

On January 29, 1737, Thomas Paine was born in Thetford, England as the son of a poor corseter. By the age of 12, Thomas had failed out of school. The young Paine began apprenticing for his father, but again, he failed. So at 19 Paine went to sea. This adventure didn't last too long, and by 1768 he found himself as an excise (tax) officer in England. Thomas didn't exactly excel at the role, getting discharged from his post twice in four years, but as an inkling of what was to come, he published *The Case of the Officers of Excise* (1772), arguing for a pay raise for officers. In 1774, by happanstance, he met Benjamin Franklin in London, who helped him emigrate to Philadelphia.

His career turned to journalism while in Philadelphia. In 1776, he published *Common Sense*, a strong defense of American Independence from England. Declaring as it did that "Government, even in its best state, is but a necessary evil; in its worst state an intolerable one," the pamphlet attacked British monarchy and added fuel to the fire which was soon to bring the colossus of its colonial rule down in flames. Paine declared that the crisis with which the North American colonies were then faced could only be solved by an appeal to man's instincts and common sense and to "the clear, uniform and irresistibly obeyed" impulses of conscience. The booklet was warmly received in the colonies both as a justification for their cause of independence and as an encouragement to the painfully fighting people. Paine became a major influence in the American Revolution. He joined the Continental Army and wasn't a success as a soldier, but he produced *The Crisis* (1776—1783), which helped inspire the Army.

But, instead of continuing to help the Revolutionary cause, he returned to Europe and pursued other ventures, including working on a smokeless candle and an iron bridge. In 1791—1792, he wrote *The Rights of Man* in response to criticism of the French Revolution. This work caused Paine to be labeled an outlaw in England for his anti-monarchist views. He would have been arrested, but he fled for France to join the National Convention.

By 1793, he was imprisoned in France for not endorsing the execution of Louis X VI. During his imprisonment, he wrote and distributed the first part of what was to become his most famous work at the time, the anti-church text, *The Age of Reason* (1794—1796), in which the "age of Revolutions" bore a post-Voltairean and post-Jeffersonian fruit. Paine proclaimed his theism and a faith in a broad egalitarian morality of "doing justice, loving mercy, and endeavoring to make our fellow-creatures happy". He turned down all forms of established, defined, or "revealed" religion by treating the nature of "revelation" as if it were little more than hearsay. The authority of the Bible was disposed of with much the same verve. The books of the Old Testament were dismissed as a collection of "obscene stories ... voluptuous debaucheries ... cruel and torturous executions and unrelenting vindictiveness". The Gospels stroke him as merely anecdotal mystifications. "The world of God", he proclaimed in capital letters, "is **THE CREATION WE BEHOLD**," and God himself stood for "moral truth" not "mystery or obscurity".

Paine was freed in 1794 (narrowly escaping execution), thanks to the efforts of James Monroe, then U. S. Minister to France. Paine remained in France until 1802 when he returned to America on an invitation from Thomas Jefferson. Paine discovered that his contributions to the American Revolution had been all but eradicated due to his religious views. Derided by the public and abandoned by his friends, he died on June 8, 1809 at the age of 72 in New York.

■ Selected Reading

from *The American Crisis*

These are the times that try men's souls. The summer soldier and the sunshine patriot will, in this crisis, shrink from the service of their country; but he that stands it *now*, deserves the love and thanks of man and woman. Tyranny, like hell, is not easily conquered; yet we have this consolation with us, that the harder the conflict, the more glorious the triumph. What we obtain too cheap, we esteem too lightly: it is dearness only that gives every thing its value. Heaven knows how to put a proper price upon its goods; and it would be strange indeed if so celestial an article as *freedom* should not be highly rated. Britain, with an army to enforce her tyranny, has declared that she has a right not only to *tax* but "to *bind* us in *all cases whatsoever*"; and if being *bound in that manner* is not slavery, then is there not such a thing as slavery upon earth. Even the expression is impious; for so unlimited a power can belong only to God.

...

I have as little superstition in me as any man living, but my secret opinion has ever been, and still is, that God Almighty will not give up a people to military destruction, or leave them unsupportedly to perish, who have so earnestly and so repeatedly sought to avoid the calamities of war, by every decent method which wisdom could invent. Neither have I so much of the infidel[4] in me as to suppose that He has relinquished the government of the world, and given us up to the care of devils; and as I do not, I cannot see on what grounds the king of Britain can look up to heaven for help against us: a common murderer, a highwayman, or a housebreaker, has as good a

---

4   **infidel**: unbeliever.

pretense as he.

...

I once felt all that kind of anger "which a man ought to feel against the mean [5] principles that are held by the Tories: [6] a noted one, who kept a tavern at Amboy, was standing at his door, with as pretty a child in his hand, about eight or nine years old, as I ever saw, and after speaking his mind as freely as he thought was prudent, finished with this unfatherly expression, "Well! Give me peace in my day." Not a man lives on the continent but fully believes that a separation must some time or other finally take place, and a generous parent should have said, "If there must be trouble, let it be in my day, that my child may have peace"; and this single reflection, well applied, is sufficient to awaken every man to duty. Not a place upon earth might be so happy as America. Her situation is remote from all the wrangling world, and she has nothing to do but to trade with them. A man can distinguish himself between temper and principle, and I am as confident, as I am that God governs the world, that America will never be happy till she gets clear of foreign dominion. Wars, without ceasing, will break out till that period arrives, and the continent must in the end be conqueror; for though the flame of liberty may sometimes cease to shine, the coal can never expire.

■ Study Questions

1. According to the first paragraph, whom is Paine criticizing? Whom is he praising?

2. According to the first paragraph, what is the purpose of Britain's army? What has Britain declared?

3. What "secret opinion" does Paine state in his second paragraph?

4. What does the third paragraph state about the possibility of happiness in America? What does it say must be accomplished before America can be happy?

5. What is the price of freedom, according to Paine? For what is Paine, therefore, criticizing the "summer soldiers," the "sunshine patriots," and the tavern keeper in Amboy?

6. To what emotions does Paine appeal when he describes the king of Britain? Where in this selection does Paine rely on reason rather than emotion?

7. The "crisis" Paine speaks of was nothing less than the potential defeat of the American armies. Do you think Paine's words have a more general application as well?

8. What do you think of the prose of Paine?

Thomas Jefferson (1743—1826)

As an important revolutionary statesman during the American War of Independence, the main drafter of The Declaration of Independence, an active and devoted politician, **Thomas Jefferson** has branded his democratic ideas into the veins of the American people generation after generation.

Thomas Jefferson was born in Albemarle County, Virginia. When he stayed on in Williamsburg to read law

---

5   **mean**: narrow-minded.

6   **Tories**: Here colonists loyal to Great Britain.

after graduation from William and Mary College, his election to the Virginia House of Burgesses in 1769 drew him into public life. After that, he was almost constantly in the political service of Virginia and of the nation except a withdrawal from 1781 to 1784. During these four years, he completed his only book, *Notes on the State of Virginia.*

In 1776, Jefferson was elected to draft a declaration of independence in the five-member committee. He was almost wholly responsible for the spirit and expressing of The Declaration of Independence, although Franklin made fundamental contributions and the influence of John Adams is evident. On July 4, the Declaration was passed after some changes during debate. Jefferson was unhappy with the changes made by the Congress to his draft because these changes went contrary to some of his basic arguments. [7] However, the document still reflects the authorship of Jefferson, his precise clarity and powerful grace of thought. Moreover, it remains the most noble, famous, and powerful statement of the basis of government ever written. It is unique. It has shaped a people and a nation, and it has helped to shape the world.

The Declaration of Independence made Jefferson internationally famous. And its spirit of pursuing freedom, liberty, happiness and life found practical expressions throughout not only the distinguished range of Jefferson's public offices—member of Congress, Governor of Virginia, Minister to France, Secretary of State, Vice President, and President, twice—but also the multiplicity of his interests and inventions. All these undoubtedly made him unique among the Founding Fathers of America.

In the final 17 years of his life, Jefferson's major accomplishment was the founding (1819) of the University of Virginia at Charlottesville. He conceived it, planned it, designed it, and supervised both its construction and the hiring of faculty. The university was the last of three contributions by which Jefferson wished to be remembered; they constituted a trilogy of interrelated causes: freedom from Britain (drafting The Declaration of Independence), freedom of conscience (writing and supporting *The Virginia Statute for Religious Freedom*, 1786), and freedom maintained through education (founding the University of Virginia). On July 4, 1826, the 50th anniversary of The Declaration of Independence, Jefferson died at Monticello.

■ Selected Reading

The Declaration of Independence

In Congress, July 4, 1776

The unanimous Declaration of the thirteen united States of America. [8]

When in the Course of human events, it becomes necessary for one people to dissolve the political bands which have connected them with another, and to assume among the powers of the

---

7   The philosophical and political ideals expressed in the Declaration can be traced far back in history, and their immediate roots are found in 18th-century thought, while the final draft represented a consensus among the delegates.

8   Richard Henry Lee of Virginia, on June 7, 1776, proposed a resolution in Congress that "these united Colonies are, and of right ought to be, free and independent States." Final action was postponed, but on June 11 the committee of five was appointed, which on June 28 presented the draft of the Declaration. On July 2, Lee's original resolution was passed. On July 4, the Declaration was passed after some changes; the Liberty Bell rang from the State House steeple in Philadelphia, and that night printed broadside copies were hastily run off for public distribution. On August 2, an engrossed parchment copy was signed by all the delegates but three, who also signed shortly after. Printed copies, with all the signatures, appeared in January, 1777.

earth, the separate and equal station to which the Laws of Nature and of Nature's God entitle them, a decent respect to the opinions of mankind requires that they should declare the causes which impel them to the separation.

We hold these truths to be self-evident, that all men are created equal, that they are endowed by their Creator with certain unalienable Rights; that among these are Life, Liberty and the pursuit of Happiness. [9] That to secure these rights, Governments are instituted among Men, deriving their just Powers from the consent of the governed; That whenever any Form of Government becomes destructive of these ends, it is the Right of the People to alter or to abolish it, and to institute new Government, laying its foundation on such principles and organizing its powers in such form, as to them shall seem most likely to effect their Safety and Happiness. Prudence, indeed, will dictate that Governments long established should not be changed for light and transient causes; and accordingly all experience hath shown that mankind are more disposed to suffer, while evils are sufferable, than to right themselves by abolishing the forms to which they are accustomed. But when a long train of abuses and usurpations, [10] pursuing invariably the same Objects, evinces a design to reduce them under absolute Despotism, [11] it is their right, it is their duty, to throw off such Government, and to provide new guards for their future security. Such has been the patient sufferance of these Colonies; and such is now the necessity which constrains [12] them to alter their former Systems of Government. The history of the present King of Great Britain [13] is a history of repeated injuries and usurpations, all having in direct object the establishment of an absolute Tyranny over these States. To prove this, let facts be submitted to a candid [14] world.

He has refused his Assent to Laws, the most wholesome and necessary for the public good.

He has forbidden his Governors to pass Laws of immediate and pressing importance, unless suspended in their operation till his Assent should be obtained; and when so suspended, he has utterly neglected to attend to them.

He has refused to pass other Laws for the accommodation of large districts of people, unless those people would relinquish the right of Representation in the Legislature, a right inestimable to them and formidable to tyrants only.

He has called together legislative bodies at places unusual, uncomfortable, and distant from the depository of their Public Records, for the sole purpose of fatiguing them into compliance with

---

9   In his *Second Treatise on Government* (1689), John Locke defined man's natural rights to "life, liberty, and property." Jefferson substituted happiness for property.

10   **usurpations**: unlawful seizures of power.

11   **Despotism**: tyranny.

12   **constrains**: forces.

13   **the present King of Great Britain**: George Ⅲ (1760—1820), was the responsible engineer of those policies of his government which evoked rebellion.

14   **candid**: impartial.

his measures.

He has dissolved Representative Houses repeatedly, for opposing with manly firmness his invasions on the rights of the people.

He has refused for a long time, after such dissolutions, to cause others to be elected; whereby the Legislative Powers, incapable of Annihilation, have returned to the People at large for their exercise; the State remaining in the mean time exposed to all the dangers of invasion from without, and convulsions within.

He has endeavored to prevent the population of these States; for that purpose obstructing the Laws for Naturalization of Foreigners; refusing to pass others to encourage their migrations hither, and raising the conditions of new Appropriations of Lands.

He has obstructed the Administration of Justice, by refusing his Assent to Laws for establishing Judiciary Powers.

He has made Judges dependent on his Will alone, for the tenure of their offices, and the amount and payment of their salaries.

He has erected a multitude of New Offices, and sent hither swarms of Officers to harass our People, and eat out their substance.

He has kept among us, in times of peace, Standing Armies without the Consent of our legislatures.

He has affected to render the Military independent of and superior to the Civil Power.

He has combined with others[15] to subject us to a jurisdiction foreign to our constitution, and unacknowledged by our laws; giving his Assent to their Acts of pretended Legislation:

For Quartering large bodies of armed troops among us;

For protecting them, by a mock Trial, from Punishment for any Murders which they should commit on the Inhabitants of these States;

For cutting off our Trade with all parts of the world;

For imposing Taxes on us without our Consent;

For depriving us in many cases, of the benefits of Trial by Jury;

For transporting us beyond seas to be tried for pretended offences;

For abolishing the free system of English Laws in a neighboring Province,[16] establishing therein an Arbitrary government, and enlarging its Boundaries so as to render it at once an example and fit instrument for introducing the same absolute rule into these Colonies;

For taking away our Charters, abolishing our most valuable Laws, and altering fundamentally the forms of our Governments;

For suspending our own Legislature, and declaring themselves invested with power to legislate for us in all cases whatsoever.

---

15   **others**: the British Parliament.

16   **abolishing... neighboring Province**: In 1774 the British, having captured Quebec, forced strict laws on colonists there.

He has abdicated Government here, by declaring us out of his Protection and waging War against us.

He has plundered our seas, ravaged our Coasts, burnt our towns, and destroyed the lives of our people.

He is at this time transporting large Armies of foreign Mercenaries [17] to complete the works of death, desolation and tyranny, already begun with circumstances of Cruelty and perfidy [18] scarcely paralleled in the most barbarous ages, and totally unworthy the Head of a civilized nation.

He has constrained our fellow Citizens taken Captive on the high Seas to bear Arms against their Country, to become the executioners of their friends and Brethren [19], or to fall themselves by their Hands.

He has excited domestic insurrections amongst us, and has endeavored to bring on the inhabitants of our frontiers, the merciless Indian Savages, whose known rule of warfare is an undistinguished destruction of all ages, sexes and conditions.

In every stage of these Oppressions we have Petitioned for Redress in the most humble terms: Our repeated Petitions have been answered only by repeated injury. A Prince, whose character is thus marked by every act which may define a Tyrant, is unfit to be the ruler of a free people.

Nor have we been wanting in attention to our British brethren. We have warned them from time to time of attempts by their legislature [20] to extend an unwarrantable jurisdiction over us. We have reminded them of the circumstances of our emigration and settlement here. We have appealed to their native justice and magnanimity, and we have conjured them by the ties of our common kindred to disavow these usurpations, which, would inevitably interrupt our connections and correspondence. They too have been deaf to the voice of justice and of consanguinity. [21] We must, therefore, acquiesce in the necessity, which denounces [22] our Separation, and hold them, as we hold the rest of mankind, Enemies in War, in Peace Friends.

We, therefore, the Representatives of the united States of America, in General Congress, Assembled, appealing to the Supreme Judge of the world for the rectitude of our intentions, do, in the Name, and by Authority of the good People of these Colonies, solemnly publish and declare that these United Colonies are, and of Right ought to be Free and Independent States; that they are absolved from all Allegiance to the British Crown, and that all political connection between them and the State of Great Britain, is and ought to be totally dissolved; and that as Free and Independent States, they have full Power to levy War, conclude Peace, contract Alliances, establish Commerce, and to do all other Acts and Things which Independent States may of right

---

17　**large Armies of Foreign Mercenaries**: German soldiers, particularly Hessians, hired by the British for colonial Service.

18　**perfidy**: betrayal of trust.

19　**Brethren**: brothers (archaic except in religious contexts).

20　**their legislature**: British Parliament.

21　**consanguinity**: blood relationship.

22　**denounces**: here, announces, proclaims.

do.

And for the support of this Declaration, with a firm reliance on the protection of Divine Providence, we mutually pledge to each other our Lives, our Fortunes and our sacred Honor.

■ Study Questions

1. According to the second paragraph, by whom are the thirteen United States entitled to declare their independence? What does "a decent respect to the opinions of mankind" require?

2. According to the third paragraph, what are the inalienable rights of men? What is the purpose of government, and when should a government be replaced?

3. Moving from a theory of government to the situation in 1776, what does Jefferson claim King George's "direct object" has been in the colonies? How does Jefferson set out to prove his claim?

4. What does Jefferson say the Americans have done "in every stage of these Oppressions"? To what does he say "our British brethren" have been deaf?

5. What does the final paragraph "publish and declare"?

6. How is the faith in reason characteristic of the 18th century reflected in the opening paragraph? In Jefferson's remarks about Prudence in the third paragraph? In the description of the colonists' peaceful attempts to redress their grievances?

7. What is the primary aim of The Declaration of Independence?

8. In The Declaration of Independence, God is named four times as: ① a law giver ("the laws of nature and of nature's God"); ② a maker (the "Creator"); ③ a judge ("the Supreme Judge of the world") and ④ a protector ("Divine Providence"). What are reasons for doing so?

9. In the final sentence of the Declaration, the signers pledge their "Fortunes", or fate. What do you think their fate would have been if Britain had been the victor in the Revolution?

LITERARY FOCUS

Literary Criticism

Literary criticism, in the words of Mathew Arnold—the 19th-century English critic, is "a disinterested endeavor to learn and propagate the best that is known and thought in the world." Implicit in this definition is that literary criticism is a disciplined activity that attempts to describe, study, analyze, justify, interpret, and evaluate a literary work. Modern literary criticism is often informed by **literary theory**, which in a strict sense is the systematic study of the nature of literature and of the methods for analyzing literature. Though the two activities are closely related, literary critics are not always, and have not always been, theorists.

When its function and its relationship to the text are concerned, literary criticism can hardly be accepted as a discipline in and of itself, for it must be connected with something else—that is, a literary work. Without the literary work, the activity of literary criticism cannot exist. And it is through this discerning activity that we can knowingly explore the questions that help define our humanity, critique our culture, evaluate our actions, or simply increase our appreciation and enjoyment of both a literary work and our fellow human beings.

Traditionally, literary critics involve themselves in either theoretical or practical criticism. **Theoretical criticism** formulates the theories, principles, and tenets of the nature and value of art. By citing general aesthetic and moral principles of art, theoretical criticism provides the necessary framework for practical criticism. **Practical criticism**, or applied criticism, applies the theories and principles of theoretical criticism to particular work. Using the theories and principles of theoretical criticism, the practical critic defines the standards of taste and explains, evaluates, or justifies a particular piece of literature. A further distinction is made between the practical critic who posits that there is only one theory or set of principles a critic may use when evaluating a literary work— the absolute critic—and the relativistic critic, one who uses various and even contradictory theories in critiquing a text.

The basis for any kind of critic, or any form of criticism, is literary theory. Consciously or unconsciously, we have developed a mind-set or framework that accommodates our expectations when reading a novel, short story, poem, or any other type of literature. In addition, what we choose to value or uphold as good or bad, moral or immoral, or beautiful or ugly within a given text actually depends on this ever-evolving framework. When we can clearly articulate the mental framework when reading a text and explain how this mind-set directly influences our values and aesthetic judgments about the text, we are well on our way to developing a coherent, unified literary theory.

Because anyone who responds to a text is already a practicing literary critic and because practical criticism is rooted in the reader's preconditioned expectations—the mind-set—when reading a text, every reader espouses some sort of literary theory. It can be conscious or unconscious, whole or partial, informed or ill informed, eclectic or unified. While unclear theory usually leads to illogical, unsound, and haphazard interpretations, clearly articulated theory makes it possible for the reader to establish principles to justify and clarify his or her appraisal of a text in a consistent manner.

■ Thinking About Literary Criticism

- The value of literary criticism has been questioned by some prominent artists. Vladimir Nabokov argued that good readers don't read books, and particularly literary masterpieces, "for the academic purpose of indulging in generalizations." Stephen J. Joyce, grandson of James Joyce, at a 1986 academic conference of Joyceans in Copenhagen, said "If my grandfather was here, he would have died laughing… *Dubliners* and *A Portrait of the Artist as a Young Man* can be picked up, read, and enjoyed by virtually anybody without scholarly guides, theories, and intricate explanations, as can *Ulysses*, if you forget about all the hue and cry." And he questioned if anything is added to the legacy of Joyce's art, by the 261 books of literary criticism stored by the Library of Congress; he summed up that Academics are "people who want to brand this great work with their mark. I don't accept that." What do you think about Nabokov's and S. Joyce's view? What is your opinion about the function and significance of literary criticism?

READING FOR APPRECIATION

The Sound of Prose

Any piece of writing has sound. People hear the words in their heads, and so the sounds that a piece of writing creates can draw people's attention. In addition, at the right moments, the writer can be much like a music composer, working with sound to create feeling. The skillful writer has sounds in mind.

Read the last paragraph but one of The Declaration of Independence *aloud silently* or *silently aloud* as we always do when we read any literary writing that originally functions as a public speech:

> We, therefore, the Representatives of the United States of America, in General Congress, Assembled, appealing to the Supreme Judge of the world for the rectitude of our intentions, do, in the Name, and by Authority of the good People of these Colonies, solemnly publish and declare that these United Colonies are, and of Right ought to be Free and Independent States; that they are absolved from all Allegiance to the British Crown, and that all political connection between them and the State of Great Britain, is and ought to be totally dissolved; and that as Free and Independent States, they have full Power to levy War, conclude Peace, contract Alliances, establish Commerce, and to do all other Acts and Things which Independent States may of right do.

You may immediately realize that this by-no-means-short paragraph is made up of ONE sentence. As you read on, you may also come at the importance of the use of those commas and semicolons, with which you are aware of where to pause and able to read on smoothly, and without which you will be completely lost and get nowhere. If you read it time and again, you may even sense how the Declaration was originally read by those fathers of the United States to the public. Getting the sound, then, is a large part of the pleasure of reading any writing we call literature.

How can you start thinking in terms of sound? Consider these commonly used sound devices first:

Alliteration: the repetition of initial sounds of stressed syllables.

> *... and we have conjured them by the ties of our common kindred to disavow these usurpations, which, would inevitably interrupt our connections and correspondence.*

Assonance: the close juxtaposition of vowel sounds. "Asleep under a tree" is an example. "Time and tide" is another.

Consonance: a type of near rhyme, a pleasing sound, where there is a close juxtaposition of consonant sounds, as in "boats... into the past." The words "cool" and "soul" have consonance.

Euphony: lines that are musically pleasant to the ear bring euphony.

Onomatopoeia: words whose sound is suggestive of its meaning. For animal sounds, words like quack (duck), moo (cow), bark or woof (dog), roar (lion), meow or purr (cat) and baa (sheep) are typically used in English.

These devices, of course, are more than often used in poetry. Therefore, a rather different approach to that used for the analysis of poetry is usually adopted in the analysis of *rhythm* and other sound features in prose. As the reading of the last paragraph but one of the Declaration shows, *prose rhythm* can be analyzed by looking at the punctuation marks in a given prose passage, as these are written indicators of *intonational units* in the passage. Another consideration which may be of significance in the analysis of the *sound features* of *prose*, is the use of unconventional *spelling* (usually in a fiction) to represent the *style* or *dialect* of the speech of certain characters (see, for example, Simon Wheeler's speech in "The Celebrated Jumping Frog of Calaveras County" by Mark Twain). The use of italics, underlining, and capital letters, may also represent the emphasis that the writer, narrator or character puts on certain words, which is obviously the case in many places of the capitalization used in the Declaration of the Independence:

> *And for the support of this Declaration, with a firm reliance on the protection of Divine Providence,*
> *we mutually pledge to each other our **Lives**, our **Fortunes** and our sacred **Honor.***

VOICE OF THE AGE

Liberty

Most of the American voices in this unit, from the famous to the anonymous, carry the message of the Declaration of Independence. These voices mainly about life and death belong to the Age of Reason: though strongly emotional, they are still logical, coherent, and organized. In particular, they share a vision of the liberty and the freedom that would allow Americans to think and feel as independent individuals long after the Revolution:

Franklin: **I** *took upon me to assert my Freedom...*

Patrick Henry [23]: *If we wish to be free, if we mean to preserve inviolate those inestimable privileges... we must fight* !

Anonymous [24]: *I will sing you a song concerning liberty. / Concerning liberty, my boys, the truth I will unfold, / Of the bold Americans, who scorn to be controlled.*

Jefferson: *We hold these truths to be self-evident, that all men are created equal, that they are endowed by their*

---

23   Patrick Henry (1736—1799): an orator and politician who led the movement for independence in Virginia in the 1770s. Leading the opposition to the Stamp Act, Henry is well remembered for his "Give me Liberty, or give me Death!" speech.

24   "The Bold American" was circulated as an anonymous broadside, a large printed piece of paper, in late 1775 or early 1776. Unlike other songs of the time that uttered wholeheartedly for complete independence, "The Bold American" offered a compromise, reminding us that in the beginning most Americans wanted both a measure of liberty and continued affiliation with England.

Creator with certain unalienable Rights, that among these are Life, Liberty and the pursuit of Happiness.

Paine: *For though the flame of liberty may sometimes cease to shine, the coal can never expire.*

Jean de Crèvecoeur[25]: *The American ought therefore to love this country much better than that wherein either he or his forefathers were born. Here the rewards of his industry follow with equal steps the progress of his labor; his labor is founded on the basis of nature, self-interest; can it want a stronger allurement?*

Freedom in American literary expression had helped to create the American political system. Writing about liberty helped to make liberty possible. The literature in this unit helped to found the nation on the basis of private and public independence.

As the new United States continued to grow, American literature also continued to grow. Literature helped the nation to achieve an identity by defining its characteristics, its problems, and its goals. Liberty is one of those characteristics. It is part of the answer to Crevecoeur's question, "What then is the American, this new man?" The American is someone free to create a new literature, to found a new tradition, to speak in a new voice.

---

[25]　Michel Guillaume Jean de Crèvecœur (1735—1813) left for England and then Canada from France where he was born and lived for 19 years. After traveling throughout the American colonies as a surveyor, he settled on a farm near Chester, New York, in 1769. There he began writing his Letters from an American Farmer, published in London in 1782.

Chapter 3

NATIVE GROUNDS 1800—1840

INTRODUCTION

A Prosperous New Nation

The establishment of the United States as an independent country marked by the inauguration of George Washington in 1789 stood for the complete success of the American Revolution. But the new nation faced a bunch of problems, many of which were physical. In an age of few good roads and no rapid and reliable means of transportation or communication, it was difficult for the 13 states to conceive of themselves and act as a single nation. Regional rivalries and even separate cultures had to be reconciled. In 1810 the population of the 17 states totaled little more than 7 million. 51 years later, at the beginning of the Civil War, the number of states had doubled, and the number of Americans had increased to more than 31 millions. Could a modern republic—a nation without a king or a hereditary aristocracy—withstand the tensions of a large and varied population? Would there be economic prosperity? More critical were questions beyond the material sphere. Would there be real democracy? Would the new Constitution stand the test of time? As Lincoln asked during the Civil War, could a nation "conceived in liberty and dedicated to the proposition that all men are created equal... long endure" ?

In fact the nation did prosper, did expand, and did overcome the dangers it faced. Jefferson's Louisiana Purchase in 1803 vastly enlarged the territory. The War of 1812 offered a challenge to the proud new nation, and the victory reasserted American independence. By 1821 ten new states had joined the original thirteen. Through the first half of the 19th century American pioneers pushed the frontier line of settlement beyond the Mississippi to the Great Plains. The nation's center of population gradually shifted westward from the eastern seaboard, across the Appalachians, Ohio, and the West rose as a sectional power to challenge the political dominance of the East and the South. In 1828 the election of the frontier hero Andrew Jackson as the 7th President of the United States brought an effective end to the "Virginia Dynasty" of American Presidents. By the 1840s the age of the Common Man had arrived. Voting restrictions were ceased. The Jeffersonian concept of a natural aristocracy was now replaced by the egalitarian belief that all white men were literally equal and most of them were capable of political leadership. What's more, the improvement of roads and waterways, the establishment of new factories and mills, and the invention of new machines and equipment rapidly moved the nation away from a largely agricultural economy toward a more urban and industrialized society.

By the 1850s the level of education and literacy had risen significantly. State legislatures had started to enact compulsory school attendance laws. More Americans began to read books, magazines, and newspapers. Improvements in the printing press and the expansion of the postal service made possible the rapid production and wide distribution of periodicals. Compensation for magazine contributors was almost unknown until the 1820s, and long thereafter payment remained slight and uncertain. But by midcentury, magazines were paying Henry Wadsworth Longfellow $50 for a poem and James Fenimore Cooper $10 for a page of his prose.

"Our Own Books"

Therefore, with the turn of the century, the young republic entered upon an era of expansion and development which can be described only as marvelous. It is unnecessary to attempt a full historical outline of that period of growth and change except to note that coincidentally with this expansive period of material prosperity and growth, the national literature entered upon what may not be inaptly termed its golden age—the age of its best essayists, novelists and poets, the real American men of letters.

We have traced the slow steps of literary effort recorded in the several colonies to the close of their existence as colonies; and, immediately after the period of revolution, we have recognized the new and fresh impulse of expressing a sense of national pride, creating a new culture and a new literature, and in short, demonstrating the Americanism. Now as Americans continued to build the nation, they came increasingly to feel less like transported Europeans. The native grounds of the Old World—the European environment, its traditions and customs, its languages and literatures—gave way to the native grounds of the New World. The playwright Royall Tyler saw what was needed: "that we write our own books… and that they exhibit our own manners."

During the first decades of the American republic, a great deal of *writing* was done, but very little of it possessed that mysterious vitality that made it *literature*. As the century progressed, however, a new national literature with an artistic excellence felt and enjoyed by all gradually emerged and became increasingly important to command recognition by the people of England and the Continent. There were evidences of literary activity in Boston, in Philadelphia, and in New York. Little groups of *literati*, as they liked to call themselves, mightily interested in the development of a national literature, gave an atmosphere that was helpful to literary effort; and they themselves accomplished what could be accomplished by interest, patriotism, and industry when joined with talent, modest if not mediocre.

In 1820 it was still possible for a British critic, Sydney Smith, to ask, "Who reads an American book?" Smith, like many other Europeans, wondered why any intelligent person would want to bother reading books from such an unformed, uncultured, unsophisticated place as America. Yet in the same year that Smith asked his mocking question, Washington Irving's *Sketch Book* was published in England. American literature of lasting value was beginning to be created. The next year William Cullen Bryant gained fame for his poem *Thanatopsis*. James Fennimore Cooper brought out the first of the Leatherstocking novels, *The Pioneers*, in 1823. Edgar Allan Poe published his first volume of poetry in 1827.

Who were the people who produced this first American literature, and what made their work unmistakably American? In the first place they were *writers*, not soldiers of fortune like John Smith, business leaders like Ben

Franklin, or government leaders like Thomas Jefferson. Though they sometimes had to do other things to make a living, they thought of themselves as writers, and they were thought of as writers by their growing public. Second, they began writing about American people in American places dealing with American problems. This accomplishment may seem like something to take for granted, but it is important to remember that no one had ever done it before. Their characters and settings were not *always* American, and their forms were usually British, but they did take the first steps. They celebrated American meadows, groves, and streams, its endless prairies, dense forests, and vast oceans. They praised American heroes and American artists and told American tales. Such nationalism also stimulated a greater interest in America's language and its common people. In 1828 Noah Webster published *An American Dictionary of the English Language*. American character types speaking local dialects appeared in poetry and fiction with increasing frequency. Literature began to celebrate American farmers, the poor, the unlettered, children, and noble savages (red and white) untainted by society. In short, their subjects "were freedom, expansion, the individual—definitely not European subjects. "

The Romantic Writers

The first half of the 19th century was the Romantic Period for American literature. As we have asserted, a rising America with its ideals of democracy and equality, its industrialization, its westward expansion, and a variety of foreign influences such as Sir Walter Scott were among the many important factors which made literary expansion and expression not only possible but also inevitable in the period immediately following the nation's political independence. The spirit of revolution and the love of the still crude country drew American men of letters close to Romanticism, a reaction to Classicism, the Age of Reason movement in the arts that attempted to duplicate the order and balance in the art of Greece and Rome. While Classicism stressed reason over emotion and social concerns over personal ones, Romantic writers stressed personal experience and were often highly emotional.

Originally, Romanticism referred to the characteristics of romances, or fanciful stories, whose extravagances carried pejorative connotations. But in the 18th century the term came to designate a kind of exotic landscape which evoked feelings of pleasing melancholy (At this time there developed a taste for the Gothic). The term Romantic as a designation for a school of literature opposed to the Classic was first used by the German critic Friedrich Schlegel at the beginning of the 19th century. From Germany, this meaning was carried to England, France, and America.

Since individual Romantics are often in conflict and since no single figure or literary school displays all the characteristics labeled "Romantic", general definition tends to be imprecise. But there are six characteristics that can give us a general definition of the American Romanticism: 1) a profound love of nature; 2) a focus on the self and the individual; 3) a fascination with the supernatural, the mysterious, and the gothic; 4) a yearning for the picturesque and the exotic; 5) a deep-rooted idealism; and 6) a passionate nationalism, or love of country.

One quality of Romantic writers, then, is a deep feeling for nature. Close observation of the natural world usually gives a Romantic writer an insight into all life, especially human life. We can find this kind of detailed observation of nature in Irving, Cooper, and Bryant—particularly in Bryant's poems and in Cooper's breadth of feeling for the unspoiled wilderness.

Romantic writers also reveal with emotion their own personal visions and delve deeply into the individual personalities of their characters. Poe is the best representative of this strain of Romanticism, for he often displays the tortured minds and hearts of inward-looking characters. It is Poe who also demonstrates a fascination with the gothic—the dark, irrational side of the imagination.

One generalization about Romantic writing fits all four of the authors in this unit. Romantic writers were often interested in the picturesque and the exotic, in times and places other than their own, especially the past. Sometimes this interest in the past offers an escape from an oppressive or unromantic present. To trace the story of Irving's "Rip Van Winkle", we have to make "a voyage up the Hudson River" to "a dismembered branch of the great Appalachian family and ... to the west swelling up to a noble height and lording it over the surrounding country." Besides, the story is wrapped in legend, rumor, suggestion, and fantasy. Cooper's hero, the frontiersman Natty Bumppo, lived in an America that was already a legendary past for Cooper's readers. Bryant's *Thanatopsis* moves deep into the past of the human race. Poe's story, "The Fall of the House of Usher", is not set in any country at all or in any time that we can easily recognize.

Irving, Cooper, and Bryant often wrote with a fervent idealism, a belief in a heroic mode of behavior that would make life worthwhile. Nationalism, too, was a part of the imaginative lives of these writers—men who were completely aware of the importance of establishing an *American* literary art.

These four writers of the first half of the 19th century began an American Romantic tradition that would be developed by Emerson, Hawthorne, Melville, Whitman, and Faulkner, writers you will meet later in this book. We continue to read the four writers in this unit, however, not only because of their historical importance but because they still offer exciting and meaningful imaginative experiences.

Washington Irving (1783—1859)

Washington Irving was the first American to achieve an international literary reputation. Combining elegance and folklore, humor and history, nostalgia and satire, Irving achieved what no American writer had done before: He became an American writer admired and accepted by Europe.

Born in New York City on April 3, 1783, the last of 11 children of a wealthy family, Irving was named after George Washington. While modeling his early prose on the graceful *Spectator* papers by Joseph Addison, Irving was delighted by many other writers, including Shakespeare, Oliver Goldsmith, and Laurence Sterne. Like Ben Franklin in the preceding unit, Irving had begun to publish witty and satiric letters in a newspaper edited by his brother. In 1809 Irving began work on *A History of New York*, at first conceiving it as a parody of Samuel Latham Mitchell's pompously titled *The Picture of New York*, then taking on a variety of satiric targets, including President Jefferson, whom he portrayed as an early Dutch governor of New Amsterdam, William the Testy. Then the *History* was launched by a charming publicity campaign. First a newspaper noted the disappearance of a "small elderly gentleman, dressed in an old black coat and cocked hat by the name of KNICKERBOCKER," adding that there were "some reasons for believing he is not entirely in his right mind", After further "news" items the old man's fictitious landlord announced that he had found in Knickerbocker's room a "very curious kind of a written book" which he intended to dispose of to pay the bill that was owed him. And the book at last appeared, ascribed to Diedrich Knickerbocker, entitled *History of New York from the Beginning of the World to the End of the Dutch Dynasty*. Knickerbocker gave Irving an opportunity to mix old tales and satiric opinions with a bit of history. The *History* entertained its readers with hilarious sketches of the customs, manners, families, and "history" of old New York. It was enormously popular and established Irving as a celebrity. Reprinted in England, the *History* reached Sir Walter Scott, who declared that it made his sides hurt from laughter.

In 1819 Irving began sending *The Sketch Book* to the United States for publication in installments. When the full version was printed in England the next year, it made Irving famous and brought him the friendship of many of the leading British writers of the time. The disguised storyteller, an elegant English gentleman named Geoffrey Crayon this time, became universally recognized. Over the next years selections from *The Sketch Book* entered the classroom as models of English prose just as selections from Addison had long been used.

Irving himself knew that part of his British success derived from general astonishment that a man born in the United States could write in such an English way about English scenes. However, the memory of his hometown and the imaginative power thus inspired gave rise to his most vigorous writings. "Rip Van Winkle" and "The Legend of the Sleepy Hollow", the two stories that anyone then reading them knew instantly that they were among the literary treasures of the language, were set in rural New York. The old Knickerbocker, rather than Geoffrey Crayon, told these two famous tales, now classics among any list of American literature. Here we find the most distinctive characteristic of Irving's writing, i. e. his ability to blend European sophistication and American flavor.

Irving's next book, *Bracebridge Hall* (1822), a worshipful tribute to old-fashioned English country life, was, as the author realized, a feeble follow-up, and *Tales of a Traveller* (1824) was widely taken as a sign that he had written himself out. Though he continued writing travel books, histories, biographies of Columbus and Washington, more tales and sketches, none of them retained the strength of his earlier works.

■ Selected Reading

"Rip Van Winkle", *a short story based on German folk tales, is one of America's most beloved. It has been adapted for other media for the last two centuries, from stage plays to an operetta to cartoons to films.*

Narration is writing that tells a story, moving from event to event, usually in chronological order. A narrative may be factual, like William Bradford's Of Plymouth Plantation, or fiction like "Rip Van Winkle." Sometimes a fictional narrative will have elements that make it seem factual. In the following story Irving uses the narrator, Diedrich Knickerbocker, to help make his fictional narrative seem like fact. Knickerbocker is supposed to be a historian, and so his reputation lends the story believability. Besides, the quotation at the beginning of the story emphasizes that "Truth is a thing that ever I will keep" so as to make the reader believe that this outlandish tale actually happened. What's more, Knickerbocker cites his sources of information and even tells the reader that there are a few details of which he is not quite sure (implying that everything else is absolutely correct). These devices give the narrative the ring of truth.

Rip Van Winkle[26]

...

Whoever has made a voyage up the Hudson must remember the Catskill Mountains. They are a dismembered branch of the great Appalachian family, and are seen away to the west of the river, swelling up to a noble height, and lording it over the surrounding country. Every change of season, every change of weather, indeed, every hour of the day, produces some change in the magical hues and shapes of these mountains, and they are regarded by all the good wives, far and near, as perfect barometers. When the weather is fair and settled, they are clothed in blue and purple, and print their bold outlines on the clear evening sky; but sometimes, when the rest of the landscape is cloudless, they will gather a hood of gray vapors about their summits, which, in the

---

[26] "Rip Van Winkle" was the last of the sketches printed in May 1819 the first installment of *The Sketch Book*.

last rays of the setting sun, will glow and light up like a crown of glory.

At the foot of these fairy mountains the voyager may have descried the light smoke curling up from a village whose shingle roofs gleam among the trees, just where the blue tints of the upland melt away into the fresh green of the nearer landscape. It is a little village of great antiquity, having been founded by some of the Dutch colonists, in the early times of the province, just about the beginning of the government of the good Peter Stuyvesant[27] (may he rest in peace!), and there were some of the houses of the original settlers standing within a few years, with lattice windows, gable fronts surmounted with weathercocks, and built of small yellow bricks brought from Holland.

In that same village, and in one of these very houses (which, to tell the precise truth, was sadly time-worn and weather-beaten), there lived many years since, while the country was yet a province of Great Britain, a simple, good-natured fellow, of the name of Rip Van Winkle. He was a descendant of the Van Winkles who figured so gallantly in the chivalrous days of Peter Stuyvesant, and accompanied him to the siege of Fort Christina. He inherited, however, but little of the martial character of his ancestors. I have observed that he was a simple, good-natured man; he was, moreover, a kind neighbor and an obedient, henpecked husband. Indeed, to the latter circumstance might be owing that meekness of spirit which gained him such universal popularity; for those men are most apt to be obsequious and conciliating abroad who are under the discipline of shrews at home. Their tempers, doubtless, are rendered pliant and malleable in the fiery furnace of domestic tribulation, and a curtain lecture is worth all the sermons in the world for teaching the virtues of patience and long-suffering. A termagant wife may, therefore, in some respects, be considered a tolerable blessing; and if so, Rip Van Winkle was thrice blessed.

Certain it is that he was a great favorite among all the good wives of the village, who, as usual with the amiable sex, took his part in all family squabbles, and never failed, whenever they talked those matters over in their evening gossipings, to lay all the blame on Dame Van Winkle. The children of the village, too, would shout with joy whenever he approached. He assisted at their sports, made their playthings, taught them to fly kites and shoot marbles, and told them long stories of ghosts, witches, and Indians. Whenever he went dodging about the village, he was surrounded by a troop of them, hanging on his skirts, clambering on his back, and playing a thousand tricks on him with impunity; and not a dog would bark at him throughout the neighborhood.

The great error in Rip's composition was an insuperable aversion to all kinds of profitable labor. It could not be from the want of assiduity or perseverance; for he would sit on a wet rock, with a rod as long and heavy as a Tartar's lance, and fish all day without a murmur, even though he should not be encouraged by a single nibble. He would carry a fowling piece on his shoulder, for hours together, trudging through woods and swamps, and up hill and down dale, to shoot a few

---

[27] **Peter Stuyvesant**: Last governor of the Dutch province of New Netherlands (1592—1672), in 1655 (as mentioned below) defeated Swedish colonists at Fort Christina, near what is now Wilmington, Delaware.

squirrels or wild pigeons. He would never even refuse to assist a neighbor in the roughest toil, and was a foremost man at all country frolics for husking Indian corn, or building stone fences. The women of the village, too, used to employ him to run their errands, and to do such little odd jobs as their less obliging husbands would not do for them; in a word, Rip was ready to attend to anybody's business but his own; but as to doing family duty, and keeping his farm in order, it was impossible.

In fact, he declared it was of no use to work on his farm; it was the most pestilent little piece of ground in the whole country; everything about it went wrong, and would go wrong, in spite of him. His fences were continually falling to pieces; his cow would either go astray or get among the cabbages; weeds were sure to grow quicker in his fields than anywhere else; the rain always made a point of setting in just as he had some outdoor work to do; so that though his patrimonial estate had dwindled away under his management, acre by acre, until there was little more left than a mere patch of Indian corn and potatoes, yet it was the worst-conditioned farm in the neighborhood.

His children, too, were as ragged and wild as if they belonged to nobody. His son Rip, an urchin begotten in his own likeness, promised to inherit the habits, with the old clothes of his father. He was generally seen trooping like a colt at his mother's heels, equipped in a pair of his father's cast-off galligaskins, which he had much ado to hold up with one hand, as a fine lady does her train in bad weather.

Rip Van Winkle, however, was one of those happy mortals, of foolish, well-oiled dispositions, who take the world easy, eat white bread or brown, whichever can be got with least thought or trouble, and would rather starve on a penny than work for a pound. If left to himself, he would have whistled life away, in perfect contentment; but his wife kept continually dinning in his ears about his idleness, his carelessness, and the ruin he was bringing on his family. Morning, noon, and night, her tongue was incessantly going, and everything he said or did was sure to produce a torrent of household eloquence. Rip had but one way of replying to all lectures of the kind, and that, by frequent use, had grown into a habit. He shrugged his shoulders, shook his head, cast up his eyes, but said nothing. This, however, always provoked a fresh volley from his wife, so that he was fain to draw off his forces, and take to the outside of the house—the only side which, in truth, belongs to a henpecked husband.

Rip's sole domestic adherent was his dog Wolf, who was as much henpecked as his master; for Dame Van Winkle regarded them as companions in idleness, and even looked upon Wolf with an evil eye, as the cause of his master's so often going astray. True it is, in all points of spirit befitting an honorable dog, he was as courageous an animal as ever scoured the woods—but what courage can withstand the ever-during and all-besetting terrors of a woman's tongue? The moment Wolf entered the house his crest fell, his tail drooped to the ground, or curled between his legs; he sneaked about with a gallows air, casting many a sidelong glance at Dame Van Winkle, and at the least flourish of a broomstick or ladle would fly to the door with yelping precipitation.

Times grew worse and worse with Rip Van Winkle as years of matrimony rolled on; a tart temper never mellows with age, and a sharp tongue is the only edged tool that grows keener by constant use. For a long while he used to console himself, when driven from home, by frequenting a kind of perpetual club of the sages, philosophers, and other idle personages of the village, which held its sessions on a bench before a small inn, designated by a rubicund portrait of his majesty George the Third. Here they used to sit in the shade, of a long lazy summer's day, talking listlessly over village gossip, or telling endless sleepy stories about nothing. But it would have been worth any statesman's money to have heard the profound discussions which sometimes took place, when by chance an old newspaper fell into their hands, from some passing traveler. How solemnly they would listen to the contents, as drawled out by Derrick Van Bummel, the schoolmaster, a dapper, learned little man, who was not to be daunted by the most gigantic word in the dictionary; and how sagely they would deliberate upon public events some months after they had taken place.

The opinions of this junto were completely controlled by Nicholas Vedder, a patriarch of the village, and landlord of the inn, at the door of which he took his seat from morning till night, just moving sufficiently to avoid the sun, and keep in the shade of a large tree; so that the neighbors could tell the hour by his movements as accurately as by a sun-dial. It is true, he was rarely heard to speak, but smoked his pipe incessantly. His adherents, however (for every great man has his adherents), perfectly understood him, and knew how to gather his opinions. When anything that was read or related displeased him, he was observed to smoke his pipe vehemently, and send forth short, frequent, and angry puffs; but when pleased, he would inhale the smoke slowly and tranquilly, and emit it in light and placid clouds, and sometimes taking the pipe from his mouth, and letting the fragrant vapor curl about his nose, would gravely nod his head in token of perfect approbation.

From even this stronghold the unlucky Rip was at length routed by his termagant wife, who would suddenly break in upon the tranquility of the assemblage, and call the members all to naught; nor was that august personage, Nicholas Vedder himself, sacred from the daring tongue of this terrible virago, who charged him outright with encouraging her husband in habits of idleness.

Poor Rip was at last reduced almost to despair; and his only alternative, to escape from the labor of the farm and clamor of his wife, was to take gun in hand and stroll away into the woods. Here he would sometimes seat himself at the foot of a tree, and share the contents of his wallet with Wolf, with whom he sympathized as a fellow-sufferer in persecution. "Poor Wolf," he would say, "thy mistress leads thee a dog's life of it; but never mind, my lad, while I live thou shalt never want a friend to stand by thee!" Wolf would wag his tail, look wistfully in his master's face, and if dogs can feel pity, I verily believe he reciprocated the sentiment with all his heart.

In a long ramble of the kind on a fine autumnal day, Rip had unconsciously scrambled to one of the highest parts of the Catskill Mountains. He was after his favorite sport of squirrel shooting, and the still solitudes had echoed and reechoed with the reports of his gun. Panting and fatigued, he threw himself, late in the afternoon, on a green knoll, covered with mountain herbage, that crowned the brow of a precipice. From an opening between the trees he could overlook all the lower country for many a mile of rich woodland. He saw at a distance the lordly Hudson, far, far below him, moving on its silent but majestic course, the reflection of a purple cloud, or the sail of a lagging bark, here and there sleeping on its glassy bosom, and at last losing itself in the blue highlands.

On the other side he looked down into a deep mountain glen, wild, lonely, and shagged, the bottom filled with fragments from the impending cliffs, and scarcely lighted by the reflected rays of the setting sun. For some time Rip lay musing on this scene; evening was gradually advancing; the mountains began to throw their long blue shadows over the valleys; he saw that it would be dark long before he could reach the village, and he heaved a heavy sigh when he thought of encountering the terrors of Dame Van Winkle.

As he was about to descend, he heard a voice from a distance, hallooing, "Rip Van Winkle! Rip Van Winkle!" He looked around, but could see nothing but a crow winging its solitary flight across the mountain. He thought his fancy must have deceived him, and turned again to descend, when he heard the same cry ring through the still evening air: "Rip Van Winkle! Rip Van Winkle!" —at the same time Wolf bristled up his back, and giving a low growl, skulked to his master's side, looking fearfully down into the glen. Rip now felt a vague apprehension stealing over him; he looked anxiously in the same direction, and perceived a strange figure slowly toiling up the rocks, and bending under the weight of something he carried on his back. He was surprised to see any human being in this lonely and unfrequented place, but supposing it to be some one of the neighborhood in need of assistance, he hastened down to yield it.

On nearer approach, he was still more surprised at the singularity of the stranger's appearance. He was a short, square-built old fellow, with thick bushy hair, and a grizzled beard. His dress was of the antique Dutch fashion—a cloth jerkin strapped around the waist—several pair of breeches, the outer one of ample volume, decorated with rows of buttons down the sides, and bunches at the knees. He bore on his shoulders a stout keg, that seemed full of liquor, and made signs for Rip to approach and assist him with the load. Though rather shy and distrustful of this new acquaintance, Rip complied with his usual alacrity, and mutually relieving one another, they clambered up a narrow gully, apparently the dry bed of a mountain torrent. As they ascended, Rip every now and then heard long rolling peals, like distant thunder, that seemed to issue out of a deep ravine, or rather cleft between lofty rocks, toward which their rugged path conducted. He paused for an instant, but supposing it to be the muttering of one of those transient thunder showers which often take place in mountain heights, he proceeded. Passing through the ravine, they came to a hollow, like a small amphitheater, surrounded by perpendicular precipices, over the brinks of which impending trees shot their branches, so that you only caught glimpses of the azure sky and the bright evening cloud. During the whole time, Rip and his companion had labored on in silence; for though the former marveled greatly what could be the object of carrying a keg of liquor up this wild mountain, yet there was something strange and incomprehensible about the unknown that inspired awe and checked familiarity.

On entering the amphitheater, new objects of wonder presented themselves. On a level spot in the center was a company of odd-looking personages playing at ninepins[28]. They were dressed in a quaint, outlandish fashion: some wore short doublets, others jerkins, with long knives in their belts, and most had enormous breeches, of similar style with that of the guide's. Their visages, too, were peculiar: one had a large head, broad face, and small, piggish eyes; the face of another seemed to consist entirely of nose, and was surmounted by a white sugar-loaf hat set off with a little red cock's tail. They all had beards, of various shapes and colors. There was one who seemed to be the commander. He was a stout old gentleman, with a weather-beaten countenance; he wore a laced doublet, broad belt and hanger, high-crowned hat and feather, red stockings, and high-heeled shoes, with roses in them. The whole group reminded Rip of the figures in an old Flemish painting, in the parlor of Dominie Van Schaick, the village parson, and which had been brought over from Holland at the time of the settlement.

What seemed particularly odd to Rip, was that though these folks were evidently amusing themselves, yet they maintained the gravest faces, the most mysterious silence, and were, withal, the most melancholy party of pleasure he had ever witnessed. Nothing interrupted the stillness of the scene but the noise of the balls, which, whenever they were rolled, echoed along the mountains like rumbling peals of thunder.

As Rip and his companion approached them, they suddenly desisted from their play, and stared at him with such fixed statue-like gaze, and such strange, uncouth, lack-luster countenances, that his heart turned within him, and his knees smote together. His companion now emptied the contents of the keg into large flagons, and made signs to him to wait upon the company. He obeyed with fear and trembling; they quaffed the liquor in profound silence, and then returned to their game.

By degrees, Rip's awe and apprehension subsided. He even ventured, when no eye was fixed upon him, to taste the beverage, which he found had much of the flavor of excellent Hollands. He was naturally a thirsty soul, and was soon tempted to repeat the draught. One taste provoked another, and he reiterated his visits to the flagon so often, that at length his senses were overpowered, his eyes swam in his head, his head gradually declined, and he fell into a deep sleep.

On awaking, he found himself on the green knoll from whence he had first seen the old man of the glen. He rubbed his eyes—it was a bright sunny morning. The birds were hopping and twittering among the bushes, and the eagle was wheeling aloft and breasting the pure mountain breeze. "Surely," thought Rip, "I have not slept here all night." He recalled the occurrences

---

28　**Ninepins**: It is a game (or sport) in which a participant rolls wooden balls on a lane in an attempt to knock down nine bottle-shaped wooden pins arranged in the shape of a diamond. The participant may bowl up to three balls to knock down all the pins. Ninepins is similar to the modern sport of bowling.

before he fell asleep. The strange man with a keg of liquor—the mountain ravine—the wild retreat among the rocks—the woe-begone party at ninepins—the flagon—" Oh! that flagon! that wicked flagon!" thought Rip—" what excuse shall I make to Dame Van Winkle?"

He looked round for his gun, but in place of the clean, well-oiled fowling piece, he found an old firelock lying by him, the barrel incrusted with rust, the lock falling off, and the stock worm-eaten. He now suspected that the grave roysters of the mountain had put a trick upon him, and having dosed him with liquor, had robbed him of his gun. Wolf, too, had disappeared, but he might have strayed away after a squirrel or partridge. He whistled after him, shouted his name, but all in vain; the echoes repeated his whistle and shout, but no dog was to be seen.

He determined to revisit the scene of the last evening's gambol, and if he met with any of the party, to demand his dog and gun. As he rose to walk, he found himself stiff in the joints, and wanting in his usual activity. "These mountain beds do not agree with me," thought Rip, "and if this frolic should lay me up with a fit of the rheumatism, I shall have a blessed time with Dame Van Winkle." With some difficulty he got down into the glen; he found the gully up which he and his companion had ascended the preceding evening; but to his astonishment a mountain stream was now foaming down it, leaping from rock to rock, and filling the glen with babbling murmurs. He, however, made shift to scramble up its sides, working his toilsome way through thickets of birch, sassafras, and witch-hazel, and sometimes tripped up or entangled by the wild grape vines that twisted their coils and tendrils from tree to tree, and spread a kind of network in his path.

At length he reached to where the ravine had opened through the cliffs to the amphitheater; but no traces of such opening remained. The rocks presented a high, impenetrable wall, over which the torrent came tumbling in a sheet of feathery foam, and fell into a broad, deep basin, black from the shadows of the surrounding forest. Here, then, poor Rip was brought to a stand. He again called and whistled after his dog; he was only answered by the cawing of a flock of idle crows, sporting high in air about a dry tree that overhung a sunny precipice; and who, secure in their elevation, seemed to look down and scoff at the poor man's perplexities. What was to be done? The morning was passing away, and Rip felt famished for want of his breakfast. He grieved to give up his dog and gun; he dreaded to meet his wife; but it would not do to starve among the mountains. He shook his head, shouldered the rusty firelock, and, with a heart full of trouble and anxiety, turned his steps homeward.

As he approached the village, he met a number of people, but none whom he knew, which somewhat surprised him, for he had thought himself acquainted with every one in the country round. Their dress, too, was of a different fashion from that to which he was accustomed. They all stared at him with equal marks of surprise, and whenever they cast their eyes upon him, invariably stroked their chins. The constant recurrence of this gesture induced Rip, involuntarily, to do the same, when, to his astonishment, he found his beard had grown a foot long!

He had now entered the skirts of the village. A troop of strange children ran at his heels, hooting after him, and pointing at his gray beard. The dogs, too, none of which he recognized for his old acquaintances, barked at him as he passed. The very village was altered: it was larger and more populous. There were rows of houses which he had never seen before, and those which had been his familiar haunts had disappeared. Strange names were over the doors—strange faces at the windows—everything was strange. His mind now began to misgive him; he doubted whether both he and the world around him were not bewitched. Surely this was his native village, which he had left but the day before. There stood the Catskill Mountains—there ran the silver Hudson at a distance—there was every hill and dale precisely as it had always been—Rip was sorely perplexed—"That flagon last night," thought he, "has addled my poor head sadly!"

It was with some difficulty he found the way to his own house, which he approached with silent awe, expecting every moment to hear the shrill voice of Dame Van Winkle. He found the house gone to decay—the roof fallen in, the windows shattered, and the doors off the hinges. A half-starved dog, that looked like Wolf, was skulking about it. Rip called him by name, but the cur snarled, showed his teeth, and passed on. This was an unkind cut indeed—"My very dog," sighed poor Rip, "has forgotten me!"

He entered the house, which, to tell the truth, Dame Van Winkle had always kept in neat order. It was empty, forlorn, and apparently abandoned. This desolateness overcame all his connubial fears—he called loudly for his wife and children—the lonely chambers rung for a moment with his voice, and then all again was silence.

He now hurried forth, and hastened to his old resort, the little village inn—but it too was gone. A large rickety wooden building stood in its place, with great gaping windows, some of them broken, and mended with old hats and petticoats, and over the door was painted, "The Union Hotel, by Jonathan Doolittle." Instead of the great tree which used to shelter the quiet little Dutch inn of yore, there now was reared a tall naked pole, with something on the top that looked like a red nightcap, and from it was fluttering a flag, on which was a singular assemblage of stars and stripes—all this was strange and incomprehensible. He recognized on the sign, however, the ruby face of King George, under which he had smoked so many a peaceful pipe, but even this was singularly metamorphosed. The red coat was changed for one of blue and buff, a sword was stuck in the hand instead of a scepter, the head was decorated with a cocked hat, and underneath was painted in large characters, GENERAL WASHINGTON.

There was, as usual, a crowd of folk about the door, but none whom Rip recollected. The very character of the people seemed changed. There was a busy, bustling, disputatious tone about it, instead of the accustomed phlegm and drowsy tranquility. He looked in vain for the sage Nicholas Vedder, with his broad face, double chin, and fair long pipe, uttering clouds of tobacco smoke instead of idle speeches; or Van Bummel, the schoolmaster, doling forth the contents of an ancient newspaper. In place of these, a lean, bilious-looking fellow, with his pockets full of handbills, was haranguing vehemently about rights of citizens—election—members of Congress—liberty—Bunker's Hill—heroes of '76—and other words, that were a perfect Babylonish jargon to the bewildered Van Winkle.

The appearance of Rip, with his long grizzled beard, his rusty fowling piece, his uncouth dress, and the army of women and children that had gathered at his heels, soon attracted the attention of the tavern politicians. They crowded around him, eying him from head to foot, with great curiosity. The orator bustled up to him, and drawing him partly aside, inquired "on which side he voted?" Rip stared in vacant stupidity. Another short but busy little fellow pulled him by the arm, and raising on tiptoe, inquired in his ear, "whether he was Federal or Democrat." Rip was equally at a loss to comprehend the question; when a knowing, self-important old gentleman, in a sharp cocked hat, made his way through the crowd, putting them to the right and left with his elbows as he passed, and planting himself before Van Winkle, with one arm akimbo, the other resting on his cane, his keen eyes and sharp hat penetrating, as it were, into his very soul, demanded, in an austere tone, "what brought him to the election with a gun on his shoulder, and a mob at his heels, and whether he meant to breed a riot in the village?" "Alas! gentlemen," cried Rip, somewhat dismayed, "I am a poor quiet man, a native of the place, and a loyal subject of the king, God bless him!"

Here a general shout burst from the bystanders—"A Tory! A Tory! A spy! A refugee! Hustle him! Away with him!" It was with great difficulty that the self-important man in the cocked hat restored order; and having assumed a tenfold austerity of brow, demanded again of the unknown culprit, what he came there for, and whom he was seeking. The poor man humbly assured him that he meant no harm; but merely came there in search of some of his neighbors, who used to keep about the tavern.

"Well—who are they? —name them."

Rip bethought himself a moment, and then inquired, "Where's Nicholas Vedder?"

There was silence for a little while, when an old man replied in a thin, piping voice, "Nicholas Vedder? why, he is dead and gone these eighteen years! There was a wooden tombstone in the churchyard that used to tell all about him, but that's rotted and gone, too."

"Where's Brom Dutcher?"

"Oh, he went off to the army in the beginning of the war; some say he was killed at the battle of Stony Point—others say he was drowned in a squall, at the foot of Antony's Nose. I don't know—he never came back again."

"Where's Van Bummel, the schoolmaster?"

"He went off to the wars, too, was a great militia general, and is now in Congress."

Rip's heart died away, at hearing of these sad changes in his home and friends, and finding himself thus alone in the world. Every answer puzzled him, too, by treating of such enormous lapses of time, and of matters which he could not understand: war—Congress—Stony Point! —he had no courage to ask after any more friends, but cried out in despair, "Does nobody here know Rip Van Winkle?"

"Oh, Rip Van Winkle!" exclaimed two or three, "Oh, to be sure! that's Rip Van Winkle yonder, leaning against the tree."

Rip looked, and beheld a precise counterpart of himself, as he went up the mountain: apparently as lazy, and certainly as ragged. The poor fellow was now completely confounded. He doubted his own identity, and whether he was himself or another man. In the midst of his bewilderment, the man in the cocked hat demanded who he was, and what was his name?

"God knows," exclaimed he, at his wit's end; "I'm not myself—I'm somebody else—that's me yonder—no—that's somebody else, got into my shoes—I was myself last night, but I fell asleep on the mountain, and they've changed my gun, and everything's changed, and I'm changed, and I can't tell what's my name, or who I am!"

The bystanders began now to look at each other, nod, wink significantly, and tap their fingers against their foreheads. There was a whisper, also, about securing the gun, and keeping the old fellow from doing mischief; at the very suggestion of which, the self-important man in the cocked hat retired with some precipitation. At this critical moment a fresh, likely woman pressed through the throng to get a peep at the gray-bearded man. She had a chubby child in her arms, which, frightened at his looks, began to cry. "Hush, Rip," cried she, "hush, you little fool, the old man won't hurt you." The name of the child, the air of the mother, the tone of her voice, all awakened a train of recollections in his mind. "What is your name, my good woman?" asked he.

"Judith Gardenier."

"And your father's name?"

"Ah, poor man, his name was Rip Van Winkle; it's twenty years since he went away from home with his gun, and never has been heard of since—his dog came home without him; but whether he shot himself, or was carried away by the Indians, nobody can tell. I was then but a little girl."

Rip had but one question more to ask; but he put it with a faltering voice:—

"Where's your mother?"

"Oh, she too had died but a short time since; she broke a blood vessel in a fit of passion at a New England peddler."

There was a drop of comfort, at least, in this intelligence. The honest man could contain himself no longer. —He caught his daughter and her child in his arms. —"I am your father!" cried he—"Young Rip Van Winkle once—old Rip Van Winkle now! —Does nobody know poor Rip Van Winkle!"

All stood amazed, until an old woman, tottering out from among the crowd, put her hand to her brow, and peering under it in his face for a moment, exclaimed, "Sure enough! it is Rip Van Winkle—it is himself. Welcome home again, old neighbor. —Why, where have you been these twenty long years?"

Rip's story was soon told, for the whole twenty years had been to him but as one night. The neighbors stared when they heard it; some where seen to wink at each other, and put their tongues in their cheeks; and the self-important man in the cocked hat, who, when the alarm was over, had returned to the field, screwed down the corners of his mouth, and shook his head—upon which there was a general shaking of the head throughout the assemblage.

It was determined, however, to take the opinion of old Peter Vanderdonk, who was seen slowly advancing up the road. He was a descendant of the historian of that name, who wrote one of the earliest accounts of the province. Peter was the most ancient inhabitant of the village, and well versed in all the wonderful events and traditions of the neighborhood. He recollected Rip at once, and corroborated his story in the most satisfactory manner. He assured the company that it was a fact, handed down from his ancestor the historian, that the Catskill Mountains had always been haunted by strange beings. That it was affirmed that the great Hendrick Hudson, the first discoverer of the river and country, kept a kind of vigil there every twenty years, with his crew of the *Half-Moon*, being permitted in this way to revisit the scenes of his enterprise, and keep a guardian eye upon the river, and the great city called by his name. That his father had once seen them in their old Dutch dresses playing at ninepins in a hollow of the mountain; and that he himself had heard, one summer afternoon, the sound of their balls, like long peals of thunder.

To make a long story short, the company broke up, and returned to the more important concerns of the election. Rip's daughter took him home to live with her; she had a snug, well-furnished house, and a stout cheery farmer for a husband, whom Rip recollected for one of the urchins that used to climb upon his back. As to Rip's son and heir, who was the ditto of himself, seen leaning against the tree, he was employed to work on the farm; but evinced a hereditary disposition to attend to anything else but his business.

Rip now resumed his old walks and habits; he soon found many of his former cronies, though all rather the worse for the wear and tear of time; and preferred making friends among the rising generation, with whom he soon grew into great favor.

Having nothing to do at home, and being arrived at that happy age when a man can do nothing with impunity, he took his place once more on the bench, at the inn door, and was reverenced as one of the patriarchs of the village, and a chronicle of the old times "before the war". It was some time before he could get into the regular track of gossip, or could be made to comprehend the strange events that had taken place during his torpor. How that there had been a revolutionary war—that the country had thrown off the yoke of old England—and that, instead of being a subject of his Majesty, George Ⅲ., he was now a free citizen of the United States. Rip, in fact, was no politician; the changes of states and empires made but little impression on him; but there was one species of despotism under which he had long groaned, and that was—petticoat government; happily, that was at an end; he had got his neck out of the yoke of matrimony, and could go in and out whenever he pleased, without dreading the tyranny of Dame Van Winkle. Whenever her name was mentioned, however, he shook his head, shrugged his shoulders, and cast up his eyes; which might pass either for an expression of resignation to his fate, or joy at his deliverance.

He used to tell his story to every stranger that arrived at Dr. Doolittle's hotel. He was observed, at first, to vary on some points every time he told it, which was, doubtless, owing to his having so recently awaked. It at last settled down precisely to the tale I have related, and not a man, woman, or child in the neighborhood but knew it by heart. Some always pretended to doubt the reality of it, and insisted that Rip had been out of his head, and this was one point on which he always remained flighty. The old Dutch inhabitants, however, almost universally gave it full credit. Even to this day they never hear a thunder-storm of a summer afternoon, about the Catskills, but they say Hendrick Hudson and his crew are at their game of ninepins; and it is a common wish of all henpecked husbands in the neighborhood, when life hangs heavy on their hands, that they might have a quieting draught out of Rip Van Winkle's flagon.

■ Study Questions

1. When and where did the story happen?

2. Why did Rip Van Winkle frequently leave his house? How did Rip escape his wife after she came to the inn?

3. Why was Rip suspected of being disloyal on his return?

4. Even though he was a failure as a farmer, Rip Van Winkle was a success as a human being. What were the most praiseworthy qualities that he possessed?

5. When Rip returns to his village, he learns that Dame Van Winkle has died and that his fellow Americans liberated themselves from English rule in a revolutionary war. What do the war and the death of Rip's wife have in common in terms of how Rip will live the rest of his life?

6. Where are the "travelling notes" after the tale picked up? What are they mainly about? In what way are these notes connected with Rip?

7. Identify the similar and different situations in the village for Rip before and after his 20-year sleep. How did Rip view the changes of states and empires? Do you think Rip symbolizes man's desire to flee from responsibility? Why?

8. This selection is a good illustration of the humorous characteristic of Irving. Analyze how Irving creates humor.

James Fenimore Cooper (1789—1851)

James Fenimore Cooper was a prolific and popular American writer of the early 19th century. He is best remembered for his historical romances[29] about the American frontier, particularly the Leatherstocking Tales, featuring frontiersman Natty Bumppo. Among them, *The Last of the Mohicans* (1826) is widely accepted as his masterpiece.

Born in Burlington, New Jersey and grew up in Cooperstown, a settlement established by his father William in New York State, James Cooper (The "Fenimore" was legally added only in 1826) never experienced the danger and struggle of pioneer life. By 1789, the frontier had moved farther west, and there were few pioneers left. "I was never among the Indians," Cooper admitted. "All that I know

---

29　Like Irving, Cooper wrote tales that passed as history, by mimicking history's methods of truth-telling and formal realism. Cooper, as we have examined how well Irving did in this realm, jumbled events and sources and invented new ones in a way that was almost impossible to disentangle fact from fiction. But unlike historical writing during this period, Cooper novels (again like Irving's sketches) offered space for detailing the lives of everyday Americans: the losers as well as the victors, whereas historical writing concentrated on the victors.

of them is from reading, and from hearing my father speak of them. " From his home Cooper watched wagon trains heading west; he left the rest up to his imagination.

After several years as a sailor and then as an officer, Cooper married and settled down to the life of a gentleman farmer with money inherited from his father. Tradition says that one day he tossed aside the British novel he was reading and exclaimed to his wife, "*I could write you a better book than that myself*!" His first novel, *Precaution* (1820), was rather a failure if compared with the Leatherstocking Tales, yet its reception was pleasant enough to encourage Cooper to continue. Then *The Spy* (1821) was an immediate success. Here for the first time Cooper adapted the historical romance of Sir Walter Scott to an array of themes suggested by the American Revolution: the legitimacy of the rebellion, the failure of the British army, the random violence of paramilitary groups of self-proclaimed patriots, the patriarchal benevolence of Washington as the "father of his country," and the cultural centrality of the outcast spy of the title, Harvey Birch. It was an immediate success and, together with Washington Irving's *The Sketch Book* (1820) and William Cullen Bryant's *Poems* (1821), was cited as evidence that American culture had at last begun to produce a worthwhile democratic art.

In 1823, Cooper published *The Pioneers*, the first of the *Leatherstocking Tales*. In it he was to investigate what it meant to inherit the American history of conflict over possession of the landscape, setting the claims of Native Americans, British Loyalists, American Patriots, roaming hunters, and forest-clearing farmers against each other. If the novel wistfully resolves all these conflicts in the marriage of the children of all the contending parties, it nevertheless succeeds brilliantly as a thoroughly American fiction, not least in its invention of the central figure, Natty Bumppo, Cooper's essential American hero. Natty has many names—Leatherstocking, Deerslayer, Pathfinder—but his character never changes. He is strong, brave, resourceful, independent, and absolutely honorable, with a profound understanding of nature. The *Leatherstocking Tales*—*The Deerslayer* (1841), *The Last of the Mohicans* (1826), *The Pathfinder* (1840), *The Prairie* (1827), and *The Pioneers* (1823)—make up an American epic,[30] chronicling the westward march of civilization and the destruction of the wilderness.

More works followed in quick succession. Besides novels, he also wrote travel books and history books (particularly those on American Navy). By the time of his death Cooper had developed an international reputation as America's "national novelist"[31] and was probably more successful and respected abroad than at home. But both at home and abroad Cooper was best known for the mythic sweep and power of his Leatherstocking series, which represents, in D. H. Lawrence's words, "a decrescendo of reality, and a crescendo of beauty. " In fact, all his novels engaged historical themes and helped to form the popular sense of American history and romantic historiography in the 19th century.

The weaknesses of Cooper's fiction are "famous". James Russell Lowell called attention to Cooper's undemocratic class-consciousness and to the limitations of his female characters. Mark Twain hilariously skewered

---

30 Here the *Leatherstocking Tales* are not listed in the time sequence in which they were written but in their order of events. Thus the stories respectively took place in the year(s) 1740—1745, 1757, 1757, 1793, and 1804, while the hero was in his 20s, 40s, 40s, 70s, and 90s. Allan Nevins, who has edited a one-volume version of the series, calls these five novels "the nearest approach yet to an American epic. "

31 Before Cooper, novelists struggled to identify themselves against England and the cultural superiority of Europe, but it was Cooper who first stood as an "American novelist" as he drew extensively on the frontier wilderness as his setting and created abundant characters who are also uniquely American, particularly in their racial make-up. The interpenetration of racial types is everywhere in *The Last of the Mohicans*: Cora is white with a taint of black blood. Magua is a mixed blood Indian. Hawkeye is a white who has been raised by Indians.

the excesses of Cooper's romanticism. All his fictions reflect his didactic concern to educate his audience in the requirements of democracy. Moreover, His plots are often improbable and his language unrealistic.

In spite of all these shortcomings, Cooper has established himself as a great American writer. He charges his works with an energy that makes them immensely popular. His characters (including women) are often more richly developed than is usually recognized and compose a remarkable gallery of American types. In particular, he achieves through Natty Bumppo what few writers ever succeed in doing: He brings before us a character so original and so influential that it has become a myth. As a result, the novels constitute a record of American life and society and at their best present a richness, depth, and complexity that was unsurpassed in American fiction before the works of Hawthorne and Melville.

■ Selected Reading

The Last of the Mohicans, *"A Narrative of 1757,"* *is the 1826 sequel to the now less-famous The Pioneers (1823) and the prequel to The Prairie (1827). Cooper uses the French and Indian war to trace out the essential nature of America as he understood it in 1826. He describes the downfall of genteel, English society and of dark-skinned Americans, that paves the way for the emergence of a middle-class white America. As the novel begins, we are already three years into the conflict. At Fort Edward, General Webb receives news that a French attack under Montcalm is coming to Fort William Henry, which is only guarded by the small force of the Scotsman Munro. Captain Duncan Heyward is dispatched to take Munro's daughters to that Fort along with the renegade Native American runner Magua, known as Le Renard Subtil (The Cunning Fox). We follow their journey as they meet the magnificent Chingachgook whose son Uncas is the last of the Mohican tribe, and find that Magua is actually preventing their progress and is allied to the French. We meet the character Hawkeye and follow him and his Indian companions as they become involved in the bloody war. Hawkeye is seemingly the last decent white man as he respects the Indians customs in this exciting adventure story full of battles, captures and rescues.*

Chapter 12 traces the process of Cora and four other Englishmen being trapped by Magua, while the Hawkeye and his Indian friends followed the tracks they left behind them. The moment Magua and his men intended to end the lives of the English, the Hawkeye, Chingachgook and his son were before them. Wrestles were inevitable, which ended with the rescue of the English, while Magua escaped on a narrow margin.

from *The Last of the Mohicans*

Chapter 12

Clown: *I am gone, sire,*

And anon, sire,

I'll be with you again.

TWELFTH NIGHT

The Hurons stood aghast at this sudden visitation of death on one of their band. But as they regarded the fatal accuracy of an aim which had dared to immolate an enemy at so much hazard to a friend, the name of La Longue Carabine[32] burst simultaneously from every lip, and was succeeded by a wild and a sort of plaintive howl. The cry was answered by a loud shout from a

---

32 **La Longue Carabine**: French name for "the long rifle."

1992 Hollywood Adaptation
of the novel with Daniel Day-
Lewis as Hawkeye

little thicket, where the incautious party had piled their arms; and at the next moment, Hawkeye, too eager to load the rifle he had regained, was seen advancing upon them, brandishing the clubbed weapon, and cutting the air with wide and powerful sweeps. Bold and rapid as was the progress of the scout, it was exceeded by that of a light and vigorous form which, bounding past him, leaped, with incredible activity and daring, into the very center of the Hurons, where it stood, whirling a tomahawk, and flourishing a glittering knife, with fearful menaces, in front of Cora. Quicker than the thoughts could follow those unexpected and audacious movements, an image, armed in the emblematic panoply of death, glided before their eyes, and assumed a threatening attitude at the other's side. The savage tormentors recoiled before these warlike intruders, and uttered, as they appeared in such quick succession, the often repeated and peculiar exclamations of surprise, followed by the well-known and dreaded appellations of:

"Le Cerf Agile! Le Gros Serpent! [33]"

But the wary and vigilant leader of the Hurons was not so easily disconcerted. Casting his keen eyes around the little plain, he comprehended the nature of the assault at a glance, and encouraging his followers by his voice as well as by his example, he unsheathed his long and dangerous knife, and rushed with a loud whoop upon the expected Chingachgook. It was the signal for a general combat. Neither party had firearms, and the contest was to be decided in the deadliest manner, hand to hand, with weapons of offense, and none of defense.

Uncas answered the whoop, and leaping on an enemy, with a single, well-directed blow of his tomahawk, cleft him to the brain. Heyward tore the weapon of Magua from the sapling, and rushed eagerly toward the fray. As the combatants were now equal in number, each singled an opponent from the adverse band. The rush and blows passed with the fury of a whirlwind, and the swiftness of lightning. Hawkeye soon got another enemy within reach of his arm, and with one sweep of his formidable weapon he beat down the slight and inartificial defenses of his antagonist, crushing him to the earth with the blow. Heyward ventured to hurl the tomahawk he had seized, too ardent to await the moment of closing. It struck the Indian he had selected on the forehead, and checked for an instant his onward rush. Encouraged by this slight advantage, the impetuous young man continued his onset, and sprang upon his enemy with naked hands. A single instant was enough to assure him of the rashness of the measure, for he immediately found himself fully engaged, with all his activity and courage, in endeavoring to ward the desperate thrusts made with the knife of the Huron. Unable longer to foil an enemy so alert and vigilant, he threw his arms about him, and succeeded in pinning the limbs of the other to his side, with an iron grasp, but

---

33   **Le Gros Serpent**: the large snake, French name given to Chingachgook. He was so called because of his wisdom, cunning, and prudence.

one that was far too exhausting to himself to continue long. In this extremity he heard a voice near him, shouting:

"Extarminate the varlets! no quarter to an accursed Mingo [34]!"

At the next moment, the breech of Hawkeye's rifle fell on the naked head of his adversary, whose muscles appeared to wither under the shock, as he sank from the arms of Duncan, flexible and motionless.

When Uncas had brained his first antagonist, he turned, like a hungry lion, to seek another. The fifth and only Huron disengaged at the first onset had paused a moment, and then seeing that all around him were employed in the deadly strife, he had sought, with hellish vengeance, to complete the baffled work of revenge. Raising a shout of triumph, he sprang toward the defenseless Cora, sending his keen axe as the dreadful precursor of his approach. The tomahawk grazed her shoulder, and cutting the withes which bound her to the tree, left the maiden at liberty to fly. She eluded the grasp of the savage, and reckless of her own safety, threw herself on the bosom of Alice, striving with convulsed and ill-directed fingers, to tear asunder the twigs which confined the person of her sister. Any other than a monster would have relented at such an act of generous devotion to the best and purest affection; but the breast of the Huron was a stranger to sympathy. Seizing Cora by the rich tresses which fell in confusion about her form, he tore her from her frantic hold, and bowed her down with brutal violence to her knees. The savage drew the flowing curls through his hand, and raising them on high with an outstretched arm, he passed the knife around the exquisitely molded head of his victim, with a taunting and exulting laugh. But he purchased this moment of fierce gratification with the loss of the fatal opportunity. It was just then the sight caught the eye of Uncas. Bounding from his footsteps he appeared for an instant darting through the air and descending in a ball he fell on the chest of his enemy, driving him many yards from the spot, headlong and prostrate. The violence of the exertion cast the young Mohican at his side. They arose together, fought, and bled, each in his turn. But the conflict was soon decided; the tomahawk of Heyward and the rifle of Hawkeye descended on the skull of the Huron, at the same moment that the knife of Uncas reached his heart.

The battle was now entirely terminated with the exception of the protracted struggle between Le Renard Subtil [35] and Le Gros Serpent. Well did these barbarous warriors prove that they deserved those significant names which had been bestowed for deeds in former wars. When they engaged, some little time was lost in eluding the quick and vigorous thrusts which had been aimed at their lives. Suddenly darting on each other, they closed, and came to the earth, twisted together like twining serpents, in pliant and subtle folds. At the moment when the victors found themselves unoccupied, the spot where these experienced and desperate combatants lay could only be distinguished by a cloud of dust and leaves, which moved from the center of the little plain

---

34　**Mingo**: a name scornfully applied by the Mohicans to their enemies, the Hurons.

35　**Le Renard Subtil**: the clever fox, French name for Magua because of his sly craftiness.

toward its boundary, as if raised by the passage of a whirlwind. Urged by the different motives of filial affection, friendship and gratitude, Heyward and his companions rushed with one accord to the place, encircling the little canopy of dust which hung above the warriors. In vain did Uncas dart around the cloud, with a wish to strike his knife into the heart of his father's foe; the threatening rifle of Hawkeye was raised and suspended in vain, while Duncan endeavored to seize the limbs of the Huron with hands that appeared to have lost their power. Covered as they were with dust and blood, the swift evolutions of the combatants seemed to incorporate their bodies into one. The death-like looking figure of the Mohican, and the dark form of the Huron, gleamed before their eyes in such quick and confused succession, that the friends of the former knew not where to plant the succoring blow. It is true there were short and fleeting moments, when the fiery eyes of Magua were seen glittering, like the fabled organs of the basilisk through the dusty wreath by which he was enveloped, and he read by those short and deadly glances the fate of the combat in the presence of his enemies; ere, however, any hostile hand could descend on his devoted head, its place was filled by the scowling visage of Chingachgook. In this manner the scene of the combat was removed from the center of the little plain to its verge. The Mohican now found an opportunity to make a powerful thrust with his knife; Magua suddenly relinquished his grasp, and fell backward without motion, and seemingly without life. His adversary leaped on his feet, making the arches of the forest ring with the sounds of triumph.

"Well done for the Delawares[36]! victory to the Mohicans!" cried Hawkeye, once more elevating the butt of the long and fatal rifle; a finishing blow from a man without a cross will never tell against his honor, nor rob him of his right to the scalp. But at the very moment when the dangerous weapon was in the act of descending, the subtle Huron rolled swiftly from beneath the danger, over the edge of the precipice, and falling on his feet, was seen leaping, with a single bound, into the center of a thicket of low bushes, which clung along its sides. The Delawares, who had believed their enemy dead, uttered their exclamation of surprise, and were following with speed and clamor, like hounds in open view of the deer, when a shrill and peculiar cry from the scout instantly changed their purpose, and recalled them to the summit of the hill.

"'Twas like himself!" cried the inveterate forester, whose prejudices contributed so largely to veil his natural sense of justice in all matters which concerned the Mingoes; "a lying and deceitful varlet as he is. An honest Delaware now, being fairly vanquished, would have lain still, and been knocked on the head, but these knavish Maquas cling to life like so many cats-o'-the-mountain. Let him go—let him go; 'tis but one man, and he without rifle or bow, many a long mile from his French commerades; and like a rattler that lost his fangs, he can do no further mischief, until such time as he, and we too, may leave the prints of our moccasins over a long reach of sandy plain. See, Uncas," he added, in Delaware, "your father if flaying the scalps already. It may be well to go round and feel the vagabonds that are left, or we may have another of them loping

---

36 **Delawares**: Mohicans.

through the woods, and screeching like a jay that has been winged. "

So saying the honest but implacable scout made the circuit of the dead, into whose senseless bosoms he thrust his long knife, with as much coolness as though they had been so many brute carcasses. He had, however, been anticipated by the elder Mohican, who had already torn the emblems of victory from the unresisting heads of the slain.

But Uncas, denying his habits, we had almost said his nature, flew with instinctive delicacy, accompanied by Heyward, to the assistance of the females, and quickly releasing Alice, placed her in the arms of Cora. We shall not attempt to describe the gratitude to the Almighty Disposer of Events which glowed in the bosoms of the sisters, who were thus unexpectedly restored to life and to each other. Their thanksgivings were deep and silent; the offerings of their gentle spirits burning brightest and purest on the secret altars of their hearts; and their renovated and more earthly feelings exhibiting themselves in long and fervent though speechless caresses. As Alice rose from her knees, where she had sunk by the side of Cora, she threw herself on the bosom of the latter, and sobbed aloud the name of their aged father, while her soft, dove-like eyes, sparkled with the rays of hope.

"We are saved! we are saved!" she murmured; "to return to the arms of our dear, dear father, and his heart will not be broken with grief. And you, too, Cora, my sister, my more than sister, my mother; you, too, are spared. And Duncan," she added, looking round upon the youth with a smile of ineffable innocence, even our own brave and noble Duncan has escaped without a hurt. "

To these ardent and nearly innocent words Cora made no other answer than by straining the youthful speaker to her heart, as she bent over her in melting tenderness. The manhood of Heyward felt no shame in dropping tears over this spectacle of affectionate rapture; and Uncas stood, fresh and blood-stained from the combat, a calm, and, apparently, an unmoved looker-on, it is true, but with eyes that had already lost their fierceness, and were beaming with a sympathy that elevated him far above the intelligence, and advanced him probably centuries before, the practices of his nation.

During this display of emotions so natural in their situation, Hawkeye, whose vigilant distrust had satisfied itself that the Hurons, who disfigured the heavenly scene, no longer possessed the power to interrupt its harmony, approached David, and liberated him from the bonds he had, until that moment, endured with the most exemplary patience.

"There," exclaimed the scout, casting the last withe behind him, "you are once more master of your own limbs, though you seem not to use them with much greater judgment than that in which they were first fashioned. If advice from one who is not older than yourself, but who, having lived most of his time in the wilderness, may be said to have experience beyond his years, will give no offense, you are welcome to my thoughts; and these are, to part with the little tooting instrument in your jacket to the first fool you meet with, and buy some we'pon with the money, if it be only the barrel of a horseman's pistol. By industry and care, you might thus come to some prefarment; for by this time, I should think, your eyes would plainly tell you that a carrion crow is a better bird than a mocking-thresher. The one will, at least, remove foul sights from before the face of man, while the other is only good to brew disturbances in the woods, by cheating the ears of all that hear them. "

"Arms and the clarion for the battle, but the song of thanksgiving to the victory!" answered the liberated David. "Friend," he added, thrusting forth his lean, delicate hand toward Hawkeye, in kindness, while his eyes twinkled and grew moist, "I thank thee that the hairs of my head still grow where they were first rooted by Providence; for, though those of other men may be more glossy and curling, I have ever found mine own well suited to the brain they shelter. That I did not join myself to the battle, was less owing to disinclination, than to the bonds of the heathen. Valiant and skillful hast thou proved thyself in the conflict, and I hereby thank thee, before proceeding to discharge other and more important duties, because thou hast proved thyself well worthy of a Christian's praise. "

"The thing is but a trifle, and what you may often see if you tarry long among us," returned the scout, a good deal softened toward the man of song, by this unequivocal expression of gratitude. "I have got back my old companion, killdeer," he added, striking his hand on the breech of his rifle; "and that in itself is a victory. These Iroquois are cunning, but they outwitted themselves when they placed their firearms out of reach; and had Uncas or his father been gifted with only their common Indian patience, we should have come in upon the knaves with three bullets instead of one, and that would have made a finish of the whole pack; yon loping varlet, as well as his commerades. But 't was all fore-ordered, and for the best. "

"Thou sayest well," returned David, "and hast caught the true spirit of Christianity. He that is to be saved will be saved, and he that is predestined to be damned will be damned. This is the doctrine of truth, and most consoling and refreshing it is to the true believer. "

The scout, who by this time was seated, examining into the state of his rifle with a species of parental assiduity, now looked up at the other in a displeasure that he did not affect to conceal, roughly interrupting further speech.

"Doctrine or no doctrine," said the sturdy woodsman, "'tis the belief of knaves, and the curse of an honest man. I can credit that yonder Huron was to fall by my hand, for with my own eyes I have seen it; but nothing short of being a witness will cause me to think he has met with any reward, or that Chingachgook there will be condemned at the final day. "

"You have no warranty for such an audacious doctrine, nor any covenant to support it," cried David who was deeply tinctured with the subtle distinctions which, in his time, and more especially in his province, had been drawn around the beautiful simplicity of revelation, by endeavoring to penetrate the awful mystery of the divine nature, supplying faith by self-sufficiency, and by consequence, involving those who reasoned from such human dogmas in absurdities and doubt; "your temple is reared on the sands, and the first tempest will wash away its foundation. I demand your authorities for such an uncharitable assertion (like other advocates of a system,

David was not always accurate in his use of terms). Name chapter and verse; in which of the holy books do you find language to support you?"

"Book!" repeated Hawkeye, with singular and ill-concealed disdain; "do you take me for a whimpering boy at the apronstring of one of your old gals; and this good rifle on my knee for the feather of a goose's wing, my ox's horn for a bottle of ink, and my leathern pouch for a cross-barred handkercher to carry my dinner? Book! what have such as I, who am a warrior of the wilderness, though a man without a cross, to do with books? I never read but in one, and the words that are written there are too simple and too plain to need much schooling; though I may boast that of forty long and hard-working years."

"What call you the volume?" said David, misconceiving the other's meaning.

"'Tis open before your eyes," returned the scout; and he who owns it is not a niggard of its use. I have heard it said that there are men who read in books to convince themselves there is a God. I know not but man may so deform his works in the settlement, as to leave that which is so clear in the wilderness a matter of doubt among traders and priests. If any such there be, and he will follow me from sun to sun, through the windings of the forest, he shall see enough to teach him that he is a fool, and that the greatest of his folly lies in striving to rise to the level of One he can never equal, be it in goodness, or be it in power."

The instant David discovered that he battled with a disputant who imbibed his faith from the lights of nature, eschewing all subtleties of doctrine, he willingly abondoned a controversy from which he believed neither profit nor credit was to be derived. While the scout was speaking, he had also seated himself, and producing the ready little volume and the iron-rimmed spectacles, he prepared to discharge a duty, which nothing but the unexpected assault he had received in his orthodoxy could have so long suspended. He was, in truth, a minstrel of the western continent— of a much later day, certainly, than those gifted bards, who formerly sang the profane renown of baron and prince, but after the spirit of his own age and country; and he was now prepared to exercise the cunning of his craft, in celebration of, or rather in thanksgiving for, the recent victory. He waited patiently for Hawkeye to cease, then lifting his eyes, together with his voice, he said, aloud:

"I invite you, friends, to join in praise for this signal deliverance from the hands of barbarians and infidels, to the comfortable and solemn tones of the tune called Northampton."

He next named the page and verse where the rhymes selected were to be found, and applied the pitch-pipe to his lips, with the decent gravity that he had been wont to use in the temple. This time he was, however, without any accompaniment, for the sisters were just then pouring out those tender effusions of affection which have been already alluded to. Nothing deterred by the smallness of his audience, which, in truth, consisted only of the discontented scout, he raised his voice, commencing and ending the sacred song without accident or interruption of any kind.

Hawkeye listened while he coolly adjusted his flint and reloaded his rifle; but the sounds, wanting the extraneous assistance of scene and sympathy, failed to awaken his slumbering emotions. Never minstrel, or by whatever more suitable name David should be known, drew upon his talents in the presence of more insensible auditors; though considering the singleness and sincerity of his motive, it is probably that no bard of profane song ever uttered notes that ascended so near to that throne where all homage and praise is due. The scout shook his head, and muttering some unintelligible words, among which throat and Iroquois were alone audible, he walked away, to collect and to examine into the state of the captured arsenal of the Hurons. In this office he was now joined by Chingachgook, who found his own, as well as the rifle of his son, among the arms. Even Heyward and David were furnished with weapons; nor was ammunition wanting to render them all effectual.

When the foresters had made their selection, and distributed their prizes, the scout announced that the hour had arrived when it was necessary to move. By this time the song of Gamut had ceased, and the sisters had learned to still the exhibition of their emotions. Aided by Duncan and the younger Mohican, the two latter descended the precipitous sides of that hill which they had so lately ascended under so very different auspices, and whose summit had so nearly proved the scene of their massacre. At the foot they found the Narragansetts browsing the herbage of the bushes, and having mounted, they followed the movements of a guide, who, in the most deadly straits, had so often proved himself their friend. The journey was, however, short. Hawkeye, leaving the blind path that the Hurons had followed, turned short to his right, and entering the thicket, he crossed a babbling brook, and halted in a narrow dell, under the shade of a few water elms. Their distance from the base of the fatal hill was but a few rods, and the steeds had been serviceable only in crossing the shallow stream.

The scout and the Indians appeared to be familiar with the sequestered place where they now were; for, leaning their rifle against the trees, they commenced throwing aside the dried leaves, and opening the blue clay, out of which a clear and sparkling spring of bright, glancing water, quickly bubbled. The white man then looked about him, as though seeking for some object, which was not to be found as readily as he expected.

"Them careless imps, the Mohawks, with their Tuscarora and Onondaga brethren, have been here slaking their thirst," he muttered, "and the vagabonds have thrown away the gourd! This is the way with benefits, when they are bestowed on such disremembering hounds! Here has the Lord laid his hand, in the midst of the howling wilderness, for their good, and raised a fountain of water from the bowels of the 'arth, that might laugh at the richest shop of apothecary's ware in all the colonies; and see! the knaves have trodden in the clay, and deformed the cleanliness of the place, as though they were brute beasts, instead of human men."

Uncas silently extended toward him the desired gourd, which the spleen of Hawkeye had hitherto prevented him from observing on a branch of an elm. Filling it with water, he retired a short distance, to a place where the ground was more firm and dry; here he coolly seated himself, and after taking a long, and, apparently, a grateful draught, he commenced a very strict examination of the fragments of food left by the Hurons, which had hung in a wallet on his arm.

"Thank you, lad!" he continued, returning the empty gourd to Uncas; "now we will see how these rampaging Hurons lived, when outlying in ambushments. Look at this! The varlets know the better pieces of the deer; and one would think they might carve and roast a saddle, equal to the best cook in the land! But everything is raw, for the Iroquois are thorough savages. Uncas, take my steel and kindle a fire; a mouthful of a tender broil will give natur'a helping hand, after so long a trail."

Heyward, perceiving that their guides now set about their repast in sober earnest, assisted the ladies to alight, and placed himself at their side, not unwilling to enjoy a few moments of grateful rest, after the bloody scene he had just gone through. While the culinary process was in hand, curiosity induced him to inquire into the circumstances which had led to their timely and unexpected rescue:

"How is it that we see you so soon, my generous friend, he asked, and without aid from the garrison of Edward?"

"Had we gone to the bend in the river, we might have been in time to rake the leaves over your bodies, but too late to have saved your scalps," coolly answered the scout. "No, no; instead of throwing away strength and opportunity by crossing to the fort, we lay by, under the bank of the Hudson, waiting to watch the movements of the Hurons."

"You were, then, witnesses of all that passed?"

"Not of all; for Indian sight is too keen to be easily cheated, and we kept close. A difficult matter it was, too, to keep this Mohican boy snug in the ambushment. Ah! Uncas, Uncas, your behavior was more like that of a curious woman than of a warrior on his scent."

Uncas permitted his eyes to turn for an instant on the sturdy countenance of the speaker, but he neither spoke nor gave any indication of repentance. On the contrary, Heyward thought the manner of the young Mohican was disdainful, if not a little fierce, and that he suppressed passions that were ready to explode, as much in compliment to the listeners, as from the deference he usually paid to his white associate.

"You saw our capture? Heyward next demanded."

"We heard it," was the significant answer. "An Indian yell is plain language to men who have passed their days in the woods. But when you landed, we were driven to crawl like sarpents, beneath the leaves; and then we lost sight of you entirely, until we placed eyes on you again trussed to the trees, and ready bound for an Indian massacre."

"Our rescue was the deed of Providence. It was nearly a miracle that you did not mistake the path, for the Hurons divided, and each band had its horses."

"Ay! there we were thrown off the scent, and might, indeed, have lost the trail, had it not been for Uncas; we took the path, however, that led into the wilderness; for we judged, and judged rightly, that the savages would hold that course with their prisoners. But when we had followed it for many miles, without finding a single twig broken, as I had advised, my mind misgave me; especially as all the footsteps had the prints of moccasins."

"Our captors had the precaution to see us shod like themselves," said Duncan, raising a foot, and exhibiting the buckskin he wore.

"Aye, 'twas judgmatical and like themselves; though we were too expart to be thrown from a trail by so common an invention."

"To what, then, are we indebted for our safety?"

"To what, as a white man who has no taint of Indian blood, I should be ashamed to own; to the judgment of the young Mohican, in matters which I should know better than he, but which I can now hardly believe to be true, though my own eyes tell me it is so."

"'Tis extraordinary! will you not name the reason?"

"Uncas was bold enough to say, that the beasts ridden by the gentle ones," continued Hawkeye, glancing his eyes, not without curious interest, on the fillies of the ladies, planted the legs of one side on the ground at the same time, which is contrary to the movements of all trotting four-footed animals of my knowledge, except the bear. "And yet here are horses that always journey in this manner, as my own eyes have seen, and as their trail has shown for twenty long miles."

"'Tis the merit of the animal! They come from the shores of Narrangansett Bay, in the small province of Providence Plantations, and are celebrated for their hardihood, and the ease of this peculiar movement; though other horses are not unfrequently trained to the same."

"It may be—it may be," said Hawkeye, who had listened with singular attention to this explanation; "though I am a man who has the full blood of the whites, my judgment in deer and beaver is greater than in beasts of burden. Major Effingham has many noble chargers, but I have never seen one travel after such a sidling gait."

"True; for he would value the animals for very different properties. Still is this a breed highly esteemed and, as you witness, much honored with the burdens it is often destined to bear."

The Mohicans had suspended their operations about the glimmering fire to listen; and, when Duncan had done, they looked at each other significantly, the father uttering the never-failing exclamation of surprise. The scout ruminated, like a man digesting his newly-acquired knowledge, and once more stole a glance at the horses.

"I dare to say there are even stranger sights to be seen in the settlements!" he said, "at length natur' is sadly abused by man, when he once gets the mastery. But, go sidling or go straight, Uncas had seen the movement, and their trail led us on to the broken bush. The outer branch, near the prints of one of the horses, was bent upward, as a lady breaks a flower from its stem, but all the rest were ragged and broken down, as if the strong hand of a man had been tearing them! So I concluded that the cunning varments had seen the twig bent, and had torn the rest, to make us believe a buck had been feeling the boughs with his antlers."

"I do believe your sagacity did not deceive you; for some such thing occurred!"

"That was easy to see," added the scout, in no degree conscious of having exhibited any extraordinary sagacity; "and a very different matter it was from a waddling horse! It then struck me the Mingoes would push for this spring, for the knaves well know the vartue of its waters!"

"Is it, then, so famous?" demanded Heyward, examining, with a more curious eye, the secluded dell, with its bubbling fountain, surrounded, as it was, by earth of a deep, dingy brown.

"Few red-skins, who travel south and east of the great lakes but have heard of its qualities. Will you taste for yourself?"

Heyward took the gourd, and after swallowing a little of the water, threw it aside with grimaces of discontent. The scout laughed in his silent but heartfelt manner, and shook his head with vast satisfaction.

"Ah! you want the flavor that one gets by habit; the time was when I liked it as little as yourself; but I have come to my taste, and I now crave it, as a deer does the licks. Your high-spiced wines are not better liked than a red-skin relishes this water; especially when his natur' is ailing. But Uncas has made his fire, and it is time we think of eating, for our journey is long, and all before us. "

Interrupting the dialogue by this abrupt transition, the scout had instant recourse to the fragments of food which had escaped the voracity of the Hurons. A very summary process completed the simple cookery, when he and the Mohicans commenced their humble meal, with the silence and characteristic diligence of men who ate in order to enable themselves to endure great and unremitting toil.

When this necessary, and, happily, grateful duty had been performed, each of the foresters stooped and took a long and parting draught at that solitary and silent spring, around which and its sister fountains, within fifty years, the wealth, beauty and talents of a hemisphere were to assemble in throngs, in pursuit of health and pleasure. Then Hawkeye announced his determination to proceed. The sisters resumed their saddles; Duncan and David grasped their rifles, and followed on footsteps; the scout leading the advance, and the Mohicans bringing up the rear. The whole party moved swiftly through the narrow path, toward the north, leaving the healing waters to mingle unheeded with the adjacent brooks and the bodies of the dead to fester on the neighboring mount, without the rites of sepulture; a fate but too common to the warriors of the woods to excite either commiseration or comment.

■ Study Questions

1. Who is Le Gros Serpent? Apart from him, who else take part in the sudden attack against the Hurons? Why do they fight "hand to hand" with the Hurons? Retell the details of the combat "in the deadliest manner. "

2. Who is Le Renard Subtil? Why does he suddenly relinquish his grasp and fall back motionless during the fierce fight with the Mohican?

3. In Paragraph 11, Cooper writes, "He had, however, been anticipated by the elder Mohican, who had already torn the emblems of victory from the unresisting heads of the slain. " What does "emblems of victory" here refer to?

4. What drives Alice to say that Cora is "more than sister" after they are saved?

5. Upon what subject do David and Hawkeye argue after the combat? What are their disputes?

6. According to Hawkeye, how did he and the Mohicans manage to follow the Hurons?

7. When the Hawkeye is about to give a "finishing blow" to Magua, he calls himself "a man without a cross", and says his act will "never tell against his honor, nor rob him of his right to the scalp." What does he mean by saying that? What does Cooper actually intend to say through the term "a man without a cross"?

8. At the end of the chapter, Cooper describes the different reactions of the Hawkeye and Major Heyward toward the water they drink. Cooper also makes the Hawkeye contrast the water with the "high-spiced wines". What is Cooper's intention here?

9. Most of Cooper's readers lived in towns and cities. Why would a romance of the wilderness such as *The Last of the Mohicans* appeal to them?

William Cullen Bryant (1794—1878)

William Cullen Bryant, the "father of American poetry," grew up in a small village in western Massachusetts. Bryant was interested in poetry ever since his childhood. His work, written in an English romantic style and celebrating the countryside of New England, was well received. His first book of verse, *The Embargo*, was published in 1808, his first published poem appearing at age ten. Bryant's first critically acclaimed work, "Thanatopsis", was published in the *North American Review* (an important Boston literary magazine) in 1817 [37] at age 23, addressing the theme of death's definite occurrence for all. Bryant refined and expanded this poem as the years passed. "Thanatopsis" was one of the most popular poems in circulation in its time. Bryant's father, a prominent doctor, encouraged him to continue writing poetry but recommended that he become a lawyer in order to make a living.

After a short time as a lawyer, however, Bryant began a career as one of the nation's most distinguished journalists. He became the editor-in-chief of the influential *New York Evening Post* and used his position to put forth his strong political and social views. Bryant was a lifelong political activist; later in life he became a founder of the Republican Party. He supported the early labor movement, free speech, a free press, and the abolition of slavery. He was a fervent supporter of Abraham Lincoln's presidential bid in 1860; in fact, it was Bryant who introduced Lincoln to the voters of New York. For the last thirty years of his life, Bryant was New York City's most prominent citizen.

Yet he continued to write poetry. Among his best known poems are "To A Waterfowl", "The Rivulet", "The West Wind", "The Forest Hymn", and "The Fringed Gentian". These noble and romantic verses, often based on the American landscape, established him as the first American poet to have an enduring reputation.

Bryant received great praise for his poetry, but the critics did not give him unconditional laurels, due to the absence of a full range of poetry, such as epics, elegies, and verse drama—as we have seen, he didn't publish enough. He looked at art as something demanding time and reflection, something not afforded to him on his travels or by his work at the paper. He did publish *The Letters of a Traveller* in 1850, a series of letters he had written to the *Evening Post*, describing his tours of Europe, Mexico, Cuba, and South America. In 1866, after the death of his wife, Bryant took up translation and editing anthologies as he did less and less with the newspaper, and he

---

[37]   The poem first appeared in the NAR in 1817, vol. 5. issue 13, pp. 338-339.

resumed translating the *Iliad* and subsequently the *Odyssey*. He published a collected edition, a final one, in 1876.

Bryant's place in literary history is not altogether secure. He is regarded as falling somewhat short of his potential. Although he published little as he became immersed in the journalistic life, he was extremely popular in his time and even one time was named as a candidate for President. Bryant died in 1878 of complications from an accidental fall. At his death, New York City's flags flew at half-mast. In 1884, New York City's Reservoir Square, at the intersection of 42nd Street and 6th Avenue, was renamed Bryant Park in his honor.

■ Selected Reading

*Bryant probably wrote "**Thanatopsis**" when he was about 19. Several years later his father sent it to the* North American Review. *As it was published anonymously, according to the custom of the magazine, readers could not believe that it had been written by a young man, or even by an American. Even the editors of the magazine thought that Bryant's father had actually written it. As successful as the poem was, Bryant later revised it. He added the beginning section (Lines 1-11) and the ending (Lines 66-81).*

The title of the poem is a Greek word meaning "view of death" (It is a compound Greek word made by "thanatos" meaning "death" while "opsis" meaning "think" or "look at"). The poem is, however, much more than that. "Thanatopsis" is a Romantic poet's vision of what it means to be a human being—to be both a mortal individual and a part of enduring nature.

The poem is written in blank verse, namely, in unrhymed iambic pentameter, for the advantage to express with more freedom.

Kindred Spirits, 1849, Asher B. Durand. Bryant and the painter Thomas Cole share their Romantic awe of nature

Thanatopsis

To him who in the love of Nature holds
Communion with her visible forms,[38] she Speaks
A various language; for his gayer hours
She has a voice of gladness, and a Smile
5   And eloquence of beauty, and she glides
Into his darker musings, with a mild
And healing sympathy, that steals away
Their sharpness, ere he is aware. When thoughts
Of the last bitter hour come like a blight
10   Over thy spirit, and sad images
Of the stern agony, and shroud, and pall,
And breathless darkness, and the narrow house[39],

---

38   **holds communion… forms:** shares or exchanges thoughts or feelings with the objective existence in nature.

39   **narrow house:** coffin.

Make thee to shudder, and grow sick at heart?
Go forth, under the open sky, and list[40]
15 To Nature's teachings, while from all around?
Earth and her waters, and the depths of air?[41]
Comes a still voice: —Yet a few days, and thee
The all-beholding sun shall see no more
In all his course; nor yet in the cold ground,
20 Where thy pale form was laid, with many tears,
Nor in the embrace of ocean, shall exist
Thy image. Earth, that nourished thee, shall claim
Thy growth, to be resolved to earth again,
And, lost each human trace, surrendering up
25 Thine individual being, shalt thou go
To mix forever with the elements,
To be a brother to the insensible rock
And to the sluggish clod, which the rude swain[42]
Turns with his share and treads upon. The oak
30 Shall send his roots abroad, and pierce thy mold.
Yet not to thine eternal resting place
Shalt thou retire alone, nor couldst thou wish
Couch[43] more magnificent. Thou shalt lie down
With patriarchs of the infant world[44]—with kings,
35 The powerful of the earth—the wise, the good,
Fair forms, and hoary seers of ages past,
All in one mighty sepulcher. The hills
Rock-ribbed and ancient as the sun—the vales
Stretching in pensive quietness between;
40 The venerable woods—rivers that move
In majesty, and the complaining brooks
That make the meadows green; and, poured round all,
Old Ocean's gray and melancholy waste—
Are but the solemn decorations all

40　**list**: listen.

41　**the depths of air**: the highest level of heaven.

42　**swain**: country youth.

43　**Couch**: bed.

44　**patriarchs of the infant world**: the prominent figures of the ancient time; the infant world is the early stage of human history.

45 Of the great tomb of man. The golden sun,
    The planets, all the infinite host of heaven,
    Are shining on the sad abodes of death,
    Through the still lapse of ages. All that tread
    The globe are but a handful to the tribes
50 That slumber in its bosom. [45] Take the wings
    Of morning, [46] pierce the Barcan wilderness, [47]
    Or lose thyself in the continuous woods
    Where rolls the Oregon[48] and hears no sound,
    Save his own dashings—yet the dead are there:
55 And millions in those solitudes, since first
    The flight of years began, have laid them down
    In their last sleep—the dead reign there alone,
    So shalt thou rest, and what if thou withdraw
    In silence from the living, and no friend
60 Take note of thy departure? All that breathe
    Will share thy destiny. The gay will laugh
    When thou art gone, the solemn brood of care
    Plod on, and each one as before will chase
    His favorite phantom; yet all these shall leave
65 Their mirth and their employments, and shall come
    And make their bed with thee. As the long train
    Of ages glides away, the sons of men,
    The youth in life's fresh spring, and he who goes
    In the full strength of years, matron[49]and maid,
70 The speechless babe, and the gray-headed man—
    Shall one by one be gathered to thy side,
    By those, who in their turn shall follow them.
    So live, that when thy summons comes to join
    The innumerable caravan, which moves
75 To that mysterious realm where each shall take
    His chamber in the silent halls of death,

---

45 **All that tread... in its bosom:** All those people who now walk arrogantly on earth are just a few compared to those who are sleeping peacefully in their tombs.
46 **Take... morning:** from Psalm 139:9, in which the psalmist sings of flying away to distant places.
47 **Barcan wilderness:** the deserts of Barca in North Africa.
48 **Oregon:** American Indian name for the Columbia River.
49 **matron:** married woman; middle-aged or elderly married woman, esp. one with a dignified appearance.

Thou go not, like the quarry-slave at night.

Scourged to his dungeon, but, sustained and soothed

By an unfaltering trust, approach thy grave,

80 Like one who wraps the drapery of his couch

About him, and lies down to pleasant dreams.

■ Study Questions

1. According to Lines 1-8, to whom does nature speak? To what two different human moods does nature respond?

2. What do Lines 14-17 recommend to those who "grow sick at heart" when they think of death?

3. According to Lines 22-30, what will happen to all people? What two points should people remember, according to Lines 31-33?

4. What do Lines 61-66 tell the readers will happen after their own deaths?

5. What simile does Bryant use in Lines 80-81 to suggest the way the reader should "approach thy grave"?

6. What lesson about death does the poet expect us to learn from closely observing nature? What is the overall relationship between human beings and nature, according to the poet?

7. What comforting observation about human experience does the poet make repeatedly throughout the poem (Lines 31-32, 48-50, 60-61, 64-66, 70-72, and 75-76)?

8. With what emotion does Bryant suggest people face death?

9. In what way does the subject matter of the poem reflect the Romantic interest in the self, or the individual?

10. Poets often use the image of the seasons for human life. Tell in your own words what this expression means. How does the image of human seasons reflect the central idea of Bryant's poem?

Edgar Allan Poe (1809—1849)

Edgar Allan Poe was one of the leaders of the American Romantic Movement. Best known for his tales of the macabre and mystery, Poe was one of the early American practitioners of the short story and a progenitor of detective fiction[50] and crime fiction. He is also credited with contributing to the emergent science fiction genre. [51] The short, unhappy life of Edgar Allan Poe was marked by poverty, restlessness, and feverish creative activity. Nevertheless, this struggling, sometimes overwhelmingly lonely man became, after his death, one of the most widely read and influential American writers.

Edgar Poe was born in Boston, the son of traveling actors. His father abandoned their family in 1810. His mother died a year later from "consumption" (now more commonly known as tuberculosis). Poe was then taken into the home of John Allan, a successful Scottish tobacco merchant in Richmond, Virginia. Although his middle name is often misspelled as "Allen" (even in encyclopedias), it is actually "Allan", which he had chosen as a

---

50 Poe has greatly influenced the development of the 19th century detective novel. J. L. Borges, R. L. Stevenson, and a vast general readership, have been impressed by the stories which feature Poe's detective Dupin ("The Murders in the Rue Morgue", 1841; "The Purloined Letter", 1845) and the morbid metaphysical speculation of "The Facts in the Case of M. Waldermar" (1845).

51 Thomas M. Disch has argued in his *The Dreams Our Stuff Is Made Of* (1998) that it was actually Poe who was the originator of the modern science fiction. One of Poe's tales, "Mellonta Taunta" (1840) describes a future society. "The Thousand-and-Second Tale of Sceherazade" and "A Descent into the Maelstrom" are also in this vein. However, Poe was not concerned with any specific scientific concept but mostly explored different realities, one of the central concerns of science fiction ever since.

sign of respect towards this family. He then received a good education and seemed to be headed for the life of a gentleman when he entered the University of Virginia. However, heavy gambling debts and a wild life forced him to drop out.

Refusing to join his foster father's business, Poe fled to Boston and, under an assumed name, joined the United States Army. At the age of 18, he published his first book of poetry[52] and in 1829, a second book. The next year, his foster father (only according to the regard of his foster mother who died in 1829) helped him win an appointment to the U. S. Military Academy at West Point, but once again a rigid life seemed incompatible with the writing Poe wanted to do. He deliberately broke rules and behaved in a way that made it necessary for West Point to expel him. His third book of poems (*Poems, Second Edition*), published soon after his expulsion, was dedicated to "the U. S. Corps, of Cadets. "

The daguerreotype of Poe was taken less than a year before his death at the age of 40.

Poe knew that he was not going to inherit the Allans' fortune and that he would have to make his own way in the world. He moved from city to city, from job to job, usually as an editor or journalist, continuing to write poems, short stories, and reviews. His steadiest income came as the editor of a newly founded magazine, the *Southern Literary Messenger*.

In 1838 Poe published his only novel, *The Narrative of Arthur Gordon Pym*, a mysterious sea adventure. His *Tales of the Grotesque and Arabesque* came out in 1840, as he continued to contribute stories and poems to an assortment of journals. Nevertheless, Poe was unable to escape his spirit-breaking poverty. Even "The Raven," his most popular work, brought him little money. When his beloved wife, Virginia, died in 1847, Poe found his deep sorrow difficult to bear. On October 3, 1849, Poe was found on the streets of Baltimore delirious and "in great distress, and... in need of immediate assistance," according to the friend who found him. He was taken to the Washington College Hospital, where he died early on the morning of October 7. Some sources say Poe's final words were "Lord help my poor soul. " Poe suffered from bouts of depression and madness, and he may have attempted suicide in 1848. The precise cause of Poe's death is disputed and has aroused great controversy.

Poe was a proponent and supporter of magazine literature, and felt that short stories, or "tales" as they were called in the early 19th century, which were usually considered "vulgar" or "low art" along with the magazines that published them, were legitimate art forms on par with the novel or epic poem. His insistence on the artistic value of the short story was influential in the short story's rise to prominence in later generations. Poe was also one of the most prolific literary journalists in American history, one whose extensive body of reviews and criticism has yet to be collected fully. James Russell Lowell once wrote about Poe: "Three fifths of him genius and two fifths sheer fudge. "

Poe associated the aesthetic aspect of art with pure ideality claiming that the mood or sentiment created by a work of art elevates the soul, and is thus a spiritual experience. He championed art for art's sake (before the term itself was coined). He was consequentially an opponent of didacticism, arguing in his literary criticisms that the role of moral or ethical instruction lies outside the realm of poetry and art, which should only focus on the production of a beautiful work of art. He criticized James Russell Lowell in a review for being excessively didactic and moralistic in his writings, and argued often that a poem should be written "for a poem's sake. "

Poe's work and his theory of "pure poetry" were early recognized especially in France, where his influence

---

52   Entitled *Tamerlane and Other Poems*, it was released anonymously as "a Bostonian. " A surviving copy of this rare book has sold for $200,000.

was associated with such big names of Modern French literature as Charles Baudelaire, Paul Valéry, and Stéphane Mallarmé. Since then, Poe's works have had a broad influence on American and world literature, and even on the art world beyond literature. He has been accepted as "this marvelous lord of rhythmic expression" (Oscar Wilde) and "an enormously talented writer" (Fyodor Dostoevsky) and followed by a great many famous modern writers from France, Britain, Russia, Spain, Argentina, Japan, etc.

Poe's literary reputation was greater abroad than in the United States, perhaps as a result of America's general revulsion towards the macabre. A few American writers have found Poe's writing unpolished and juvenile: Emerson called him "the jingle man", and Mark Twain said he would read Poe only if someone paid him to do so. Yet there are still a good many American writers and critics who have admired Poe, at times even more than any other American writer. Among them, authors as diverse as Herman Melville, Walt Whitman, H. P. Lovecraft and William Faulkner have been influenced by Poe's works. Today Poe is largely praised for his extraordinary ability to create moods and atmospheres, his unforgettable images, his rhythmical language, and his awareness of universal human fears. Even those who do not like him cannot turn a blind eye to this enormous figure in American literary history. He has become, to borrow from Poe himself, "The Man That Was Used Up."

■ Selected Readings

In his essay "The Poetic Principle", Poe would argue that there is no such thing as a long poem, since the ultimate purpose of art is aesthetic, that is, its purpose is the effect it has on its audience, and this effect can only be maintained for a brief period of time (the time it takes to read a lyric poem, or watch a drama performed, or view a painting, etc.). He argued that an epic, if it has any value at all, must be actually a series of smaller pieces, each geared towards a single effect or sentiment, which "elevates the soul".

Virginia Poe, in a painting created after her death.

"To Helen" shows how a Romantic poet can use classical images for his own purposes. Inspired by the beauty of the mother of one of his friends, Poe uses Helen of Troy— "the face that launched a thousand ships" —to represent that beauty. Helen may also be an allusion to the Greek goddess of light, but whatever the specific reference Poe intended, she is clearly the poet's timeless ideal of pure beauty.

To Helen [53]

Helen, thy beauty is to me
　　Like those Nicean barks [54] of yore,
That gently, o'er a perfumed sea,
　　The weary, way-worn wanderer bore
5　　To his own native shore.

53　The text is that of 1845, with errors of indentation corrected. The poem was first published in 1831 where, among other differences, Lines 9 and 10 read: "To the beauty of fair Greece, / And the Grandeur of old Rome."

54　**Nicean**: Of or from Nicea (also spelled Nicaea), a city in ancient Bithynia (part of present-day Turkey) near the site of the Trojan War. By Nicean Barks, Poe may be referring to boats from this shipbuilding city in Asia Minor. It is likely, however, that he created the phrase for its melodious sound.

On desperate seas long wont[55] to roam,

Thy hyacinth[56] hair, thy classic face,

Thy Naiad[57] airs have brought me home

To the glory that was Greece,

10   And the grandeur that was Rome. [58]

Lo! in yon brilliant window niche

How statue-like I see thee stand,

The agate lamp within thy hand

Ah, Psyche,[59] from the regions which

15   Are Holy Land![60]

■ Study Questions

1. To what does the poet compare Helen's beauty in the first stanza? Who is brought "to his own native shore"?

2. What images describe Helen in the second stanza? Who is brought home in this stanza? To what is he brought home?

3. What is Helen doing in the third stanza? With whom is she associated in Line 14? Where does she come from?

4. State in your own words the condition the speaker was in before encountering Helen.

5. Considering the places to which Helen brings the speaker and the place from which she comes, name the three kinds of joys or comforts she seems to provide. What might the agate lamp represent? What has Helen done for the speaker to explain why he calls her Psyche?

6. In what way is this poem idealistic? Which of the other characteristics of Romanticism (listed in the Introduction to this unit) does this poem display?

Poe said that when he set out to write a poem with a melancholy effect, the word "nevermore" was the first word that came into his mind, both for its sound and for its meaning. The subject of the following poem, he decided, had to be the death of a beautiful woman, "unquestionably, the most poetical topic in the world." His first thought was to have "nevermore" repeated by a parrot, but he saw greater possibilities in a raven, "the bird of ill omen," an emblem of "Mournful and Never-ending Remembrance."

The poem comes out to tell the following story: It is midnight on a cold evening in December in the 1840s. In a

---

55 **wont**: accustomed to (usually followed by an infinitive, like "to roam" in this line).

56 **Hyacinth**: wavy and perfumed.

57 **Naiad**: Naiads were minor nature goddesses in Greek and Roman mythology. They inhabited and presided over rivers, lakes, streams, and fountains. **Naiad airs**: Peaceful, gentle breezes or qualities.

58 **the glory that... Rome**: These last two lines, beginning with *the glory that was*, are among the most frequently quoted lines in world literature. Writers and speakers quote these lines to evoke the splendor of classical antiquity.

59 **Psyche**: goddess of the soul. In Greek and Roman mythology, Psyche was a beautiful princess dear to the god of love, Eros (Cupid), who would visit her in a darkened room in a palace. One night she used an agate lamp to discover his identity. Later, at the urging of Eros, Zeus gave her the gift of immortality. Eros then married her.

60 **from... Holy Land**: from ancient Greece and Rome; from the memory Poe had of the beauty.

dark and shadowy bedroom, wood burns in the fireplace as a man laments the death of Lenore[61], a woman he deeply loved. To occupy his mind, he reads a book of ancient stories. But a tapping noise disturbs him. When he opens the door to the bedroom, he sees nothing—only darkness. When the tapping persists, he opens the shutter of the window and discovers a raven, which flies into the room and lands above the door on a bust of Athena (Pallas in the poem), the goddess of wisdom and war in Greek mythology. It says "Nevermore" to all his thoughts and longings. The raven, a symbol of death, tells the man he will never again ("nevermore") see his beloved; never again hold her— even in heaven.

The Raven

Once upon a midnight dreary, while I pondered, weak and weary,
Over many a quaint[62] and curious volume of forgotten lore[63]—
While I nodded, nearly napping, suddenly there came a tapping,
As of someone gently rapping, rapping at my chamber[64] door—
5   "'Tis some visitor," I muttered, "tapping at my chamber door—
        Only this and nothing more."

Ah, distinctly I remember it was in the bleak December;
And each separate dying ember[65] wrought its ghost upon[66] the floor.
Eagerly I wished the morrow—vainly I had sought to borrow
10   From my books surcease[67] of sorrow—sorrow for the lost Lenore—
For the rare and radiant maiden whom the angels name Lenore—
        Nameless here for evermore.

And the silken, sad, uncertain rustling of each purple curtain
Thrilled me—filled me with fantastic terrors never felt before;
15   So that now, to still the beating of my heart, I stood repeating
"'Tis some visitor entreating entrance at my chamber door—
Some late visitor entreating entrance at my chamber door—
        This it is and nothing more."

Presently my soul grew stronger; hesitating then no longer,

---

61   It is possible that Lenore, the idealized deceased woman in the poem, represents Poe's beloved wife, Virginia, who was in poor health when Poe wrote "The Raven." She died two years after the publication of the poem, when she was quite young.

62   **quaint**: archaic, old.

63   **volume of forgotten lore**: book of knowledge or myth.

64   **chamber**: bedroom or study. *Chamber* is used apparently because of its dark and mysterious connotation.

65   **ember**: glowing wood fragment in fireplace.

66   **wrought its ghost upon**: formed ash.

67   **surcease**: an end, a pause, a delay.

20   "Sir," said I, "or Madam, truly your forgiveness I implore;

But the fact is I was napping, and so gently you came rapping,

And so faintly you came tapping, tapping at my chamber door,

That I scarce was sure I heard you" —here I opened wide the door—

Darkness there and nothing more.

25   Deep into that darkness peering, long I stood there wondering, fearing,

Doubting, dreaming dreams no mortal ever dared to dream before;

But the silence was unbroken, and the stillness gave no token.

And the only word there spoken was the whispered word, "Lenore?"

This I whispered, and an echo murmured back the word, "Lenore!"

30   Merely this and nothing more.

Back into the chamber turning, all my soul within me burning,

Soon again I heard a tapping somewhat louder than before.

"Surely," said I, "surely that is something at my window lattice;

Let me see, then, what thereat is, and this mystery explore—

35   Let my heart be still a moment and this mystery explore—

'Tis the wind and nothing more!"

Open here I flung the shutter, when, with many a flirt and flutter,

In there stepped a stately Raven of the saintly days of yore[68].

Not the least obeisance made he; not a minute stopped or stayed he;

40   But with mien of lord or lady, perched above my chamber door—

Perched upon a bust of Pallas[69] just above my chamber door—

Perched, and sat and nothing more,

Then this ebony bird beguiling my sad fancy into smiling.

By the grave and stern decorum of the countenance it wore[70]

45   "Though thy crest be shorn and shaven, thou," I said, "art sure no craven,

Ghastly grim and ancient Raven wandering from the Nightly shore—

Tell me what thy lordly name is on the Night's Plutonian shore!"[71]

Quoth the Raven "Nevermore."

---

68   **yore:** the distant past.

69   **Pallas:** Athena, Greek goddess of wisdom.

70   **decorum of the countenance it wore:** look on its face.

71   The narrator believes the raven is from the shore of the River Styx in the Underworld, the abode of the dead in Greek mythology. "Plutonian" is a reference to Pluto, the god of the Underworld.

Much I marveled this ungainly fowl to hear discourse so plainly,
50   Though its answer little meaning—little relevancy bore;
for we cannot help agreeing that no living human being
Ever yet was blessed with seeing bird above his chamber door—
Bird or beast upon the sculptured bust above his chamber door,
        With such name as "Nevermore."

55   But the Raven, sitting lonely on the placid bust, spoke only
That one word, as if his soul in that one word he did outpour.
Nothing farther then he uttered—not a feather then he fluttered—
Till I scarcely more than muttered "Other friends have flown before—
On the morrow he will leave me, as my Hopes have flown before."
60   Then the bird said "Nevermore."

Startled at the stillness broken by reply so aptly spoken,
"Doubtless," said I, "what it utters is its only stock and store
Caught from some unhappy master whom unmerciful Disaster
Followed fast and followed faster till his songs one burden bore—
65   Till the dirges of his Hope that melancholy burden bore
        Of 'Never—nevermore,'"

But the Raven still beguiling my sad fancy into smiling,
Straight I wheeled a cushioned seal in front of bird and bust and door;
Then, upon the velvet sinking, I betook myself to linking
70   Fancy unto fancy, thinking what this ominous bird of yore—
What this grim, ungainly, ghastly, gaunt, and ominous bird of yore
        Meant in croaking "Nevermore."

This I sat engaged in guessing, but no syllable expressing
To the fowl whose fiery eyes now burned into my bosom's core,
75   This and more I sat divining, with my head at ease reclining
On the cushion's velvet lining that the lamplight gloated o'er.
But whose velvet violet lining with the lamplight gloating o'er,
        She shall press, ah, nevermore!

Then, methought, the air grew denser, perfumed from an unseen censer

80   Swung by seraphim[72] whose footfalls tinkled on the tufted floor.
"Wretch," I cried,"thy God hath lent thee—by these angels he hath sent thee
Respite—respite and nepenthe[73] from thy memories of Lenore;
Quaff, oh quaff this kind nepenthe and forget this lost Lenore!"
　　　Quoth the Raven "Nevermore."

85   "Prophet!" said I,"thing of evil! —prophet still, if bird or devil! —
Whether Tempter sent, or whether tempest tossed thee here ashore,
Desolate yet all undaunted, on this desert land enchanted—
On this home by Horror haunted—tell me truly, I implore—
is there—is there balm in Gilead[74]—tell me—tell me, I implore!"
90　　　Quoth the Raven "Nevermore."

"Prophet!" said I,"thing of evil! —prophet still, if bird or devil!
By that Heaven that bends above us—by that God we both adore—
Tell this soul with sorrow laden if, within the distant Aidenn[75],
It shall clasp a sainted maiden whom the angels name Lenore—
95   Clasp a rare and radiant maiden whom the angels name Lenore."
　　　Quoth the Raven "Nevermore."

"Be that word our sign of parting, bird or fiend!" I shrieked, upstarting—
"Get thee back into the tempest and the Night's Plutonian shore!
Leave no black plume as a token of that lie thy soul hath spoken!
100 Leave my loneliness unbroken! —quit the bust above my door!
Take thy beak from out my heart, and take thy form from off my door!"
　　　Quoth the Raven "Nevermore."

And the Raven, never flitting, still is sitting, still is sitting
On the pallid bust of Pallas just above my chamber door;
105 And his eyes have all the seeming of a demon's that is dreaming,
And the lamplight o'er him streaming throws his shadow on the floor;
And my soul from out that shadow that lies floating on the floor
　　　Shall be lifted—nevermore!

---

72   **seraphim**: angels.

73   **nepenthe**: in classical mythology a drink that banishes sorrow.

74   **balm to Gilead**: Poe's version of "Is there no balm in Gilead?" (Jeremiah 8: 22), referring to a healing ointment made in
Gilead in ancient Palestine; therefore, a relief from suffering.

75   **Aidenn**: Arabic for "Eden" or heaven.

■ Study Questions

1. In Stanzas 1-3 what is the speaker doing when he first hears the tapping? What does he seek "to borrow"? What does he say "to still the beating" of his heart?

2. In Stanzas 4-5 what does the speaker see when he opens the door? What does he whisper?

3. Who does the speaker hope is making the tapping noise in Stanza 6? What happens when he opens the shutter?

4. What is the only word the raven speaks? In Stanza 9 what does the speaker think the word relates to? How does he explain the word when the raven first repeats it (Lines 62-66)?

5. What does the speaker begin to think about when he wheels his chair in front of the raven (Lines 69-72)?

6. What question does the speaker ask in Lines 88-90? And what question in Lines 93-95? What does the raven reply? What does it say when ordered to leave?

7. Where is the raven now? What will never be lifted from the raven's shadow?

8. Does the speaker believe the words he says in Lines 16-18 and Line 36? How do you know?

9. Who is "she" in Line 78? Who is the "wretch" in Line 81? Trace the speaker's thoughts in Lines 78-83.

10. What does the speaker interpret "nevermore" in Line 84 and in Line 96 to mean? What do you know about the raven's answers that the speaker does not realize?

11. What does the raven come to represent for the speaker? What does "Plutonian shore" (Line 98) suggest about the speaker's final evaluation of the raven? Of himself?

12. Evaluate the speaker's emotional state at the beginning of the poem, in the next-to-the-last stanza, and in the last stanza. What does the future probably hold for the speaker?

13. Describe the mood of the poem. Which expressions in Stanzas 1-2 help establish the mood?

14. Poe felt the death of a beautiful woman was "the most poetical topic in the world," What do you think makes a topic "poetical"? Name at least three topics you find poetical, and tell why they are suitable for poetry.

LITERARY FOCUS

The Single Effect

In a review of *Twice-Told Tales* by his contemporary, Nathaniel Hawthorne, Poe asserted that a work of literature must arrange all of its elements so that they combine to achieve a single effect. In fact, Poe believed that a poet or a short story writer must begin with an idea of a single effect and then create the characters and incidents to produce that effect. He said, "In the whole composition there should be no word written, of which the tendency, direct or indirect, is not to the one preestablished design." He added, "If [an author's] very initial sentence tends not to the out-bringing of this [single] effect, then he has failed in his first step."

Poe believed, in other words, that one clear, powerfully felt emotion should carry the reader through the work. Of course, literature may display many different emotions, but Poe believed they must all ultimately combine into one over-whelming feeling for the reader.

■ Thinking About Single Effect

1. What is the single effect of "The Raven"?

2. Discuss the first sentence of "The Raven," pointing out how each element of it contributes to the single effect.

Sound Devices

Poe's use of sound devices in poetry is as important as his subject matter. The particular music of his verses creates mood, reveals character, and conveys ideas, in addition to providing that pleasure in sound that only poetry can provide.

Most sound devices are kinds of **repetition. Alliteration**, for example, is the repetition of consonant sounds at the beginnings of words and of sounds within words. Poe uses alliteration to create an almost hypnotic effect in phrases like "weak and weary" and "silken, sad, uncertain rustling." (**Consonance** is the repetition in nearby words of similar consonant sounds preceded by different accented vowels.)

Assonance is the repetition of vowel sounds, and Poe uses assonance mainly to create mood. The most conspicuous example in "The Raven" is the open *o* sound, with its deep mournful effect: "s*o*rrow—s*o*rrow f*o*r the l*o*st Len*o*re."

Poe uses the assonance of the *o* sound as the basis for the poem's most common rhyme. **Rhyme** is a kind of repetition, and it also can be used to create mood. Notice, for example, how many times the poet rhymes that long moaning sound: "neverm*ore*," "d*oor*," "Len*ore*," "impl*ore*," "y*ore*," "b*ore*," and so on. Rhyme can reinforce meaning; the poet emphasizes the absence of his beloved when he rhymes *Lenore* with *nevermore*.

Internal rhyme is rhyme that occurs within a single line:

Ah, distinctly I *remember* it was in the bleak *December*.

Poe uses internal rhyme as another kind of repeated sound, like alliteration or assonance, for hypnotic effect, for mood, and simply for the pleasure of the repetition itself.

Poe also employs **onomatopoeia**, the use of words with sounds that suggest their meanings. For example, the words *tapping* and *rapping*, in addition to meaning "knocking," actually suggest the sound of someone or something knocking at the door. Poe repeats the words in the first stanza, just as a knock at the door is repeated.

To achieve his musical effect, Poe also adopts a regular pattern of accented and unaccented syllables, i. e. a pattern using a stressed syllable followed by an unstressed syllable, with a total of 16 syllables in each line (iambic octave meter). Here is an example (the first line of the poem):

ONCE uPON a MID night DREARy, WHILE i PONDered WEAK and WEARy

In this line, the capitalized letters represent the stressed syllables and the lower-cased letters, the unstressed ones. Notice that the line has 16 syllables in all. Notice, too, that the line has internal rhyme (*dreary* and *weary*) and alliteration (while, weak, weary).

■ Thinking About Sound Devices

- Find at least two more examples in "The Raven" of alliteration, assonance, internal rhyme, and onomatopoeia. Tell how Poe's use of each of these sound devices contributes to the meaning or the mood of the poem.

READING FOR APPRECIATION

Significant Detail

Our greatest delight as readers lies in the details of what we are reading. In fact, the pleasure of reading literature comes from responding to the actual words as they appear before our eyes. If we fully respond to the details of "Rip Van Winkle," "Thanatopsis," *The Last of Mohicans*, or "The Raven," we will sense some of the pleasure that Irving, Bryant, Cooper, and Poe had as they created their texts. If we read too quickly, without attention, looking only for some abstract "meaning," reading is likely to become a chore rather than a pleasure. We must attend to the details. In fact, it is only from the details that the specific meaning arises.

Each good story or poem is different from all others, even if it shares its themes, its forms, its language with thousands of other works. That difference, that unique sound and texture, is what we try to capture as we read. We might try to sum up "Thanatopsis," for example, in this way. "We will all die, but we should be comforted by the thought that we will all be gathered into nature with every man and woman who lived before us." Here we have the main idea of the poem but none of its pleasure. If we are to enjoy "Thanatopsis," or any poem, it will be because we give ourselves up to the specific movements of its verse, to the sound carrying us from line to line, to the details and images that make us feel the thought. Our pleasure is not always in "happy" thoughts, but in the perfection, the rightness of the language:

> To be a brother to the insensible rock
> And to the sluggish clod which the rude swain
> Turns with his share and treads upon. The oak
> Shall send his roots abroad, and pierce thy mold.

From this feeling of negation, we move with and in the language of the poem toward a more positive and comforting feeling:

> So live, that when thy summons comes to join
> The innumerable caravan...
> Thou go not, like the quarry-slave at night,
> Scourged to his dungeon, but, sustained and soothed
> By an unfaltering trust...

To take just one detail, ask yourself why innumerable is so right here. For one thing, innumerable caravan suggests along and stately procession moving toward a definite goal, rather than a disorderly or panic driven mob. For another, innumerable is the only word in the poem with as many as five syllables, and the sense that many syllables suddenly come together in one word supports the sense that many (in fact, innumerable) people are moving together in this caravan. In itself, innumerable is not a particularly interesting word at all. Yet placed within its context in this poem, it becomes a source of delight.

VOICE OF THE AGE

Other Times, Other Places

One of the paradoxes of Romantic literature is that it can be passionately nationalistic and still long for foreign places and ancient ages. Romantic authors, like those in this unit, insist on the value of their own land, their own customs and language, their own time in history. Yet these same authors often dream of old tales and exotic settings, as the following quotations reveal:

Irving: *At the foot of these fairy mountains the voyager may have descried the light smoke curling up from a village whose shingle roofs gleam among the trees, just where the blue tints of the upland melt away into the fresh green of the nearer landscape. It is a little village of great antiquity, having been founded by some of the Dutch colonists, in the early times of the province, just about the beginning of the government of the good Peter Stuyvesant (may he rest in peace!), and there were some of the houses of the original settlers standing within a few years, with lattice windows, gable fronts surmounted with weathercocks, and built of small yellow bricks brought from Holland.*

Cooper: *The incidents of this tale occurred between the years 1740 and 1745, when the settled portions of the colony of New York we confined to the four Atlantic counties... A bird's eye view of the whole region east of the Mississippi must then have offered one vast expanse of woods, relieved by a comparatively narrow fringe of cultivation along the sea, dotted by the glittering surfaces of lakes, and intersected by the waving tines of rivers. In such a vast picture of solemn solitude, the district of country we design to paint sinks into insignificance. ... (From the beginning of* The Deerslayer)

Bryant: *... Thou shalt lie down / With patriarchs of the infant world—with kings, / The powerful of the earth—the wise, the good, / Pair forms, and hoary seers of ages past, ...*

Poe: *Thy Naiad airs have brought me home / To the glory that was Greece, / And the grandeur that was Rome.*

These writers established a national identity for American literature in the first part of the 19th century. They helped define the character of the New World, but they never gave up the marvels of the past.

Chapter 4

NEW ENGLAND RENAISSANCE
1840—1855

INTRODUCTION

American Renaissance

New England Renaissance, or the **American Renaissance**[76], refers to the remarkable outburst of creativity in the mid-19th century, especially during the period roughly from 1840 to 1855, when many of the works most widely considered American masterpieces were produced.

A renaissance is a rebirth, a vital period in a culture, a ripeness that calls forth a concentration of great writers and artists. Such flowering periods took place in ancient Athens, in 15th- and 16th-century Italy, and in Elizabethan England. The United States, by the mid-19th century, began to flower.

After over 200 years on this continent, why was this time ripe? There is nothing comparable in so short a period in Europe. Is there any relationship between this literary outburst and the conflicts which would soon lead to war?

As is so often true, there are no good answers, but lots of good speculation. Culturally there was time for literature and art; the practical matters such as the essential of making a living and establishing political independence had been squared. There were American publishers and even more important, copyright laws protected writers from having their works printed, without their permission or pay, in England. There were readers, often women eager to expand their minds. It was actually possible to make a kind of living as a writer, although it was difficult and limited, making these writers agonize over the problem of "vocation." There was also a strong national pride, self-conscious and anti-British.

Politically the time was ripe. The 18th century left a heritage of optimism about man's possibilities and

---

76   The period was first named and critically discussed by F. O. Matthiessen in his 1941 book *American Renaissance*: *Art and Expression in the Age of Emerson and Whitman*. It continues as a central term in American studies.

perfectibility. The lofty ideals of democracy asserted the value of individuals, regardless of class, and education. Of course, these values primarily applied to white males. In fact, tensions were building which cried out for creative release. Inequality, not equality, was the rule for many, especially women and slaves. The clash of these realities with the idealistic rhetoric led writers to take extremes, championing individualism yet also seeing the darker sides of a fragmenting society.

Further observations upon the American economic, religious, scientific, and aesthetic situations around this period all direct at the same point—then and there came the time ripe for the concentration of great writers and artists.

The Literary Response

Americans had always produced a vital literary response to their experience: the Native Americans, the Puritans, the planters, the revolutionaries, the early Romantics. Yet many American writers—even Irving and Cooper—seemed to be still a bit provincial, still under the influence of English and other European writers. The first steps taken by Irving, Cooper, Bryant, and Poe had to be lengthened, and now came the giant strides.

A convenient historical marker is Emerson's stirring lecture *The American Scholar* (1837), often called America's intellectual declaration of independence. Emerson exclaimed, "We will walk on our own feet; we will work with our own hands; we will speak our own minds." The nation listened and took the words to heart.

Increasingly, American writers, many of them directly inspired by Emerson, began to free themselves from European models. During a relatively few years, concentrating around Boston and the village of Concord, a number of writers appeared whom we now think of as "classic." Some of them, such as Emerson and Hawthorne, were well known in their time; others, like Thoreau, were uncelebrated until years after their deaths. Their influence, especially Emerson's, reached Walt Whitman in New York and Emily Dickinson in western Massachusetts. We say these writers arc great because their work has for many readers a vitality and originality that endures, that transcends time and place. They produced work that has a scope and a depth that still reach us, still inspire us, still make us ask the great questions and face the most mysterious of realities. At times this literature celebrates the American, even the human, spirit. At times it criticizes the easy optimism that also marked the first half of the 19th century.

The Transcendentalists

Transcendentalism was a group of new ideas in literature, religion, culture, and philosophy that emerged in New England in the early- to mid-19th century. It is sometimes called **American Transcendentalism** to distinguish it from other uses of the word *transcendental*. To transcend something is to rise above it, to pass beyond its limits.

Transcendentalism began as a protest against the general state of culture and society at the time, and in particular, the state of intellectualism at Harvard and the doctrine of the Unitarian church which was taught at Harvard Divinity School. Among their core beliefs was an ideal spiritual state that "transcends" the physical and empirical and is only realized through the individual's intuition, rather than through the doctrines of established religions.

Transcendentalist is a fairly loose term referring to a large group of men and women who were very different from one another both as individuals and as writers. They did not have a strict doctrine or code to which they all subscribed. Emerson himself in his 1842 lecture "The Transcendentalist" suggested that the goal of a purely Transcendental outlook on life was impossible to attain in practice, "You will see by this sketch that there is no such thing as a Transcendental *party*; that there is no pure Transcendentalist; that we know of no one but prophets and heralds of such a philosophy..." Prominent Transcendentalists included Ralph Waldo Emerson, Henry David Thoreau, Margaret Fuller, as well as Bronson Alcott, Orestes Brownson, William Ellery Channing, Frederick Henry Hedge, Theodore Parker, George Putnam, and Sophia Peabody, the wife of Nathaniel Hawthorne.

Transcendentalism is more of a tendency, an attitude, than it is a philosophy in any well-defined way. Nevertheless, we are able to define some aspects of it. Nature played an important role in the transcendental view. To Emerson as well as most other transcendentalists, nature was divine, alive with spirit; the human mind could read nature, find truth in it; to live in harmony with nature, to allow one's deepest intuitive being to communicate with nature, was a source of goodness and inspiration.

The Transcendentalists desired to ground their "religion" and "philosophy" in transcendental principles: principles not based on, or falsifiable by, sensuous experience, but deriving from the inner, spiritual or mental essence of the human. Kant had called "all knowledge transcendental which is concerned not with objects but with our mode of knowing objects."

The Transcendentalists believed that this deep intuition of spiritual reality is available to us only if we allow ourselves to be individuals, and Transcendentalist writing places a strong emphasis on *individualism*. Transcendentalism is also very *democratic*, asserting that the power of the individual mind and soul are equally available to all people. These powers are not dependent upon wealth or background or education. We all have a potential equality as spiritual beings, and the divinity within each of us can be realized by the laborer and the farmer as well as by the learned minister and the scholar. For Emerson, every person can be a kind of poet, releasing individual imaginative power.

Such thoughts and feelings led the Transcendentalists to intense moral enthusiasm and concerns. Society, with its emphasis on material success, is often seen as a source of corruption. The Transcendentalist wants to do the right thing, the moral thing. The very desire brought many Transcendentalists into efforts to reform society, to create a Utopia—a perfect social and political system. They worked toward their ideal through Utopian communities such as Brook Farm, through the antislavery movement (like Thoreau's imprisonment for disobedience), and through a sometimes vigorous feminism (as in the case of Margaret Fuller). The tone of Transcendentalist writing is often intensely optimistic and aspiring. It frequently suggests that the individual, in harmony with the divine universe, can transform the world.

The Darker Visions

The optimism of the Transcendentalists was not shared by all the great writers of the time. There were those—Hawthorne and Melville are the outstanding examples—who saw the universe as a more confusing and difficult place. Nature, they thought, is ambiguous, not easy to read, interpret, and harmonize. Evil and suffering had to be accounted for and were not to be brushed airily aside. Human nature was obstinate. Life was, as it always had been and always would be, mysterious.

Emerson could not read Hawthorne with pleasure, for he found Hawthorne's tales too gloomy. Hawthorne admired Emerson but thought him "a mystic, stretching his hand out of cloud-land, in vain search for something real." Melville had no use at all for Transcendentalism and the optimism of Emerson. To him it was all "nonsense," a much too easy dismissal of life's "disagreeable facts." For Melville life was a matter of compromises, not ideals—spectacle of disappointment and illusion. It is, of course, one's privilege to have preferences, but there is no need to take sides between Emerson and Hawthorne / Melville. As readers, however, we must be fully aware of two elements common to all these writers: the power of their writing and the sincerity of their search.

The American Romance

An important development in American writing began to take shape with the writing of Hawthorne and Melville. This was the idea of the romance.

With Irving, Cooper, Bryant, and Poe, America began to have her "own" novelists and poets. These writers distinguished themselves from their European romantic "colleagues" not only in that they largely made use of materials that are American in their works but also because they began to break the genre itself away from its European origin. Gilbert Highet, in *The Classical Tradition: Greek and Roman Influences on Western Literature*, lists the main elements of classical romance: 1) separated lovers who remain true to each other, while the woman's chastity is preserved; 2) an intricate plot, including stories within stories; 3) exciting and unexpected chance events; 4) travel to faraway settings; 5) hidden and mistaken identity; and 6) written in an elaborate and elegant style. Classical romance, Highet noted, is "escape literature"; American romance, on the contrary, brings the reader closer to truth, not further from it. The American pastoral is a literary form in which happy country life is only portrayed as a contrast to the complexity and anxiety of the urban society. Such a contrast may be seen in the American Romanticists' use of the frontier, Indian society, Arcadian communities, Puritan villages, and shipboard societies. Few of the characters are strictly outside the urban society to which they provide contrast. It is clearly related to Hawthorne's creation of "a theater, a little removed from the highway of ordinary travel, where the creatures of his brain may play their phantasmagoric antics, without exposing them to too close a comparison with the actual events of real lives," and to his calling for a "license with regard to everyday probability." Therefore Hawthorne, like any other American Romanticist, created a form that—at first glance, seems ancient and traditional—he borrowed from classical romance, adapted pastoral themes, incorporated Gothic elements, and always with the reality in his mind.

But it is Hawthorne, rather than any of his contemporary Americans, that is generally accepted as the symbol of the 19th century American author and his predicament. This is because he was the first American writer to make a critical distinction between a romance and a novel, an important distinction that is useful in helping us to define just what it is that makes an American narrative different from a European one.

Hawthorne described what he meant by romance in the Preface to *The House of the Seven Gables* (similar views can also be found in Prefaces to *The Blithedale Romance* and *The Marble Faun*):

> When a writer calls his work a Romance, it need hardly be observed that he wishes to claim a certain latitude, both as to its fashion and material, which he would not have felt himself entitled to assume, had he professed to be writing a Novel. The latter form of composition is presumed to aim at a very minute fidelity, not merely to the possible, but to the probable and ordinary course of man's experience. The former—while, as a work of art, it must rigidly subject itself to laws, and while it sins unpardonably so far as it may swerve aside from the truth of the human heart—as fairly a right to present that truth under circumstances, to a great extent, of the writer's own choosing or creation."

Hawthorne's statement makes clear that he thought a romance, though should not be alienated from reality, need not be totally faithful to it. A romance can make greater use of the marvelous, the improbable, the eccentric, and even the completely unbelievable. A romance need not tie itself to an accurate portrait of real people in the real social and physical world—as a novel does—as long as it is true to the human heart. Hawthorne's story "Young Goodman Brown" is built on a highly improbable situation, but it remains faithful to larger human emotions. Melville's *Moby-Dick* contains characters and events that we never would expect to find in the real world, yet this great novel never fails to strike a reader as a voyage into authentic human experience.

Unable to feel any confidence in the reality of the subjective, and unable, despite the long effort of his notebooks, to come to terms with the solid earth, Hawthorne evolved his conception of the "romance." Whereas the novelist was limited to "the probably and ordinary course of man's experience," the romancer tried to create a realm midway between private thought and the objective world. This doctrine, which is the burden of those prefaces, betrayed an intellectual as well as a literary problem. Hawthorne was anxious not merely to draw the literary distinction between the novel and the romance but also, and more fundamentally, to fix the status of the romance in an almost metaphysical sense. As Hawthorne wrote, it would be a great mistake for a reader to try to bring "his fancy pictures almost into positive contact with the realities of the moment." For Hawthorne—and for many of the American novelists to follow him—an American "novel" should only be judged as a romance.

Ralph Waldo Emerson (1803—1882)

Ralph Waldo Emerson was an American essayist, poet, and leader of the Transcendentalist movement in the mid-19th century.

Outwardly Emerson's life was quiet and well ordered, but inwardly it overflowed with new ideas. Emerson was born in Boston to the Rev. William Emerson, a Unitarian minister in a famous line of ministers. His father, who called him "a rather dull scholar," died when he was eight years old. The young Emerson was subsequently sent to the Boston Latin School in 1812; then in October 1817, at the age of 14, Emerson went to Harvard College and was appointed Freshman's President. He studied theology there, and became a Unitarian minister himself in 1829. In that year he was also married, but his beloved wife, Ellen, died only 16 months later. In 1832, for reasons of conscience, Emerson felt obliged to resign his ministry. In 1835, after his trip to Europe, where he met the English writers Wordsworth, Coleridge, and Carlyle, Emerson bought a house on the Cambridge Turnpike, in Concord, Massachusetts. He remarried, began his lifelong career as lecturer and writer, and quickly became one of the leading citizens in the town. There he became a member of the Transcendental Club and was surrounded by a remarkable group of men and women. Emerson also associated himself with Nathaniel Hawthorne and Henry David Thoreau and often took walks with them. He even encouraged Thoreau's talent and early career, though their close relationship later fractured and his eulogy to Thoreau is largely credited with Thoreau's negative reputation during the 19th century.

It was at Concord that Emerson composed his first book, *Nature* (1836). His address called "*The American Scholar*" (1837) has been an inspiration to generations of young Americans, but Emerson did not achieve national fame until his *Essays* appeared in 1841. Then came *Essays: Second Series* (1844), *Representative Men* (1849), and *The Conduct of Life* (1860). Emerson was noted as a very abstract and difficult writer who nevertheless drew large crowds for his speeches. The heart of Emerson's writing was from his "Savings Bank" —his direct observations in his journals and remarkable notes on his wide reading, which he started keeping as a teenager at Harvard. The journals and notes were elaborately indexed. Emerson went back to his journals and notes, his "bank" of experiences and ideas, and took out relevant passages, which were joined together in his dense, concentrated lectures. He later revised and polished his lectures for his essays and sermons.

As he became increasingly famous as an American "prophet", he traveled widely throughout the country, delivering lectures that enraptured crowds with his deep voice, his enthusiasm, and his egalitarian respect for his audience. The lectures, polished and improved with many deliveries, often became the basis for the essays that were important influences upon so many American writers, including Thoreau, Whitman, Dickinson, and Frost. Yet Emerson's great influence extended beyond the literary community to the American people at large. His optimism, his belief in the vast possibilities of mind and spirit, and his doctrine of self-reliance well suited a democratic, progressive nation.

Not all his lectures, however, were well received. His outspoken, uncompromising support for abolitionism later in life caused protest and jeers from crowds when he spoke on the subject. He continued to speak on abolition without concern for his popularity and with increasing radicalism. He attempted, with difficulty, not to join the public arena as a member of any group or movement, and always retained a stringent independence that reflected his individualism. He always insisted that he wanted no followers, but sought to give man back to himself, as a self-reliant individual. Asked to sum up his work late in life, he said it was his doctrine of "the infinitude of the private man" that remained central.

It is easy to find oversimplified, watered-down versions of Emersonian aspiration, optimism, and individualism. Simplifications of his thought often lead toward the very opposite of what he meant. When Emerson spoke, for example, of the potential powers of the self-reliant individual—"A man is stronger than a city" —he did not mean that we should become irresponsibly obsessed with our selves. He did not mean that individualism is a license to do as, we wish as we grasp for power and wealth. For Emerson, individualism is idealistic. He would have us trust in "divine providence", live in harmony with nature and with what he called the Oversoul, the universal spirit that is the source of all unity and growth. Emerson believed that if we "see truly" we will "live truly".

■ Selected Readings

Nature was published anonymously in 1836. *It was in this essay that the foundation of transcendentalism was put forth*, *a belief system that espoused a non-traditional appreciation of nature. Recent advances in zoology, botany, and geology confirmed Emerson's intuitions about the intricate relationships of Nature at large. Emerson defined nature as an all-encompassing divine entity inherently* **known** *to us in our unfettered innocence, rather than as merely a component of a world ruled by a divine, separate being* **learned** *by us through passed-on teachings in our experience.*

Many scholars identify Emerson as one of the first writers (with others, notably Walt Whitman) to develop a literary style and vision that is uniquely American, rather than following in the footsteps of Longfellow and others who were strongly influenced by their British cultural heritage. Nature *was the first significant work to establish this new way of looking at The Americas and its raw, natural environment. In England, all natural things were a reference to layers of historical events, a reflection of human beings. However, in America, all of nature was relatively new to Western Civilization with no man-made meaning. With this clean slate, as it were, Emerson was enabled to see nature through new eyes and rebuild nature's role in the world. In the book Emerson explains his stay in the Woods as a thriving transcendentalist.*

from *Nature*

To go into solitude, a man needs to retire as much from his chamber as from society. I am not solitary whilst I read and write, though nobody is with me. But if a man would be alone, let him look at the stars. The rays that come from those heavenly worlds will separate between him and what he touches. One might think the atmosphere was made transparent with this design, to give man, in the heavenly bodies, the perpetual presence of the sublime. Seen in the streets of cities, how great they are! If the stars should appear one night in a thousand years, how would men believe and adore, and preserve for many generations the remembrance of the city of God which had been shown! But every night come out these envoys of beauty, and light the universe with their admonishing smile.

The stars awaken a certain reverence because, though always present, they are inaccessible; but all natural objects make a kindred impression when the mind is open to their influence. Nature never wears a mean appearance. Neither does the wisest man extort her secret and lose his curiosity by finding out all her perfection. Nature never became a toy to a wise spirit. The flowers, the animals, the mountains reflected the wisdom of his best hour, as much as they had delighted the simplicity of his childhood...

To speak truly, few adult persons can see nature. Most persons do not see the sun. At least they have a very superficial seeing. The sun illuminates only the eye of the man, but shines into the eye and the heart of the child. The lover of nature is he whose inward and outward senses are still truly adjusted to each other, who has retained the spirit of infancy even into the era of manhood. His intercourse with heaven and earth becomes part of his daily food. In the presence of nature a wild delight runs through the man, in spite of real sorrows. Nature says: He is my creature, and maugre[77] all his impertinent griefs, he shall be glad with me. Not the sun or the summer alone, but every hour and season yields its tribute of delight; for every hour and change corresponds to and authorizes a different state of the mind, from breathless noon to grimmest midnight. Nature is a setting that fits equally well a comic or a mourning piece. In good health, the air is a cordial[78] of incredible virtue. Crossing a bare common,[79] in snow puddles, at twilight, under a clouded sky, without having in my thoughts any occurrence of special good fortune, I have enjoyed a perfect exhilaration. I am glad to the brink of fear. In the woods, too, a man casts off his years, as the snake his slough, and at what period soever of life is always a child. In the woods is perpetual youth. Within these plantations of God, a decorum[80] and sanctity reign; a perennial festival is dressed, and the guest sees not how he should tire of them in a thousand years. In the woods, we return to reason and faith. There I feel that nothing can befall me in life—no disgrace, no calamity (leaving me my eyes), which nature cannot repair. Standing on the bare ground—my head bathed by the blithe air and uplifted into infinite space— all mean egotism vanishes. I become a transparent eyeball; I am nothing; I see all; the currents of the Universal Being circulate through me; I am part or particle of God. The name of the

---

77   **mangre**: in spite of.

78   **cordial**: stimulating medicine or drink.

79   **common**: area of open public land.

80   **decorum**: rightness; harmony.

nearest friend sounds then foreign and accidental: to be brothers, to be acquaintances, master or servant, is then a trifle and a disturbance. I am the lover of uncontained and immortal beauty. In the wilderness, I find something more dear and connate[81] than in streets or villages. In the tranquil landscape, and especially in the distant line of the horizon, man beholds somewhat as beautiful as his own nature.

The greatest delight which the fields and woods minister is the suggestion of an occult relation between man and the vegetable. I am not alone and unacknowledged. They nod to me, and I to them. The waving of the boughs in the storm is new to me and old. It takes me by surprise, and yet is not unknown. Its effect is like that of a higher thought or a better emotion coming over me, when I deemed I was thinking justly or doing right.

Yet it is certain that the power to produce this delight does not reside in nature, but in man, or in a harmony of both. It is necessary to use these pleasures with great temperance. For nature is not always tricked[82] in holiday attire; but the same scene which yesterday breathed perfume and glittered as for the frolic of the nymphs is overspread with melancholy today. Nature always wears the colors of the spirit. To a man laboring under calamity, the heat of his own fire hath sadness in it. Then there is a kind of contempt of the landscape felt by him who has just lost by death a dear friend. The sky is less grand as it shuts down over less worth in the population.

■ Study Questions

1. Near the end of Paragraph 3, what does Emerson mean when he describes himself as "a transparent eyeball" when in the woods? How does this state of mind affect his relationship with God?

2. Summarize the first sentence of Paragraph 4. Be sure to use your own words in the summary.

3. Where does Emerson believe the power for a true relationship between man and God comes from, according to Paragraph 5?

4. What do you think is the difference between the kind of meaning Emerson finds in nature and the meaning a botanist, a geographer, or an astrophysicist finds in nature?

"Self-Reliance," published in 1841, is the other best-known and most influential essay by Emerson. While "Nature" is a lyrical expression of the harmony the auther feels between himself and nature. "Self-Reliance" is an essay that urges readers to trust in their own intuition and common sense—rather than automatically following popular opinion and conforming to the will of the majority. An ancient Latin quotation precedes the essay: Ne te quaesiveris extra. (Do not look outside of yourself for the truth.) The Roman satirist and poet Aulus Persius Flaccus (34-63 AD)—usually referred to simply as those words Persius wrote in Book 1, Line 7, of his Satires. The quotation is an apt introductory aphorism for Emerson's essay, for it sums up the central idea of "Self-Reliance" and the transcendental philosophy behind it: that one should rely on his own inner voice—his own intuition and instinct—to make important decisions and put his life on a righteous path. Emerson follows the Latin quotation with an English quotation from the epilogue of a verse drama by playwrights Franics Beaumont and John Fletcher, the 17th Century

---

81   **connate**: closely related.

82   **tricked**: dressed.

contemporaries of Shakespeare. That quotation, which begins with the words "Man is his own star," reinforces the view expressed in the Latin quotation.

from *Self-Reliance*

I read the other day some verses written by an eminent painter which were original and not conventional. The soul always hears an admonition in such lines, let the subject be what it may. The sentiment they instill is of more value than any thought they may contain. To believe your own thought, to believe that what is true for you in your private heart is true for all men, that is genius. Speak your latent conviction, and it shall be the universal sense; for the inmost in due time becomes the outmost, and our first thought is rendered back to us by the trumpets of the Last Judgment. Familiar as the voice of the mind is to each, the highest merit we ascribe to Moses, Plato, and Milton is, that they set at naught books and traditions, and spoke not what men but what they thought. A man should learn to detect and watch that gleam of light which flashes across his mind from within, more than the lustre of the firmament of bards and sages. Yet he dismisses without notice his thought, because it is his. In every work of genius we recognize our own rejected thoughts: they come back to us with a certain alienated majesty. Great works of art have no more affecting lesson for us than this. They teach us to abide by our spontaneous impression with good-humored inflexibility then most when the whole cry of voices is on the other side. Else, tomorrow a stranger will say with masterly good sense precisely what we have thought and felt all the time, and we shall be forced to take with shame our own opinion from another.

...

Trust thyself: every heart vibrates to that iron string. Accept the place the divine providence has found for you, the society of your contemporaries, the connection of events. Great men have always done so, and confided themselves childlike to the genius of their age, betraying their perception that the absolutely trustworthy was seated at their heart, working through their hands, predominating in all their being. And we are now men, and must accept in the highest mind the same transcendent destiny; and not minors and invalids in a protected corner, not cowards fleeing before a revolution, but guides, redeemers, and benefactors, obeying the Almighty effort, and advancing on Chaos and the Dark.

...

A foolish consistency is the hobgoblin of little minds, adored by little statesmen and philosophers and divines. With consistency a great soul has simply nothing to do. He may as well concern himself with his shadow on the wall. Speak what you think now in hard words, and tomorrow speak what tomorrow thinks in hard words again, though it contradict every thing you said today. Ah, so you shall be sure to be misunderstood. Is it so bad, then, to be misunderstood? Pythagoras was misunderstood, and Socrates, and Jesus, and Luther, and Copernicus, and Galileo, and Newton, and every pure and wise spirit that ever took flesh. To be great is to be misunderstood.

I suppose no man can violate his nature. All the sallies of his will are rounded in by the law of his being, as the inequalities of Andes and Himmaleh are insignificant in the curve of the sphere. Nor does it matter how you gauge and try him. A character is like an acrostic or Alexandrian stanza; read it forward, backward, or across, it still spells the same thing. In this pleasing, contrite wood-life which God allows me, let me record day by day my honest thought without prospect or retrospect, and, I cannot doubt, it will be found symmetrical, though I mean it not, and see it not. My book should smell of pines and resound with the hum of insects. The swallow over my window should interweave that thread or straw he carries in his bill into my web also. We pass for what we are. Character teaches above our wills. Men imagine that they communicate their virtue or vice only by overt actions, and do not see that virtue or vice emit a breath every moment.

...

Man is timid and apologetic; he is no longer upright; he dares not say "I think," "I am," but quotes some saint or sage. He is ashamed before the blade of grass or the blowing rose. These roses under my window make no reference to former roses or to better ones; they are for what they are; they exist with God today. There is no time to them. There is simply the rose; it is perfect in every moment of its existence. Before a leaf-bud has burst, its whole life acts; in the full-blown flower there is no more; in the leafless root there is no less. Its nature is satisfied, and it satisfies nature, in all moments alike. But man postpones or remembers; he does not live in the present, but with reverted eye laments the past, or, heedless of the riches that surround him, stands on tiptoe to foresee the future. He cannot be happy and strong until he too lives with nature in the present, above time.

This should be plain enough. Yet see what strong intellects dare not yet hear God himself, unless he speak the phraseology of I know not what David, or Jeremiah, or Paul. We shall not always set so great a price on a few texts, on a few lives. We are like children who repeat by rote the sentences of grandames and tutors, and, as they grow older, of the men of talents and character they chance to see—painfully recollecting the exact words they spoke; afterwards, when they come into the point of view which those had who uttered these sayings, they understand them, and are willing to let the words go; for, at any time, they can use words as good when occasion comes. If we live truly, we shall see truly. It is as easy for the strong man to be strong, as it is for the weak to be weak. When we have new perception, we shall gladly disburden the memory of its hoarded treasures as old rubbish. When a man lives with God, his voice shall be as sweet as the murmur of the brook and the rustle of the corn.

...

So use all that is called Fortune. Most men gamble with her, and gain all, and lose all, as her wheel rolls. But do thou leave as unlawful these winnings, and deal with Cause and Effect, the chancellors of God. In the Will work and acquire, and thou hast chained the wheel of Chance, and shalt sit hereafter out of fear from her rotations. A political victory, a rise of rents, the recovery of your sick, or the return of your absent friend, or some other favorable event, raises your spirits, and you think good days are preparing for you. Do not believe it. Nothing can bring you peace but yourself. Nothing can bring you peace but the triumph of principles.

■ Study Questions

1. In Paragraph 1 (also the beginning of the original essay), Emerson applies three kinds of personae. What are they? Distinguish them from each other.

2. Explain two lessons that 1) nature, and 2) great figures of the past teach us about the concept of self-reliance.

3. In your opinion, does Emerson express optimism or pessimism about human nature and human potential? What seems to the basis of his belief? Support your answer with specific references to the essay.

4. Explain how Emerson's moral philosophy serves as an expression of Transcendentalism.

5. Explain to what extent the concept of self-reliance can be considered a fundamental American idea. Support your answer with references to works that you have read in this book as well as to other aspects of American life and history.

Nathaniel Hawthorne (1804—1864)

Nathaniel Hawthorne, a novelist and short story writer brought up in the same New England giving birth to the hopeful visions of the Transcendentalists, developed a troubled vision towards the world. Generally seen as a key figure in the development of American literature for his tales of the nation's colonial history, however, he has obtained a secure position in the history of American literature.

Nathaniel Hawthorne was born in Salem, Massachusetts into the sixth generation of a once prominent Puritan family. Two aspects of his heritage were especially to affect his imagination. The Hathornes (Nathaniel added the "w" to the name in his 20s) had been involved in religious persecution with their first American forebear, William, and John Hathorne was one of the three judges at the 17th-century Salem witchcraft trials. Further, the family had over the generations gradually declined from its early prominence and prosperity into relative obscurity and indigence. Thus the Pyncheons and the Maules of Hawthorne's Salem novel The House of the Seven Gables (1851) represent the two different faces of his ancestors, and his feelings about his birthplace were mixed. With deep and unbreakable ties to Salem, he nevertheless found its physical and cultural environment as chilly as its prevalent east wind.

Nathaniel's father, a sea captain, died of yellow fever in Dutch Guiana in 1808, leaving his wife and three children dependent on relatives. Nathaniel spent his early years in Salem and in Maine. A leg injury immobilized the boy for a considerable period, during which he developed an exceptional taste for reading and contemplation. His childhood was calm, a little isolated but far from unhappy—as a handsome and attractive only son of the family, he was idolized by his mother and his two sisters. With the aid of his prosperous maternal uncles, the Mannings, Hawthorne attended Bowdoin College from 1821 to 1825, where he made steadfast friends with his classmates Henry Wadsworth Longfellow, Franklin Pierce, and Horatio Bridge, who remained devoted to him throughout life and all rendered him timely assistance. At Bowdoin, Hawthorne read widely and received solid instruction in English composition and the classics, particularly in Latin.

Returning from Bowdoin, Hawthorne spent from 1825 to 1837 in his mother's Salem household. Later he looked back upon these years as a period of dreamlike isolation and solitude. The "solitary years" were, however, his literary apprenticeship, during which he learned to write tales and sketches that are still unrivaled and unique. Hawthorne gathered his material by observing and listening to others. He roamed around the town, moving among old sailors on the docks, farmers from the country, men clustered in taverns, and the old wives at the market. He listened to their talks filled with New England lore, legend, and superstition. He made annual excursions into Vermont and New Hampshire and absorbed hints for stories on these jaunts. He even read the annals and chronicles of the Puritan world. He filled his notebooks and his thoughts with these scraps of impressions and memories, and after a few years began pouring them out as marvelously wrought tales.

Most of Hawthorne's early stories, including his first novel, *Fanshawe* (1829), were published anonymously. In his own words, he was "for a good many years, the obscurest man of letters in America." In 1837 the publication of his first collection of stories, *Twice-Told Tales*, somewhat lifted this spell of darkness. He supplemented *The Twice-Told Tales* with two later collections, *Mosses from an Old Manse* (1846) and *The Snow-Image* (1851), along with *Grandfather's Chair* (1841), a history for children of New England through the Revolution; the *Journal of an African Cruiser* (1845), edited from the observations of his friend Horatio Bridge while he was purser on an American frigate; and the second edition of the *Tales* (1842).

By Hawthorne's own account it was his love of his Salem neighbor Sophia Peabody that brought him out into the world. Unable to support himself by writing and editing, he took a job at the Boston customhouse and then spent part of 1841 in the famous Brook Farm community in hopes of finding a pleasant and economical haven for Sophia and himself. It is curious that the seclusive Hawthorne was always interested in experiments in community living in Brook Farm, in the New England Shaker settlements, and later in Greenwich Hospital in London. He was to record his mingled feelings of sympathy and skepticism about Brook Farm in *The Blithedale Romance* (1852).

At any rate, Hawthorne and Sophia, whom he married in 1842, resorted not to Brook Farm but to the Old Manse in Concord, where they spent several years of idyllic happiness in as much solitude as they could achieve. Concord, however, contained Ralph Waldo Emerson, Henry David Thoreau, and Ellery Channing, and Hawthorne was in frequent contact with these important thinkers, though his was not a nature for transcendental affirmations.

The Old Manse in Concord, MA

Facing the world once more, Hawthorne obtained in 1846 the position of surveyor in the Salem Custom House, from which as a Democrat he was expelled after the Whig victory in the 1848 presidential election. He did not leave without a fight and considerable bitterness, and he took revenge in "Custom-House," the introduction to *The Scarlet Letter* (1850), and in *The House of the Seven Gables*, in which he portrayed his chief Whig enemy as the harsh and hypocritical Judge Pyncheon. His dismissal, however, turned out to be a blessing, since it gave him leisure in which to write his greatest and crucial success, *The Scarlet Letter*. With his first successful "romance", his literary career divided into two distinct parts, since he now almost wholly abandoned the shorter tale.

The period 1850—1853 was Hawthorne's most prolific time. Doubtless stimulated by the enthusiastic reception accorded *The Scarlet Letter*, he went on with *The House of the Seven Gables* and *The Blithedale Romance*, along with *A Wonder Book* (1852) and *Tanglewood Tales* (1853, exquisitely fanciful stories for children from Greek mythology). During 1850 the Hawthornes lived at the Red House in Lenox in the Berkshire Hills, and Hawthorne formed a memorable friendship with Herman Melville, whose Arrowhead Farm was some miles away on the outskirts of Pittsfield. The association was more important to Melville than to Hawthorne, since Melville was 15 years younger and much the more impressionable of the two men. It left its mark in Melville's celebrated review of *Mosses from an Old Manse*, in the dedication of his *Moby-Dick*, and in some wonderful letters. Hawthorne's share in their correspondence has not survived, but he clearly aided Melville with insight and sympathy.

In 1852 Franklin Pierce was elected to the presidency of the United States, and Hawthorne was appointed to the important overseas post of American consul at Liverpool, England. After many years in Europe, he returned to America but, with the exception of *The Marble Faun* (1860), the inspiration for which he found during his visit to Rome, he was unable to complete any major work during his later years.

Hawthorne listened to conversations at Emerson's house and went boating with Thoreau, but his spirit was very different from theirs. As Emerson and Thoreau assert human freedom, Hawthorne reminds us of human limitations. He called his tales "allegories of the heart." An allegory is a story with a symbolic meaning used to teach a moral principle. Hawthorne's allegories are stories of how pride and isolation frustrate our capacity for love and sympathy. Isolation or "alienation" is Hawthorne's principal theme and problem, and loss of contact with reality is the ultimate penalty he envisions. Characteristically, this results from a separation of the "head," or intellect, and the "heart," a term that includes the emotions, the passions, and the unconscious. The heart is the custodian of man's deepest potentialities for good and evil, and it is man's vital connection with reality. Too much "head" leads always to a fatal intellectual pride, which distorts and finally destroys the wholeness of the real world. This, for Hawthorne, is the worst sin or calamity that man is heir to.

■ Selected Reading

*Published in 1850, the year in which the Clay Compromise postponed the American Civil War, **The Scarlet Letter** is a romance set in the years from 1642 to 1649, when Puritans were fighting the English civil war over the ultimate meaning of England Puritans in the Boston of Hawthorne's story attempt to label Hester Prynne. A woman taken in adultery, she must wear the letter **A** on her chest for all to see, yet she surrounds it with beautiful stitching, so that it advertises not only her shame, but also her skill as a seamstress. She refuses to name her lover, the Reverend Mr. Arthur Dimmesdale; keeps her word not to reveal the identity of her husband, now calling himself Roger Chillingworth; and raises her daughter, Pearl, on her own, living at the edge of town, near the wild forest and the open sea.*

As its title suggests, the book is about labeling, about the Puritan and later the American desire to eliminate ambiguity, to get the meanings right. The tale shows that even so simple a label as the first letter of the alphabet is

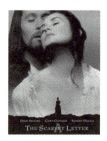

*full of burgeoning meanings dependent upon changing contexts. After Hester's competence and usefulness to the community become evident, some think the letter stands for "able." When an **A** appears in the sky at Governor John Winthrop's death, they think it stands for "angel." Since historical Puritans convicted of adultery were made to wear the letters AD on their sleeves, critics have noted that these are Dimmesdale's initials and concluded that the **A** also represents Arthur. Anne Hutchinson[84] of the Antinomian Controversy is explicitly mentioned in the text, so the letter also represents Anne and Antinomian. Readers may well*

A Hollywood adaptation[83]

*conclude that the **A** can mean almost anything, even America, where people still struggle to*

83   The 1995 film *The Scarlet Letter* is directed by Roland Joffé and stars Demi Moore as Hester. This version is "freely adapted" from Hawthorne according to the opening credits and takes liberties with the original story.

84   Mentioned in "The Prison Door," Chapter 1 of the novel, was a religious dissenter (1591—1643). In the 1630s she was excommunicated by the Puritans and exiled from Boston and moved to Rhode Island.

reinscribe the labels that others put on them.

*Destroyed by his lie and guilt, Dimmesdale dies in Hester's arms, and some see a scarlet **A** on his chest. Destroyed by his single-minded quest for vengeance, Chillingworth bequeaths his vast estates to Pearl, who leaves America to live abroad, depriving America of all she represents. The book ends with an allusion to Andrew Marvell's poem "The Unfortunate Lover," in which the lover lives on in story. So does Hester Prynne, perhaps the first fully realized female character in American fiction, whose meanings continue to attract new readers.*

from *The Scarlet Letter*

Chapter 12 stands out as the first point in **The Scarlet Letter** that could be identified as the book's "climax."[85] Presenting the second of three crucial scaffold scenes, this chapter appears exactly in the middle of the novel. As Dimmesdale watches a meteor trace a letter "A" in the sky, he confronts his role in Hester's sin and realizes that he can no longer deny his deed and its consequences. The key characters confront one another when Hester and Pearl join Dimmesdale in an "electric chain" as he holds his vigil on the marketplace scaffold, the location of Hester's original public shaming. Chillingworth appears in this scene as well. Again, Hawthorne gathers all of his major characters in one place—this time in a chapter so foreboding, so convincing in its psychology, and so rich in its symbolism that it is unquestionably one of the most powerful in the novel.

In his description of Dimmesdale's actions while alone on the scaffold, Hawthorne demonstrates his mastery of psychological realism (though the term appeared much later and is usually related to Henry James). The sudden changes in mood that take place in the minister's tired mind, the self-condemnation for his cowardice, the near-insanity of his scream, and his impulse to speak to Mr. Wilson all are developed convincingly. The first scaffold scene took place during the noon hours and concentrated on Hester's guilt and punishment. This second scene, occurring at the midnight hours, puts both "sinners" on the scaffold and concentrates on Dimmesdale's guilt and punishment. All the major characters of the first scene are again present. The town, although present, sleeps or is otherwise unaware of the action.

In the previous chapters, readers can see Dimmesdale's conscious mind attempting to reason through the problem of his concealed guilt. In contrast, in this chapter, they see the tortured workings of his subconscious mind, which is the real source of his agony. When Dimmesdale is forced by Pearl's repeated question to bring the issue into the open, his fear of confession still dominates his subconscious desire to confess.

As in the first scaffold scene, this chapter abounds in both major and minor symbols: the scaffold itself; Dimmesdale's standing on it; the three potential observers representing Church, State, and the World of Evil; the "electric chain" of Hester, Pearl, and

---

85 The other occurs in Chapter 23, at the end of the book. Here, the characters' secrets are publicly exposed and their fates sealed. Dimmesdale, Hester, and Chillingworth not only acknowledge their secrets to themselves and to each other; they push these revelations to such extremes that they all must leave the community in one way or another.

Dimmesdale; Pearl's appeal to Dimmesdale; the revealing light from the heavens; and the variation on the letter **A**.

XII *THE MINISTER'S VIGIL*

Walking in the shadow of a dream, as it were, and perhaps actually under the influence of a species of somnambulism, Mr. Dimmesdale reached the spot where, now so long since, Hester Prynne had lived through her first hours of public ignominy. The same platform or scaffold, black and weather-stained with the storm or sunshine of seven long years, and foot-worn, too, with the tread of many culprits who had since ascended it, remained standing beneath the balcony of the meeting-house. The minister went up the steps.

It was an obscure night in early May. An unvaried pall of cloud muffled the whole expanse of sky from zenith to horizon. If the same multitude which had stood as eye-witnesses while Hester Prynne sustained her punishment could now have been summoned forth, they would have discerned no face above the platform nor hardly the outline of a human shape, in the dark grey of the midnight. But the town was all asleep. There was no peril of discovery. The minister might stand there, if it so pleased him, until morning should redden in the east, without other risk than that the dank and chill night air would creep into his frame, and stiffen his joints with rheumatism, and clog his throat with catarrh and cough; thereby defrauding the expectant audience of tomorrow's prayer and sermon. No eye could see him, save that ever-wakeful one which had seen him in his closet, wielding the bloody scourge[86]. Why, then, had he come hither? Was it but the mockery of penitence? A mockery, indeed, but in which his soul trifled with itself! A mockery at which angels blushed and wept, while fiends rejoiced with jeering laughter! He had been driven hither by the impulse of that Remorse which dogged him everywhere, and whose own sister and closely linked companion was that Cowardice which invariably drew him back, with her tremulous gripe, just when the other impulse had hurried him to the verge of a disclosure. Poor, miserable man! What right had infirmity like his to burden itself with crime? Crime is for the iron-nerved, who have their choice either to endure it, or, if it press too hard, to exert their fierce and savage strength for a good purpose, and fling it off at once! This feeble and most sensitive of spirits could do neither, yet continually did one thing or another, which intertwined, in the same inextricable knot, the agony of heaven-defying guilt and vain repentance.

And thus, while standing on the scaffold, in this vain show of expiation[87], Mr. Dimmesdale was overcome with a great horror of mind, as if the universe were gazing at a scarlet token on his naked breast, right over his heart. On that spot, in very truth, there was, and there had long been, the gnawing and poisonous tooth of bodily pain. Without any effort of his will, or power to restrain himself, he shrieked aloud: an outcry that went pealing through the night, and was beaten

---

86 **scourge**: a whip used for flogging.

87 **expiation**: atonement; to pay a penalty for something.

back from one house to another, and reverberated from the hills in the background; as if a company of devils, detecting so much misery and terror in it, had made a plaything of the sound, and were bandying it to and fro.

"It is done!" muttered the minister, covering his face with his hands. "The whole town will awake and hurry forth, and find me here!"

But it was not so. The shriek had perhaps sounded with a far greater power, to his own startled ears, than it actually possessed. The town did not awake; or, if it did, the drowsy slumberers mistook the cry either for something frightful in a dream, or for the noise of witches, whose voices, at that period, were often heard to pass over the settlements or lonely cottages, as they rode with Satan through the air. The clergyman, therefore, hearing no symptoms of disturbance, uncovered his eyes and looked about him. At one of the chamber-windows of Governor Bellingham's mansion, which stood at some distance, on the line of another street, he beheld the appearance of the old magistrate himself with a lamp in his hand a white night-cap on his head, and a long white gown enveloping his figure. He looked like a ghost evoked unseasonably from the grave. The cry had evidently startled him. At another window of the same house, moreover appeared old Mistress Hibbins, the Governor's sister, also with a lamp, which even thus far off revealed the expression of her sour and discontented face. She thrust forth her head from the lattice, and looked anxiously upward. Beyond the shadow of a doubt, this venerable witch-lady had heard Mr. Dimmesdale's outcry, and interpreted it, with its multitudinous echoes and reverberations, as the clamour of the fiends and night-hags, with whom she was well known to make excursions in the forest.

Detecting the gleam of Governor Bellingham's lamp, the old lady quickly extinguished her own, and vanished. Possibly, she went up among the clouds. The minister saw nothing further of her motions. The magistrate, after a wary observation of the darkness—into which, nevertheless, he could see but little further than he might into a mill-stone—retired from the window.

The minister grew comparatively calm. His eyes, however, were soon greeted by a little glimmering light, which, at first a long way off was approaching up the street. It threw a gleam of recognition, on here a post, and there a garden fence, and here a latticed window-pane, and there a pump, with its full trough of water, and here again an arched door of oak, with an iron knocker, and a rough log for the door-step. The Reverend Mr. Dimmesdale noted all these minute particulars, even while firmly convinced that the doom of his existence was stealing onward, in the footsteps which he now heard; and that the gleam of the lantern would fall upon him in a few moments more, and reveal his long-hidden secret. As the light drew nearer, he beheld, within its illuminated circle, his brother clergyman—or, to speak more accurately, his professional father, as well as highly valued friend—the Reverend Mr. Wilson, who, as Mr. Dimmesdale now conjectured, had been praying at the bedside of some dying man. And so he had. The good old minister came freshly from the death-chamber of Governor Winthrop, who had passed from earth to heaven within that very hour. And now surrounded, like the saint-like personage of olden times, with a radiant halo, that glorified him amid this gloomy night of sin—as if the departed Governor had left him an inheritance of his glory, or as if he had caught upon himself the distant shine of the celestial city, while looking thitherward to see the triumphant pilgrim pass within its gates—now, in short, good Father Wilson was moving homeward, aiding his footsteps with a lighted lantern! The glimmer of this luminary suggested the above conceits to Mr. Dimmesdale, who smiled—nay, almost laughed at them—and then wondered if he was going mad.

As the Reverend Mr. Wilson passed beside the scaffold, closely muffling his Geneva cloak[88] about him with one arm, and holding the lantern before his breast with the other, the minister could hardly restrain himself from speaking—

"A good evening to you, venerable Father Wilson. Come up hither, I pray you, and pass a pleasant hour with me!"

Good Heavens! Had Mr. Dimmesdale actually spoken? For one instant he believed that these words had passed his lips. But they were uttered only within his imagination. The venerable Father Wilson continued to step slowly onward, looking carefully at the muddy pathway before his feet, and never once turning his head towards the guilty platform. When the light of the glimmering lantern had faded quite away, the minister discovered, by the faintness which came over him, that the last few moments had been a crisis of terrible anxiety, although his mind had made an involuntary effort to relieve itself by a kind of lurid playfulness.

Shortly afterwards, the like grisly sense of the humorous again stole in among the solemn phantoms of his thought. He felt his limbs growing stiff with the unaccustomed chilliness of the night, and doubted whether he should be able to descend the steps of the scaffold. Morning would break and find him there.

The neighbourhood would begin to rouse itself. The earliest riser, coming forth in the dim twilight, would perceive a vaguely-defined figure aloft on the place of shame; and half-crazed betwixt alarm and curiosity, would go knocking from door to door, summoning all the people to behold the ghost—as he needs must think it—of some defunct transgressor. A dusky tumult would flap its wings from one house to another. Then—the morning light still waxing stronger—old patriarchs would rise up in great haste, each in his flannel gown, and matronly dames, without pausing to put off their night-gear. The whole tribe of decorous personages, who had never heretofore been seen with a single hair of their heads awry, would start into public view with the disorder of a nightmare in their aspects. Old Governor Bellingham would come grimly forth, with his King James' ruff fastened askew, and Mistress Hibbins, with some twigs of the forest clinging to her skirts, and looking sourer than ever, as having hardly got a wink of sleep after her night ride; and good Father Wilson too, after spending half the night at a death-bed, and liking ill to be disturbed, thus early, out of his dreams about the glorified saints. Hither, likewise, would come the elders and deacons of Mr. Dimmesdale's church, and the young virgins who so idolized their

---

88 **Geneva cloak**: a black cloak that Calvinist ministers wore.

minister, and had made a shrine for him in their white bosoms, which now, by-the-bye, in their hurry and confusion, they would scantly have given themselves time to cover with their kerchiefs. All people, in a word, would come stumbling over their thresholds, and turning up their amazed and horror-stricken visages around the scaffold. Whom would they discern there, with the red eastern light upon his brow? Whom, but the Reverend Arthur Dimmesdale, half-frozen to death, overwhelmed with shame, and standing where Hester Prynne had stood!

Carried away by the grotesque horror of this picture, the minister, unawares, and to his own infinite alarm, burst into a great peal of laughter. It was immediately responded to by a light, airy, childish laugh, in which, with a thrill of the heart—but he knew not whether of exquisite pain, or pleasure as acute—he recognised the tones of little Pearl.

"Pearl! Little Pearl!" cried he, after a moment's pause; then, suppressing his voice— "Hester! Hester Prynne! Are you there?"

"Yes; it is Hester Prynne!" she replied, in a tone of surprise; and the minister heard her footsteps approaching from the side-walk, along which she had been passing. "It is I, and my little Pearl."

"Whence come you, Hester?" asked the minister. "What sent you hither?"

"I have been watching at a death-bed," answered Hester Prynne "at Governor Winthrop's death-bed, and have taken his measure for a robe, and am now going homeward to my dwelling."

"Come up hither, Hester, thou and little Pearl," said the Reverend Mr. Dimmesdale. "Ye have both been here before, but I was not with you. Come up hither once again, and we will stand all three together."

She silently ascended the steps, and stood on the platform, holding little Pearl by the hand. The minister felt for the child's other hand, and took it. The moment that he did so, there came what seemed a tumultuous rush of new life, other life than his own pouting like a torrent into his heart, and hurrying through all his veins, as if the mother and the child were communicating their vital warmth to his half-torpid system. The three formed an electric chain.

"Minister!" whispered little Pearl.

"What wouldst thou say, child?" asked Mr. Dimmesdale.

"Wilt thou stand here with mother and me, tomorrow noontide?" inquired Pearl.

"Nay; not so, my little Pearl," answered the minister; for, with the new energy of the moment, all the dread of public exposure, that had so long been the anguish of his life, had returned upon him; and he was already trembling at the conjunction in which—with a strange joy, nevertheless—he now found himself—"not so, my child. I shall, indeed, stand with thy mother and thee one other day, but not tomorrow."

Pearl laughed, and attempted to pull away her hand. But the minister held it fast.

"A moment longer, my child!" said he.

"But wilt thou promise," asked Pearl, "to take my hand, and mother's hand, tomorrow noontide?"

"Not then, Pearl," said the minister; "but another time."

"And what other time?" persisted the child.

"At the great judgment day," whispered the minister; and, strangely enough, the sense that he was a professional teacher of the truth impelled him to answer the child so. "Then, and there, before the judgment-seat, thy mother, and thou, and I must stand together. But the daylight of this world shall not see our meeting!"

Pearl laughed again.

But before Mr. Dimmesdale had done speaking, a light gleamed far and wide over all the muffled sky. It was doubtless caused by one of those meteors, which the night-watcher may so often observe burning out to waste, in the vacant regions of the atmosphere. So powerful was its radiance, that it thoroughly illuminated the dense medium of cloud betwixt the sky and earth.

The great vault brightened, like the dome of an immense lamp. It showed the familiar scene of the street with the distinctness of midday, but also with the awfulness that is always imparted to familiar objects by an unaccustomed light. The wooden houses, with their jutting storeys and quaint gable-peaks; the doorsteps and thresholds with the early grass springing up about them; the garden-plots, black with freshly-turned earth; the wheel-track, little worn, and even in the market-place margined with green on either side—all were visible, but with a singularity of aspect that seemed to give another moral interpretation to the things of this world than they had ever borne before. And there stood the minister, with his hand over his heart; and Hester Prynne, with the embroidered letter glimmering on her bosom; and little Pearl, herself a symbol, and the connecting link between those two. They stood in the noon of that strange and solemn splendour, as if it were the light that is to reveal all secrets, and the daybreak that shall unite all who belong to one another.

There was witchcraft in little Pearl's eyes; and her face, as she glanced upward at the minister, wore that naughty smile which made its expression frequently so elvish. She withdrew her hand from Mr. Dimmesdale's, and pointed across the street. But he clasped both his hands over his breast, and cast his eyes towards the zenith.

Nothing was more common, in those days, than to interpret all meteoric appearances, and other natural phenomena that occurred with less regularity than the rise and set of sun and moon, as so many revelations from a supernatural source. Thus, a blazing spear, a sword of flame, a bow, or a sheaf of arrows seen in the midnight sky, prefigured Indian warfare. Pestilence was known to have been foreboded by a shower of crimson light. We doubt whether any marked event, for good or evil, ever befell New England, from its settlement down to revolutionary times, of which the inhabitants had not been previously warned by some spectacle of its nature. Not seldom, it had been seen by multitudes. Oftener, however, its credibility rested on the faith of some lonely eye-witness, who beheld the wonder through the coloured, magnifying, and distorted medium of his imagination, and shaped it more distinctly in his after-thought. It was, indeed, a majestic idea that the destiny of nations should be revealed, in these awful hieroglyphics, on the cope[89] of heaven. A scroll so wide might not be deemed too expensive for Providence to write a people's doom upon. The belief was a favourite one with our forefathers, as betokening that their infant commonwealth was under a celestial guardianship of peculiar intimacy and strictness. But what shall we say, when an individual discovers a revelation addressed to himself alone, on the same vast sheet of record. In such a case, it could only be the symptom of a highly disordered mental state, when a man, rendered morbidly self-contemplative by long, intense, and secret pain, had extended his egotism over the whole expanse of nature, until the firmament itself should appear no more than a fitting page for his soul's history and fate.

We impute it, therefore, solely to the disease in his own eye and heart that the minister, looking upward to the zenith, beheld there the appearance of an immense letter—the letter A— marked out in lines of dull red light. Not but the meteor may have shown itself at that point, burning duskily through a veil of cloud, but with no such shape as his guilty imagination gave it, or, at least, with so little definiteness, that another's guilt might have seen another symbol in it.

There was a singular circumstance that characterised Mr. Dimmesdale's psychological state at this moment. All the time that he gazed upward to the zenith, he was, nevertheless, perfectly aware that little Pearl was pointing her finger towards old Roger Chillingworth, who stood at no great distance from the scaffold. The minister appeared to see him, with the same glance that discerned the miraculous letter. To his feature as to all other objects, the meteoric light imparted a new expression; or it might well be that the physician was not careful then, as at all other times, to hide the malevolence with which he looked upon his victim. Certainly, if the meteor kindled up the sky, and disclosed the earth, with an awfulness that admonished Hester Prynne and the clergyman of the day of judgment, then might Roger Chillingworth have passed with them for the arch-fiend, standing there with a smile and scowl, to claim his own. So vivid was the expression, or so intense the minister's perception of it, that it seemed still to remain painted on the darkness after the meteor had vanished, with an effect as if the street and all things else were at once annihilated.

"Who is that man, Hester?" gasped Mr. Dimmesdale, overcome with terror. "I shiver at him! Dost thou know the man? I hate him, Hester!"

She remembered her oath, and was silent.

"I tell thee, my soul shivers at him!" muttered the minister again. "Who is he? Who is he? Canst thou do nothing for me? I have a nameless horror of the man!"

"Minister," said little Pearl, "I can tell thee who he is!"

"Quickly, then, child!" said the minister, bending his ear close to her lips. "Quickly, and as low as thou canst whisper."

Pearl mumbled something into his ear that sounded, indeed, like human language, but was only such gibberish as children may be heard amusing themselves with by the hour together. At all

---

89   **cope**: a vestmentworn by priests for certain ceremonies. Here, anything that covers like a cope, a canopy over, or the sky.

events, if it involved any secret information in regard to old Roger Chillingworth, it was in a tongue unknown to the erudite clergyman, and did but increase the bewilderment of his mind. The elvish child then laughed aloud.

"Dost thou mock me now?" said the minister.

"Thou wast not bold! —thou wast not true!" answered the child.

"Thou wouldst not promise to take my hand, and mother's hand, tomorrow noontide!"

"Worthy sir," answered the physician, who had now advanced to the foot of the platform— "pious Master Dimmesdale! can this be you? Well, well, indeed! We men of study, whose heads are in our books, have need to be straitly looked after! We dream in our waking moments, and walk in our sleep. Come, good sir, and my dear friend, I pray you let me lead you home!"

"How knewest thou that I was here?" asked the minister, fearfully.

"Verily, and in good faith," answered Roger Chillingworth, "I knew nothing of the matter. I had spent the better part of the night at the bedside of the worshipful Governor Winthrop, doing what my poor skill might to give him ease. He, going home to a better world, I, likewise, was on my way homeward, when this light shone out. Come with me, I beseech you, Reverend sir, else you will be poorly able to do Sabbath duty tomorrow. Aha! See now how they trouble the brain— these books! —these books! You should study less, good sir, and take a little pastime, or these night whimsies will grow upon you."

"I will go home with you," said Mr. Dimmesdale.

With a chill despondency, like one awakening, all nerveless, from an ugly dream, he yielded himself to the physician, and was led away.

The next day, however, being the Sabbath, he preached a discourse which was held to be the richest and most powerful, and the most replete with heavenly influences, that had ever proceeded from his lips. Souls, it is said, more souls than one, were brought to the truth by the efficacy of that sermon, and vowed within themselves to cherish a holy gratitude towards Mr. Dimmesdale throughout the long hereafter. But as he came down the pulpit steps, the grey-bearded sexton met him, holding up a black glove, which the minister recognised as his own.

"It was found," said the Sexton, "this morning on the scaffold where evil-doers are set up to public shame. Satan dropped it there, I take it, intending a scurrilous[90] jest against your reverence. But, indeed, he was blind and foolish, as he ever and always is. A pure hand needs no glove to cover it!"

"Thank you, my good friend," said the minister, gravely, but startled at heart; for so confused was his remembrance, that he had almost brought himself to look at the events of the past night as visionary. "Yes, it seems to be my glove, indeed!"

"And, since Satan saw fit to steal it, your reverence must needs handle him without gloves henceforward," remarked the old sexton, grimly smiling. "But did your reverence hear of the

---

90 **scurrilous**: vulgar, indecent, abusive.

portent that was seen last night? a great red letter in the sky—the letter A, which we interpret to stand for Angel. For, as our good Governor Winthrop was made an angel this past night, it was doubtless held fit that there should be some notice thereof!"

"No," answered the minister, "I had not heard of it."

■ Study Questions

1. Where did the story of this chapter happen? According to the beginning of this chapter, what had drawn Mr. Dimmesdale back to the spot? Was it but the mockery of penitence? What had taken place at the same spot?

2. What kind of picture carried the minister away? What did he do? What did he hear then? Why should he recognize it "with a thrill of the heart"?

3. What did Pearl ask the minister to do "tomorrow noontide"? How did the minister reply to this request? Was Pearl satisfied?

4. What message did Mr. Dimmesdale intend to get from Hester? Why did the latter refuse to give him the answer?

5. Where did Roger Chillingworth stay to observe the minister? What did Chillingworth mean when he said that Governor Winthrop was "going home to a better world"?

6. What was "the portent that was seen last night"? How did people interpret it? Did the minister see it? How did he respond to it?

7. Chillingworth talked about evil and Satan with Dimmesdale towards the end of the chapter. What do the major characters in the novel understand and feel about the subject? What is the author's attitude and feeling behind his characters' views?

8. Discuss ways in which Hester Prynne, Arthur Dimmesdale, Roger Chillingworth, and Pearl complement each other thematically.

9. Given your earlier study of Puritan literature, trace elements of Puritanism in *The Scarlet Letter* and discuss the extent to which Hawthorne himself embraces or critiques Puritan ideology. (Compare actual Puritans you have studied with Hawthorne's fictional characters, e. g. Anne Bradstreet with Hester Prynne.)

10. Consider Hawthorne's presentation of women and children in his fiction. What attitudes inform his portrait of Hester Prynne? And his portrait of Pearl?

Henry Wadsworth Longfellow (1807—1882)

Longfellow is the best-known among the Fireside Poets and probably the best loved of American poets. Many of his lines are as familiar to Chinese readers as rhymes and words from nursery songs like "Two Rabbits". Like these rhymes and melodies, they remain in the memory and accompany us through life. A number of his phrases, such as "ships that pass in the night," "the patter of little feet," and "I shot an arrow into the air," have become a common property.

There are two reasons for the popularity and significance of Longfellow's poetry. First, he had the gift of easy rhyme. He wrote poetry as a bird sings, with natural grace and melody. Read or heard once or twice, his rhyme and meters cling to the mind long after the sense may be forgotten. Second, Longfellow wrote on obvious themes which appeal to all kinds of people. Though his works ranged as widely as from sentimental pieces like "The Village Blacksmith" to translations of Dante, his poems are always easily understood;

they sing their way into the consciousness of those who read them. Above all, there is a joyousness in them, a spirit of optimism and faith in the goodness of life which evokes immediate response in the emotions of his readers.

Born in Maine, Longfellow attended Bowdoin College, where one of his classmates was Nathaniel Hawthorne. He loved languages and became so skilled in them that for most of his life, first at Bowdoin, later at Harvard, he taught a great variety of languages and literatures, even writing his own language textbooks. As a result of his attachment to languages and his broad knowledge of European literature, and through his work as a teacher, anthologist, and poet, Longfellow did much to bring European culture to America.

But if that had been the only contribution Longfellow made to the American culture, it would be insecure to say that Americans owe a great debt to him. Longfellow lived in the day when "the flowering of New England" (as Van Wyck Brooks terms the period) took place, and he made a great contribution to it. He lived when giants walked on the New England earth, giants of intellect and feeling who established the New Land as a source of greatness. Emerson, Thoreau, Hawthorne, Melville, Oliver Wendell Holmes, and William Prescott were a few of the great minds and spirits among whom Longfellow took his place as a singer and as a representative of America. He was among the first of American writers to use native themes. He wrote about the American scene and landscape, the American Indian (*Song of Hiawatha*, 1855), and American history and tradition (*Evangeline*, 1847; *The Courtship of Miles Standish*, 1858). Longfellow's later poetry reflects his interest in establishing an American mythology, though at times with materials borrowed from European culture. Among his other works are *Tales of a Wayside Inn* (1863), a translation of Dante's *The Divine Comedy* (1865—1867) and *Christus: A Mystery* (1872), a trilogy dealing with Christianity from its beginnings. As a matter of fact, Longfellow wrote noble and elevated verse built around romanticized characters and heroic sentiments throughout his life. His versatility and enthusiasm won him a large audience, but, more important, he helped to popularize poetry itself in America.

Longfellow had already become so revered in his lifetime that his 75th birthday was celebrated in schoolrooms across the land. After he died in Cambridge on March 24, 1882, a memorial bust was placed in the Poet's Corner of Westminster Abbey in London. He is still the only American so honored. "Of all the suns of the New England morning," says Van Wyck Brooks, "he was the largest in his golden sweetness."

■ Selected Readings

*Longfellow said of "**A Psalm of Life**": "I kept it some time in manuscript, unwilling to show it to any one, it being a voice from my inmost heart, at a time when I was rallying from depression." Before it was published in the Knickerbocker Magazine, October, 1838, it was read by the poet to his college class at the close of a lecture on Goethe. Its title, though used now exclusively for this poem, was originally, in the poet's mind, a generic one. He notes from time to time that he has written a psalm, a psalm of death, or another psalm of life. The "psalmist" is thus the poet himself. When printed in the Knickerbocker it bore as a motto the lines from Crashaw: "Life that shall send / A challenge to its end, / And when it comes, say, Welcome, friend." Literally, the psalmist is of course King David.*

A Psalm of Life

What the Heart of the Young Man Said to the Psalmist.

Tell me not, in mournful numbers[91],

---

[91]   **numbers**: verses (meters and rhythms).

"Life is but an empty dream!"
For the soul is dead that slumbers,
      And things are not what they seem.

5   Life is real! Life is earnest!
      And the grave is not its goal;
"Dust thou art, to dust returnest,"
      Was not spoken of the soul.

Not enjoyment, and not sorrow,
10   Is our destined end or way;
But to act, that each tomorrow
      Find us farther than today.

Art is long, and Time is fleeting,[92]
      And our hearts, though stout and brave,
15   Still, like muffled drums, are beating
      Funeral marches to the grave.

In the world's broad field of battle,
      In the bivouac[93] of Life,
Be not like dumb, driven cattle!
20   Be a hero in the strife!

Trust no Future, howe'er pleasant!
      Let the dead Past bury its dead!
Act, —act in the living Present!
      Heart within, and God o'erhead!

25   Lives of great men all remind us
      We can make our lives sublime,
And, departing, leave behind us
      Footprints on the sands of time;

Footprints, that perhaps another,

---

92   **Art... fleeting**: A paraphrase of Seneca's complaint, "Vita brevis est, ars longa."
93   **bivouac**: temporary camp.

30   Sailing o'er life's solemn main[94],

       A forlorn and shipwrecked brother,

         Seeing, shall take heart again.

       Let us, then, be up and doing,

         With a heart for any fate;

35   Still achieving, still pursuing,

         Learn to labor and to wait.

*Both "**A Psalm of Life**" and "**The Tide Rises, the Tide Falls**" offer large views of life. However, the tone, or poet's attitude, is different in the two poems. In the first the young Longfellow urges us to live vigorously in spite of hardships. In the second the same poet, now older, gazes back on life with a sense of melancholy.*

The Tide Rises, the Tide Falls

       The tide rises, the tide falls,

       The twilight darkens, the curlew[95] calls;

       Along the sea-sands damp and brown

       The traveller hastens toward the town,

5   And the tide rises, the tide falls.

       Darkness settles on roofs and walls,

       But the sea, the sea in darkness calls;

       The little waves, with their soft, white hands,

       Efface the footprints in the sands,

10   And the tide rises, the tide falls.

       The morning breaks, the steeds in their stalls

       Stamp and neigh, as the hostler calls;

       The day returns, but nevermore

       Returns the traveller to the shore,

15   And the tide rises, the tide falls.

■ Study Questions

A Psalm Of Life

1. What was the poet preoccupied with when he wrote the poem?

2. What demand does the speaker make in Lines 1-2? What opinion does he proclaim in Line 5?

---

94   **main**: ocean.

95   **curlew**: large wading bird whose call is associated with evening.

3. According to Stanza 3, what is "our destined end or way"?

4. What figure of speech does the poet employ by referring to the "muffled drums"?

5. According to Stanza 6, when should we act? What do we learn from the lives of the great, according to Stanza 7?

6. What does "solemn main" mean in Line 30?

7. Find out in the poem images with symbolic meaning. Explain the symbolic meaning in your own words and summarize the speaker's advice for living.

8. Why is the image in Stanza 5 of a "field of battle" appropriate to the speaker's view of life?

9. Based on the last two stanzas, explain how the speaker feels that we can help future generations. What, specifically, might the image in Line 28 refer to?

10. In what respects is Emerson's idea of self-reliance echoed by the speaker of this poem?

The Tide Rises, the Tide Falls

1. What is the setting of the poem?

2. According to Stanza 2, what evidence does the traveler leave behind? What happens to this evidence?

3. What line is repeated throughout the poem?

4. What returns in the 3rd stanza? What never returns?

5. Does the action of the tide suggest permanence or impermanence? Why?

6. Find out in the poem images with symbolic meaning. Explain the symbolic meaning in your own words.

7. What does the poet suggest about the nature and about human life in Lines 13-14?

8. How does repetition underscore the meaning of the poem?

9. Longfellow wrote "A Psalm of Life" when he was young and "The Tide Rises, the Tide Falls" when he was old. How do you think the first poem represents the visions and ideals of a young person? What elements in the second poem indicate the view of a mature and experienced person looking back and assessing life?

10. Have you read other poems which express similar attitude with this one? Have you read any other poet who holds at different stages of life similar attitudes with Longfellow? Make comparisons between the poems and the poets.

LITERARY FOCUS

Repetition in Poetry

The most basic device of poetry—the one that gives poetry most of its musical quality—is repetition. It includes not only the repetition of sounds and rhythms but the repetition of words and lines.

Often individual words are repeated in a poem for emphasis. For example, in "The Tide Rises, the Tide Falls" Longfellow repeats the words *tide* and *sea* a number of times, suggesting the importance of these words to the meaning of the poem. Entire lines may also be repeated in a poem. A repeated line or group of lines is called a **refrain.** Like a musical refrain—the chorus of a song, for example—a poetic refrain occurs at regular intervals. "The tide rises, the tide falls" is both the title and the refrain of Longfellow's poem.

■ Thinking About Repetition

- Find and discuss at least two examples of word repetition in "A Psalm of Life." Tell what the repetition contributes to the meaning of the poem.

Rhythm in Poetry

Rhythm is the arrangement of stressed and unstressed syllables in a poem. When the rhythm forms a regular pattern, it is called **meter**.

The rhythm of "The Tide Rises, the Tide Falls" is irregular. For example, the first two lines of the poem swing forward and backward like a pendulum:

> The TIDE RIS es, the TIDE FALLS,
> The TWI light DAR kens, the CUR-LEW CALLS.

This rhythm suits the meaning, suggesting the rise and fall of the tide itself.

The "rising-falling" rhythm is created in part by punctuation, usually a comma, that interrupts certain lines, such as Line 1. The resulting pause, **a caesura**, accentuates the "rising" and the "falling" of the line.

Lines 3-4 of the poem have a more regular rhythm, and no comma interrupts their flow:

> a LONG the SEA sands DAMP and BROWN
> The TRA veler HAS tens to WARD the TOWN.

The contrast between the rhythms of the first two lines and the rhythm of the next two lines echoes the contrast between the tide and the traveler that the poet wishes to make.

Sometimes the sense and the grammatical structure of a line flow into the next line, as Line 3 flows into Line 4. This is a **run-on line**. If a line does not flow on to another line, it is called an **end-stopped line**.

■ Thinking About Rhythm

- How does the regular rhythm, or meter, of "A Psalm of Life" echo the meaning of the poem?

READING FOR APPRECIATION

The Sound of Poetry

Poems began with the human voice singing or chanting. Now that we see most poems in print rather than hear them recited, we can easily forget that one of the pleasures of poetry is the sound it makes.

Perhaps we should say: the sound we make for it, or of it. A printed poem, like a musical score, is only an indication of what can happen in "performance," even if we are reading silently. Yet the sound of poetry is not pure like the sound of a piano: It is part of the words. When we read a poem, we do not want the sense to overwhelm the verse; we do not want the verse to overwhelm the sense.

Look at the rhythm of Whittier's *Snow-Bound*[96], for example. Possible heavy or long pauses are marked with //, and light or short pauses with /. Try to read aloud these lines, taking no pause at all or just the hint of a pause at the ends of lines, unless a pause is indicated:

> The moon / above the eastern wood /
>
> Shone at its full; // the hill range stood
>
> Transfigured in the silver flood, /
>
> Its blown snows dashing / cold and keen,/
>
> Dead white, // save where some sharp ravine
>
> Took shadow, / or the somber green
>
> Of hemlocks turned to pitchy black /
>
> Against the whiteness at their back, //

You may disagree with this phrasing; the point, however, is that we can avoid a monotonous sing-song:

> The MOON a BOVE the EAST ern WOOD
>
> Shone AT its FULL; the HILL range STOOD

and so forth. There are subtler and more pleasant rhythms than that. At the same time we do not want to turn the poem into prose. Whittier did not write: "The moon above the eastern wood shone at its hill; the hill range stood transfigured in the silver flood..."

All poems do not sound alike, although the poems of a single poet do sometimes take on the "voice" of that poet. Find a "music" appropriate to some poems. Longfellow's "A Psalm of Life" and "The Tide Rises, the Tide Falls" would be good candidates. Allow the English language to have its natural way, and allow the verse to have its way as well.

VOICE OF THE AGE

Self-Reliance

Self-reliance in all its forms seems always to have been a part of American culture. During the New England Renaissance, however, it was given special attention and special expression.

---

96   This is Whittier's most famous poem that idealized his boyhood on a Massachusetts farm. The excerption is from "The Hearth at Night," a typical section that encompasses in its imagery, many changes of scene and a variety of moods.

Emerson：*Trust thyself*：*every heart vibrates to that iron string. Accept the place the divine providence has found for you... Speak what you think now in hard words, and tomorrow speak what tomorrow thinks in hard words again, though it contradict everything you said today... To be great is to be misunderstood.*

Hawthorne：*The belief was a favourite one with our forefathers, as betokening that their infant commonwealth was under a celestial guardianship of peculiar intimacy and strictness. But what shall we say, when an individual discovers a revelation addressed to himself alone, on the same vast sheet of record. In such a case, it could only be the symptom of a highly disordered mental state, when a man, rendered morbidly self-contemplative by long, intense, and secret pain, had extended his egotism over the whole expanse of nature, until the firmament itself should appear no more than a fitting page for his soul's history and fate.*

Longfellow：Be not like dumb, driven cattle. ／ Be a hero in the strife!

As a true American idea, self-reliance has withstood the extremes of optimism and pessimism. It has lifted some people to glorious visions when it distorted, isolated some people to the point of destruction. It has been the basis for a great variety of philosophical ideas, and it has inspired many political thinkers. Every period of American literature, every unit in this book, reveals in some way that self-reliance is an idea continually defining and redefining the American imagination.

Chapter 5

CONFLICT AND CELEBRATION
1855—1880

INTRODUCTION

Why a Separate Period

There is one but sufficient reason for getting this period start at the year 1855. This year, Whitman published the first edition of his *Song of Myself*, in which he cried out loudly, "I sound my barbaric yawp over the roofs of the world." There was indeed something elemental, unmannered and unmannerly, in the new language American writers found themselves using. This was something that the preceding American Romanticists or romancers could not have expected. Those Romanticists and romancers, no matter what kind of vision they held, optimistic or dark, were either born or raised under the influence of the European tradition. The Whitman generation (though some of them were born into the same decade as the late New Englanders, they published their masterpieces and earned their fame much later) were born Americans. While the Romanticists and romancers made great efforts to shake away the traces of the European influence from themselves, the Whitman generation never bothered to distinguish themselves from any one else. They *were* Americans, they took pride in their *own* experience, and they only needed to sing a song of themselves. And then Whitman came out and became the first and foremost singer. While Melville the boldest New Englander introduced himself timidly to the cruel world: "I am Ishmael," Whitman sounded his most "barbaric yawp over the roofs of the world." Whitman grew up in a culturally independent new nation and he absorbed it. He invented new expressions to describe the new nation's experience; he generated new rhythms and new forms for her new literature. He became the new country in his poetry, and his songs became America's new self-portrait.

Ending the period by the year 1880 is an unusual choice, as most literary histories would choose 1900 (the turn of the century) or 1914 (when WWI started) as the dividing line. Though, as usual, literary works were published in this year, there was not a book that deserves our speculation. What could be rendered as special was that in 1880 *The Dial* magazine founded U. S. population estimate 50 million, which was later proved by the seventh American census. The great route explored by Whitman was further treaded by his contemporaries and followers. There did occur a significant change concerning literature—while the first two decades after the outbreak of the Civil War remained "poetic," the last two decades of the 19th century and the beginning decade of the 20th century were dominated by prose writing. The years immediately after the Civil War witnessed the undiminished enthusiasm and efforts of Whitman and the Fireside Poets as well; the then unknown Emily Dickson would not stop composing her fantastic verses until her death (1886). Then people saw the puissant rise of the prose. The change, however, did not occur abruptly at any particular time. Instead, it had emerged when Mark Twain took a ride with his "celebrated jumping frog." Therefore, 1880—because of its convenience for memory— is chosen to separate two periods with close correlation but slight differences.

"A House Divided Against Itself"

Mrs. Stowe

At mid-19th century the United States, in politics as in literature, was at a turning point. Civil war loomed on the horizon. Among those who suggested social reformation none spoke more effectively than Harriet Beecher Stowe (1811—1896). As an abolitionist and novelist, Mrs. Stowe combined sentiment with realism in *Uncle Tom's Cabin* (1852) and severely attacked the cruelty of slavery. The *Cabin* reached millions as a novel and play, and became influential as well in Britain. It made the political issues of the 1850s regarding slavery tangible to millions, energizing anti-slavery forces in the North, while angering and embittering the South. The impact was summed up by Abraham Lincoln when he met Stowe, "So you're the little woman who wrote the book that made this great great war!"

Lincoln was only a little bit exaggerated, as the coexistence of a slave-owning agricultural South and an increasingly anti-slavery industrial North was the primary cause of the war. In the beginning Lincoln did not propose federal laws against slavery where it already existed, but he had, in his 1858 House Divided Speech[97], expressed a desire to "arrest the further spread of it, and place it where the public mind shall rest in the belief that it is in the course of ultimate extinction." Much of the political battle in the 1850s focused on the expansion of slavery into the newly created territories. Southern fears of losing control of the federal government to antislavery forces, and northern fears that the slave power already controlled the government, brought the crisis to a head in the late 1850s. Sectional disagreements over the morality of slavery, the scope of democracy and the economic merits of free labor vs. slave plantations caused the Whig and "Know-Nothing" parties to collapse, and new ones to arise (the Free Soil Party in 1848, the Republicans in 1854, the Constitutional Union in 1860). In 1860, the last remaining national political party, the Democratic Party, split along sectional lines.

Every year the debates grew fiercer. Besides slavery, other issues covered by the debates included states'

97　An address given by Lincoln in Springfield, Illinois. The speech created a lasting image of the danger of disunion because of slavery, and it rallied Republicans across the North. Along with the Gettysburg Address and his second inaugural address, this became one of the best-known speeches of his career. The speech contains the quotation "A house divided against itself cannot stand," which is taken from *Matthew* 12:25: "Every kingdom divided against itself is brought to desolation; and every city or house divided against itself shall not stand."

rights, modernization, sectionalism, the Nullification Crisis[98] over a tariff and economic differences between the North and South. When Abraham Lincoln was elected President in 1860, the Southern states took action. In December of 1860, South Carolina seceded from the Union; within a month six more states followed, and four others joined the new Confederacy soon after. With the firing at Fort Sumter on April 12, 1861, the Civil War began.

It is difficult to express what a civil war means to a nation. "Cousin against cousin" is a tired phrase, but it tells the truth. The young Mark Twain of Hannibal, Missouri, joined a Confederate militia; his brother accepted a Union appointment and moved to the Nevada Territory. The war was fought on a scale that America had never before seen. On land and sea, in the Mississippi Valley and in Virginia Wilderness, across Pennsylvania, Tennessee, and Georgia, in massive battles and unrecorded skirmishes—people fought and died. Bull Run, Shiloh, Chancellorsville, Gettysburg, Vicksburg, Atlanta—early Southern victories eventually gave way to Northern ones. On April 9, 1865, after a long and bitter war that some people had thought would take only a few weeks, Robert E. Lee, General of the Confederate Armies, surrendered to the Union Commander, General Ulysses S. Grant, at Appomattox Court House. For the new nation, the Civil War, or War Between the States, was a tragedy of the great magnitude. The war decimated generation and left the nation its most painful legacy.

The Gilded Age

The post-war period was an era of development and celebration, which saw unprecedented economic, industrial, and population expansion. The era overlaps with Reconstruction (which ended in 1877) in the South and includes the Panic of 1873. The era was characterized by an unusually rapid growth of railroads, small factories, banks, stores, mines and other family-owned enterprises, together with dramatic expansion into highly fertile western farmlands. There was a great increase in ethnic diversity from immigrants drawn by the promotions of steamship and railroad companies which emphasized the availability of jobs and farmland. The United States Census of 1880 determined the resident population of the United States to be 50,189,209, an increase of 30.2 percent over the 38,558,371 persons enumerated during the 1870 Census. With the rapid population increase, villages became towns, towns became cities, and cities grew to a size and with a speed that would have astonished the Founding Fathers.

The wealth of the period is highlighted by the American upper class's opulent self-indulgence, but also the rise of the American philanthropy (Andrew Carnegie called it the "Gospel of Wealth") that endowed thousands of colleges, hospitals, museums, academies, schools, opera houses, public libraries, symphony orchestras, and charities.

The end of the period coincided with the Panic of 1893[99], a deep depression. The depression lasted until 1897 and marked a major political realignment in the election of 1896. After that came the Progressive Era. This period overlaps with the nadir of American race relations, during which African Americans lost many of the civil rights obtained during the Reconstruction period. Increased racist violence, as well as exile of African Americans from the Southern states to the Midwest, started as soon as 1879.

This was the "Gilded Age." The term was coined by Mark Twain and Charles Dudley Warner in their book,

---

[98]   **The Nullification Crisis** was a sectional crisis during the presidency of Andrew Jackson around the question of whether a state can refuse to recognize or to enforce a federal law passed by the United States Congress. It was precipitated by protective tariffs, specifically the Tariff of 1828. The issue incited a debate over states' rights that ultimately threatened violent hostilities between South Carolina and the federal government, and the dissolution of the Union.

[99]   The Panic of 1893 was a serious decline in the economy of the United States that began in 1893 and was precipitated in part by a run on the gold supply. The Panic was the worst economic crisis to hit the nation in its history to that point.

The Gilded Age: A Tale of Today (1873). The term originates in Shakespeare's *King John* (1595): "To gild refined gold, to paint the lily… is wasteful and ridiculous excess." The Gilded Age, like gilding the lily (which is already beautiful and not in need of further adornment), was excessive and wasteful—it was a period characterized by showy displays of wealth and excessive opulence.

The toil of the slaves, the bloodshed of battle, the celebration of a reunited America, the boom in technology, the populating of the American frontier, and the displacement of the Indian cultures were dramatic experiences. Out of such experiences came memorable contributions to American literature.

Characteristics of the Literature

Literature before the Civil War was usually characterized by a romanticism that included the novels or romances of James Fenimore Cooper, Nathaniel Hawthorne, and Herman Melville, the transcendental essays of Ralph Waldo Emerson and Henry David Thoreau, and the genteel poetry of Henry Wadsworth Longfellow, John Greenleaf Whittier, and James Russell Lowell.

Though the Gilded Age saw some continuation of both romanticism and the genteel tradition, the more significant pattern was the gradual rise of realism, that is, a realistic—and sometimes quite critical—portrayal of life, replacing the romantic idealism characteristic of the pre-Civil War period, and producing works that significantly influenced the development of literature in the 20th century.

Among poets, Walt Whitman and Emily Dickinson led the way in rejecting previous poetic forms and introducing a new, less structured, psychological approach. Whitman, especially, also dealt with topics previously considered inappropriate. His *Leaves of Grass*, first published in 1855 and reissued in revised and enlarged editions until his death in 1892, stands as a major work in world literature. Though romantic in many ways, his poetry clearly abandoned the genteel tradition as it gloried in democracy, in the scenes and rhythms of New York City, and in the faces and forms of working people. He dealt, too, with topics often considered inappropriate for public print, including intimate relationships and the human body.

Emily Dickinson, whose poetry was first published in 1890, after her death, rejected the formal structures of most previous verse, and probed depths of anxiety and emotion. The American language shaped the sound of Emily Dickinson's poetry as well, but it is the quieter, drier, crisper tone of New England speech we hear in her poems. Most of early American poets wrote in a language close to the "literary" style of England, but the poems of Dickinson—like those of Whitman—take on the characteristic turns and twists of American speech. Her poems deal with the profound matters that New England writers had always explored, but her voice takes on an irony and reveals a sensibility that still seems modern today.

During the Gilded Age, American novelists became increasingly realistic. The towering novelist of this era was Mark Twain, whose *Huckleberry Finn* (1885) may be read at many levels, from a nostalgic account of boyhood adventures to profound social satire. In this masterpiece, Twain reproduced the everyday speech of unschooled whites and blacks, poked fun at social pretensions of the day, scorned the Old South myth, and challenged prevailing, racially biased attitudes toward African-Americans. Twain picked up similar themes in his other novels and especially in his essays, which often made explicit the political messages that lay buried in his novels.

Wherever Americans were going after the war, they were not returning to the past. The old forms and many of the old ideals had died in the war. New ones were not easily found. Perhaps Mark Twain's Huckberry Finn best sums up the direction many Americans felt they had to take: "But I reckon I got to light out for the Territory ahead of the rest, because Aunt Sally she's going to adopt me and sivilize me and I can't stand it. I been there before."

Walt Whitman (1819—1892)

Walter Whitman, proclaimed the "greatest of all American poets" by many foreign observers a mere four years after his death, is among the most influential and controversial poets in the American canon. His works, a "rude shock" and "the most audacious and debatable contribution yet made to American literature," have even been translated into more than 25 languages. Whitman largely abandoned the metrical structures of European poetry for an expansionist freestyle verse—"irregular" but "beautifully rhythmic" —which represented his philosophical view that America was destined to reinvent the world as emancipator and liberator of the human spirit.

Whitman was born on Long Island, New York, into a devout Quaker family. He grew up in Brooklyn, where he left school at 11 to become, in turn, an office boy, a doctor's helper, a printer's assistant, a journalist, a typesetter, and a printer. Thus he split his early manhood in New York City, soaking up its sights and sounds. At twenty-seven he became editor of the *Brooklyn Daily Eagle*, but he left the job when the paper took a proslavery stand.

He self-published an early edition of *Leaves of Grass* in 1855. Except for his own anonymous reviews, the early edition of the book received little attention. One exception was Ralph Waldo Emerson, who praised *Leaves of Grass* in a letter to Whitman which said, "I greet you at the beginning of a great career." Whitman republished the letter in the second edition of *Leaves of Grass* without Emerson's permission. Emerson was furious, but continued to recommend the book.

It was not until 1864 that *Leaves of Grass* found a publisher other than Whitman. After Secretary of the Interior, James Harlan, read it, he said he found it offensive and fired Whitman from his job at the Interior Department. Whitman remained undaunted. He kept arranging, rearranging, and adding to *Leaves of Grass* throughout his lifetime, envisioning all of his work as one vast poem.

In December of 1862, Whitman was first exposed to the tragedy of the Civil War when he traveled to Virginia in search of his brother George who had been wounded in battle. Whitman spent several days at camp hospitals of the Army of the Potomac at Falmouth, Virginia. He was so moved by the scene at the battlefield hospital that he traveled to Washington, D. C. , and spent much of the next three years working occasionally as an unofficial nurse in several army hospitals in and around the city.

Out of these experiences in the Civil War grew his *Drum-Taps* (1865), a sequence of 43 poems standing as the finest war poetry written by an American. In these poems Whitman presents, often in innovative ways, his emotional experience of the Civil War. The sequence as a whole traces Whitman's varying responses, from initial excitement (and doubt), to direct observation, to a deep compassionate involvement with the casualties of the armed conflict. The mood of the poems varies dramatically, from excitement to woe, from distant observation to engagement, from belief to resignation. Written ten years after "Song of Myself," these poems are more concerned with history than the self, more aware of the precariousness of America's present and future than of its expansive promise. In "Drum-Taps" Whitman projects himself as a mature poet, directly touched by human suffering, in clear distinction to the ecstatic, naive, electric voice which marked the original edition of *Leaves of Grass*.

Later Whitman added the poems from *Drum-Taps* to *Leaves of Grass*. To it he also added poems that have since been recognized as among the greatest of American expressions: the elegy to Abraham Lincoln, "When Lilacs Last in the Dooryard Bloom'd," "Crossing Brooklyn Ferry," and "Out of the Cradle Endlessly Rocking." Even in old age Whitman kept working, attempting to put "a Person, a human being (myself, in the latter half of the Nineteenth Century, in America) freely, fully and truly on record." In the final, "deathbed" edition of *Leaves of*

Grass（1891）there were 383 titled poems, and the person they put on record was one of the most remarkable America has ever produced.

■ Selected Readings

In the 1855 *edition of Leaves of Grass,* "**Song of Myself**" *came first in the series of* 12 *untitled poems, dominating the volume not only by its sheer bulk, but also by its brilliant display of Whitman's innovative techniques and original themes. Whitman left the poem in the lead position in the 1856 edition and gave it its first title,* "*Poem of Walt Whitman, an American,*" *shortened to* "*Walt Whitman*" *in the 3rd edition of 1860. By the time Whitman had shaped Leaves of Grass into its final structure in 1881, he left the poem (its lines now grouped into 52 sections) in a lead position, preceded only by the epigraph-like cluster* "*Inscriptions*" *and the programmatic* "*Starting from Paumanok*".*

Like most poetic works of genius, "*Song of Myself*" *has defied attempts to provide a definitive interpretation. In a very real sense, no reading of the poem has clarified the sum of its many mysteries. Critics have provided useful readings, concentrating on one or another dimension of the poem: Carl F. Strauch on the solidity of a fundamental structure, Randall Jarrell on the brilliance of individual lines, James E. Miller, Jr., on the portrayal of an* "*inverted mystical experience,*" *Richard Chase on the often-overlooked comic aspects, Malcolm Cowley on the affinities with the inspired prophecies of antiquity, Robert K. Martin on the resemblance to a* "*dream vision based on sexual* [*essentially homosexual*] *experience.*" *In addition, Edwin Haviland Miller has provided a guide through the various readings in Walt Whitman's* "*Song of Myself*": *A Mosaic of Interpretations* (1989). *In the final analysis, readers must find their own way through* "*Song of Myself*". *They will know that they are on the right path when they begin to feel something of the* "*great power*" *that Ralph Waldo Emerson felt in 1855.*

from *Song of Myself*

1

I celebrate myself, and sing myself,

And what I assume you shall assume,

For every atom belonging to me as good belongs to you.

I loaf and invite my soul,

5　I lean and loaf at my ease observing a spear of summer grass.

My tongue, every atom of my blood, formed from this soil, this air,

Born here of parents born here from parents the same, and their parents the same,

I, now thirty-seven years old in perfect health begin,

Hoping to cease not till death.

10　Creeds and schools in abeyance,[100]

Retiring back a while sufficed at what they are, but never forgotten,

---

100　**Creeds... in abeyance**: When I am singing myself and wandering, I'd like to leave all the (religious) doctrines and theories (of particular groups of scholars) aside, having them retire back; in abeyance: the condition of not being in use or in force.

I harbor for good or bad, I permit to speak at every hazard,

Nature without check with original energy.

6

A child said *What is the grass?*　fetching it to me with full hands;

How could I answer the child? I do not know what it is any more than he.

I guess it must be the flag of my disposition, out of hopeful green stuff woven.

Or I guess it is the handkerchief of the Lord,

5　A scented gift and remembrancer[101] designedly dropped,[102]

Bearing the owner's name someway in the corners, that we may see and remark, and say

　　Whose?

...

What do you think has become of the young and old men?

And what do you think has become of the women and children?

They are alive and well somewhere,

10　The smallest sprout shows there is really no death,

And if ever there was it led forward life, and does not wait at the end to arrest it,

And ceased the moment life appeared.

All goes onward and outward, nothing collapses,

And to die is different from what any one supposed, and luckier.

17

These are really the thoughts of all men in all ages and lands, they are not original with me,

If they are not yours as much as mine they are nothing, or next to nothing,

If they are not the riddle and the untying of the riddle they are nothing,

If they are not just as close as they are distant they are nothing.

5　This is the grass that grows wherever the land is and the water is,

　This is the common air that bathes the globe.

101　**a scented gift or remembrancer**: a pleasantly smelt gift or souvenir.

102　**designedly dropped**: intentionally dropped for others to pick up (In old times, a handkerchief is often used as a keepsake between lovers.)

51

The past and present wilt—I have filled them, emptied them,
And proceed to fill my next fold of the future.

Listener up there! what have you to confide to me?
Look in my face while I snuff the sidle of evening,[103]
5 (Talk honestly, no one else hears you, and I stay only a minute longer.)

Do I contradict myself?
Very well then I contradict myself,
(I am large, I contain multitudes.)

I concentrate toward them that are nigh[104], I wait on the door-slab.
10 Who has done his day's work? who will soonest be through with his supper?
Who wishes to walk with me?

Will you speak before I am gone? will you prove already too late?

52

The spotted hawk swoops by and accuses me, he complains of my gab and
     my loitering.

I too am not a bit tamed, I too am untranslatable,
I sound my barbaric yawp over the roofs of the world.

The last scud[105] of day holds back for me,
5 It flings my likeness after the rest and true as any on the shadow'd wilds,
It coaxes me to the vapor and the dusk.

I depart as air, I shake my white locks at the runaway sun,
I effuse[106] my flesh in eddies, and drift it in lacy jags.

---

103 **snuff... evening**: put out the light of day, which is moving sideways across the sky.
104 **nigh**: near.
105 **scud**: low, dark, wind-driven clouds.
106 **effuse**: pour forth.

I bequeath myself to the dirt to grow from the grass I love,

10   If you want me again look for me under your boot soles.

You will hardly know who I am or what I mean,

But I shall be good health to you nevertheless,

And filter and fiber your blood.

Failing to fetch me at first keep encouraged,

15   Missing me one place search another,

I stop somewhere waiting for you.

■ Study Questions

1. According to Line 1 of Section 1, who is the poet celebrating? Whom do Lines 2-3 also include in the celebration?

2. Who fetches the grass in Section 6? What does Whitman guess the grass might be? What does the "smallest sprout" show?

3. According to Section 17, are Whitman's thoughts original? Whose thoughts are they?

4. In Section 51 what explanation does the poet give for contradicting himself?

5. What animal does Whitman compare himself to in Section 52? What does he sound "over the roofs of the world"? Where does he tell us to look for him if we want him again?

6. Describe the relationship Whitman sets up with the reader in the first section.

7. Name as many characteristics of Whitman's "self" as you can. Which characteristics seem the most prominent?

8. Consider the image of the grass in Sections 6 and 52. What does the grass have to do with life and death?

9. By associating himself with the grass, what does the poet suggest about himself? Summarize Whitman's attitude towards nature.

10. Why might Whitman have called his volume of poetry *Leaves of Grass*?

*Whitman wrote the following dirge for the death of Abraham Lincoln in 1865. Published to immediate acclaim in the New York City Saturday Press, "**O Captain! My Captain!**" was widely anthologized during his lifetime. In the 1880s, when Whitman gave public lectures and readings, he was asked to recite the poem so often that he said: "I'm almost sorry I ever wrote [it]," though it had "certain emotional immediate reasons for being."*

While Whitman is renowned as the most innovative of American poets, this poem is a rare example of his use of rhymed, rhythmically regular verse, which serves to create a somber yet exalted effect. Whitman had envisioned Lincoln as an archangel captain, and reportedly dreamed the night before the assassination about a ship entering harbor under full sail.

*Restlessly creative, Whitman was still revising "**O Captain! My Captain!**" decades after its creation. Pictured here are an 1887 revision and a proof sheet of the poem, with his corrections, which was readied for publication in 1888. The editors apparently had erred by picking up earlier versions of punctuation and whole lines that had appeared in the poem prior to Whitman's 1871 revision.*

O Captain! My Captain!

O Captain! My Captain! Our fearful trip is done,
The ship has weather'd every rack, the prize we sought is won,
The port is near, the bells I hear, the people all exulting,
While follow eyes the steady keel, the vessel grim and daring;
5   But O heart! heart! heart!
          O the bleeding drops of red,
            Where on the deck my Captain lies,
              he Fallen cold and dead.

1887 revision

O Captain! My Captain! Rise up and hear the bells,
10 Rise up—for you the flag is flung—for you the bugle trills,
For you bouquets and ribbon'd wreaths—for you the shores acrowding,
For you they call, the swaying mass, their eager faces turning;
      Here Captain! Dear Captain!
       This arm beneath your head!
15   It is some dream that on the deck,
         You've fallen cold and dead.

My Captain does not answer, his lips are pale and still,
My father does not feel my arm, he has no pulse nor will,
The ship is anchor'd safe and sound, its voyage closed and done
20 From fearful trip the victor ship comes in with object won;
      Exult O shores, and ring O bell!
       But I with mournful tread,
        Walk the deck my Captain lies,
         Fallen cold and dead.

■ Study Questions

1. Why do people on the shores exult and bells ring, while the speaker remains so sad?
2. According to Stanza 2, what are people doing?
3. What is the response of "Captain" according to Stanza 3?
4. Why is the word "Captain" capitalized throughout the poem?
5. What overall metaphor does the poet employ in this poem?
6. Find out the rhyme and rhythm of this poem. What kind of effect do you think they create?
7. Compare this poem with Whitman's free verses. What are some merits and demerits of a rhymed verse? Why might Whitman have said sorry for composing this poem?

Emily Dickinson (1830—1886)

Though virtually unknown in her lifetime, **Emily Dickinson** has come to be regarded, along with Walt Whitman, as one of the two quintessential American poets of the 19th century. Dickinson lived an introverted and hermetic life. Although she wrote, at the last count, 1,789 poems, only a handful of them were published during her lifetime—all anonymously and some perhaps without her knowledge. One of the great poets of the English language had lived and died unknown to the public.

Dickinson was born in Amherst, Massachusetts, the middle child of a prominent lawyer and one-term United States congressional representative. She attended the Mount Holyoke Female Seminary (now Mount Holyoke College) in nearby South Hadley. With the exception of a trip to Washington, D. C., in the late 1850s and a few trips to Boston for eye treatments in the early 1860s, Dickinson remained in Amherst, living in the same house on Main Street from 1855 until her death. As she grew older, she communicated with fewer and fewer people. Her neighbors knew there was something extraordinary about this radiant yet isolated woman. At the age of 56 Dickinson died in the house in which she had been born.

Dickinson enjoyed the King James Version of the Bible, as well as English writers such as Shakespeare, Milton, Dickens, Elizabeth Barrett Browning, George Eliot, and Thomas Carlyle. But her poetry, in form or in content, is closer to that of her fellow American authors (Even here, she does not let any of their influence overshadow her own spirit). Dickinson's terse, frequently imagistic style is even more modern and innovative than Whitman's. She never uses two words when one will do, and combines concrete things with abstract ideas in an almost proverbial, compressed style. Her best poems have no fat; many mock current sentimentality, and some are even heretical. She sometimes shows a terrifying existential awareness. Like Poe, she explores the dark and hidden part of the mind, dramatizing death and the grave. Yet she also celebrated simple objects—a flower, a bee, or the like. Her poetry exhibits great intelligence and often evokes the agonizing paradox of the limits of the human consciousness trapped in time. She had an excellent sense of humor, and her range of subjects and treatment is amazingly wide. Her poems are generally known by the numbers assigned them in Thomas H. Johnson's standard edition (*The Complete Poems*) of 1955. They bristle with odd capitalizations and dashes.

In the early stages of her career, Dickinson's handwritten lyrics imitated the formalities of print, and her poetic techniques were conventional, but she later began to attend to the visual aspects of her work. For example, she arranged and broke lines of verse in highly unusual ways to underscore meaning and she created extravagantly shaped letters of the alphabet to emphasize or play with a poem's sense. She also incorporated cutouts from novels, magazines, and even the Bible to augment her own use of language.

Although few of Dickinson's poems were formally published during her lifetime, she herself "published" by sending out at least 1/3 of her poems in the more than 1,000 letters she wrote to at least 100 different correspondents. Dickinson's method of binding about 800 of her poems into 40 manuscript books and distributing several hundred of them in letters is now widely recognized as her particular form of self-publication. She also read her poems aloud to several people, including her cousins Louise and Frances Norcross, over a period of three decades.

Dickinson's poems, generally accepted as her magnificent personal confession, continue to intrigue critics, who often disagree about them. Some stress her mystical side; some emphasizes her sensitivity to nature; many note her odd, exotic appeal. One modern critic, R. P. Blackmur, comments that Dickinson's poetry sometimes feels as if "a cat came at us speaking English." Her clean, clear, chiseled poems are some of the most fascinating and challenging in American literature.

■ Selected Readings

*Everybody requires a successful life. However, who is able to understand the meaning of "success"? It is not those who were born into the high society, nor those who had easily taken the critical position. It is those people who had been striving with every effort and had been badly wounded but never gratified that are able to catch, in their last breath, the music of victory. "**Success is counted sweetest**" is a song for the common people.*

Success is counted sweetest

Success is counted sweetest
By those who ne'er succeed. [107]
To comprehend a nectar[108]
Requires sorest need.

5 Not one of all the purple host
Who took the flag today
Can tell the definition,
So clearly, of victory.

As he, defeated—dying—
10 On whose forbidden ear
The distant strains of triumph
Burst, agonized and clear.

■ Study Questions

1. According to the first stanza, to whom is success "sweetest"? What is required to "comprehend a nectar"?
2. Who are "the purple host"? What do they achieve? What are they unable to do?
3. Who is "he" in the last stanza?
4. Why is success "counted sweetest by those who ne'er succeed"?
5. How is the rest of the poem related to this observation?
6. Do you agree that "Success is counted sweetest by those who ne'er succeeded"? Why or why not?

*If the word "great" means anything in poetry, "**Because I could not stop for Death**" can be, one of the greatest in the English language. The rhythm charges with movement. Every image is precise and, moreover, not merely beautiful, but fused with the central idea. Every image extends and intensifies every other. The content of death in the poem eludes explicit definition. He is a gentleman taking a lady out for a drive. But note the restraint that keeps the poet from carrying this so far that it becomes ludicrous and incredible; and note the subtly interfused*

---

[107] **Success... succeed**: More generally, that people tend to desire things more acutely when they do not have them.
[108] **nectar**: a symbol of triumph, luxury.

erotic motive, which the idea of death has presented to most romantic poets, love being a symbol interchangeable with death. The terror of death is objectified through the figure of the genteel driver, who is made ironically to serve the end of Immortality. This is the heart of the poem: the poet presented a typical Christian theme in its final irresolution, without making any final statements about it. There is no solution to the problem; there can be only a presentation of it in the full context of intellect and feeling. A construction of the human will, elaborated with all the abstracting powers of the mind, is put to the concrete test of experience; the idea of immortality is confronted with the fact of physical disintegration. We are not told what to think; we are told to look at the situation.

The framework of the poem is, in fact, the two abstractions: mortality and eternity, which are made to associate in equality with the images: she sees the ideas and thinks the perceptions. We must use the logical distinctions, even to the extent of paradox, if we are to form any notion of this rare quality of mind. Unless we prefer the feeble poetry of moral ideas that flourished in New England in the 1880s, we must conclude that her intellectual deficiency contributes at least negatively to her great distinction. Dickinson is probably the only Anglo-American poet of her century whose work exhibits the perfect literary situation—in which is possible the fusion of sensibility and thought. Unlike her contemporaries, she never succumbs to her ideas, to easy solutions, to her private desires.

Because I could not stop for Death

Because I could not stop for Death—
He[109] kindly stopped for me—
The Carriage[110] held but just Ourselves—
And Immortality.

5 We slowly drove—He knew no haste
And I had put away
My labor and my leisure too,
For His Civility—

We passed the School, where Children strove
10 At Recess—in the Ring—
We passed the fields of Gazing Grain—
We passed the Setting Sun—[111]

Or rather—He passed Us—
The Dews drew quivering and chill—
15 For only Gossamer, my Gown[112]—

---

109 **He**: death.
110 **Carriage**: hearse; carriage for carrying a coffin at a funeral.
111 **School... Fields of Gazing Grain... Setting Sun**: there stages of life—youth, mature period, and the end of life.
112 **Gown**: grave clothes.

My Tippet[113]—only Tulle[114]—

We paused before a House[115] that seemed
A Swelling of the Ground—
The Roof was scarcely visible—
20   The Cornice—in the Ground—

Since then—'tis Centuries—and yet
Feels shorter than the Day
I first surmised the Horses' Heads
Were toward Eternity—

Emily Dickinson displays an obsession with pain and suffering; there is an eagerness in her to examine pain, to measure it, to calculate it, to intellectualize it as fully as possible. Emily says "I like a look of Agony." Many readers have been even more intrigued by Dickinson's ability to probe the fact of human death. She often adopts the pose of having already died before she writes her lyric. She can look straight at approaching death.

Emily Dickinson's theological orientation was Puritan—she was taught all the premises of Calvinistic dogma—but she reacted strenuously against two of them: infant damnation and God's sovereign election of His own. There was another force alive in her time that competed for her interests: that was the force of literary transcendentalism. This explains a kind of paradoxical or ambivalent attitude toward matters religious. She loved to speak of a compassionate Savior and the grandeur of the Scriptures, but she disliked the hypocrisy and arbitrariness of institutional church. In one of her poems she approached God in prayer, but she could only worship, she could not pray. In another she addressed Him progressively as "Burglar, Banker, Father." There are other lyrics which express grave doubt.

In the following poem, Dickinson boldly images and describes the process of dying and presents her vision of death. From this poem, we can see that Dickinson's poetry is a clear illustration of her religious-ethical ideas, though in a bitter ironical way.

I heard a fly buzz—when I died— [116]

I heard a fly buzz—when I died—
The stillness in the Room
Was like the Stillness in the Air—
Between the Heaves of Storm—

5   The Eyes around—had wrung them dry[117]—

---

113 **Tippet**: shoulder cape or scarf.
114 **Tulle**: thin net.
115 **House**: garve.
116 This poem is a description of the moment of death. In Christian culture, people believe that God will come to take the dead person's soul to heaven. But in this poem, it is not God, but a fly, that comes to welcome the dead.
117 **The Eyes around had wrung them dry**: the relatives and friends had cried and cried so that there were no tears any more.

And Breaths were gathering firm

For that last Onset—when the king[118]

Be witnessed—in his Room—

I willed my Keepsakes—Signed away

10   What portion of me be

Assignable—and then it was

There interposed a Fly—

With blue—uncertain, stumbling buzz[119]—,

Between the light—and me—

15   And then the windows failed—and then

I could not see to see—

■ Study Questions

Because I could not stop for Death

1. According to Stanza 1, why did Death stop for the speaker? What is the poet's attitude towards death?

2. What three things did the speaker and Death pass in the third stanza? Where did they pause in Stanza 5?

3. According to Stanza 6, how much time has passed since the day of Death's visit? What does that time feel shorter than?

4. What metaphor does Dickinson use for Death? How does she maintain it throughout the poem?

5. What does the word "kindly" in Line 2 suggest? Does it carry any religious meaning? What does "death" mean to the author?

6. What is the function of those dashes used in the poem?

I heard a fly buzz—when I died—

1. According to the first stanza, what was the stillness like?

2. What are people expecting in the second stanza?

3. What has the speaker signed away in the third stanza? How can a buzz be blue? How can it stumble? What do the two "see" mean?

4. What is happening to the speaker? Who are the other people in the room?

5. What do the windows and the fly symbolize? Why is the fly's appearance somewhat ironic? What basic message about death is suggested to the poet by the appearance of the fly?

6. Emily Dickinson frequently voices ideas of independence and individualism, of reaction against conformity and obeisance to tradition, providing us a poetic variation upon the theme of self-reliance. There is also the romantic notion of the relationship between beauty and truth. Can you find out traces in her poetry that reveal Dickinson's relationship with the Emersonian tradition?

7. It has been characteristic of New England people to be shy, withdrawn, to say little, but to convey much. Emily never writes a long poem, but tends toward epigrammatic, the concentrated, carefully wrought, gemlike lyric,

---

118   **The King**: the God of death.

119   **With blue, uncertain, stumbling Buzz**: the sight of the dying became dim and listening became weak.

whose mastery of ambiguity, of allusion, of compressed syntax, of the lyric outburst, is a central concern. Can you find out traces in her poetry that reveal Dickinson's relationship with the New England tradition?

8. There is possible influence of William Cullen Bryant and Henry Thoreau upon Dickinson. On the one hand, she shared with her romantic and transcendental predecessors who believed that a mythical bond between man and nature existed, that nature revealed to man things about mankind and universe. On the other hand, she felt strongly about nature's inscrutability and indifference to the life and interests of human beings. Can you find out traces in her poetry that reveal Dickinson's relationship with the nature poetry tradition?

9. Dickinson read a great deal and enjoyed the writings of 17th century authors. Her imagery and metaphors derive both from an acute observation of nature and from an imagination often as playful in thought and witty in expression as that of the English metaphysical poets of the 17th century. Can you find out traces in her poetry that reveal Dickinson's relationship with the metaphysical tradition?

Mark Twain (1835—1910)

Mark Twain, born Samuel Langhorne Clemens, was an American writer, journalist, and humorist. During his lifetime, Twain became a friend to presidents, artists, leading industrialists, and European royalty. He also enjoyed immense public popularity, and his keen wit and incisive satire earned him praise from both critics and peers. Twain even won a worldwide audience for his stories of youthful adventures of Tom Sawyer and Huckleberry Finn. Sensitive to the sound of language, Twain introduced colloquial speech into American fiction. In *Green Hills of Africa*, Ernest Hemingway wrote: "All modern American literature comes from one book by Mark Twain called *Huckleberry Finn*..." William Faulkner called Twain "the father of American literature."

Samuel Langhorne Clemens was born in Florida, Missouri, and brought up chiefly in the river town of Hannibal. After his father's death in 1847, Twain was apprenticed to a printer and wrote for his brother's newspaper. Twain worked later as a licensed Mississippi river-boat pilot (1857—1861), adopting his name from the call ("Mark twain!" —meaning by the mark of two fathoms) used when sounding river shallows. But this isn't the full story: he had also satirized an older writer, Isaiah Sellers, who called himself Mark Twain. The Civil War put an end to the steamboat traffic and Clemens moved to Virginia City, where he edited two years *Territorial Enterprise*. On February 3, 1863, "Mark Twain" was born when he signed a humorous travel account with that pseudonym ("I believe that our Heavenly Father invented man because he was disappointed in the monkey.").

In 1864 Twain left for California, and worked in San Francisco as a reporter. During a period when he was out of work, he lived in a primitive cabin on Jackass Hill and tried his luck as a gold-miner. Twain heard a story about a frog, and made an entry in his notebook: "Coleman with his jumping frog—bet a stranger $50. —Stranger had no frog and C. got him one: —In the meantime stranger filled C's frog full of shot and he couldn't jump. The stranger's frog won." He published "Jim Smiley and his Jumping Frog" in *The Saturday Press* of New York on the 18th of November in 1865. It was reprinted all over the country and became the foundation stone of *The Celebrated Jumping Frog of Calaveras County, and Other Sketches* (1867). This work marked the beginning of Twain's literary career, and set the tone of his subsequent stories. Twain focused on not the outcome of the story but the manner of telling.

In 1867, as a correspondent for the *Alta California*, Twain set out for Europe and the Middle East. This journey provided the material for *Innocents Abroad* (1869), a sharp-tongued look at raw American travelers that quickly became a best seller, and a chance for him to meet Charles Langdon and see a picture of Langdon's sister Olivia. Twain claimed to have fallen in love at first sight. They met in 1868, were engaged a year later, and married in 1870 in New York. In 1871, Clemens moved his family to Hartford, Connecticut. There he became good friends with fellow author William Dean Howells and Charles Dudley Warner, the most influential literary critic of the day. Another huge success, *Roughing It* (1872), recounted Clemens' experiences in the "Wild West." With Warner Twain collaborated on *The Gilded Age* (1874), a satire that gave its name to the era of corrupt materialism that followed the Civil War. In Howells' *Atlantic Monthly* Twain recounted his experiences as a riverboat pilot in a series, "Old Times on the Mississippi," later developed into *Life on the Mississippi* (1883).

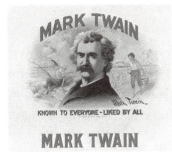

Twain's next major publication was *The Adventures of Tom Sawyer* which drew on his youth in Hannibal. The character of Tom Sawyer was modeled on Twain as a child. The book also introduced Huckleberry Finn as a supporting character. *Tom Sawyer* established Twain as a master of fiction, and its sequel, *The Adventures of Huckleberry Finn* (1883), as one of the greatest novelists America has ever produced. Mark Twain did not write a story; he told it. His mastery of American speech—the native vernacular—and his ability "to spin a yarn" are unrivaled; and whether his yarn spinning is aimed at pure entertainment or at social satire, his humor is irresistible. His realism and detail influenced many later writers of American fiction.

Plagued by financial misfortunes and the deaths of loved ones, Twain's later years saw him frequently embittered, his work given 10 dark satire and philosophic brooding. *A Connecticut Yankee in King Arthur's Court* (1889) is a biting satire set in the Middle Ages; *Pudd'nhead Wilson* (1894) is an attack on racial discrimination. *The Man That Corrupted Hadleyburg* (1900) is probably the best of the powerful pessimistic tales.

■ Selected Reading

"The Celebrated Jumping Frog of Calaveras County" is Mark Twain's most famous western tale. It is actually a story within a frame story: The first narrator introduces us to a second narrator, Simon Wheeler, who then tells the tale. Our pleasure is in the company of Wheeler himself, a man who loves to talk and who could, as we see at the end, go on spinning his tall tales forever.

Twain on "Celebrated Jumping Frog." Frederick Waddy, 1872.

The Celebrated Jumping Frog of Calaveras County

In compliance with the request of a friend of mine, who wrote me from the East, I called on good-natured, garrulous old Simon Wheeler, and inquired after my friend's friend, Leonidas W. Smiley, as requested to do, and I hereunto append the result. I have a lurking suspicion that *Leonidas W.* Smiley is a myth; that my friend never knew such a personage; and that he only conjectured that if I asked old Wheeler about him, it would remind him of his infamous *Jim* Smiley, and he would go to work and bore me to death with some exasperating reminiscence of him as long and as tedious as it should be useless to me. If that was the design, it succeeded.

I found Simon Wheeler dozing comfortably by the barroom stove of the dilapidated tavern in the decayed mining camp of Angel's, and I noticed that he was fat and baldheaded, and had an expression of winning gentleness and simplicity upon his tranquil countenance. He roused up, and gave me good day. I told him that a friend of mine had commissioned me to make some inquiries about a cherished companion of his boyhood named *Leonidas W. Smiley—Rev. Leonidas W. Smiley*, a young minister of the gospel, who he had heard was at one time a resident of Angel's Camp. I added that if Mr. Wheeler could tell me anything about this Rev. Leonidas W. Smiley, I would feel under many obligations to him.

Simon Wheeler backed me into a corner and blockaded me there with his chair, and then sat down and reeled off the monotonous narrative which follows this paragraph. He never smiled, he never frowned, he never changed his voice from the gentle-flowing key to which he tuned his initial sentence, he never betrayed the slightest suspicion of enthusiasm; but all through the interminable narrative there ran a vein of impressive earnestness and sincerity, which showed me plainly that, so far from his imagining that there was anything ridiculous or funny about his story, he regarded it as a really important matter, and admired its *two* heroes as men of transcendent genius in *finesse*. I let him go on in his own way, and never interrupted him once.

"Rev. Leonidas W. H'm, Reverend Le—well, there was a feller here once by the name of *Jim* Smiley, in the winter of '49—or maybe it was the spring of '50—I don't recollect exactly, somehow, though what makes me think it was one or the other is because I remember; big flume[120] warn't finished when he first come to the camp; but anyway, he was the curiousest man about always betting on anything it turned up you ever see, if he could get anybody to bet on the other side; and if he couldn't he'd change sides. Any way that suited the other man would suit *him*—any way just so's he got a bet, *he* was satisfied. But still he as lucky, uncommon lucky; he most always come out winner. He was always ready and laying for a chance; there couldn't be no solitary thing mentioned but that feller'd offer to bet in it, and take ary side you please, as I was list telling you. If there was a horse race, you'd find him flush or you'd find him busted at the end of it; if there was a dog fight, he'd bet on it; if there was a cat fight, he'd bet on it; if there was a chicken fight, he'd bet on it; why, if there was two birds setting on a fence, he would bet you which one would fly first; or if there was a camp meeting,[121] he would be there reg'lar to bet on Parson Walker, which judged to be the best exhorter about here, so he was too, and a good man. If he even a straddle bug[122] start to go anywheres, he would bet you how long it would take him to get to—to wherever he was going to, and if you took him up, he would foller that straddle to Mexico but what he would find out where he was bound for and how long he was on the road. Lots of the boys here has seen that Smiley, and can tell you about him. Why, it never made no difference to *him*—he'd bet on *any* thing—the dangdest feller. Parson Walker's wife laid very sick once, for a good and it seemed as if they warn't going to save her; but one morning he come in,

---

120 **flume**: artificial inclined channel for conducting water to provide power and transport objects.

121 **camp meeting**: religious meeting and service held in the mining camp.

122 **straddle bug**: long-legged beetle.

and up and asked him how she was, and he said he was consid'rable better—thank the Lord for his inf 'nit' mercy—and coming on so that with the blessing of Prov'dence get well yet; and Smiley, before he thought, says, "Well, I'll resk two-and-a-half she don't anyway."

"Thish-yer Smiley had a mare—the boys called her the fifteen-minute nag, but that was only in fun, you know, because of course she was faster than that—and he used to win money on that horse, for all she was so slow and always had the asthma, or the distemper, or the consumption, or something of that kind. They used to give her two or three hundred yards' start, and then pass her underway; but always at the fag end[123] of the race she'd get excited and desperate like, and come cavorting and straddling up, and scattering her legs around limber, sometimes in the air, and sometimes out to one side among the fences, and kicking up m-o-r-e dust and raising m-o-r-e racket with her coughing and sneezing and blowing her nose—and *always* fetch up at the stand just about a neck ahead, as near as you could cipher it down.

"And he had a little small bull pup, that to look at him you'd think he warn't worth a cent but to set around and look ornery and lay for a chance to steal something. But as soon as money was up on him he was a different dog; his under-jaw'd begin to stick out like the fo'castle of a steamboat, and his teeth would uncover and shine like the furnaces. And a dog might tackle him and bullyrag him, and bite him, and throw him over his shoulder two or three times, and Andrew Jackson[124]—which was the name of the pup—Andrew Jackson would never let on but what *he* was satisfied, and hadn't expected nothing else—and the bets being doubled and doubled on the other side all the time, till the money was all up; and then all of a sudden he would grab that other dog jest by the j'int of his hind leg and freeze to it—not chaw, you understand, but only just grip and hang on till they throwed up the sponge, if it was a year. Smiley always come out winner on that pup, till he harnessed a dog once that didn't have no hind legs, because they'd been sawed off in a circular saw, and when the thing had gone along far enough, and the money was all up, and he come to make a snatch for his pet holt, he see in a minute how he'd been imposed on, and how the other dog had him in the door, so to speak, and he' peared surprised, and then he looked sorter discouraged-like, and didn't try no more to win the fight, and so he got shucked out bad. He give Smiley a look, as much as to say his heart was broke, and it was *his* fault, for putting up a dog that hadn't no hind legs for him to take holt of, which was his main dependence in a fight, and then he limped off a piece and laid down and died. It was a good pup, was that Andrew Jackson, and would have made a name for hisself if he'd lived, for the stuff was in him and he had genius—I know it, because he hadn't no opportunities to speak of, and it don't stand to reason that a dog could make such a fight as he could under them circumstances if he hadn't no talent. It always makes me feel sorry when I think of that last fight of his'n, and the way it turned out.

---

123   **fag end**: last part.

124   **Andrew Jackson**: after the general and seventh President of the United States.

"Well, thish-yer Smiley had rat terriers[125] and chicken cocks[126] and tomcats and all them kind of things, till you couldn't rest, and you couldn't fetch nothing for him to bet on but he'd match you. He ketched a frog one day, and took him home, and said he cal'lated to educate him; and so he never done nothing for three months but set in his back yard and learn that frog to jump. And you bet you he *did* learn him, too. He'd give him a little punch behind, and the next minute you'd see that frog whirling in the air like a doughnut—see him turn one summerset, or maybe a couple, if he got a good start, and come down flatfooted and all right, like a cat. He got him up so in the matter of ketching flies, and kep' him in practice so constant, that he'd nail a fly every time as fur as he could see him. Smiley said all a frog wanted was education, and he could do 'most anything—and I believe him. Why, I'v seen him set Dan'l, Webster[127] down here on this floor—Dan'l Webster—was the name of the frog—and sing out, 'Flies, Dan'l, flies!' and quicker'n you could wink he'd spring straight up and snake a fly off 'n the counter there, and flop down on the floor ag'in as solid as a gob of mud, and fall to scratching the side of his head with his hind foot as indifferent as if he hadn't no idea he'd been doin' any more'n any frog might do. You never see a frog so modest and straightfor'ard as he was, for all he was so gifted. And when it come to fair and square jumping on a dead level, he could get over more ground at one straddle than any animal of his breed you ever see. Jumping on a dead level was his strong suit, you understand; and when it come to that, Smiley would ante up money on him as long as he had a red. Smiley was monstrous proud of his frog, and well he might be, for fellers that had traveled and been everywheres all said he laid over any frog that ever *they* see.

"Well, Smiley kep' the beast in a little lattice box, and he used to fetch him downtown sometimes and lay for a bet. One day a feller—a stranger in the camp, he was—come acrost him with his box, and says:

"'What might it be that you've got in the box?'

"And Smiley says, sorter indifferent-like, 'It might be a parrot, or it might be a canard maybe, but it ain't—it's only just a frog.'

"And the feller took it, and looked at it careful, and turned it round this way and that and says, 'H'm—so' tis. Well, what's *by* good for?'

"'Well,' Smiley says, easy and careless, 'he's good enough for *one* thing, I should judge—ha can outjump any frog in Calaveras County.'

"The feller took the box again, and took another long, particular look, and give it back to Smiley, and says, very deliberate, 'Well,' he says, 'I don't see no p'ints about that frog that's any better'n any other frog.'

"'Maybe you don't,' Smiley says. 'Maybe you understand frogs and maybe you don't

---

125　**rat terriers**：dogs skilled in catching rats.

126　**chicken cocks**：here, roosters trained for fights on which bets were made.

127　**Dan'l Webster**：after Daniel Webster, the American statesman and orator.

understand 'em; maybe you've had experience, and maybe you ain't only a amature, as it were. Anyways, I've got *my* opinion, and I'll risk forty dollars that he can outjump any frog in Calaveras County.'

"And the feller studied a minute, and then says, kinder sad-like, 'Well, I'm only a stranger here, and I ain't got no frog; but if I had a frog, I'd bet you.'

"And then Smiley says, 'That's all right—that's all right—if you'll hold my box a minute, I'll go and get you a frog.' And so the feller took the box, and put up his forty dollars along with Smiley's, and set down to wait.

"So he set there a good while thinking and thinking to himself, and then he got the frog out and prized his mouth open and took a teaspoon and filled him full of quailshot[128]—filled him pretty near up to his chin—and set him on the floor. Smiley he went to the swamp and slopped around in the mud for a long time, and finally he ketched a frog, and fetched him in, and give him to this feller, and says:

"'Now, if you're ready, set him alongside of Dan'l, with his fore paws just even with Dan'l's, and I'll give the word.' Then he says, 'One—two—three—*git*! ' and him and the feller touched up the frogs from behind, and the new frog hopped off lively, but Dan'l give a heave, and hysted up his shoulders—so—like a Frenchman, but it warn't no use—he couldn't budge; he was planted as solid as a church, and he couldn't no more stir than if he was anchored out. Smiley was a good deal surprised, and he was disgusted too, but he didn't have no idea what the matter was, of course.

"The feller took the money and started away; and when he was going out at the door, he sorter jerked his thumb over his shoulder—so—at Dan'l, and says again, very deliberate, 'Well, ' he says, 'I don't see no p'ints about that frog that's any better'n any other frog.'

"Smiley he stood scratching his head and looking down at Dan'l a long time, and at last he says, 'I do wonder what in the nation that frog throw'd off for—I wonder if there ain't something the matter with him—he 'pears to look mighty baggy, somehow.' And he ketched Dan'l by the nap of the neck, and hefted him, and says, 'Why blame my cats if he don't weigh five pound! ' and turned him upside down and he belched out a double handful of shot. And then he see how it was, and he was the maddest man—he set the frog down and took out after that feller, but he never ketched him. And—'

Here Simon Wheeler heard his name called from the front yard, and got up to see what was wanted. And turning to me as he moved away, he said: "Just set where you are, stranger, and rest easy—I ain't going to be gone a second. "

But, by your leave, I did not think that a continuation of the history of the enterprising vagabond *Jim* Smiley would be likely to afford me much information concerning the Rev. *Leonidas W.* Smiley, and so I started away.

---

[128] **quailshot**: small lead pellets used for shooting quail.

At the door I met the sociable Wheeler returning, and he buttonholed me and recommenced:

"Well, thish-yer Smiley had a yaller one-eyed cow that didn't have no tail, only jest a short stump like a bannanner, and—"

However, lacking both time and inclination, I did not wait to hear about the afflicted cow, but took my leave.

■ Study Questions

1. With what adjectives does the narrator describe Wheeler and Wheeler's reminiscences in the first paragraph?

2. Whom does the narrator ask Wheeler about? Whom does Wheeler speak about?

3. According to Wheeler's opening paragraph, what was Jim Smiley "the curiousest man" about?

4. How did Smiley's bullpup surprise people? What eventually became of the dog?

5. What did Smiley train his frog to do? Summarize what the stranger did to the frog and Smiley's reaction.

6. The narrator tells us that Wheeler bored him to death. Do you think Twain expects the reader to have the same reaction? How can you tell?

7. Does Wheeler's account of what happened to Smiley's dog make sense? Does it matter? Why or why not?

8. What kind of person is Jim Smiley, presented by Wheeler presents?

9. Who is really the main character in this story, and why?

10. Why do you think people love to tell tall tales—and to listen to them?

Abraham Lincoln (1809—1865)

"We cannot escape history," Abraham Lincoln once said. Lincoln himself was caught in history and proved to be one of history's greatest and most tragic personalities.

Born in a log cabin in Kentucky, Lincoln spent his boyhood in Indiana where he struggled to get an education, taking every opportunity to read the books that were available to him. In 1830 his family, plagued by poverty, moved to Illinois where Lincoln became interested in politics. Two years later he ran for the Illinois state legislature—and lost. He continued to pursue a political career, however, and moved steadily into public view. In 1858 he debated Stephen Douglas, his opponent in the Illinois Senate race, and became nationally known as a brilliant, compelling speaker.

Elected the nation's sixteenth President in 1860, Lincoln saw as his chief duty the preservation of the Union. In speech after speech, he inspired Americans at a time of dark despair. His dream was that the nation be reunited "with malice toward none; and charity for all." But five days after Lee's surrender at Appomattox, Lincoln was shot in a Washington theater, and his plans for a harmonious reunion died with him.

Lincoln's speeches were written to express his convictions and convince others to share them. His language is masterful: plain, powerful, dignified, as in the Gettysburg Address. On November 19, 1863, Lincoln attended the dedication of a national cemetery at Gettysburg, the site of a great but costly Union victory. The main speaker was Edward Everett, one of the most admired orators in the country. Everett gave a lengthy address, and Lincoln's aim was to make a few pertinent remarks following Everett's performance. Afterward, however, Everett wrote to Lincoln:"I should be glad if I could flatter myself that I came as near to the central idea of the occasion in two hours, as you did in two minutes." In the ten sentences that appear below, Lincoln gave the world a masterpiece of oratory and one of the greatest speeches ever written by an American.

■ Selected Reading

The Gettysburg Address

Four score and seven years ago our fathers brought forth on this continent, a new nation, conceived in Liberty, and dedicated to the proposition that all men are created equal.

Now we are engaged in a great civil war, testing whether that nation, or any nation so conceived and so dedicated, can long endure. We are met on a great battlefield of that war. We have come to dedicate a portion of that field, as a final resting place for those who here gave their lives that that nation might live. It is altogether fitting and proper that we should do this.

But, in a larger sense, we can not dedicate—we can not consecrate—we can not hallow—this ground. The brave men, living and dead, who struggled here, have consecrated it, far above our poor power to add or detract. The world will little note, nor long remember what we say here, but it can never forget what they did here. It is for us the living, rather, to be dedicated here to the unfinished work which they who fought here have thus far

Mount Rushmore[129]

so nobly advanced. It is rather for us to be here dedicated to the great task remaining before us—that from these honored dead we take increased devotion to that cause, for which they gave the last full measure of devotion—that we here highly resolve that these dead shall not have died in vain—that this nation, under God, shall have a new birth of freedom—and that government of the people, by the people, for the people, shall not perish from the earth.

■ Study Questions

1. What happened "four score and seven years ago" ?

2. What is happening "now", according to Paragraph 2?

3. According to Paragraph 3, what is the "great task remaining before us" ?

4. State in your own words the kind of nation that Lincoln says is having its endurance tested by the Civil War.

5. In your own words, state the main point of Lincoln's speech. What does he argue for?

6. What chief emotion or feeling does Lincoln's speech appeal to?

7. Do you think the Gettysburg Address is more as a written speech for reading in silence or for an oral presentation? Why?

---

[129]   Mount Rushmore is a memorial to the birth, growth, preservation, and development of USA. Gutzen Borglum sculpted busts of Presidents George Washing, Thomas Jefferson, Theodore Roosevelt, and Abraham Lincoln high in the Black Hills to represent the first 150 years of American history.

LITERARY FOCUS

Types of Poetry

Poetry is often classified as **narrative**, **dramatic**, or **lyric**. These categories are more clear-cut in some poems than in others. The category in which we place a poem will often depend on what we consider the main purpose of the poem to be.

The main purpose of a narrative poem is to tell a story. Narrative poetry includes the **epic**, a long poem that recounts the adventures of heroic figures in polished, elevated language. Narrative poetry also includes the **mock-epic**, a poem about a comical or foolhardy hero that parodies epic grandeur. The **ballad** is a shorter narrative poem.

The main purpose of a dramatic poem is to reveal character through dialogue and monologue. A dramatic poem may contain narrate elements, but it usually presents characters in a particular situation rather than in a series events. The focus of the dramatic poem is on character, not events.

The main purpose of a lyric poem is to communicate the emotions of the poet. Lyric poems are generally short and attempt to achieve a single, unified effect. By far, most poetry falls into the category. Lyric poems, too, may contain narrative or dramatic elements, but the focus of the lyric is on the personal feelings of the poet.

Free Verse

Free verse is poetry that has an irregular rhythm and line length and that attempts to avoid any predetermined verse structure; instead, it uses the cadences of natural speech. While it alternates stressed and unstressed syllables as stricter verse forms do, free verse does so in a looser way.

Whitman's poetry is an example of free verse at its most impressive. Listen, for instance, to a line from "Song of Myself":

A child said *What is the grass?* fetching it to me with full hands;

Here, question and answer create a rising and falling effect, ending in a stop. Whitman continues:

How could I answer the child? I do not know what it is any more than he.

The same question-and-answer pattern is repeated, the same rising and falling effect. This is not prose but poetry. It is arranged rhythmically, tightened and loosened by the poet. It has a plan, although the plan seems to "grow" organically—like its subjects, nature and human beings.

Although free verse had been used before Whitman—notably in Italian opera and in the King James translation of the Bible—it was Whitman who pioneered the form and made it acceptable in

American poetry. It has since been used by Ezra Pound, T. S. Eliot, William Carlos Williams, Wallace Stevens, and other major American poets of the 20th century.

READING FOR APPRECIATION

Meaning

As we read, most of us ask some version of the question, "What does it mean?" But in order to get the most out of what we read, we ought to first stop and ask ourselves the odd question, "What do we mean by 'mean'?" It will help to make a few distinctions.

To begin with, we should recognize the fact that no statement about a poem or a story, no summary of it, can take the place of the work itself. For convenience we sometimes make such statements and summaries. To do so is fine as long as we know that they are not the same as the poem or story as it is written.

Surely, we want to interpret a work so that as many of its multiple meanings as possible are brought to light. These meanings will include much more than whatever "message" we may find—and we must not turn ourselves exclusively into "message seekers." The meanings of a work will also include the way the specific language works, the tone of a work, its shape, its movements. In short, the complete meaning of a work of literature is its total effect.

As we read we must ask not only what does this say, but also how does this work, and what happens in it? For the way the poem or story happens is part of its meaning. We may say, for example, that Whitman's "As Toilsome I Wander'd Virginia's Woods" can be paraphrased or restated, as follows: "The poet remembers coming across the grave of an unknown soldier in the woods and an inscription nailed to a nearby tree. Long after that incident he still sees the grave and the inscription. The memory comes back to him suddenly." Compare this version of the poem with the poem itself. You will sense at once how much of the meaning is missing.

In the paraphrase, for one thing, the repeated retrain is missing—the important line that makes its effect by its very repetition. All the poem's rhythms disappear in a paraphrase, and you can hear at once how the phrasing of the words creates the poem's effect. In the refrain, for example, there are three short words—"Bold," "cautious," "true" —followed by a long phrase—"and my loving comrade" —which suggests the sudden rush of emotion that sprang into the poet's heart. If you are moved by the way that phrase is positioned twice within the poem, then you will see how hard it is to isolate meaning from the total effect of the work. The meaning is what happens in the poem as it happens.

VOICE OF THE AGE

The Shadow of War

The writers in this unit lived through a turbulent time in American history. The Civil War brought many Americans face to face with suffering and death. It also shocked many people into an intense awareness of the value of human life itself. Whether they faced war's violence publicly as soldiers or privately as poets, the writers in this unit confronted the harsh facts of war with honesty and courage. They found strength and refuge in a larger vision of the compassionate individual.

Lincoln: *It is rather for us to be here dedicated to the great task remaining before us—that from these honored dead we take increased devotion to that cause for which they gave the last full measure of devotion—that we here highly resolve that these dead shall not have died in vain.*

Whitman: *Beat! beat! drums! —blow! bugles! blow! / Through the windows—through doors—burst like a ruthless force, / Into the solemn church, and scatter the solemn congregation / Into the school where the scholar is studying.*

Dickinson: *Not one of all the purple Host / Who took the Flag today / Can tell the definition / So clear of Victory // As he defeated—dying—/ On whose forbidden ear / The distant strains of triumph / Burst agonized and clear!*

Americans endured the war with a combination of realism and idealism. The American voice spoke of victory and of defeat, of compassion deeply felt, and of hard lessons learned. The period to come would reflect in its realistic literature both that surviving compassion and the effects of those hard lessons.

Chapter 6

REGIONALISM AND REALISM
1880—1910

INTRODUCTION

Multiple Directions

In the decades around the turn of the century, America continued its energetic expansion and its growth in population, wealth, and military power. The Civil War had challenged the nation's self-confidence and had put an end to the optimism of the mid-19th century. After the war a new, more varied, bewildering America emerged. In the Puritan age, in the revolutionary age, in the age of the western frontier, America seemed to have a single, clear direction. Now it seemed to be moving in many different directions at once.

Iron Horse by Paul Detlefsen

The war had devastated the nation. Throughout the South people suffered from the continued effects of economic collapse. In the North industry flourished, having been spurred by the production demands of the war. The movement west continued as established American families and new immigrants searching for a better life spread out and populated new territories. The isolated frontier was becoming only a memory as railroads continued to crisscross the continent.

Thomas Jefferson's dream of an agrarian America, with small towns and family farms, was vanishing. The United States was becoming a wealthy industrial nation. By the 1890s there were over 4,000 American millionaires, and some whose wealth greatly exceeded a mere million dollars. Yet as we have examined in the previous unit, this was no more than the surface of a "Gilded Age." As wealth grew more conspicuous, however, poverty became more visible. In the Midwest a series of natural disasters forced farmers to move from state to state in order to eke from the soil the barest means of existence. In the West wheat growers battled the railroads, whose owners were condemned in works such as Frank Norris' *The Octopus* (1901). Drawing the most criticism were the burgeoning urban centers: Journalist Lincoln Steffens called poverty and slums "the shame of the cities," attacking too the urban phenomenon of political corruption and "bossism." Other "muckraking" journalists, such as Upton

In Days Gone By by Paul Detlefsen

Sinclair and Ida Tarbell, criticized corrupt business practices and urged governmental reforms.

Responding to the new conditions of social life (as is on most occasions a distinctive characteristic of literature), American literature of the decades just before and after 1900 became multiply oriented. While the literary mainstream continued to turn away from Romanticism and Transcendental optimism toward a franker portrayal, or a realistic reflection of society and of human nature, Southern literature with its usual distinctive flavor "suddenly" gained widespread national popularity toward the end of the 19th century. Of course, the romantic and genteel tradition was far from extinct; it not only found frequent entry into the "local color" works but also occasionally showed itself up in the nostalgic pieces of the most prominent realists. Meanwhile, some realists made up their mind to break completely away from any fancy of romanticism by turning themselves into "extreme realists," that is, naturalists. American literature in the years 1880—1910 was preparing itself for another renaissance.

Local Color and Regionalism[130]

The national spirit that emerged after the Civil War reunited the country paradoxically encouraged the acceptance of divergent regional identities. As the United States grew geographically, and transportation and communication innovations began to connect the regions, Americans wanted to know more about their far-flung compatriots. Furthermore, increasing urbanization and industrialization spurred an increasing fascination with the remaining rural areas. These factors, combined with the emergence of several large-circulation magazines, led to the development of the local color genre. Short stories and poems celebrating the individual regions appeared first in the national magazines and then often were collected in books. Soon local color writers began producing full-length novels.

Local Color as a literary genre bears the full weight of the concept of region, for its typical stories and sketches offer highly particularized visions of "locale" that are "colored" by regionally defined characters, settings, folkways, and dialects. The paradox, and thus the richness, of this often discounted form lies in the tension between local and national that its core texts embody. Local color fiction stresses isolation and otherness, but also makes, however uneasily, a case for the nation's ability to reconcile and accept divergent regional identities. Local color writers might be seen as promoting a separatist view of region through their attention to difference and unique detail, but they might also be seen as arguing an early brand of diversity by depicting attractive communities that could access cross-regional agreements about values that defused troubling surface differences.

Although the beginning of the local color movement is usually dated from the first publication in the *Overland Monthly* in 1868 of Bret Harte's stories of California mining camps, a disproportionate number of contributors of local color stories to national magazines were southerners. The southern writer, particularly after the Civil War, saw the necessity of devising a literary agenda to advance a political one and found in local color writing a successful

---

130　Although the terms regionalism and local color are sometimes used interchangeably, regionalism generally has broader connotations. Whereas local color is often applied to a specific literary mode that flourished in the late 19th century, regionalism implies recognition from the colonial period to the present of differences among specific areas of the country. Additionally, regionalism refers to an intellectual movement encompassing regional consciousness beginning in the 1930s.

formula for this program, especially during the Reconstruction and post-Reconstruction era.

The demand that local color fiction present distinct vernacular dialect, picturesque traditions, and exotic characters found fulfillment almost too easily in the diversities of the 19th century South. And in no respect was the South more different than in its underlying political structures. Both before and after the war, the South had unusual accents and vernacular vocabularies, and it was linked in the national mind with a unique

Shooting for the Beef by George Caleb

plantation economic base that influenced its secular traditions as well as its religious habits. But most importantly, the South had race, America's most visible metaphor of human difference, and one enshrined both in social manners and political practices designed specifically to identify and control "the Different." In many stories written about life in the antebellum South there was an idealization of the way things were before the war; the South was often pictured in these stories not as it actually had been but as it "might have been." Although not all southern local color writing depicted the South in such romanticized terms, the exotic and quaint characteristics of this region were dominant motifs.

Realism

Local Color became America's first national literature of race. It also became a powerful tool through which American women could develop a distinctive, even heroic vision of lives too often pejoratively labeled "ordinary" and "small time." Through local color fiction southern women writers could critique their placement in a paternalistic hierarchy made possible by the exploitation of both racial and gender difference. Women came to dominate the genre of local color in the South, where they often focused on black-white family relations or upper-lower class divisions in ways that challenged the elitist and paternalistic message of works by white male counterparts. It is possible that the feminization of local color contributed to the genre's loss of popularity, as southern women writers bravely broke away from the genteel tradition and portrayed a crueler but more realistic picture of life.

But we cannot say that local color literature thus gave way to realism, as the former had always been part, or a peculiar form, of the latter. To understand it, we need to come at a rough idea about realism first.

In part, realism was a reaction against romanticism. Realism turned from an emphasis on the strange toward a faithful rendering of the ordinary, a slice of life as it is really lived. Objectivity in presentation becomes increasingly important: overt authorial comments or intrusions diminish as the century progresses. The realist writers avoided the improbabilities of such romantic tales as Washington Irving's "Rip Van Winkle" and Edgar Allan Poe's "Fall of the House of Usher." Events in a realistic novel will usually be plausible as the novel generally avoids the sensational, dramatic elements of romances. They render reality closely and in comprehensive detail. In a sense, the realist work is a selective presentation of reality with an emphasis on verisimilitude, at times even at the expense of a well-made plot. Class is important; the realist work has traditionally served the interests and aspirations of an insurgent middle class. In a realistic work character is more important than action and plot. Characters appear in their real complexity of temperament and motive; they are in explicable relation to nature, to each other, to their social class, and to their own past. The realist diction is natural vernacular, not heightened or poetic; his tone may be comic, satiric, or matter-of-fact.

Many realist writers found the greatest sources for literature in the daily life that immediately surrounded them. Yet it is not exact to say that realism is literature about the normal or the ordinary. If things are too normal, too ordinary, there may be no imaginative lure to the writing. It is more accurate to say the realist literature finds the drama and the tension beneath the ordinary surface of life. A realist writer is more objective than subjective, more descriptive than symbolic. A realist writer gets to the heart of human experience without ever swerving too far from verisimilitude, or lifelikeness. Realists looked for Truth in everyday truths.

In American literature, the term "realism" encompasses the period of time from the Civil War (or a decade before) to the turn of the century (the period that is generally accepted as "gilded") during which William Dean Howells, Henry James, Mark Twain, and others wrote fiction devoted to accurate representation and an exploration of American lives in various contexts.

Naturalism: A New Direction

Dramatic changes took place in the United States around the 1880s when many American young writers then felt that the United States needed a more robust literature to understand the changing times. The changes primarily included the closing of the frontier; an end to the great days of railroad building, an industry that had helped propel the economy; the late 19th-century rise of science; the mid-to late-19th-century influences of Charles Darwin as well as the later influences of Sigmund Freud; and a large influx of immigrants that helped lead to the creation of urban slums (with bad sanitation, poor living conditions, crime gross poverty, and ward politics). In a land that had once believed in the dream of progress, poverty was now a growing nightmare. All of this made realism seem obsolete and naturalism necessary.

The term *naturalism* describes a type of literature that attempts to apply scientific principles of objectivity and detachment to its study of human beings. Unlike realism, which focuses on literary technique, naturalism implies a philosophical position: for naturalistic writers, since human beings are, in Emile Zola's phrase, "human beasts," characters can be studied through their relationships to their surroundings. Zola's 1880 description of this method in *Le roman experimental* (*The Experimental Novel*, 1880) follows Claude Bernard's medical model and the historian Hippolyte Taine's observation that "virtue and vice are products like vitriol and sugar" —that is, that human beings as "products" should be studied impartially, without moralizing about their natures.

Through this objective study of human beings, naturalistic writers believe that the laws behind the forces that govern human lives might be studied and understood. Naturalistic writers thus use a version of the scientific method to write their novels; they study human beings governed by their instincts and passions as well as the ways in which the characters' lives are governed by forces of heredity and environment.

There were plenty of reasons for American writers' preference of naturalism to realism toward the end of the 19th century; the following were the major ones. By the 1890s, realism's individual problems seemed nothing compared to crushing forces seemingly outside human control. Not only did the notion of self-reliance seem an illusion but the idea of the individual negotiating his own fate also appeared ridiculous. People deluded themselves into believing that there are real choices in the world; life to them was no longer beneficent but downright hostile. Realism's concern with everyday life seemed a luxury compared to events from social and economic forces. The notion of a "surface" world (reality) seemed obsolete compared with determinants from "below" (economics, basic physical needs, sexual drives, natural and social environment, etc.).

All these thoughts are reflected in the world of naturalist fiction. Characters are motivated by sexual desire, greed, and mob psychology; many are stereotypes and absolutes. Society is divided into the have and have-nots, predator and prey. Life is ugly, brutal, and short; men and women are not far removed from the animal world.

Nature and fate are indifferent to humans; free will is an illusion; words like "courage" and "virtue" have no meaning. The world is made up of random events; everything and everyone is shaped by blind chance and environmental determinism.

Bret Harte (1836—1902)

Bret Harte was born an Easterner, yet in a handful of stories, he captured much of the humor and romance that make up the myth of the American West. Although his finest stories were written during the 1860s, Harte stands as the first writer of the local color movement that continued until approximately the turn of the century.

Born in Albany, New York, Harte moved to California in 1854, later working there in a number of capacities, including miner, teacher, messenger, and journalist. He spent part of his life in the northern California coast town now known as Arcata, at the time it was just a mining camp on Humboldt Bay.

In the 1850s California was a booming, turbulent, and colorful frontier. The discovery of gold in 1848 had drawn prospectors and adventurers from all over the United States and the rest of the world. Mining towns had sprung up; small towns had turned into cities; fortunes had been made and lost; and people from all walks of life had been thrown together in rough, sometimes violent circumstances. History was being made, and a whole new way of life was being forged. The colorful incidents of western life and vivid anecdotes of "old-timers" fired the imagination of Bret Harte, who began to turn this material into fiction.

First as a journalist, Harte wrote for *The Northern Californian*. At the beginning of 1859, Harte lost the job after he used the paper to denounce the townspeople who had massacred a tribe of peaceful Native Americans that were holding a religious festival near Eureka. In 1864 Harte was appointed to the branch mint at San Francisco. He held that office for four years, when he was invited to become the editor of the *Overland Monthly*, a literary magazine. Harte met Mark Twain during this time: the later claimed Harte taught him how to write.

Harte used ubiquitous newspapers to break into the literary market. "The Luck of Roaring Camp" (1868), the first of his scenic stories of the West, was published in the *Overland Monthly*. Later, stories like "The Outcasts of Poker Flat" and "Brown of Calaveras" and the poem "The Plain Language from Truthful James" cemented Harte's fame. These stories and poems were spectacularly successful both in the United States and in England, among readers eager for descriptions of California and the Wild West. Because of the stir his short stories were causing, Harte was flooded with offers for his work. However, when Fields, Osgood and Company (in Boston), after publishing *The Luck of Roaring Camp and Other Stories* offered Harte $10,000 in April of 1870 for the exclusive rights to the rest of his work over a twelve-month period, Harte accepted.

The return east was a disappointment, however; Harte's later stories did not match the early ones in quality and were less successful with readers. Harte spent most of his remaining years abroad, in Germany, Scotland, and England, continuing to write and working as a diplomat. Harte died from throat cancer in England on May 6, 1902. In 1987 he appeared on a $5 U.S. Postage stamp, as part of the "Great Americans" Series of issues.

■ Selected Reading

*In his early stories, particularly in "**The Outcasts of Poker Flat**," Harte painted a romantic portrait of the*

West that has endured. The local color of the West, its particular time and place, are described as well as in many of Mark Twain's sketches. Characters like John Oakhurst, the gambler with nerves of steel, have become fixtures in America's collective imagination.

The following lines from "The Plain Language from Truthful James" betray Harte's view on the aim and style of his own writing: "Which I wish to remark / And my language is plain / That for ways that are dark / And for tricks that are vain / The heathen Chinee is peculiar."

The Outcasts of Poker Flat

As Mr. John Oakhurst, gambler, stepped into the main street of Poker Flat on the morning of the twenty-third of November, 1850, he was conscious of a change in its moral atmosphere since the preceding night. Two or three men, conversing earnestly together, ceased as he approached, and exchanged significant glances. There was a Sabbath lull in the air, which, in a settlement unused to Sabbath influences, looked ominous.

Mr. Oakhurst's calm, handsome face betrayed small concern in these indications. Whether he was conscious of any predisposing cause, was another question. "I reckon they're after somebody," he reflected; "likely it's me." He returned to his pocket the handkerchief with which he had been whipping away the red dust of Poker Flat from his neat boots, and quietly discharged his mind of any further conjecture.

In point of fact, Poker Flat was "after somebody." It had lately suffered the loss of several thousand dollars, two valuable horses, and a prominent citizen. It was experiencing a spasm of virtuous reaction, quite as lawless and ungovernable as any of the acts that had provoked it. A secret committee[131] had determined to rid the town of all improper persons. This was done permanently in regard of two men who were then hanging from the boughs of a sycamore in the gulch, and temporarily in the banishment of certain other objectionable characters. I regret to say that some of these were ladies. It is but due to the sex, however, to state that their impropriety was professional, and it was only in such easily established standards of evil that Poker Flat ventured to sit in judgment.

Mr. Oakhurst was right in supposing that he was included in this category. A few of the committee had urged hanging him as a possible example, and a sure method of reimbursing themselves from his pockets of the sums he had won from them. "It's agin[132] justice," said Jim Wheeler, "to let this yer young man from Roaring Camp—an entire stranger—carry away our money." But a crude sentiment of equity residing in the breasts of those who had been fortunate enough to win from Mr. Oakhurst overruled this narrower local prejudice.

Mr. Oakhurst received his sentence with philosophic calmness, none the less coolly that he was aware of the hesitation of his judges. He was too much of a gambler not to accept Fate. With

---

131　**secret committee**: vigilance committee; a group of vigilantes organized to suppress and punish crime summarily when the processes of law appear inadequate.

132　**agin**: dialect variation of *against*.

him life was at best an uncertain game, and he recognized the usual percentage in favor of the dealer.

A body of armed men accompanied the deported wickedness of Poker Flat to the outskirts of the settlement. Besides Mr. Oakhurst, who was known to be a coolly desperate man, and for whose intimidation the armed escort was intended, the expatriated party consisted of a young woman familiarly known as "The Duchess"; another, who had won the title of "Mother Shipton";[133] and "Uncle Billy," a suspected sluice-robber[134] and confirmed drunkard. The cavalcade provoked no comments from the spectators, nor was any word uttered by the escort. Only, when the gulch which marked the uttermost limit of Poker Flat was reached, the leader spoke briefly and to the point. The exiles were forbidden to return at the peril of their lives.

As the escort disappeared, their pent-up feelings found vent in a few hysterical tears from the Duchess, some bad language from Mother Shipton, and a Parthian[135] volley of expletives from Uncle Billy. The philosophic Oakhurst alone remained silent. He listened calmly to Mother Shipton's desire to cut somebody's heart out, to the repeated statements of the Duchess that she would die in the road, and to the alarming oaths that seemed to be bumped out of Uncle Billy as he rode forward. With the easy good-humor characteristic of his class, he insisted upon exchanging his own riding-horse, "Five Spot," for the sorry mule which the Duchess rode. But even this act did not draw the party into any closer sympathy. The young woman readjusted her somewhat draggled plumes with a feeble, faded coquetry; Mother Shipton eyed the possessor of "Five Spot" with malevolence, and Uncle Billy included the whole party in one sweeping anathema.

The road to Sandy Bar—a camp that, not having as yet experienced the regenerating influences of Poker Flat, consequently seemed to offer some invitation to the emigrants—lay over a steep mountain range. It was distant a day's severe travel. In that advanced season, the party soon passed out of the moist, temperate regions of the foot-hills into the dry, cold, bracing air of the Sierras.[136] The trail was narrow and difficult. At noon the Duchess, rolling out of her saddle upon the ground, declared her intention of going no farther, and the party halted.

The spot was singularly wild and impressive. A wooded amphitheatre, surrounded on three sides by precipitous cliffs of naked granite, sloped gently toward the crest of another precipice that overlooked the valley. It was, undoubtedly, the most suitable spot for a camp, had camping been advisable. But Mr. Oakhurst knew that scarcely half the journey to Sandy Bar was accomplished, and the party were not equipped or provisioned for delay. This fact he pointed out to his companions curtly, with a philosophic commentary on the folly of "throwing up their hand before the game was played out." But they were furnished with liquor, which in this emergency stood

---

133 **Mother Shipton**: an English witch (1488—1560) who allegedly was carried off by the devil and bore him an imp. Her prophecies were edited by S. Baker in 1797.

134 **sluice**: an inclined trough or flume for washing or separating gold from earth.

135 **Partheian**: an ancient people of southwest Asia noted for firing shots while in real or feigned retreat.

136 **Sierras**: Sierra Nevada mountain range in eastern California.

them in place of food, fuel, rest, and prescience. In spite of his remonstrances, it was not long before they were more or less under its influence. Uncle Billy passed rapidly from a bellicose state into one of stupor, the Duchess became maudlin, and Mother Shipton snored. Mr. Oakhurst alone remained erect, leaning against a rock, calmly surveying them.

Mr. Oakhurst did not drink. It interfered with a profession which required coolness, impassiveness, and presence of mind, and, in his own language, he "couldn't afford it." As he gazed at his recumbent fellow-exiles, the loneliness begotten of his pariah-trade[137], his habits of life, his very vices, for the first time seriously oppressed him. He bestirred himself in dusting his black clothes, washing his hands and face, and other acts characteristic of his studiously neat habits, and for a moment forgot his annoyance. The thought of deserting his weaker and more pitiable companions never perhaps occurred to him. Yet he could not help feeling the want of that excitement which, singularly enough, was most conducive to that calm equanimity for which he was notorious. He looked at the gloomy walls that rose a thousand feet sheer above the circling pines around him; at the sky, ominously clouded; at the valley below, already deepening into shadow. And, doing so, suddenly he heard his own name called.

A horseman slowly ascended the trail. In the fresh, open face of the new-comer Mr. Oakhurst recognized Tom Simson, otherwise known as "The Innocent" of Sandy Bar. He had met him some months before over a "little game," and had, with perfect equanimity, won the entire fortune—amounting to some forty dollars—of that guileless youth. After the game was finished, Mr. Oakhurst drew the youthful speculator behind the door and thus addressed him: "Tommy, you're a good little man, but you can't gamble worth a cent. Don't try it over again." He then handed him his money back, pushed him gently from the room, and so made a devoted slave of Tom Simson.

There was a remembrance of this in his boyish and enthusiastic greeting of Mr. Oakhurst. He had started, he said, to go to Poker Flat to seek his fortune. "Alone?" No, not exactly alone; in fact (a giggle), he had run away with Piney Woods. Didn't Mr. Oakhurst remember Piney? She that used to wait on the table at the Temperance House? They had been engaged a long time, but old Jake Woods had objected, and so they had run away, and were going to Poker Flat to be married, and here they were. And they were tired out, and how lucky it was they had found a place to camp and company. All this the Innocent delivered rapidly, while Piney, a stout, comely damsel of fifteen, emerged from behind the pine-tree, where she had been blushing unseen, and rode to the side of her lover.

Mr. Oakhurst seldom troubled himself with sentiment, still less with propriety; but he had a vague idea that the situation was not fortunate. He retained, however, his presence of mind sufficiently to kick Uncle Billy, who was about to say something, and Uncle Billy was sober enough to recognize in Mr. Oakhurst's kick a superior power that would not bear trifling. He then endeavored to dissuade Tom Simson from delaying further, but in vain. He even pointed out the

---

137 **pariah trade**: despicable occupation. A pariah is one who is despised, an outcast.

fact that there was no provision, nor means of making a camp. But, unluckily, the Innocent met this objection by assuring the party that he was provided with an extra mule loaded with provisions, and by the discovery of a rude attempt at a log-house near the trail. "Piney can stay with Mrs. Oakhurst," said the Innocent, pointing to the Duchess, "and I can shift for myself."

Nothing but Mr. Oakhurst's admonishing foot saved Uncle Billy from bursting into a roar of laughter. As it was, he felt compelled to retire up the cañon[138] until he could recover his gravity. There he confided the joke to the tall pinetrees, with many slaps of his leg, contortions of his face, and the usual profanity. But when he returned to the party, he found them seated by a fire—for the air had grown strangely chill and the sky overcast—in apparently amicable conversation. Piney was actually talking in an impulsive, girlish fashion the Duchess, who was listening with an interest and animation she had not shown for many days.

The Innocent was holding forth, apparently with equal effect, to Mr. Oakhurst and Mother Shipton, who was actually relaxing into amiability. "Is this yer a d—d picnic?" said Uncle Billy, with inward scorn, as he surveyed the sylvan group, the glancing firelight, and the tethered animals in the foreground. Suddenly an idea mingled with the alcoholic fumes that disturbed his brain. It was apparently of a jocular nature, for he felt impelled to slap his leg again and cram his fist into his mouth.

As the shadows crept slowly up the mountain, a slight breeze rocked the tops of the pine-trees, and moaned through their long and gloomy aisles. The ruined cabin, patched and covered with pine-boughs, was set apart for the ladies. As the lovers parted, they unaffectedly exchanged a kiss, so honest and sincere that it might have been heard above the swaying pines. The frail Duchess and the malevolent Mother Shipton were probably too stunned to remark upon this last evidence of simplicity, and so turned without a word to the hut. The fire was replenished, the men lay down before the door, and in a few minutes were asleep.

Mr. Oakhurst was a light sleeper. Toward morning he awoke benumbed and cold. As he stirred the dying fire, the wind, which was now blowing strongly, brought to his cheek that which caused the blood to leave it—snow!

He started to his feet with the intention of awakening the sleepers, for there was no time to lose. But turning to where Uncle Billy had been lying, he found him gone. A suspicion leaped to his brain and a curse to his lips. He ran to the spot where the mules had been tethered; they were no longer there. The tracks were already rapidly disappearing in the snow.

The momentary excitement brought Mr. Oakhurst back to the fire with his usual calm. He did not waken the sleepers. The Innocent slumbered peacefully, with a smile on his good-humored, freckled face; the virgin Piney slept beside her frailer sisters as sweetly as though attended by celestial guardians, and Mr. Oakhurst, drawing his blanket over his shoulders, stroked his mustaches and waited for the dawn. It came slowly in a whirling mist of snow-flakes, that dazzled

---

138 **cañon**: variant of *canyon*.

and confused the eye. What could be seen of the landscape appeared magically changed. He looked over the valley, and summed up the present and future in two words—"snowed in!" A careful inventory of the provisions, which, fortunately for the party, had been stored within the hut, and so escaped the felonious fingers of Uncle Billy, disclosed the fact that with care and prudence they might last ten days longer. "That is," said Mr. Oakhurst, *sotto voice*[139] to the Innocent, "if you're willing to board us. If you ain't—and perhaps you'd better not—you can wait till Uncle Billy gets back with provisions." For some occult reason, Mr. Oakhurst could not bring himself to disclose Uncle Billy's rascality, and so offered the hypothesis that he had wandered from the camp and had accidentally stampeded the animals. He dropped a warning to the Duchess and Mother Shipton, who of course knew the facts of their associate's defection. "They'll find out the truth about us *all* when they find out anything," he added, significantly, "and there's no good frightening them now."

Tom Simson not only put all his worldly store at the disposal of Mr. Oakhurst, but seemed to enjoy the prospect of their enforced seclusion. "We'll have a good camp for a week, and then the snow'll melt, and we'll all go back together." The cheerful gayety of the young man, and Mr. Oakhurst's calm infected the others. The Innocent, with the aid of pine-boughs, extemporized a thatch for the roofless cabin, and the Duchess directed Piney in the rearrangement of the interior with a taste and tact that opened the blue eyes of that provincial maiden to their fullest extent. "I reckon now you're used to fine things at Poker Flat," said Piney. The Duchess turned away sharply to conceal something that reddened her cheeks through its professional tint, and Mother Shipton requested Piney not to "chatter." But when Mr. Oakhurst returned from a weary search for the trail, he heard the sound of happy laughter echoed from the rocks. He stopped in some alarm, and his thoughts first naturally reverted to the whiskey, which he had prudently *cachéd*.[140] "And yet it don't somehow sound like whiskey," said the gambler. It was not until he caught sight of the blazing fire through the still-blinding storm and the group around it that he settled to the conviction that it was "square fun."

Whether Mr. Oakhurst had *cachéd* his cards with the whiskey as something debarred the free access of the community, I cannot say. It was certain that, in Mother Shipton's words, he "didn't say cards once" during that evening. Haply the time was beguiled by an accordion, produced somewhat ostentatiously by Tom Simson from his pack. Notwithstanding some difficulties attending the manipulation of this instrument, Piney Woods managed to pluck several reluctant melodies from its keys, to an accompaniment by the Innocent on a pair of bone castanets. But the crowning festivity of the evening was reached in a rude camp meeting hymn, which the lovers, joining hands, sang with great earnestness and vociferation. I fear that a certain defiant tone and

---

139 **sotto voice**: in an undertone (Latin).

140 **cachéd**: modified French for "hidden".

Covenanter's swing[141] to its chorus, rather than any devotional quality, caused it speedily to infect the others, who at last joined in the refrain:—

"I'm proud to live in the service of the Lord,

And I'm bound to die in His army."[142]

The pines rocked, the storm eddied and whirled above the miserable group, and the flames of their altar leaped heavenward, as if in token of the vow.

At midnight the storm abated, the rolling clouds parted, and the stars glittered keenly above the sleeping camp. Mr. Oakhurst, whose professional habits had enabled him to live on the smallest possible amount of sleep, in dividing the watch with Tom Simson, somehow managed to take upon himself the greater part of that duty. He excused himself to the Innocent, by saying that he had "often been a week without sleep." "Doing what?" asked Tom. "Poker!" replied Oakhurst, sententiously; "when a man gets a streak of luck,—nigger-luck,[143]—he don't get tired. The luck gives in first. Luck," continued the gambler, reflectively, "is a mighty queer thing. All you know about it for certain is that it's bound to change. And it's finding out when it's going to change that makes you. We've had a streak of bad luck since we left Poker Flat,—you come along, and slap you get into it, too. If you can hold your cards right along you're all right. For," added the gambler, with cheerful irrelevance,—

"I'm proud to live in the service of the Lord,

And I'm bound to die in His army.'"

The third day came, and the sun, looking through the white-curtained valley, saw the outcasts divide their slowly decreasing store of provisions for the morning meal. It was one of the peculiarities of that mountain climate that its rays diffused a kindly warmth over the wintry landscape, as if in regretful commiseration of the past. But it revealed drift on drift of snow piled high around the hut,—a hopeless, uncharted, trackless sea of white lying below the rocky shores to which the castaways still clung. Through the marvellously clear air the smoke of the pastoral village of Poker Flat rose miles away. Mother Shipton saw it, and from a remote pinnacle of her rocky fastness, hurled in that direction a final malediction. It was her last vituperative attempt, and perhaps for that reason was invested with a certain degree of sublimity. It did her good she privately informed the Duchess. "Just you go out there and cuss, and see." She then set herself to the task of amusing "the child," as she and the Duchess were pleased to call Piney. Piney was no chicken, but it was a soothing and original theory of the pair thus to account for the fact that she didn't swear and wasn't improper.

When night crept up again through the gorges, the reedy notes of the accordion rose and fell

---

141   **Covenanter's swing:** Covenanters are Scottish Presbyterians of the 16th and 17th centuries who bound themselves by a series of oaths or covenants to the Presbyterian doctrine and demanded separation from the Church of England. "Covenanter's swing" indicates that the hymn is sung with a vigorous rhythm with a martial beat.

142   **"I'm... army":** Refrain of the early American spiritual "Service of the Lord."

143   **nigger-luck:** very good fortune.

in fitful spasms and long-drawn gasps by the flickering camp-fire. But music failed to fill entirely the aching void left by insufficient food, and a new diversion was proposed by Piney,—story-telling. Neither Mr. Oakhurst nor his female companions caring to relate their personal experiences, this plan would have failed, too, but for the Innocent. Some months before he had chanced upon a stray copy of Mr. Pope's[144] ingenius translation of the Iliad. He now proposed to narrate the principal incidents of that poem—having thoroughly mastered the argument and fairly forgotten the words—in the current vernacular of Sandy Bar. And so for the rest of that night the Homeric demigods again walked the earth. Trojan bully and wily Greek wrestled in the winds, and the great pines in the cañon seemed to bow to the wrath of the son of Peleus.[145] Mr. Oakhurst listened with quiet satisfaction. Most especially was he interested in the fate of "Ash-heels,"[146] as the Innocent persisted in denominating the "swift-footed Achilles."

So with small food and much of Homer and the accordion, a week passed over the heads of the outcasts. The sun again forsook them, and again from leaden skies the snow-flakes were sifted over the land. Day by day closer around them drew the snowy circle, until at last they looked from their prison over drifted walls of dazzling white, that towered twenty feet above their heads. It became more and more difficult to replenish their fires, even from the fallen trees beside them, now half hidden in the drifts. And yet no one complained. The lovers turned from the dreary prospect and looked into each other's eyes, and were happy. Mr. Oakhurst settled himself coolly to the losing game before him. The Duchess, more cheerful than she had been, assumed the care of Piney. Only Mother Shipton—once the strongest of the party—seemed to sicken and fade. At midnight on the tenth day she called Oakhurst to her side. "I'm going," she said, in a voice of querulous weakness, "but don't say anything about it. Don't waken the kids. Take the bundle from under my head and open it." Mr. Oakhurst did so. It contained Mother Shipton's rations for the last week, untouched. "Give 'em to the child," she said, pointing to the sleeping Piney. "You've starved yourself," said the gambler. "That's what they call it," said the woman, querulously, as she lay down again, and, turning her face to the wall, passed quietly away.

The accordion and the bones were put aside that day, and Homer was forgotten. When the body of Mother Shipton had been committed to the snow, Mr. Oakhurst took the Innocent aside, and showed him a pair of snow-shoes, which he had fashioned from the old pack-saddle. "There's one chance in a hundred to save her yet," he said, pointing to Piney; "but it's there," he added, pointing toward Poker Flat. "If you can reach there in two days she's safe." "And you?" asked Tom Simson. "I'll stay here," was the curt reply.

The lovers parted with a long embrace. "You are not going, too?" said the Duchess, as she

144　**Mr. Pope**: Alexander Pope (1688—1744), English poet who translated Homer's *Iliad* (and *Odyssey*) into the heroic couplets for which Pope is famous.

145　**the son of Peleus**: Achilles, chief hero on the Greek side of the Trojan War.

146　**Ash-heels**: The mispronunciation emphasizes Achilles' one vulnerable spot, his heel, by which his mother, Thetis, held him when she dipped him in the river Styx to make him invulnerable.

saw Mr. Oakhurst apparently waiting to accompany him. "As far as the cañon," he replied. He turned suddenly, and kissed the Duchess, leaving her pallid face aflame, and her trembling limbs rigid with amazement.

Night came, but not Mr. Oakhurst. It brought the storm again and the whirling snow. Then the Duchess, feeding the fire, found that some one had quietly piled beside the but enough fuel to last a few days longer. The tears rose to her eyes, but she hid them from Piney.

The women slept but little. In the morning, looking into each other's faces, they read their fate. Neither spoke; but Piney, accepting the position of the stronger, drew near and placed her arm around the Duchess's waist. They kept this attitude for the rest of the day. That night the storm reached its greatest fury, and, rending asunder the protecting pines, invaded the very hut.

Toward morning they found themselves unable to feed the fire, which gradually died away. As the embers slowly blackened, the Duchess crept closer to Piney, and broke the silence of many hours: "Piney, can you pray?" "No, dear," said Piney, simply. The Duchess, without knowing exactly why, felt relieved, and, putting her head upon Piney's shoulder, spoke no more. And so reclining, the younger and purer pillowing the head of her soiled sister upon her virgin breast, they fell asleep.

The wind lulled as if it feared to waken them. Feathery drifts of snow, shaken from the long pine-boughs, flew like white-winged birds, and settled about them as they slept. The moon through the rifted clouds looked down upon what had been the camp. But all human stain, all trace of earthly travail, was hidden beneath the spotless mantle mercifully flung from above.

They slept all that day and the next, nor did they waken when voices and footsteps broke the silence of the camp. And when pitying fingers brushed the snow from their wan faces, you could scarcely have told from the equal peace that dwelt upon them, which was she that had sinned. Even the law of Poker Flat recognized this, and turned away, leaving them still locked in each other's arms.

But at the head of the gulch, on one of the largest pinetrees, they found the deuce of clubs pinned to the bark with a bowie-knife. It bore the following, written in pencil, in a firm hand: —

BENEATH THIS TREE

LIES THE BODY

OF

JOHN OAKHURST,

WHO STRUCK A STREAK OF BAD LUCK

ON THE 23D OF NOVEMBER, 1850,

AND

HANDED IN HIS CHECKS

ON THE 7TH DECEMBER, 1850.

And pulseless and cold, with a Derringer[147] by his side and a bullet in his heart, though still calm as in life, beneath the snow lay he who was at once the strongest and yet the weakest of the outcasts of Poker Flat.

■ Study Questions

1. As the story opens, what has the secret committee of Poker Flat decide to do? Who is directly affected by the committee's decision?

2. What is John Oakhurst's "profession"? How does he receive his "sentence," according to the 5th paragraph?

3. Why are Tom Simson and Piney Woods going to Poker Flat? What natural event puts them and the outcasts in danger?

4. What does Mother Shipton do to help Piney? Why does Tom leave the group?

5. When the rescue party arrives, what do they find?

6. Briefly describe John Oakhurst and his attitude toward life. Explain how his final actions relate to his philosophy of life.

7. What are Tom and Piney like? What effect do they have on Mother Shipton and on Oakhurst?

8. What forces do all the characters have to face? How do all of them except Uncle Billy behave in this crisis?

9. Have you ever read any other western fiction or seen any Western movie?[148] Which elements of this story are common elements of western fiction that you have encountered in films, TV shows, or other works about the West?

Kate Chopin (1851—1904)

Kate Chopin (*born* **Katherine O'Flaherty**) a novelist and short story writer, was mostly of a Louisiana Creole background. She is now considered to have been a forerunner of feminist authors of the 20th century.

Born in St. Louis, Missouri, Kate Chopin married at 19 and went to live in New Orleans, Louisiana. During the more than 10 years she spent there, she became fascinated by the variety of Louisiana life, the rich mixture of cultures, and the many languages and dialects. After her husband's death in 1882, she returned to St. Louis with her 6 children and began to write.

From then to 1902, she wrote short stories for both children and adults which were published in such magazines as *Atlantic Monthly*, *Vogue*, *The Century*, and *Harper's Youth's Companion*. Her major works were two short story collections, *Bayou Folk* (1884) and *A Night in Acadie* (1897). Her important short stories included "Desiree's Baby," a tale of miscegenation in antebellum Louisiana; "The Story of an Hour," and "The Storm." Chopin also wrote two novels: *At Fault* (1890) and *The Awakening* (1899).

Just as Bret Harte gave the world a vision of the American West and Sarah Orne Jewett wrote delicate sketches of rural New England, Kate Chopin was chiefly interested in Louisiana. The characters who inhabit Chopin's world

---

147　**Derringer**: Short-barreled pocket pistol, named after its 19th-century American inventor, Henry Deringer.

148　The Western is an American fiction genre, predominantly seen in film and television, but also employed in literature, painting and other visual arts. Westerns are devoted to telling stories set in the 19th Century American West, and sometimes Mexico, Canada, or the Australian Outback during the same time period, with the setting occasionally portrayed in a romanticized light.

are generally Louisiana Creoles, descendants of the original French and Spanish colonists, and Cajuns, descendants of Louisiana's French Canadian settlers. *Delicate*, *objective*, and *poignant* are words often used to describe the local color stories of Kate Chopin. A local colorist, Chopin is also a good example of an American realist, someone trying to represent life the way it actually is lived, and she acknowledged her debt to the contemporary French naturalists Emile Zola and Guy de Maupassant.

In time, however, literary critics determined that Chopin addressed the concerns of women in all places and for all times in her literature. For a time, Kate Chopin became a forgotten voice. Then her literary reputation was resuscitated by critics in the 1950s. Today her novel *The Awakening*, the story of a sensual, determined woman who insists on her independence, is widely read and highly honored as a feminist work which was decidedly ahead of its time.

■ Selected Reading

The Story of an Hour

Knowing that Mrs. Mallard was afflicted with a heart trouble, great care was taken to break to her as gently as possible the news of her husband's death.

It was her sister Josephine who told her, in broken sentences, veiled hints that revealed in half concealing. Her husband's friend Richards was there, too, near her. It was he who had been in the newspaper office when intelligence[149] of the railroad disaster was received, with Brently Mallard's name leading the list of "killed." He had only taken the time to assure himself of its truth by a second telegram, and had hastened to forestall any less careful, less tender friend in bearing the sad message.

She did not hear the story as many women have heard the same, with a paralyzed inability to accept its significance. She wept at once with sudden, wild abandonment, in her sister's arms. When the storm of grief had spent itself she went away to her room alone. She would have no one follow her.

There stood, facing the open window, a comfortable, roomy armchair. Into this she sank, pressed down by a physical exhaustion that haunted her body and seemed to reach into her soul.

She could see in the open square before her house the tops of trees that were all aquiver with the new spring life. The delicious breath of rain was in the air. In the street below a peddler was crying his wares. The notes of a distant song which some one was singing reached her faintly, and countless sparrows were twittering in the eaves.

There were patches of blue sky showing here and there through the clouds that had met and piled one above the other in the west facing her window.

She sat with her head thrown back upon the cushion of the chair, quite motionless, except when a sob came up into her throat and shook her, as a child who has cried itself to sleep continues to sob in its dreams.

---

[149] **intelligence**: information.

She was young, with a fair, calm face, whose lines bespoke repression and even a certain strength. But now there was a dull stare in her eyes, whose gaze was fixed away off yonder on one of those patches of blue sky. It was not a glance of reflection, but rather indicated a suspension of intelligent thought.

There was something coming to her and she was waiting for it, fearfully. What was it? She did not know; it was too subtle and elusive to name. But she felt it, creeping out of the sky, reaching toward her through the sounds, the scents, the color that filled the air.

Now her bosom rose and fell tumultuously. She was beginning to recognize this thing that was approaching to possess her, and she was striving to beat it back with her will—as powerless as her two white slender hands would have been.

When she abandoned herself a little whispered word escaped her slightly parted lips. She said it over and over under breath: "Free, free, free!" The vacant stare and the look of terror that had followed it went from her eyes. They stayed keen and bright. Her pulse beat fast, and the coursing blood warmed and relaxed every inch of her body.

She did not stop to ask if it were or were not a monstrous joy that held her. A clear and exalted perception enabled her to dismiss the suggestion as trivial.

She knew that she would weep again when she saw the kind, tender hands folded in death, the face that had never looked save with love upon her, fixed and gray and dead. But she saw beyond that bitter moment a long procession of years to come that would belong to her absolutely. And she opened and spread her arms out to them in welcome.

There would be no one to live for her during those coming years; she would live for herself. There would be no powerful will bending hers in that blind persistence with which men and women believe they have a right to impose a private will upon a fellow creature. A kind intention or a cruel intention made the act seem no less a crime as she looked upon it in that brief moment of illumination.

And yet she had loved him—sometimes. Often she had not. What did it matter! What could love, the unsolved mystery, count for in face of this possession of self-assertion which she suddenly recognized as the strongest impulse of her being.

"Free! Body and soul free!" she kept whispering.

Josephine was kneeling before the closed door with her lips to the keyhole, imploring for admission. "Louise, open the door! I beg; open the door—you will make yourself ill. What are you doing, Louise? For heaven's sake open the door."

"Go away. I am not making myself ill." No; she was drinking in the very elixir of life[150] through that open window.

---

[150] **she... life**: she was absorbing a genuine, sweet and aromatic, all-curing life of force. Very: true, genuine.

Her fancy was running riot[151] along those days ahead of her. Spring days, and summer days, and all sorts of days that would be her own. She breathed a quick prayer that life might be long. It was only yesterday she had thought with a shudder that life might be long.

She arose at length and opened the door to her sister's importunities. There was a feverish triumph in her eyes, and she carried herself unwittingly like a goddess of Victory. She clasped her sister's waist and together they descended the stairs. Richards stood waiting for them at the bottom.

Some one was opening the front door with a latchkey. It was Brently Mallard who entered, a little travel-stained, composedly carrying his grip-sack[152] and umbrella. He had been far from the scene of accident, and did not even know there had been one. He stood amazed at Josephine's piercing cry; at Richards' quick motion to screen him from the view of his wife.

But Richard was too late.

When the doctors came they said she had died of heart disease—of joy that kills.

■ Study Questions

1. What happens to Mr. Mallard in the beginning according to the story?

2. Why did Mrs. Mallard shut herself in her own room? When she came out of the room, however, she went down the stairs "like a goddess of Victory." In what ways does she feel herself victorious?

3. What kind of relationships do the Mallards have? Is Brently Mallard unkind to Louise Mallard, or is there some other reason for her saying "free, free, free!" when she hears of his death? How does she feel about him?

4. What happens at the end of the story? Why did Mrs. Mallard die?

5. What is the nature of Mrs. Mallard's "heart trouble"? Why would the author mention it in the first paragraph?

6. The setting of the story is very limited; it is confined largely to a room, a staircase, and a front door. How does this limitation help to express the themes of the story? Mrs. Mallard closes the door to her room so that her sister Josephine cannot get in, yet she leaves the window open. Why does Chopin make a point of telling the reader this? How might this relate to the idea of being "free" and to the implicit idea that she is somehow imprisoned? Do other words in the story relate to this idea?

7. In what ways is Paragraph 5 significant? What kinds of sensory images does this passage contain, and what senses does it address? What does the vision through the open window mean to her? Where else does she taste, smell, or touch something intangible in the story?

8. "There was something coming to her and she was waiting for it, fearfully." What is this "something" indicated here in your opinion? How do you understand the exclamation "Free! Body and soul free!"? What might Mrs. Mallard's fancy be along those days ahead of her? If this is, in some sense, a story about a symbolic journey, where does Mrs. Mallard "travel"?

9. What do Josephine and Richards represent in the story? The doctors? In what ways is the ending an ironic one? What is gained by having the doctors make such a statement rather than putting it in the mouths of Josephine or Richards?

---

151   **Her... riot**: Her imagination was wild, uncontrolled and unrestrained. Run riot: behave in a wild and uncontrolled manner; act or grow without control or restrain.

152   **grip-sack**: traveler's handbag; small suitcase.

10. What view of marriage does the story present? The story was published in 1894; does it only represent attitudes toward marriage in the 19th century, or could it equally apply to attitudes about marriage today?

Jack London (1876—1916)

Jack London, a prolific American novelist and short story writer, is still loved throughout the world for his works dealing romantically with the overwhelming power of nature and the struggle for survival. Meanwhile, he remains one of the most controversial American writers for his plagiarism, his coarse language, and his mixed and at times self-contradictory creative thoughts.

Jack London was born in San Francisco. Now it is widely accepted that he was deserted by his father[153], "Professor" William Henry Chaney, an itinerant astrologer, and raised in Oakland by his mother Flora Wellman, a music teacher and spiritualist. London's stepfather John London, whose surname he took, was a failed storekeeper. London's youth was marked by poverty. He had little formal education and worked at a series of odd jobs as he wandered about America and the rest of the world. Arrested for vagrancy near Buffalo, New York, London spent a month in jail. This was the turning point in his life.

London decided that he must have an education, and he worked hard to complete high school. He then attended the University of California for a few months but was lured away by the great Klondike Gold Rush of 1897—1898. Returning from Alaska empty-handed, London attempted to earn a living by setting his adventure down on paper.

London was fortunate in the timing of his writing career. He started just as new printing technologies enabled lower-cost production of magazines. This resulted in a boom in popular magazines aimed at a wide public, and a strong market for short fiction. In 1900, he made $2,500 in writing, the equivalent of about $75,000 today. With the publication of *The Call of the Wild* in 1903, his fortunes changed dramatically: The struggling young writer suddenly became the highest-paid author in America. *The Sea Wolf* (1904) and *White Fang* (1906) were equally successful and, like "*The Call of the Wild*," are still widely read today. Other popular works by London include the novels *The Iron Heel* and *Martin Eden*, the nonfiction *The People of the Abyss* (1903), and the autobiographical book of "alcoholic memoirs", *John Barleycorn* (1913).

Jack London was accused of plagiarism at numerous times during his career. He was vulnerable, not only because he was such a conspicuous and successful writer, but also because of his methods of working. In a letter to Elwyn Hoffman he wrote "expression, you see—with me—is far easier than invention." He purchased plots for stories and novels from the young Sinclair Lewis. And he used incidents from newspaper clippings as material on which to base stories. Egerton R. Young claimed that *The Call of the Wild* was taken from his book *My Dogs in the Northland*. Jack London's response was to acknowledge having used it as a source; he claimed to have written a letter to Young thanking him.

London was nonetheless among the most publicized figures of his day, and he used this pulpit to endorse his support of socialism, women's suffrage, and eventually, prohibition. He was among the first writers to work with the movie industry, and saw a number of his novels made into films. His novel *The Sea-Wolf* became the basis for the first full-length American movie. He was also one of the first celebrities to use his endorsement for commercial

---

153 Information about his father is not reliable. There is no sufficient proof about whether professor chaney was his father.

products in advertising, including dress suits and grape juice.

Because he was an autodidact, London's ideas lacked consistency and precision. For example, he clearly accepted the Social Darwinism and scientific racism prevalent during his time, yet he seemed troubled that the "inevitable white man," as he called him, would destroy the rich cultures of various native groups he had encountered over the years. Although he supported women's suffrage and created some of the most independent and strong female characters in American fiction, he was patriarchal toward his two wives and two daughters. His socialism was fervent, but countered by his strong drive toward individualism and capitalist success. These contradictory themes in his life and writing make him a difficult figure to reduce to simple terms.

Often troubled by physical ailments, during his thirties London developed kidney disease of unknown origin. He died of renal failure on November 22, 1916 on the ranch. Because his writings were translated in several dozen languages, he remains more widely read in some countries outside of the United States than in his home country. Study of his life and writings provides a case through which to examine the contradictions in the American character, along with key movements and ideas prominent during the Progressive era.

Following London's death, for a number of reasons a biographical myth developed in which he has been portrayed as an alcoholic womanizer who committed suicide. Recent scholarship based upon firsthand documents challenges this caricature. But its persistence has resulted in neglect of his full literary oeuvre and his significance as a seminal figure in turn-of-the-century social history.

■ Selected Reading

The Call of the Wild (1903), *remains London's most famous work, blending his experiences as a gold prospector in the Canadian wilderness with his ideas about nature and the struggle for existence. He drew these ideas from various influential figures, including Charles Darwin and Friedrich Nietzsche, a prominent German philosopher. Although The Call of the Wild is first and foremost a story about a dog, it displays a philosophical depth absent in most animal adventures.*

The Call of the Wild

CHAPTER 1　INTO THE PRIMITIVE
(Summary)

Buck, a large and handsome dog who is part St. Bernard and part Scotch sheep dog, lives on a sizable estate in California's Santa Clara Valley. He is four years old and was born on the estate, which is owned by the wealthy Judge Miller. Buck is the undisputed master of Judge Miller's place, as the locals call it, and is beloved by the Miller children and grandchildren. Buck has the run of the entire place, confident of his superiority to the pampered house pets and the fox terriers that live in the kennels.

But, unbeknownst to Buck, there is a shadow over his happy life. The year is 1897, and men from all over the world are traveling north for the gold rush that has hit the Klondike region of Canada, just east of Alaska. They need strong dogs to pull their sleds on the treacherous journey. Nor does Buck realize that Manuel, a gardener on Judge Miller's estate, is an undesirable acquaintance. Manuel's love of gambling in the Chinese lottery makes it difficult for him to support his wife and several children. One day, while the judge is away, Manuel takes Buck for a walk and leads him to a flag station where a stranger is waiting. Money changes hands, and Manuel ties a rope around Buck's neck. When the rope is tightened, Buck attacks the stranger, but he finds it impossible to break free. The man fights him; Buck's strength fails, and he blacks out and is thrown into the baggage car of the train.

When Buck regains consciousness, he feels himself being jolted around. He hears the whistle of the train and, from having traveled with the judge, recognizes the sensation of riding in a baggage car. He opens his eyes angrily and sees the kidnapper reaching for his throat. He bites the man's hand and is thrown down and choked repeatedly, then locked into a cagelike crate. He stays there for the rest of the night, and, in the morning, his crate is carried out by four men. Buck is passed from vehicle to vehicle, neither eating nor drinking for two days and two nights. He grows angrier and resolves never to let his tormentors tie a rope around his neck again.

In Seattle, Buck's crate is lifted into a small yard with high walls, while a stout man signs for him. Buck decides that this new man is his next tormentor and lunges at him inside the cage. The man smiles and brings out a hatchet and a club. He begins to break the crate, and the other men step back fearfully. Buck snarls and growls and leaps at the man with all his weight, but he feels a blow from the club. It is the first time he has been hit with a club, so he is both hurt and stunned, but he continues trying to attack until the man beats him into submission. Once Buck is exhausted and prostrate, the man brings him water and meat and pats him on the head. Buck understands that he does not stand a chance against a man with a club—it is his introduction into "primitive law," where might makes right.

Buck watches other men arrive, sometimes taking other dogs away with them, and he is glad that he is not chosen. Buck's time finally comes when a French Canadian named Perrault buys him and a Newfoundland bitch named Curly. They are taken onto a ship called the Narwhal and turned over to another French Canadian named Francois. They join two other dogs, Spitz and Dave, on the journey northward, and Buck realizes that the weather is growing colder. Finally, they arrive and step out onto a cold surface that Buck does not recognize, never having seen snow before.

CHAPTER 6   FOR THE LOVE OF A MAN
(Summary)

Buck slowly gets his strength back. John Thornton, it turns out, had frozen his feet during the previous winter, and he and his dogs are now waiting for the river to melt and for a raft to take them down to Dawson. With Thornton, Buck experiences love for the first time, developing a strong affection for the man who saved his life and who proves an ideal master. Thornton treats his dogs as if they are his own children, and Buck responds with adoration and obeys all commands. Once, to test Buck, Thornton tells him to jump off a cliff; Buck begins to obey before Thornton stops him.

Even though Buck is happy with Thornton, his wild instincts still remain strong, and he fights as fiercely as ever. Now, however, he fights in defense of Thornton. In Dawson, Thornton steps in to stop a fight in a bar, and one of the combatants lashes out at him. Immediately, Buck hurls himself at the man's throat; the man narrowly escapes having his throat ripped open when he throws up his hand, though Buck succeeds in partially ripping it open with his second try. A meeting is called on the spot to decide what to do with Buck, and the miners rule that his aggressive behavior was justified, since he acted in defense of Thornton. Soon, Buck has earned a reputation throughout Alaska for loyalty and ferocity.

Buck saves Thornton's life again when Thornton is thrown out of a boat and gets caught in fierce rapids. Buck swims to the slick rock where Thornton clings for his life, and the other men attach a rope to Buck's neck and shoulders. After several failed attempts, Thornton grabs onto his neck, and the two are pulled back to safety.

That winter, on a strange whim, Thornton boasts that Buck can start a sled with a thousand pounds loaded on it. Other men challenge his claim, betting that Buck cannot perform that task before their eyes. A man named Matthewson, who has grown rich in the gold rush, bets a thousand dollars that Buck cannot pull his sled—which is outside, loaded with a thousand pounds of flour. Thornton himself doubts it, but he makes the bet anyway, borrowing the money from a friend to cover the wager. Several hundred men come to watch, giving odds—first two to one, then three to one when the terms of the bet are clarified—that Buck cannot break out the sled, and a confident Matthewson throws on another $600 at those odds. Once Buck is harnessed in, he first breaks the sled free of the ice, then pulls it a hundred yards. The crowd of men cheers in amazement, with even Matthewson joining in the applause.

CHAPTER 7   THE SOUNDING OF THE CALL

When Buck earned sixteen hundred dollars in five minutes for John Thornton, he made it possible for his master to pay off certain debts and to journey with his partners into the East after a fabled lost mine, the history of which was as old as the history of the country. Many men had sought it; few had found it; and more than a few there were who had never returned from the quest. This lost mine was steeped in tragedy and shrouded in mystery. No one knew of the first man. The oldest tradition stopped before it got back to him. From the beginning there had been an ancient and ramshackle cabin. Dying men had sworn to it, and to the mine the site of which it marked, clinching their testimony with nuggets that were unlike any known grade of gold in the Northland.

But no living man had looted this treasure house, and the dead were dead; wherefore John Thornton and Pete and Hans, with Buck and half a dozen other dogs, faced into the East on an unknown trail to achieve where men and dogs as good as themselves had failed. They sledded seventy miles up the Yukon, swung to the left into the Stewart River, passed the Mayo and the McQuestion, and held on until the Stewart itself became a streamlet, threading the upstanding peaks which marked the backbone of the continent.

John Thornton asked little of man or nature. He was unafraid of the wild. With a handful of salt and a rifle he could plunge into the wilderness and fare wherever he pleased and as long as he pleased. Being in no haste, Indian fashion, he hunted his dinner in the course of the day's traveling; and if he failed to find it, like the Indian, he kept on traveling, secure in the knowledge that sooner or later he would come to it. So, on this great journey into the East, straight meat was the bill of fare, ammunition and tools principally made up the load on the sled, and the timecard was drawn upon the limitless future.

To Buck it was boundless delight, this hunting, fishing, and indefinite wandering through strange places. For weeks at a time they would hold on steadily, day after day; and for weeks upon end they would camp, here and there, the dogs loafing and the men burning holes through frozen muck and gravel and washing countless pans of dirt by the heat of the fire. Sometimes they went hungry, sometimes they feasted riotously, all according to the abundance of game and the fortune of hunting. Summer arrived, and dogs and men, packs on their backs, rafted across blue mountain lakes, and descended or ascended unknown rivers in slender boats whipsawed from the standing forest.

The months came and went, and back and forth they twisted through the uncharted vastness, where no men were and yet where men had been if the Lost Cabin were true. They went across divides in summer blizzards, shivered under the midnight sun on naked mountains between the timber line and the eternal snows, dropped into summer valleys amid swarming gnats and flies, and in the shadows of glaciers picked strawberries and flowers as ripe and fair as any the Southland could boast. In the fall of the year they penetrated a weird lake country, sad and silent, where wild fowl had been, but where then there was no life nor sign of life—only the blowing of chill winds, the forming of ice in sheltered places, and the melancholy rippling of waves on lonely beaches.

And through another winter they wandered on the obliterated trails of men who had gone before. Once, they came upon a path blazed throughout the forest, an ancient path, and the Lost Cabin seemed very near. But the path began nowhere and ended nowhere, and remained a mystery, as the man who made it and the reason he made it remained a mystery. Another time they chanced upon the time-graven wreckage of a hunting lodge, and amid the shreds of rotted blankets John Thornton found a long-barreled flintlock. He knew it for a Hudson Bay Company gun of the young days in the Northwest, when such a gun was worth its weight in beaver skins packed flat. And that was all—no hint as to the man who in an early day had reared the lodge and left the gun among the blankets.

Spring came on once more, and at the end of all their wandering they found, not the Lost Cabin, but a shallow placer in a broad valley where the gold showed like yellow butter across the bottom of the washing pan. They sought no farther. Each day they worked earned them thousands of dollars in clean dust and nuggets, and they worked every day. The gold was sacked in moosehide bags, fifty pounds to the bag, and piled like so much firewood outside the spruce-bough lodge. Like giants they toiled, days flashing on the heels of days like dreams as they heaped the treasure up.

There was nothing for the dogs to do, save the hauling of meat now and again that Thornton killed, and Buck spent long hours musing by the fire. The vision of the short-legged hairy man came to him more frequently, now that there was little work to be done; and often, blinking by the fire, Buck wandered with him in that other world which he remembered.

The salient thing of this other world seemed fear. When he watched the hairy man sleeping by the fire, head between his knees and hands clasped above, Buck saw that he slept restlessly, with many starts and awakenings at which times he would peer fearfully into the darkness and fling more wood upon the fire. Did they walk by the beach of a sea, where the hairy man gathered shellfish and ate them as he gathered, it was with eyes that roved everywhere for hidden danger and with legs prepared to run like the wind at its first appearance. Through the forest they crept noiselessly, Buck at the hairy man's heels; and they were alert and vigilant, the pair of them, ears twitching and moving and nostrils quivering, for the man heard and smelled as keenly as Buck. The hairy man could spring up into the trees and travel ahead as fast as on the ground, swinging by the arms from limb to limb, sometimes a dozen feet apart, letting go and catching, never falling, never missing his grip. In fact, he seemed as much at home among the trees as on the ground; and Buck had memories of nights of vigil spent beneath the trees wherein the hairy man roosted, holding on tightly as he slept.

And closely akin to the visions of the hairy man was the call still sounding in the depths of the forest. It filled him with a great unrest and strange desires. It caused him to feel a vague, sweet gladness, and he was aware of wild yearnings and stirrings for he knew not what. Sometimes he pursued the call into the forest, looking for it as though it were a tangible thing, barking softly or defiantly, as the mood might dictate. He would thrust his nose into the cool wood moss, or into the black soil where long grasses grew, and snort with joy at the fat earth smells; or he would crouch for hours, as if in concealment, behind fungus covered trunks of fallen trees, wide-eyed and wide-eared to all that moved and sounded about him. It might be, lying thus, that he hoped to surprise this call he could not understand. But he did not know why he did these various things. He was impelled to do them, and did not reason about them at all.

Irresistible impulses seized him. He would be lying in camp, dozing lazily in the heat of the day, when suddenly his head would lift and his ears cock up, intent and listening, and he would spring to his feet and dash away, and on and on, for hours, through the forest aisles and across the open spaces where the niggerheads bunched. He loved to run down dry watercourses, and to creep and spy upon the bird life in the woods. For a day at a time he would lie in the underbrush where he could watch the partridges drumming and strutting up and down. But especially he loved to run in the dim twilight of the summer midnights, listening to the subdued and sleepy murmurs of the forest, reading signs and sounds as man may read a book, and seeking for the mysterious something that called—called, waking or sleeping, at all times, for him to come.

One night he sprang from sleep with a start, eager-eyed, nostrils quivering and scenting, his mane bristling in recurrent waves. From the forest came the call—(or one note of it, for the call was many-noted), distinct and definite as never before—a long-drawn howl, like, yet unlike, any noise made by husky dog. And he knew it, in the old familiar way, as a sound heard before. He sprang through the sleeping camp and in swift silence dashed through the woods. As he drew closer to the cry he went more slowly, with caution in every movement, till he came to an open place among the trees, and looking out saw, erect on haunches, with nose pointed to the sky, a long, lean, timber wolf.

He had made no noise, yet it ceased from its howling and tried to sense his presence. Buck stalked into the open, half-crouching, body gathered compactly together, tail straight and stiff, feet falling with unwonted care. Every movement advertised commingled threatening and overture of friendliness. It was the menacing truce that marks the meeting of wild beasts that prey. But the wolf fled at sight of him. He followed, with wild leapings, in a frenzy to overtake. He ran him into a blind channel, in the bed of the creek, where a timber jam barred the way. The wolf whirled about, pivoting on his hind legs after the fashion of Joe and of all cornered husky dogs, snarling and bristling, clipping his teeth together in a continuous and rapid succession of snaps.

Buck did not attack, but circled him about and hedged him in with friendly advances. The wolf was suspicious and afraid; for Buck made three of him in weight, while his head barely reached Buck's shoulder. Watching his chance, he darted away, and the chase was resumed. Time and again he was cornered, and the thing repeated, though he was in poor condition or Buck could not so easily have overtaken him. He would run till Buck's head was even with his flank, when he would whirl around at bay, only to dash away again at the first opportunity.

But in the end Buck's pertinacity was rewarded; for the wolf, finding that no harm was intended, finally sniffed noses with him. Then they became friendly, and played about in the nervous, half-coy way with which fierce beasts belie their fierceness. After some time of this the wolf started off at an easy lope in a manner that plainly showed he was going somewhere. He made it clear to Buck that he was to come, and they ran side by side through the somber twilight, straight up the creek bed, into the gorge from which it issued, and across the bleak divide where it took its rise.

On the opposite slope of the watershed they came down into a level country where were great stretches of forest and many streams, and through these great stretches they ran steadily, hour after hour, the sun rising higher and the day growing warmer. Buck was wildly glad. He knew he was at last answering the call, running by the side of his wood brother toward the place from where the call surely came. Old memories were coming upon him fast, and he was stirring to them as of old he stirred to the realities of which they were the shadows. He had done this thing before, somewhere in that other and dimly remembered world, and he was doing it again, now, running free in the open, the unpacked earth underfoot, the wide sky overhead.

They stopped by a running stream to drink, and, stopping, Buck remembered John Thornton. He sat down. The wolf started on toward the place from where the call surely came, then returned to him, sniffing noses and making actions as though to encourage him. But Buck turned about and started slowly on the back track. For the better part of an hour the wild brother ran by his side, whining softly. Then he sat down, pointed his nose upward, and howled. It was a mournful howl, and as Buck held steadily on his way he heard it grow faint and fainter until it was lost in the distance.

John Thornton was eating dinner when Buck dashed into camp and sprang upon him in a frenzy of affection, overturning him, scrambling upon him, licking his face, biting his hand— "playing the general tom-fool," as John Thornton characterized it, the while he shook Buck back and forth and cursed him lovingly.

For two days and nights Buck never left camp, never let Thornton out of his sight. He followed him about at his work, watched him while he ate, saw him into his blankets at night and out of them in the morning. But after two days the call in the forest began to sound more imperiously than ever. Buck's restlessness came back on him, and he was haunted by recollections of the wild brother, and of the smiling land beyond the divide and the run side by side through the wide forest stretches. Once again he took to wandering in the woods, but the wild brother came no more; and though he listened through long vigils, the mournful howl was never raised.

He began to sleep out at night, staying away from camp for days at a time; and once he crossed the divide at the head of the creek and went down into the land of timber and streams. There he wandered for a week, seeking vainly for fresh sign of the wild brother, killing his meat as he traveled and traveling with the long, easy lope that seems never to tire. He fished for salmon in a broad stream that emptied somewhere into the sea, and by this stream he killed a large black bear, blinded by the mosquitoes while likewise fishing, and raging through the forest helpless and terrible. Even so, it was a hard fight, and it aroused the last latent remnants of Buck's ferocity. And two days later, when he returned to his kill and found a dozen wolverines quarreling over the spoil, he scattered them like chaff; and those that fled left two behind who would quarrel no more.

The blood-longing became stronger than ever before. He was a killer, a thing that preyed, living on the things that lived, unaided, alone, by virtue of his own strength and prowess, surviving triumphantly in a hostile environment where only the strong survived. Because of all this he became possessed of a great pride in himself, which communicated itself like a contagion to his physical being. It advertised itself in all his movements, was apparent in the play of every muscle, spoke plainly as speech in the way he carried himself, and made his glorious furry coat if anything more glorious. But for the stray brown on his muzzle and above his eyes, and for the splash of white hair that ran midmost down his chest, he might well have been mistaken for a gigantic wolf, larger than the largest of the breed. From his St. Bernard father he had inherited size and weight, but it was his shepherd mother who had given shape to that size and weight. His muzzle was the long wolf muzzle, save that it was larger than the muzzle of any wolf; and his head, somewhat broader, was the wolf head on a massive scale.

His cunning was wolf cunning, and wild cunning; his intelligence, shepherd intelligence and St. Bernard intelligence; and all this, plus an experience gained in the fiercest of schools, made him as formidable a creature as any that roamed the wild. A carnivorous animal, living on a straight meat diet, he was in full flower, at the high tide of his life, over-spilling with vigor and virility. When Thornton passed a caressing hand along his back, a snapping and crackling followed the hand, each hair discharging its pent magnetism at the contact. Every part, brain and body, nerve tissue and fiber, was keyed to the most exquisite pitch; and between all the parts there was a perfect equilibrium or adjustment. To sights and sounds and events which required action, he responded with lighting-like rapidity. Quickly as a husky dog could leap to defend from attack or to attack, he could leap twice as quickly. He saw the movement, or heard sound, and responded in less time than another dog required to compass the mere seeing or hearing. He perceived and determined and responded in the same instant. In point of fact the three actions of perceiving, determining, and responding were sequential; but so infinitesimal were the intervals of time between them that they appeared simultaneous. His muscles were surcharged with vitality, and snapped into play sharply, like steel springs. Life streamed through him in splendid flood, glad and rampant, until it seemed that it would burst him asunder in sheer ecstasy and put forth generously over the world.

"Never was there such a dog," said John Thornton one day, as the partners watched Buck marching out of camp.

"When he was made, the mold was broke," said Pete.

"Py Jingo! I think so mineself," Hans affirmed.

They saw him marching out of camp, but they did not see the instant and terrible transformation which took place as soon as he was within the secrecy of the forest. He no longer marched. At once he became a thing of the wild, stealing along softly, cat-footed, a passing shadow that appeared and disappeared among the shadows. He knew how to take advantage of every cover, to crawl on his belly like a snake, and like a snake to leap and strike. He could take a ptarmigan from its nest, kill a rabbit as it slept, and snap in mid-air the little chipmunks fleeing a second too late for the trees. Fish, in open pools, were not too quick for him; nor were beaver, mending their dams, too wary. He killed to eat, not from wantonness; but he preferred to eat what he killed himself. So a lurking humor ran through his deeds, and it was his delight to steal upon the squirrels, and, when he all but had them, to let them go, chattering in mortal fear to the tree-tops.

As the fall of the year came on, the moose appeared in greater abundance, moving slowly down to meet the winter in the lower and less rigorous valleys. Buck had already dragged down a stray part-grown calf; but he wished strongly for larger and more formidable quarry, and he came upon it one day on the divide at the head of the creek. A band of twenty moose had crossed over from the land of streams and timber, and chief among them was a great bull. He was in a savage temper, and, standing over six feet from the ground, was as formidable an antagonist as even Buck could desire. Back and forth the bull tossed his great palmated antlers, branching to fourteen points and embracing seven feet with the tips. His small eyes burned with a vicious and bitter light, while he roared with fury at sight of Buck.

From the bull's side, just forward of the flank, protruded a feathered arrow-end, which accounted for his savageness. Guided by that instinct which came from the old hunting days of the primordial world, Buck proceeded to cut the bull out from the herd. It was no slight task. He would bark and dance about in front of the bull, just out of reach of the great antlers and of the terrible splay hoofs which could have stamped his life out with a single blow. Unable to turn his back on the fanged danger and go on, the bull would be driven into paroxysms of rage. At such moments he charged Buck, who retreated craftily, luring him on by a simulated inability to escape. But when he was thus separated from his fellows, two or three of the younger bulls would charge back upon Buck and enable the wounded bull to rejoin the herd.

There is a patience of the wild—dogged, tireless, persistent as life itself—that holds motionless for endless hours the spider in its web, the snake in its coils, the panther in its ambuscade; this patience belongs peculiarly to life when it hunts its living food; and it belonged to Buck as he clung to the flank of the herd, retarding its march, irritating the young bulls, worrying the cows with their half-grown calves, and driving the wounded bull mad with helpless rage. For half a day this continued. Buck multiplied himself, attacking from all sides, enveloping the herd in a whirlwind of menace, cutting out his victim as fast as it could rejoin its mates, wearing out the patience of creatures preyed upon, which is a lesser patience than that of creatures preying.

As the day wore along and the sun dropped to its bed in the northwest (the darkness had come back and the fall nights were six hours long), the young bulls retraced their steps more and more reluctantly to the aid of their beset leader. The down-coming winter was hurrying them on to the lower levels, and it seemed they could never shake off this tireless creature that held them back. Besides, it was not the life of the herd, or of the young bulls, that was threatened. The life of only one member was demanded, which was a remoter interest than their lives, and in the end they were content to pay the toll.

As twilight fell the old bull stood with lowered head, watching his mates—the cows he had known, the calves he had fathered, the bulls he had mastered—as they shambled on at a rapid pace through the fading light. He could not follow, for before his nose leaped the merciless fanged terror that would not let him go. Three hundred weight more than half a ton he weighed; he had lived a long, strong life, full of fight and struggle, and at the end he faced death at the teeth of a creature whose head did not reach beyond his great knuckled knees.

From then on, night and day, Buck never left his prey, never gave it a moment's rest, never permitted it to browse the leaves of trees or the shoots of young birch and willow. Nor did he give the wounded bull opportunity to slake his burning thirst in the slender trickling streams they crossed. Often, in desperation, he burst into long stretches of flight. At such time Buck did not attempt to stay him, but loped easily at his heels, satisfied with the way the game was played, lying down when the moose stood still, attacking him fiercely when he strove to eat or drink.

The great head drooped more and more under its tree of horns, and the shambling trot grew weaker and weaker. He took to standing for long periods, with nose to the ground and dejected ears dropped limply; and Buck found more time in which to get water for himself and in which to rest. At such moments, panting with red lolling tongue and with eyes fixed upon the big bull, it appeared to Buck that a change was coming over the face of things. He could feel a new stir in the land. As the moose were coming into the land, other kinds of life were coming in. Forest and stream and air seemed palpitant with their presence. The news of it was borne in upon him, not by sight, or sound, or smell, but by some other and subtler sense. He heard nothing, saw nothing, yet knew that the land was somehow different; that through it strange things were afoot and ranging; and he resolved to investigate after he had finished the business in hand.

At last, at the end of the fourth day, he pulled the great moose down. For a day and a night he remained by the kill, eating and sleeping, turn and turn about. Then, rested, refreshed and strong, he turned his face toward camp and John Thornton. He broke into the long easy lope, and went on, hour after hour, never at loss for the tangled way, heading straight home through strange country with a certitude of direction that put man and his magnetic needle to shame.

As he held on he became more and more conscious of the new stir in the land. There was life abroad in it different from the life which had been there throughout the summer. No longer was this fact borne in upon him in some subtle, mysterious way. The birds talked of it, the squirrels chattered about it, the very breeze whispered of it. Several times he stopped and drew in the fresh morning air in great sniffs, reading a message which made him leap on with greater speed. He was oppressed with a sense of calamity happening, if it were not calamity already happened, and as he crossed the last watershed and dropped down into the valley toward camp, he proceeded with greater caution.

Three miles away he came upon a fresh trail that sent his neck hair rippling and bristling. It led straight toward camp and John Thornton. Buck hurried on, swiftly and stealthily, every nerve straining and tense, alert to the multitudinous details which told a story—all but the end. His nose gave him a varying description of the passage of the life on the heels of which he was traveling. He remarked the pregnant silence of the forest. The bird life had flitted. The squirrels were in hiding. One only he saw—a sleek gray fellow, flattened against a gray dead limb so that he seemed a part of it, a woody excrescence upon the wood itself.

As Buck slid along with the obscureness of a gliding shadow, his nose was jerked suddenly to the side as though a positive force had gripped and pulled it. He followed the new scent into a thicket and found Nig. He was lying on his side, dead where he had dragged himself, an arrow protruding, head and feathers, from either side of his body.

A hundred yards farther on, Buck came upon one of the sled dogs Thornton had bought in Dawson. This dog was thrashing about in a death-struggle, directly on the trail, and Buck passed around him without stopping. From the camp came the faint sound of many voices, rising and falling in a sing-song chant. Bellying forward to the edge of the clearing, he found Hans, lying on his face, feathered with arrows like a porcupine. At the same instant Buck peered out where the spruce-bough lodge had been and saw what made his hair leap straight up on his neck and shoulders. A gust of overpowering rage swept over him. He did not know that he growled, but he growled aloud with a terrible ferocity. For the last time in his life he allowed passion to usurp cunning and reason, and it was because of his great love for John Thornton that he lost his head.

The Yeehats were dancing about the wreckage of the spruce-bough lodge when they heard a fearful roaring and saw rushing upon them an animal the like of which they had never seen before. It was Buck, a live hurricane of fury, hurling himself upon them in a frenzy to destroy. He sprang at the foremost man—it was the chief of the Yeehats—ripping the throat wide open till the rent jugular spouted a fountain of blood. He did not pause to worry the victim, but ripped in passing, with the next bound tearing wide the throat of a second man. There was no withstanding him. He plunged about in their very midst, tearing, rending, destroying, in constant and terrific motion which defied the arrows they discharged at him. In fact, so inconceivably rapid were his movements, and so closely were the Indians tangled together, that they shot one another with the arrows; and one young hunter, hurling a spear at Buck in mid-air, drove it through the chest of another hunter with such force that the point broke through the skin of the back and stood out beyond. Then a panic seized the Yeehats, and they fled in terror to the woods, proclaiming as they fled the advent of the Evil Spirit.

And truly Buck was the Fiend incarnate, raging at their heels and dragging them down like deer as they raced through the trees. It was a fateful day for the Yeehats. They scattered far and wide over the country, and it was not till a week later that the last of the survivors gathered together in a lower valley and counted their losses. As for Buck, wearying of the pursuit, he returned to the desolated camp. He found Pete where he had been killed in his blankets in the first moment of surprise. Thornton's desperate struggle was fresh-written on the earth and Buck scented every detail of it down to the edge of a deep pool. By the edge, head and fore feet in the water, lay Skeet, faithful to the last. The pool itself, muddy and discolored from the sluice boxes, effectually hid what it contained, and it contained John Thornton; for Buck followed his trace into the water, from which no trace led away.

All day Buck brooded by the pool or roamed restlessly about the camp. Death, as a cessation of movement, as a passing out and away from the lives of the living, he knew, and he knew John Thornton was dead. It left a great void in him, somewhat akin to hunger, but a void which ached and ached, and which food could not fill. At times, when he paused to contemplate the carcasses of the Yeehats, he forgot the pain of it; and at such times he was aware of a great pride in himself—a pride greater than any he had yet experienced. He had killed man, the noblest game of all, and he had killed in the face of the law of club and fang. He sniffed the bodies curiously. They had died so easily. It was harder to kill a husky dog than them. They were no match at all, were it not for their arrows and spears and clubs. Thenceforward he would be unafraid of them except when they bore in their hands their arrows, spears and clubs.

Night came on, and a full moon rose high over the trees into the sky, lighting the land till it lay bathed in ghostly day. And with the coming of the night, brooding and mourning by the pool, Buck came alive to a stirring of the new life in the forest other than that which the Yeehats had made. He stood up, listening and scenting. From far away drifted a faint, sharp yelp, followed by a chorus of similar sharp yelps. As the moments passed the yelps grew closer and louder. Again Buck knew them as things heard in that other world which persisted in his memory. He walked to the center of the open space and listened. It was the call, the many-noted call, sounding more luringly and compelling than ever before. And as never before, he was ready to obey. John Thornton was dead. The last tie was broken. Man and the claims of man no longer bound him.

Hunting their living meat, as the Yeehats were hunting it, on the flanks of the migrating moose, the wolf pack had at last crossed over from the land of streams and timber and invaded Buck's valley. Into the clearing where the moonlight streamed, they poured in a silvery flood; and in the center of the clearing stood Buck, motionless as a statue, waiting their coming. they were awed, so still and large he stood, and a moment's pause fell, till the boldest one leaped straight for him. Like a flash Buck struck, breaking the neck. Then he stood, without movement, as before, the stricken wolf rolling in agony behind him. Three others tried it in sharp succession; and one after the other they drew back, streaming blood from slashed throats or shoulders.

This was sufficient to fling the whole pack forward, pellmell, crowded together, blocked and confused by its eagerness to pull down the prey. Buck's marvelous quickness and agility stood him in good stead. Pivoting on his hind legs, and snapping and gashing, he was everywhere at once, presenting a front which was apparently unbroken so swiftly did he whirl and guard from side to side. But to prevent them from getting behind him, he was forced back, down past the pool and into the creek bed, till he brought up against a high gravel bank. He worked along to a right angle in the bank which the men had made in the course of mining, and in this angle he came to bay, protected on three sides and with nothing to do but face the front.

And so well did he face it, that at the end of half an hour the wolves drew back discomfited. The tongues of all were out and lolling, the white fangs showing cruelly white in the moonlight. Some were lying down with heads raised and ears pricked forward; others stood on their feet, watching him; and still others were lapping water from the pool. One wolf, long and lean and gray, advanced cautiously, in a friendly manner, and Buck recognized the wild brother with whom he had run for a night and a day. He was whining softly, and, as Buck whined, they touched noses.

Then an old wolf, gaunt and battle-scarred, came forward. Buck writhed his lips into the preliminary of a snarl, but sniffed noses with him. Whereupon the old wolf sat down, pointed nose at the moon, and broke out the long wolf howl. The others sat down and howled. And now the call came to Buck in unmistakable accents. He, too, sat down and howled. This over, he came out of his angle and the pack crowded around him, sniffing in half-friendly, half-savage manner. The leaders lifted the yelp of the pack and sprang away into the woods. The wolves swung in behind, yelping in chorus. And Buck ran with them, side by side with the wild brother, yelping as he ran.

And here may well end the story of Buck. The years were not many when the Yeehats noted a change in the breed of timber wolves; for some were seen with splashes of brown on head and muzzle, and with a rift of white centering down the chest. But more remarkable than this the Yeehats tell of a Ghost Dog that runs at the head of the pack. They are afraid of this Ghost Dog, for it has cunning greater than they, stealing from their camps in the fierce winters, robbing their traps, slaying their dogs, and defying their bravest hunters.

Nay, the tale grows worse. Hunters there are who fail to return to the camp, and hunters there have been whom their tribesmen found with throats slashed cruelly open and with wolf prints about them in the snow greater than the prints of any wolf. Each fall, when the Yeehats follow the movement of the moose, there is a certain valley which they never enter. And women there are who become sad when the word goes over the fire of how the Evil Spirit came to select that valley for an abiding-place.

In the summers there is one visitor, however, to that valley, of which the Yeehats do not know. It is a great, gloriously coated wolf, like, and yet unlike, all other wolves. He crosses alone from the smiling timber land and comes down into an open space among the trees. Here a yellow stream flows from rotted moose-hide sacks and sinks into the ground, with long grasses growing through it and vegetable mold overrunning it and hiding its yellow from the sun; and here he muses for a time, howling once, long and mournfully, ere he departs.

But he is not always alone. When the long winter nights come on and the wolves follow their meat into the lower valleys, he may be seen running at the head of the pack through the pale moonlight or glimmering borealis, leaping gigantic above his fellows, his great throat a-bellow as he sings a song of the younger world, which is the song of the pack.

■ Study Questions

1. Where does Buck live at the beginning of the story? Who is Buck's first master? Who kidnaps Buck from his home?

2. How does Buck save John Thornton's life? What bet does Thornton win with Matthewson?

3. What quest sends Thornton and his friends into the wildness? While the men camp and look for gold, what does Buck do? What kind of animal does Buck spend four days hunting? What does Buck find when he returns from hunting? What does Buck learn when he attacks the Yeehat Indians?

4. What does Buck do at the end of the story?

5. How does *The Call of the Wild* present the human-dog relationship? To what extent does London anthropomorphize Buck—that is, present him like a human being? To what extent is he emphatically an animal?

6. What is "atavism" ? What role does it play in Buck's development as a wild animal? What is the "call of the wild" ? How does it affect Buck's behavior throughout the novel?

7. Compare the roles of John Thornton and Judge Miller. Who, from the novel's point of view, is the better master?

8. Can you read any influence of Charles Darwin's and Friedrich Nietzsche's theories on *The Call of the Wild*?

Edwin Arlington Robinson (1869—1935)

As the first major American poet of the 20th century, **Edwin Arlington Robinson** was unique in that he devoted his life to poetry and willingly paid the price of poverty and obscurity.

Edwin Arlington Robinson was born in Head Tide, Maine and grew up in Gardiner which later furnished him a setting for many of his poems as well as models for his characters throughout his career. He began writing regularly quite young and in high school attended meetings of the town's poetry society, showing no ambition but that of writing poems. In 1891 he entered Harvard University but soon Fates played jokes on the family. A series of family tragedies occurred—his father died shortly after bankruptcy; he was forced to leave Harvard for financial difficulty and his mother's failing health; his mother died from diphtheria; his brothers became a drug addict and an alcoholic respectively—which triggered a dark mood in his point of view. However, E. A. Robinson was not defeated by the miserable fate. Instead, he published his first volume of poems *The Torrent and the Night Before* in 1896 at his own expense and *The Children of the Night* in the following year with friends' help.

At the end of the 19th century, the poet left Gardiner for New York City. For the next quarter-century Robinson chose to live in poverty and write his poetry, relying on scraps of temporary work and charity from friends. In 1902 he published *Captain Craig* but received little encouragement from critics. As a result, Robinson fell into a depression, neglecting his poetry, drifting from job to job and drinking heavily.

Finally Fates showed a little sympathy. Robinson received a letter from Theodore Roosevelt in which the president expressed his fondness for his poems. Subsequently, the president arranged a job for him at the New York Customs House until 1910. Despite Roosevelt's patronage, the major magazines remained close to him. Only after the publication of *The Town Down the River* (1910) and *The Man Against the Sky* (1916) did Robinson attracted public attention. In 1917 *Merlin* appeared, the first of three long Arthurian-related poems, followed by *Lancelot* in 1920 and *Tristram* in 1927. In 1921, his *Collected Poems* was awarded the first Pulitzer Prize for poetry. He was awarded a second Pulitzer Prize in 1924 for *The Man Who Died Twice* and a third prize for *Tristram*. For the first time in his life, Robinson was financially independent, and the success exhilarated him. Otherwise, his habits remained unchanged with his full attention paid to his poetry until he died in a New York City hospital while revising the galleys of his last work, *King Jasper* (1935).

Robinson was a transitional poet at the turn of the 19th and 20th centuries. From the first, his poetry was noted for mastery of conventional forms, be it the sonnet, the quatrain, or the eight-line stanza. Due to his own painful life and the influence of the tragic vision of Thomas Hardy, he centered around futility and repression of human life. The characters in his portrait poems such as "Richard Cory," "Luke Havergal," "Aaron Stark," and "John Evereldown" are faced with failure, loneliness, defeat, despair and alienation. But on the other hand, Robinson was drawn to the individualistic idealism of Hawthorne, Whitman, Emerson and Henry James. Therefore, his limning characters failed on a materialistic level but somehow succeeded, though at great cost on a moral or spiritual level. Though Robinson cannot be categorized into modernists, he was a modern poet, holding a tragic vision in step with the modern spirit. He would turn to this theme of public failure, counterbalanced by the subject's life-affirming courage in an ironic, sympathetic and humorous tone, throughout his career.

■ Selected Readings

Form in poetry may involve not only adherence to a central story or theme, but some kind of progress or development toward a final effect to which each particular part has made its particular contribution. A simple and famous illustration is "Richard Cory." The suicide of Richard Cory is not, or ought not to be, a surprise. It is an inevitability, predetermined by the subjugation of selfhood. Even more significantly, however, the subjugated self reclaims itself in the act of suicide. Not that the poem recommends suicide as a way of asserting individuality. Rather, it observes an extreme gesture in an extreme case. To see the poem in this way is to see it as neither bitter nor negative, at least not entirely so. We read ill if we cannot see that Richard Cory is granted an oblique triumph at the end, for he has refused to suppose himself made happy by what "everyone" supposes will make him happy. In short, Richard Cory's self emerges neurotically perhaps; still it emerges triumphant over the imposed role of "success."

Richard Cory

Whenever Richard Cory went down town,
We people on the pavement looked at him:
He was a gentleman from sole to crown[154],
Clean favored[155] and imperially slim.

5   And he was always quietly arrayed[156],
And he was always human[157] when he talked;
But still he fluttered pulses[158] when he said,
"Good morning," and he glittered when he walked.

And he was rich, yes richer than a king,
10   And admirably schooled in every grace[159]:
In fine[160], we thought that he was everything
To make us wish we were in his place.

So on we worked, and waited for the light,
And went without the meat and cursed the bread;[161]
15   And Richard Cory one calm summer night,
Went home and put a bullet through his head.

---

[154]   **a gentleman from sole to crown**: gentlemanlike from top to feet; a standard gentleman.
[155]   **clean favored**: clean and tidy; neat and elegant in appearance.
[156]   **quietly arrayed**: properly dressed.
[157]   **human**: sympathetic and understanding others.
[158]   **fluttered pules**: caused people's pulses to beat irregularly.
[159]   **admirably schooled in every grace**: well educated, strictly trained in every aspect.
[160]   **In fine**: In brief.
[161]   **So... bread**: So we worked on and on after his model, and waited for the opportunities to change our fate. (For this purpose, we had to) Live a thrifty life, eating meat at long intervals or none at all, and having a little bread every day.

■ Study Questions

1. Which line in the poem identifies the speaker? Which lines tell you about the economic condition of the speaker?

2. What is Richard Cory "from sole to crown"? What effect does he have when he says "Good morning"?

3. What, "in fine," do the people think of Richard Cory?

4. What is the "surprising" ending?

5. How are the "we" of the poem different from Richard Cory?

6. What do "crown" and "imperially" indicate about the speaker's impression of Richard Cory?

7. What effect does Cory's final action seem to have on everyone in Tilbury Town? What does Tilbury Town's reaction to Cory's life and death suggest about human understanding?

"*Miniver Cheevy*" is generally regarded as a self-portrait. The tone, characteristics sketched by Robinson and shared by the poet and Miniver, and the satiric humor of the poem all lead to that interpretation. Yet, although as a satire of the poet himself, it is a delightful poem—Robinson jousts with a double-edged satiric lance. More than a clever spoof of Robinson as Miniver, the poem satirizes the age and, especially, its literary taste.

The more readily acknowledged thrust is, of course, his satire on himself. David Nivison offers as evidence that the poem is a self-parody the fact that the poet customarily found some compassion for his characters and some redeeming quality in failure. In this poem Robinson does not sympathize with Miniver, but lampoons his faults and "laughs at him without reserve in every line." Moreover, Robinson frequently made fun of himself in letters to his friends and, like Miniver, he was lean, he drank, and in the eyes of early 20th-century America he was a failure. In that materially-oriented, production-minded society, Robinson, like Miniver, was a "minimal achiever." The poem's combination of feminine endings and short final stanzaic lines contribute to the satiric effect, Ellsworth Barnard notes, as do the images and thoughts conveyed. Overtly, "Miniver Cheevy" emphasizes Miniver and gains its unity by the repetition of the name, the full name appearing at the beginning of the first and last stanzas and "Miniver" opening the intervening stanzas. Furthermore, by making his character ludicrous, Robinson makes clear within the context of the poem that Miniver is out of tune with the age.

The brilliance and sharpness, however, of the Miniver edge of the satiric blade (to use the metaphor that seems in keeping with Miniver's visions of swashbucklers) or, more precisely, the reader's tendency to see the poet in Miniver, put into shadow the other edge of the blade, the poem as a satire on the age. Although Robinson recognized himself as out of step with the time in which he lived, the anomaly was based on his choice to continue as a poet despite the public's lack of acceptance of his poetry. He objected, also, to the ideology of materialism and was not alone in criticizing the age. In "Miniver Cheevy" three aspects of 19th-and early 20th-century American culture, as analyzed by T. J. Jackson Lears, resonate: materialism, which with its components of work, action, and acquisition formed the ethos of the age and the measure of progress; militarism, a manifestation of the effort to overcome the ennui of the age and what was perceived as the feminization of American culture in the latter 19th century; and anti-modernism, an expression of the desire to escape the material-spiritual dilemmas that persisted and an effort to retrieve, if only in the imagination, the glories and principles of an earlier time. Clearly, the three are inter-related and all find satirical rendering in Robinson's poem.

Miniver Cheevy

Miniver Cheevy, child of scorn[162],
    Grew lean[163] while he assailed the seasons[164];
He wept that he was ever born,
    And he had reasons.

5   Miniver loved the days of old
    When swords were bright and steeds were prancing[165];
The vision of a warrior bold[166]
    Would set him dancing. [167]

Miniver sighed for what was not[168],
10   And dreamed, and rested from his labors;
He dreamed of Thebes and Camelot,
    And Priam's neighbors. [169]

Miniver mourned the ripe renown[170]
    That made so many a name so fragrant;
15   He mourned Romance[171], now on the town[172],
    And Art, a vagrant.

Miniver loved the Medici[173],

---

162 **child of scorn**: It's a pun. It refers to both the person who shows contempt and the person who is scorned.

163 **Grew lean**: became thin, frail.

164 **assailed the seasons**: struggled against the hard life.

165 **steeds were prancing**: horses were running quickly and proudly with a springing and dancing step.

166 **a warrior bold**: a bold warrior, an adventurous soldier.

167 **set him dancing**: excite him, cause him dance for joy.

168 **what was not**: what did not exist.

169 **He dreamed... neighbors**: Thebes was an ancient city in Boeotia, in east-central Greece northwest of Athens. Camelot was the site of King Arthur's court in Arthurian legend. Priam was the king of Troy, who was killed when his city fell to the Greeks. Here Priam's neighbors in Homer's *Iliad* are his heroic compatriots in the doomed city of Troy.

170 **mourned the ripe renown**: grieve for the brilliant achievements (in literature and art) of the old time (which have declined now).

171 **Romance**: here, literature.

172 **on the town**: on welfare, to be supported by the town, a charity case. Miniver, in other words, is the town ne'er-do-well, the town loafer.

173 **the Medici**: Family of wealthy merchants, statesmen and art patrons in Renaissance Florence, whose members were generally notorious for ruthlessness and sinfulness.

Albeit[174] he had never seen one;

He would have sinned incessantly

20   Could he have been one. [175]

Miniver cursed the commonplace

And eyed a khaki suit[176] with loathing;

He missed the medieval grace

Of iron clothing[177].

25 Miniver scorned the gold he sought,

But sore annoyed was he without it;[178]

Miniver thought, and thought, and thought,

And thought about it.

Miniver Cheevy, born too late,

30   Scratched his head and kept on thinking;

Miniver coughed, and called it fate,

And kept on drinking.

■ Study Questions

1. For what does Cheevy sigh and mourn in the first five stanzas? What does Cheevy curse in the sixth stanza?

2. What are Cheevy's feelings about gold, according to Stanza 7?

3. To what does Cheevy attribute his unhappiness in Line 31? What does he keep on doing, according to the last line of the poem?

4. What do Lines 9-10 reveal about Cheevy's character? Lines 17-18? Lines 25-26?

5. Basically, how does Cheevy see himself? How do we see him? What really causes his unhappiness?

6. Why is the fourth line of each quatrain (4-line stanza) in "Miniver Cheevy" shorter than the previous three? How is the brevity surprising, ironic, and humorous? How does the humorous surprise of the shorter lines contribute to the overall theme of the poem?

7. Could Richard Cory and Miniver Cheevy be found only in a small Maine town at the turn of the century? Explain your answer.

---

174 **Albeit**: Although.

175 **He could... one**: If he were a member of the Medici family, he would have been as ruthless and sinful.

176 **a khaki suit**: modern army uniform.

177 **iron clothing**: ancient military uniform made of iron; armor.

178 **But sore... it**: But he became anxious if he was without money.

LITERARY FOCUS

Feminist Criticism

As a distinctive and concerted approach to literature, feminist criticism was not inaugurated until late in the 1960s. Behind it, however, lie two centuries of struggle for the recognition of women's cultural roles and achievements, and for women's social and political rights, marked by such books as Mary Wollstonecraft's *A Vindication of the Rights of Woman* (1792), John Stuart Mill's *The Subjection of Women* (1869), and Margaret Fuller's *Woman in the Nineteenth Century* (1845). Much of feminist literary criticism continues in our time to be interrelated with the movement by political feminists for social, legal, and cultural freedom and equality.

An important precursor in feminist criticism was Virginia Woolf, who, in addition to her fiction, wrote *A Room of One's Own* (1929) and numerous other essays on women authors and on the cultural, economic, and educational disabilities within what she called a " patriarchal" society, dominated by men, that have hindered or prevented women from realizing their productive and creative possibilities. A much more radical critical mode, sometimes called " second-wave feminism," was launched in France by Simone de Beauvoir's *The Second Sex* (1949), a wide-ranging critique of the cultural identification of women as merely the negative object, or *Other*, to man as the dominating *Subject* who is assumed to represent humanity in general.

In America, modern feminist criticism was inaugurated by Maty Ellmann's deft and witty discussion, in *Thinking about Women* (1968), about the derogatory stereotypes of women in literature written by men, and also about alternative and subversive representations that occur in some writings by women. Even more influential was Kate Millett's hard-hitting *Sexual Politics*, published the following year. By " politics" Millett signifies the mechanisms that express and enforce the relations of power in society; she analyzes many Western social arrangements and institutions as covert ways of manipulating power so as to establish and perpetuate the dominance of men and the subordination of women.

Since 1969 there has been an explosion of feminist writings without parallel in previous critical innovations. Current feminist criticism manifests, among those who practice it, a great variety of critical vantage points and procedures, including adaptations, of psychoanalytic, Marxist, and diverse poststructuralist theories. The various feminisms, however, share certain assumptions and concepts that underlie the diverse ways that individual critics explore the factor of sexual difference and privilege in the production, the form and content, the reception, and the critical analysis and evaluation of works of literature:

1) The basic view is that Western civilization is pervasively patriarchal (ruled by the father)—that is, it
   is male-centered and controlled, and is organized and conducted in such a way as to subordinate

women to men in all cultural domains: familial, religious, political, economic, social, legal, and artistic.

2) It is widely held that while one's sex as a man or woman is determined by anatomy, the prevailing concepts of gender—if the traits that arc conceived to constitute what is masculine and what is feminine in temperament and behavior—are largely, if not entirely, social constructs that were generated by the pervasive patriarchal biases of our civilization.

3) The further claim is that this patriarchal ideology pervades those writings which have been traditionally considered great literature, and which until recently have been written mainly by men for men. Typically, the most highly regarded literary works focus on male protagonists—Captain John Smith (rather than Pocahontas), Poor Richard, Rip Van Winkle, "Hawkeye," Captain Ahab, Huck Finn, and Mr. Oakhurst—who embody masculine traits and ways of feeling and pursue masculine interests in masculine fields of action. To these males, the female characters, when they play a role, are marginal and subordinate, and are represented either as complementary and subservient to, or in opposition to, masculine desires and enterprises.

The often-asserted goal of feminist critics has been to enlarge and reorder, or in radical instances entirely to displace, the literary canon—that is, the set of works which, by a cumulative consensus, have come to be considered "major" and to serve as the chief subjects of literary history, criticism, scholarship, and teaching. Feminist studies have succeeded in raising the status of many female authors hitherto more or less scanted by scholars and critics and bringing into purview other authors who have been largely or entirely overlooked as subjects for serious consideration (among them Kate Chopin, and a number of African-American writers such as Zora Neale Hurston). Some feminists have devoted their critical attention especially to the literature written by lesbian writers, or that deals with lesbian relationships in a heterosexual culture.

■ Think About Feminist Criticism

• Find out traits in Kate Chopin's "The Story of an Hour" that conform to the contemporary feminist critical views. Taking its social and literary background into consideration, tell why most critics now believe that there is "something ahead of the time" in the story.

READING FOR APPRECIATION

The Emotional Imagination

At the end of the first unit of this book, we talked about the need each reader has to bring an active imagination to literature. This is especially important as we read about the lives of people who lived in times and places different from our own. We called this the historical imagination. Yet there is another aspect of imaginative reading that we must learn to exercise as well—the emotional imagination.

It is true that we like to see people like ourselves mirrored in art. We take pleasure in seeing a familiar reality portrayed in a painting or in a story. Most literature, however, cannot limit itself to our reality. Truly active reading means opening ourselves to ways of thinking, feeling, and seeing these that are different from our own. We shut ourselves off from a great deal of pleasure and knowledge if we resist what is strange or unfamiliar. As we read, we need to give ourselves up to the language, reading slowly, carefully, allowing the language to guide us, to take us beyond ourselves and into the lives of characters different from ourselves—and into the minds of the writers, too.

In the stories and poems in this unit, we are asked to become for a while a great many men and women. In Kate Chopin's "The Story of an Hour" we imagine what it is like to feel restricted and to allow ourselves a few moments filled with the excitement of wider horizons. We share the frustrated anger and sense of injustice of a struggling Midwestern farmer in Garland's "Under the Lion's Paw." Yet, paradoxically, what we often find as we read, giving ourselves up to "strange" experiences, is that after all there is something of ourselves in all of these characters. They are "what we might have been" or "what we might be."

Our emotional imaginations enable us to engage in the very lives of literary characters—an imaginative act that connects literature and the world of real people in which we live. How much wiser and richer we may be, and how much pleasure we may find in reading, if we are willing for an hour or two to enter—through language—the lives of others.

VOICE OF THE AGE

Down to Earth

The writers of the Realist period in American literature often shocked their contemporaries. In our own time we still see them as breaking away from some long-standing American traditions.

The Realists and Naturalists no longer took comfort from the religious vision that had supported the Puritan writers. They did not share the sense of new possibilities that had fired the imaginations of the writers of the Revolution. They did not exult with the optimism of the Transcendentalists. Instead, they brought their ideas and emotions out of the clouds and down to earth. They took long, hard looks at what those living in the world was really like in their time—without flinching from the suffering, without explaining away or softening the struggle of being human.

London: *He was beaten (he knew that); but he was not broken. He saw, once for all, that he stood no chance against a man with a club. He had learned the lesson, and in all his after life he never forgot it. That club was a revelation. It was his introduction to the reign of primitive law, and he met the introduction halfway. The* *facts of life took on a fiercer aspect and, while he faced that aspect uncowed, he faced it with all the latent cunning of his nature aroused.*

Robinson: *So on we worked, and waited for the light.*

Dreiser: *They were nearing Chicago. Signs were everywhere numerous. Trains flashed by them. Across wide stretches of flat, open prairie they could see lines of telegraph poles stalking across the fields toward the great city. Far away were indications of suburban towns, some big smokestacks towering high in the air. Frequently there were two-story frame houses standing out in the open fields, without fence or trees, lone outposts of the approaching army of homes.*

The writers in this unit reported what they saw: There were joys and times of happiness—but they were scattered within a world of struggle.

THE BLOOM OF MODERNISM
1910—1930

INTRODUCTION

Why is it the Era of Modernism

The English novelist Virginia Woolf once said that "on or about December 1910, human nature changed". Of course human nature did not change, and Woolf knew it. What she meant was that the perception of human nature and of the human condition changed, and that the new perceptions were often expressed in startling and bewildering ways.

Life in the early 20th century seemed suddenly different. New inventions allowed people to travel from place to place with a speed that was never before possible. The telephone, the

Virginia Woolf

radio, and the widespread availability of books, newspapers, and magazines all made people more aware of how others lived and thought. A person living in a remote village learned more about the variety and complexity of life on this planet than even a well-educated person living in a big city had known in the last century. The modern mind found this new knowledge exciting, but it was also bewildered by all the conflicting philosophies and ways of life.

The years from 1910 to 1930 are often called the Era of Modernism, for there seems to have been in both Europe and America a strong awareness of some sort of "break" with the past. Movements in all the arts overlapped and succeeded one another with amazing speed—Imagism, Cubism[179], Dadaism[180],

A picture of Cubism

---

179 In cubist artworks, objects are broken up, analyzed, and re-assembled in an abstracted form—instead of depicting objects from one viewpoint, the artist depicts the subject from a multitude of viewpoints to represent the subject in a greater context. Often the surfaces intersect at seemingly random angles presenting no coherent sense of depth. The background and object planes interpenetrate one another to create the ambiguous shallow space characteristic of cubism.

180 Dadaism or Dada is a cultural movement that began in World War I and peaked from 1916 to 1920. The movement concentrated its anti-war politic through a rejection of the prevailing standards in art. Dada thought that reason and logic had led people into the horrors of war, so the only route to salvation was to reject logic and embrace anarchy and irrationality.

Vorticism[181], and many others. The new artists shared a desire to capture the complexity of modern life, to focus on the variety and confusion of the 20th century by reshaping and sometimes discarding the ideas and habits of the 19th century. The Era of Modernism was indeed the era of the New.

The Lost Generation

The pivotal event of the Modernist era was World War I (1914—1918). Before the war the attitude toward the new century was one of great optimism. America was emerging from 19th century isolation: The Spanish-American War and the opening of the Panama Canal made America a world power; millions of immigrants brought new ideas and ways of life to American shores. Improved communications and transportation made Europe and the East more accessible, and American artists were able to exchange views and share ideas with their colleagues abroad.

Many American writers of this period lived in Europe for part if not all of their lives. Ezra Pound went to London in 1908; Robert Frost visited England a few years later; Gertrude Stein settled in Paris; poet Langston Hughes and playwright Eugene O'Neill traveled the world as merchant seamen. In part because of their widening experience—and in part because of their extraordinary talents—Americans for the first time were in the vanguard of the arts: Pound and T. S. Eliot shaped the poetry of the Modernist era; Stein fostered the early careers of Pablo Picasso and other modern painters.

The European and American artistic communities drew closer together. Pound acted as the London representative of *Poetry: A Magazine of Verse*, an experimental publication begun in Chicago by Harriet Monroe in 1912. The Imagist poems that Pound sent back to Chicago had their effect on Carl Sandburg in the Midwest and Amy Lowell in New England, and in Chicago poets such as Sandburg, Edgar Lee Masters, and Vachel Lindsay now had an influential magazine in which their voices could be heard. O'Neill returned to New York City's Greenwich Village to see his experimental plays performed. Hughes became a leading figure in the burst of creativity called the Harlem Renaissance. Pound encouraged Frost, influenced John Crowe Ransom, and exchanged views with his old college friend William Carlos Williams. Hilda Doolittle published the first volume of Marianne Moore's poetry. Stein assisted Sherwood Anderson and the young Ernest Hemingway. Artists writers taught one another, learned from one another, paid one another's bills, and helped one another bring new works before the public. The travelers came home from Europe and spread the Modernist message throughout America.

It was not simply going abroad, however, that made greatest difference to Americans in Europe: It was the outrage the war itself. World War I was the key event in early 20th century experience, an event that had a profound effect on the optimism that had preceded it. World War I was war on a scale that the world had had never seen, war that destroyed a generation in Europe and led tens of thousands of Americans to early graves. To many, World War I was a tragic failure of old values, of old politics, of old ideas. Now more than ever people felt they must cast off the traditions of the nineteenth century: the need for change was deep, and the mood was often one of confusion and despair. The task of the Modernist writers was, however, not only to express the waste and futility they experienced, they took up the burden of attempting to make some sense of that experience.

---

[181] Vorticism was a short lived British art movement of the early 20th century. It is considered to be the only significant British movement of the early 20th century but lasted less than 3 years. Though the style grew out of Cubism, it is more closely related to Futurism in its embrace of dynamism, the machine age and all things modern. However, Vorticism diverged from Futurism in the way that it tried to capture movement in an image. In a Vorticist painting modern life is shown as an array of bold lines and harsh colors drawing the viewer's eye into the centre of the canvas.

Modernist Literature

When we speak of Modernist literature, we speak of a broad range of artists and movements all seeking, in varying degrees, to break with the style, form, and content of the 19th century. Old ways of seeing, old ways of making sense of experience, just did not seem to work anymore for 20th century writers. "Make it new" was the cry of Ezra Pound, and most other writers of the time worked vigorously and self-consciously to make their poems, plays and novels new and different.

Modern psychology had a profound impact on the literature of the early 20th century, and most great Modernist writers were interested in the workings of the human mind. Ordinary discourse had always put thoughts in a linear, cause-and-effect order: "If this is true and that is true, then this must be true." Now came the recognition that the human mind does not always follow this straight-line pattern; we often think by leaping from association to association in what the psychologist William James called the "stream of consciousness."

Modernists took risks as they wrote in new forms and styles. Eugene O'Neill uses a number of experimental devices to reveal the flow of his characters' thoughts on stage. Ernest Hemingway opens most of his stories in the middle of the "stream," revealing background information as it comes up naturally and not in the long expository sections standard in 19th century fiction. In *The Love Song of J. Alfred Prufrock*, T. S. Eliot attempts to duplicate the "stream" of Prufrock's thoughts in a dramatic monologue. The result is a series of fragments that the reader must piece together.

Modernist literature is often fragmentary, reflecting not only the "stream of consciousness" but the Modernist perception of the 20th century as a jumble of conflicting ideas. Sometimes we are presented with only one fragment, the manner of presentation implying that there is no larger whole; the fragment "is what it is". This is true of Ezra Pound's and Doolittle's Imagist poetry, and of most of the poems of Gertrude Stein. In "This Is Just to Say", for example, Williams presents only a tiny piece of someone's life, but the poem is nevertheless satisfyingly complete; the fragment is enough.

Modernists often insist that their readers participate and draw their own conclusions. Direct statements of abstract ideas or emotions are usually avoided. The Modernist *shows* rather than *tells*. In Hemingway's stories painful and moving experience are coolly recounted by a detached narrator; the reader supplies the emotions and decides why the experiences are significant.

In the attempt to capture the bewilderment of modern life, Modernist literature is sometimes intentionally puzzling. We may sometimes miss the esoteric allusions in the poetry of Pound and Eliot, and we can never be sure why "so much depends" on Williams' red wheelbarrow. The point may be that the mystery itself is the "message". If there is something we do not know, we may not be meant to know it but rather be puzzled by it and so to think about the mystery again and again.

The degrees to which writers of this period adapted Modernist techniques vary greatly. Some writers did take comfort in the pattern and discipline of 19th century literary forms. Edna St. Vincent Millay, for example, continued to write sonnets; much of Robert Frost's poetry is traditionally rhymed and patterned.[182] In content, however, these writers are part of the Modernist era: Their subject matter shows that they could not have been writing at any other time. In fact, one of the most fascinating aspects of Modernist literature is the way each

---

[182] The best example of Robert Frost's poetry in this feature is perhaps "Stopping by Woods on a Snowy Evening", which is familiar to most of American literature learners in China.

individual writer comes to terms with the changes of the time. Each poet or novelist seems to ask, "What does being 'new' mean to me?" The responses of creative individuals produced the great variety of Modernist literature.

The Modernist Achievement

What did the modernists accomplish? They took the first great steps in the search for a new art. They broke out of old forms and styles and generated new ones. They studied the elements of the past that could still be used and showed why the rest had to be put aside. Pound demonstrated the value of ancient Chinese literature; Eliot used the tradition of the English metaphysical poets of the 17th century. They and those who followed them used the past to create a new relationship with a new world. Wallace Stevens called this relationship "the supreme fiction", a way of living in the world, creating it anew every day, and being open to change even as the world itself changes. The Modernist achievement—in poetry, fiction, drama, in music and painting, in psychology and philosophy—lies largely in throwing open for us the doors of possibility.

Ezra Pound (1885—1972)

As an American expatriate poet, musician, and critic, Ezra Weston Loomis Pound was often called "the poet's poet" because of his profound influence on early-to mid-20th century poetry. Ezra Pound, with his expression "Make it new", which served as a rallying cry for the writers of his time, was the driving force behind quite a few Modernist movements, notably Imagism and Vorticism. Pound believed that poetry is the highest of arts, and for more than 50 years his restless mind busied itself seeking new discoveries and innovations in this art. He challenged many of the common views of his time. Yet this self-styled "revolutionist" of the arts was also profoundly conservative, searching history for the "best" and most useful things he could find among the world's literature, religions, philosophies, and social systems. Pound wished to change the world's governments and economics. In this he failed, but he did change the face of literature in his time.

Pound was born in a small town in Idaho, grew up in a suburb of Philadelphia. He once studied languages at the University of Pennsylvania, and befriended there the young William Carlos Williams, who gained later fame as a poet in New York's avant-garde circles. In 1908 Pound left America for Europe, where he traveled widely and remained until 1945.

His early years in London and Paris were a whirlwind of Modernist activity. Inspired by the work of the English poet W. B. Yeats, he went to London because he thought "Yeats knew more about poetry than anybody else". Pound did learn a few poetic skills from Yeats. Meanwhile, he helped "modernize" Yeats' poetry. Before long Pound founded with Richard Aldington (1892—1962) and others the literary "Imagism", and edited its first anthology, *Des Imagistes*. Pound soon lost interest in Imagism, and after disputing with the poet Amy Lowell, Pound called the movement "Amygism". With Wyndham Lewis and the sculptor Henri Gaudier-Brzeska, he founded "Vorticism", which produced a magazine, *Blast*. Pound has also been called the "inventor" of Chinese poetry for our time. Beginning in 1913 with the notebooks of the Orientalist Ernest Fenollosa (who had lived in Japan for quite some time), he pursued a lifelong study of ancient Chinese texts, and translated among others the writings of Confucius.

As the London representative of *Poetry* magazine, Pound helped nurture the careers of many new talents. He championed the Irish novelist James Joyce, became a close friend of T. S. Eliot, and influenced the prose of the young American novelist Ernest Hemingway.

After 1925 Pound made his home in Rapallo, Italy. Here he devoted his life to social-economic thought and to his long poem the *Cantos*, one of the most beautiful but puzzling poems ever written by a great poet.

In Italy Pound became an admirer of Benito Mussolini, and his idealistic but misplaced trust in that dictator had devastating consequences. During World War Ⅱ he broadcast over the Italian radio, foolishly thinking that he was contributing to peace and to a better world. In 1945 US forces arrested him for treason at Genoa and put him for 12 years in Washington, D. C., in a hospital for the criminally insane. It has been suggested that Pound was feigning insanity to escape the death penalty. During this period he received the 1949 Bollingen Prize for his *Pisan Cantos*, which concerned his imprisonment at the camp near Pisa. After he was released, he returned to Italy, where he spent his remaining years. Pound died on November 1, 1972, in Venice.

Pound's style was clear, economical and concrete. "Great literature is simply language charged with meaning to the utmost possible degree," he once said. As an essayist Pound wrote mostly about poetry. He also argued that poetry is not "entertainment", and as an elitist he did not appreciate the common reader.

Pound considered American culture isolated from the traditions that make the arts possible, and depicted Walt Whitman as "exceedingly nauseating pill". Among Pound's most influential works are *ABC of Reading* (1934), which summarized his aesthetic theory and is said to have established the modernist poetic technique.

■ Selected Readings

*Pound said of "**In a Station of the Metro**" : "Three years ago in Paris I got out of a 'metro' train at La Concorde, and saw suddenly a beautiful face, and then another and another, and then a beautiful child's face, and then another beautiful woman, and I tried all that day to find words for what this had meant to me, and I could not find any words that seemed to me worthy, or as lovely as that sudden emotion. And that evening, as I went home along the Rue Raynouard, I was still trying, and I found, suddenly, the expression. I do not mean that I found words, but there came an equation... not in speech, but in little spotches of colour. It was just that—a 'pattern' or hardly a pattern, if by 'pattern' you mean something with a 'repeat' in it. But it was a word, the beginning, for me, of a language in colour. I do not mean that I was unfamiliar with the kindergarten stories about colours being like tones in music. I think that sort of thing is nonsense. If you try to make notes permanently correspond with particular colours, it is like tying narrow meanings to symbols."*

As a matter of fact, Pound tried very hard to find the "words". After a few unsatisfactory attempts that last actually for more than a year, he finally found them and put them down in the following two-line, haiku-like poem.

In a Station of the Metro

The apparition[183] of these faces in the crowd;
Petals on a wet, black bough.

---

[183]   **apparition**: 1) a ghostly figure, a specter; 2) a sudden or unusual sight; 3) the act of appearing, appearance.

■ Study Questions

1. Where does the scene represented in this poem take place?

2. What two images are juxtaposed, or placed next to each other, in the poem?

3. Why does the poem call the faces of pedestrians "apparition"? Why is the word "apparition" used instead of "appearance"?

4. What do "petals" and "bough" stand for respectively?

5. In what way is the poem different from the traditional poems you have read? What makes it "poetic"?

"The River-Merchant's Wife: A Letter" *was published in* 1915 *in Ezra Pound's third collection of poetry, Cathy: Translations, which contains versions of Chinese poems composed from the* 16 *notebooks of Fenollosa. Pound called the poems in English "translations" but they have been acclaimed as "poetry" for their clarity and elegance. Pound's study of the Fenollosa manuscripts led to his preoccupation with the Chinese ideogram as a medium for poetry. In fact, he realized that Chinese poets had long been aware of the image as the fundamental principle for poetic composition that he himself was beginning to formulate. Pound further maintained that the poetic image did not lose anything in translation between languages nor was it bound by time, but effectively communicated through time and across cultures, accruing meaning in the process. "The River-Merchant's Wife: A Letter" (supposed to be the version of "Chang Gan Xing,"《长干行》, by Li Bai, a Chinese poet of Tang Dynasty), for example, communicates with depth and poignancy the human experience of sorrow at separation and the human experience of enduring love. The English poem, as the original Chinese one, tells us that love endures, even in the face of loneliness by describing a married, teenage girl who is lonely as she awaits the return of her traveling-salesman husband.*

Working with the literary traditions of other cultures was typical not only of Pound, but of most of his contemporaries, who were not convinced that the only culture of value was European. However, Pound's work has significance not only for its cross-cultural innovations, but for the "cross-chronological" breakthrough notion that the human response to the world links us all, so that an American in the 20th *century can share and learn from the human experience of an* 8th *century Chinese river-merchant's wife.*

The River-Merchant's Wife: A Letter[184]

While my hair was still cut straight across my forehead
I played about the front gate, pulling flowers.
You came by on bamboo stilts, playing horse,
You walked about my seat, playing with blue plums.
5   And we went on living in the village of Chokan[185]:
Two small people, without dislike or suspicion.

---

[184]   The poem was first published in *Cathy* with the title, "The River-Merchant's Wife: A Letter, By Rihaku." Rihaku is the Japanese form of Li Bai, as the poet based it on the notebook of Fenollosa.

[185]   **Chokan**: It is the transliteration of the Japanese form of Changgan (长干), suburb of Nanjing, an ancient capital by the Yangtze River in China.

At fourteen I married My Lord you.

I never laughed, being bashful.

Lowering my head, I looked at the wall.

10   Called to, a thousand times, I never looked back.

At fifteen I stopped scowling,

I desired my dust to be mingled with yours

Forever and forever and forever.

Why should I climb the look out?

15   At sixteen you departed,

You went into far Ku-to-yen[186], by the river of swirling eddies,

And you have been gone five months.

The monkeys make sorrowful noise overhead.

You dragged your feet when you went out,

20   By the gate now, the moss is grown, the different mosses,

Too deep to clear them away!

The leaves fall early this autumn, in wind.

The paired butterflies are already yellow with August

Over the grass in the West garden;

25   They hurt me. I grow older.

If you are coming down through the narrows of the river Kiang[187], Please

let me know beforehand,

And I will come out to meet you

As far as Cho-fu-Sa[188].

■ Study Questions

1. What form does the poem take? Who is the speaker?

2. At what age did the river-merchant's wife get married? What did she stop doing at fifteen, and what did she desire? What happened when the wife was sixteen?

3. What do the monkeys do in Line 18? What do the butterflies do in Line 25? What does the wife do in Line 25?

---

186   **Ku-to-yen**: In the original Chinese poem, the line reads "瞿塘滟滪堆" and involves two terms of places: "瞿塘" refers to Qutang Gorge, one among the famous Three Gorges along the Yangtze River; "滟滪" used to be a submerged reef at the mouth of Qutang Gorge, and it is in an extremely dangerous state for the passing boats when it merged out of the water and looked like a pile of stones (as is the connotation of the Chinese word "堆"). The version, for some reason, makes a mistake as it treats "瞿塘滟" as a single place and turns it into Ku-to-yen.

187   **river Kiang**: referring to the Yangtze River.

188   **Cho-fa-Sa**: beach along the Yangtze River, a few hundred miles above Nanjing.

4. If her husband tells her when he is coming through the narrows of the river Kiang, what will the wife do?

5. How have the wife's feelings for her husband changed since she married him? How does she feel about her husband's absence?

6. Is monkeys' chattering usually described as it is here? What do the negative descriptions of the monkeys and butterflies reflect?

7. Is the tone of this poem sentimental or matter-of-fact? Cite lines to support your answer.

8. How is the attitude of the wife in this poem different from the attitude expressed in 19th century Romantic poetry that you have read? You may compare it with Poe's "*To Helen*" (Pages 80-81).

T. S. Eliot (1888—1965)

Thomas Stearns Eliot, a poet, dramatist and literary critic, received the Nobel Prize for Literature in 1948. His great reputation lies in his poems "The Love Song of J. Alfred Prufrock" (1915), *The Waste Land* (1922), "The Hollow Men" (1925), "Ash Wednesday" (1930), and *Four Quartets* (1943); the plays *Murder in the Cathedral* (1935) and *The Cocktail Party* (1949); and the essay "Tradition and the Individual Talent". Eliot was born in American, moved to the United Kingdom in 1914 (at the age of 25), became a British subject in 1927 (at the age of 39), and about the same time entered the Anglican Church.

Born into a prominent St. Louis family and educated at Harvard as a student of philosophy, T. S. Eliot first met Ezra Pound in England in 1914. The two men were outwardly different—Pound rough, wild, Bohemia; Eliot the image of a polite, conservatively dressed gentleman—yet together, both as critics and as poets, they did more than anyone else to revolutionize literary tastes in the 20th century.

In London, Eliot's poetic genius was immediately recognized by Pound, who assisted him in the publication of his work in a number of magazines, most notably "The Love Song of J. Alfred Prufrock" in *Poetry*. His first book of poems, *Prufrock and Other Observations*, was published in 1917, and immediately established him as a leading poet of the avant-garde. With the publication of *The Waste Land*, now considered by many to rank with James Joyce's novel *Ulysses* as the greatest success of Modernist movement in Anglo-American literature[189], Eliot's reputation began to grow to nearly mythic proportions; by 1930, and for the next thirty years, he was the most dominant figure in poetry and literary criticism in the English-speaking world.

Eliot has been one of the most daring innovators of the 20th century poetry. Never compromising either with the public or indeed with language itself, he has followed his belief that poetry should aim at a representation of the complexities of modern civilization in language and that such representation necessarily leads to difficult poetry. As a poet, he transmuted his affinity for the English metaphysical poets of the 17th century (most notably John Donne) and the 19th century French symbolist poets (including Baudelaire and Laforgue) into radical innovations in poetic technique and subject matter. His poems, the early ones in particular, in many respects articulated the mental crisis of a younger post-World-War- I generation with the values and conventions—both literary and social—of the

---

189　*The Waste Land* became instantly famous among literary people, many of whom thought that it spoke for the postwar generation in its suggestion that the 20th century was an emotionally and spiritually fragmented period. Few at the time saw the poem's deeply religious concern nor did they recognize that in defining the condition of the modern "waste land", Eliot was searching for something better.

Victorian era.

The crisis marked by *The Waste Land* was resolved for Eliot when he became a devout member of the Church of England. In 1927 he described himself as "classicist in literature, royalist in politics, and Anglo-Catholic in religion" —a remarkable turnaround, for as a Modernist, Eliot was "supposed" to be none of these. His spiritual journey can be traced through his poetry from *Gerontion* (1919), *The Hollow Men*, and *Ash Wednesday*[190] to one of the most profound religious poems in English, *Four Quartets*[191]. However, Eliot has always taken care not to become a religious poet and often belittled the power of poetry as a religious force—like his poems, Eliot the poet has never become less complicated, probably the result of his early study on philosophy that had almost offered him a doctorate degree.

In his later years Eliot worked for a large British publishing house. Meanwhile he wrote plays, many of them in verse. His plays *Murder in the Cathedral*, *The Family Reunion* (1939), *The Cocktail Party*, *The Confidential Clerk* (1954), and *The Elder States Man* (1959) were published in one volume in 1962, one year before his *Collected Poems* 1909—1962 appeared. He was among the few Modernist writers who made good use of blank verse. Eliot also contributed a substantial body of literary criticism and rested much of his literary reputation in this respect. His books of literary and social criticism include *The Sacred Wood* (1920), *The Use of Poetry and the Use of Criticism* (1933), *After Strange Gods* (1934), and *Notes Towards the Definition of Culture* (1940). In his essays, especially the later ones, Eliot advocated a traditionalism in religion, society, and literature that seems at odds with his pioneer activity as a poet. But although the Eliot of *Notes Towards the Definition of Culture* (1948) is an older man than the poet of *The Waste Land*, it should not be forgotten that for Eliot tradition is a living organism comprising past and present in constant mutual interaction.

Eliot was awarded the Nobel Prize in 1948 and died in London in 1965. During these years, he achieved a personal happiness that at last matched the pleasure he derived from his public life as the leading man of letters of his time.

■ Selected Reading

*"**The Love Song of J. Alfred Prufrock**" is an early poem by T. S. Eliot but is marked by an assurance in phrasing that has made many of its lines almost proverbial in our century. Its now-famous opening lines, comparing the evening sky to "a patient etherised upon a table", were considered shocking and offensive, especially at a time when the poetry of the Georgians was hailed for its derivations of the 19th century Romantic Poets. The poem is a dramatic monologue (relayed in the "stream of consciousness" form indicative of the Modernists) spoken by one J. Alfred Prufrock, whose very name seems to combine the dignity and absurdity of his public and private selves. The*

---

190 The poem is the first long poem written by Eliot after his 1927 conversion to Anglicanism. With a base of Dante's *Purgatorio*, It is richly but ambiguously allusive and deals with the aspiration to move from spiritual barrenness to hope for human salvation. The style is different from his poetry which predates his conversion. "*Ash Wednesday*" and the poems that followed had a more casual, melodic, and contemplative method.

191 Although many critics preferred his earlier work, Eliot and many other critics considered *Four Quartets* his masterpiece and it is the work which led to his receipt of the Nobel Prize. The *Four Quartets* draws upon his knowledge of mysticism and philosophy. It consists of four long poems, published separately: *Burnt Norton* (1936), *East Coker* (1940), *The Dry Salvages* (1941) and *Little Gidding* (1942), each in five sections. Although they resist easy characterization, each begins with a rumination on the geographical location of its title, and each meditates on the nature of time in some important respect— theological, historical, physical—and its relation to the human condition. Also, each is associated with one of the four classical elements: air, earth, water, and fire. They approach the same ideas in varying but overlapping ways, and are open to a diversity of interpretations.

poem follows Prufrock's conscious experience, lamenting his physical and intellectual inertia, the lost opportunities in his life and lack of spiritual progress, with the recurrent theme of carnal love unattained. Critical opinion is divided as to whether the narrator even leaves his own residence during the course of the narration. The locations described can be interpreted either as actual physical experiences, mental recollections or even as symbolic images from the subconscious mind, as, for example, in the refrain "In the room the women come and go". The poem's structure was heavily influenced by Eliot's extensive reading of Dante's Alighieri (in the Italian). References to Shakespeare's Hamlet and other literary works are present in the poem: this technique of **allusion** and **quotation** was developed in Eliot's subsequent poetry.

The Love Song of J. Alfred Prufrock

S'io credesse che mia risposta fosse
A persona che mai tornasse al mondo,
Questa fiamma staria senza piu scosse.
Ma perciocche giammai di questo fondo
Non torno vivo alcun, s'i'odo il vero,
Senza tema d'infamia ti rispondo[192]

Let us go then, you and I[193],
When the evening is spread out against the sky
Like a patient etherized upon a table;
Let us go, through certain half-deserted streets,
5   The muttering retreats[194]
Of restless nights in one-night cheap hotels[195]
And sawdust[196] restaurants with oyster-shells:
Streets that follow like a tedious argument
Of insidious intent[197]

---

[192] **S'io credesse… ti rispondo**: Its English version may run as follows, "If I believed my answer were being made / to one who could ever return / to the world, this flame would gleam no more; / but since, if what I hear is true, never from this abyss did living man return, / I answer thee without fear of infamy." In Dante's *Divine Comedy* (Inferno 27. 61～66), Guido de Montefeltro, shut up in the flame (punishment for giving false counsel), tells the shame of his evil life to Dante because he believes Dante will never return to earth to report it. Eliot suggests that Prufrock is also making a confession in this poem.

[193] **you and I**: The explanation greatly diverges. Some critics believe they are the two selves of Prufrock—a person who outwardly is a "proper" member of the "best" society, but who inwardly is lost, lonely, and suffering. The poet declared that "you" indicates an "unidentified male companion." Still some others regard "you" as a general reference to the reader.

[194] **muttering retreats**: the isolated places where people are gossiping in a low unclear voice.

[195] **one-night cheap hotels**: hotels of poor condition where one would stay for only one night.

[196] **sawdust**: used to absorb spilled beverages and food, making it easy to sweep up at the end of the day.

[197] **Streets… intent**: Going down such streets (an image that reveals the state of the poet's mind) is like being involved in a tiresome but maliciously plotted argument.

10　To lead you to an overwhelming question[198]...

　　Oh, do not ask, "What is it?"

　　Let us go and make our visit.

　　In the room the women come and go

　　Talking of Michelangelo.[199]

15　The yellow fog[200] that rubs its back upon the windowpanes,

　　The yellow smoke that rubs its muzzle on the windowpanes

　　Licked its tongue into the corners of the evening,

　　Lingered upon the pools that stand in drains,

　　Let fall upon its back the soot that falls from chimneys,

20　Slipped by the terrace, made a sudden leap,

　　And seeing that it was a soft October night,

　　Curled once about the house, and fell asleep.[201]

　　And indeed there will be time[202]

　　For the yellow smoke that slides along the street,

25　Rubbing its back upon the windowpanes;

　　There will be time, there will be time

　　To prepare a face to meet the faces that you meet;

　　There will be time to murder and create,

198　**overwhelming question**: very important question. Eliot appears to have borrowed this phrase from James Fenimore Cooper's 1823 novel, *The Pioneers*, in which one of the characters, Benjamin, asks a series of questions ending with the "overwhelming question".

199　**In the room... Michelangelo**: At a social gathering in a room, women discuss the Renaissance artist Michelangelo. These two lines repeat themselves a few times in the poem, paralleling Prufrock's going in the street. To Prufrock, the women speaking of the great artist may have no interest in him. To a conscious and keen reader, however, women talking of Michelangelo to show their gentility are part of the "streets".

200　**The yellow fog**: Yellow fog or smoke of the sordid city was a familiar detail in French symbolism. Yellow is the color of barrenness and timidity, which, in this line, intensifies the sense of the city as a wasteland.

201　Smoky haze, which is like a quiet, timid cat, spreads across the city. The speaker resembles the cat as he looks into windows or into "the room", trying to decide whether to enter and become part of the activity. Eventually, he curls up in the safety and security of his own soft arms—alone, separately.

202　**there will be time**: there's no hurry. The repetition of these words may indirectly refer to *Ecclesiastes* of the *Old Testament*: For everything there is an appointed season, and there is a proper time for every project under heaven. Some believe that this phrase replies to the opening line of "To His Coy Mistress", by Andrew Marvell (1621—1678): "Had we but world enough, and time." In Marvell's poem, the speaker urges his beloved not to be coy but instead to seize the moment—to take advantage of youth and "sport us while we may". Prufrock, however, continually postpones even meeting a woman, saying "there will be time".

And time for all the works and days[203] of hand

30 That lift and drop a question on your plate;

Time for you and time for me,

And time yet for a hundred indecisions,

And for a hundred visions and revisions,

Before the taking of a toast and tea.

35 In the room the women come and go

Talking of Michelangelo. [204]

And indeed there will be time

To wonder, "Do I dare?" and, "Do I dare?"

Time to turn back and descend the stair,

40 With a bald spot in the middle of my hair

(They will say: "How his hair is growing thin!")

My morning coat, my collar mounting firmly to the chin,

My necktie rich and modest, but asserted by a simple pin[205]

(They will say: "But how his arms and legs are thin!")

45 Do I dare

Disturb the universe?

In a minute there is time

For decisions and revisions which a minute will reverse.

For I have known them all already, known them all—

50 Have known the evenings, mornings, afternoons[206],

I have measured out my life with coffee spoons;

---

[203] **works and days**: "Works and Days" is a long poem by Hesiod, a Greek writer who lived in the 700's B. C. Here the line means there is enough time for what one wants to do.

[204] The repetition suggests that life is repetitive and dull.

[205] **simple pin**: pin inserted through the tie and shirt to hold the tie in place.

[206] **evenings, mornings, afternoons**: This phrase, as well as others focusing on time, refers obliquely to the philosophy of Henri Bergson (1859—1941), author of a revolutionary and highly influential work, "Time and Free Will: An Essay on the Immediate Data of Consciousness". In this work, he argued that the mind perceives time as a continuous process, a continuous flow, rather than as a series of measurable units as tracked by a clock or a calendar or by scientific calculation. It is not a succession, with one unit following another, but a duration in which present and past are equally real. Ordinarily, we think of a day as consisting of morning, afternoon, and evening—in that order. But, since time is a continuous flow to Prufrock, it is just as correct to think of a day as consisting of evening, morning, and afternoon. Besides, morning does follow evening.

I know the voices dying with a dying fall[207]

Beneath the music from a farther room.

So how should I presume?

55   And I have known the eyes already, known them

The eyes that fix you in a formulated phrase,[208]

And when I am formulated, sprawling on a pin,

When I am pinned and wriggling on the wall,

Then how should I begin

60   To spit out all the butt-ends of my days and ways?[209]

And how should I presume?

And I have known the arms already, known them all—

Arms that are braceleted and white and bare

(But in the lamplight, downed with light brown hair!)

65   Is it perfume from a dress

That makes me so digress[210]?

Arms that lie along a table, or wrap about a shawl.

And should I then presume?

And how should I begin?

...

70   Shall I say, I have gone at dusk through narrow streets

And watched the smoke that rises from the pipes

Of lonely men in shirtsleeves, leaning out of windows? ...

I should have been a pair of ragged claws

Scuttling across the floors of silent seas. [211]

...

75   And the afternoon, the evening, sleeps so peacefully!

---

207   **I know... dying fall**: I recognized that the voices were characterized with a falling tone and were fading in the music from a distant room. "Dying fall" is a phrase borrowed from Shakespeare's *Twelfth Night*. Duke Orsino speaks it in Line 4 of Act I, Scene I.

208   **The eyes... phrase**: The (contemptuous) women stare at you impolitely and greet you with boring words (making you feel like a small insect pinned on the wall to be studied by others.

209   In this line, Prufrock compares the rest part of his life to butt-ends (cigar or cigarette ends) and doubts how he could get out of futility.

210   **digress**: turn away or wander from the topic in speech. This line indicates Prufrock's failure to have sexual impulse in his wild imagination. Thus Prufrock, as a man, is not only timid by nature, but also sexually impotent.

211   **I should... seas**: Prufrock is tired of the human world and is likely to be a crab that "scuttling" across the seabed rather than venturing in this world to make various decisions.

Smoothed by long fingers,

Asleep... tired... or it malingers[212],

Stretched on the floor, here beside you and me.

Should I, after tea and cakes and ices,

80　Have the strength to force the moment to its crisis[213]?

But though I have wept and fasted, wept and prayed,

Though I have seen my head (grown slightly bald) brought in upon a platter,[214]

I am no prophet-and here's no great matter;

I have seen the moment of my greatness flicker,

85　And I have seen the eternal Footman[215] hold my coat, and snicker,

And in short, I was afraid.

And would it have been worth it, after all,

After the cups, the marmalade, the tea,

90　Among the porcelain, among some talk of you and me,

Would it have been worthwhile,

To have bitten off the matter with a smile,

To have squeezed the universe into a ball[216]

To roll it toward some overwhelming question,

95　To say: "I am Lazarus[217], come from the dead,

212　**malingers**: pretends to be ill in order to avoid work or duty.

213　**to force... crisis**: to regard the moment as the crisis time; to have his crucial question asked.

214　**Though... platter**: This line involves an allusion to the story about John the Baptist: Jewish prophet of the First Century A. D. who urged people to reform their lives and who prepared the way for the coming of Jesus as the Messiah. John denounced Herod Antipas (4 B. C. —39 A. D.), the Roman-appointed ruler of Galilee and Perea, for violating the law of Moses by marrying Herodias, the divorced wife of his half-brother, Philip. (Herod Antipas and Philip were sons of Herod the Great, the Roman-appointed ruler of Judea.) In retaliation, Herod Antipas imprisoned John but was afraid to kill him because of his popularity with the people. Salome, the daughter of Herodias and stepdaughter of Herod Antipas, danced at a birthday party for Herod Antipas. Her performance was so enthralling that Herod said she could have any reward of her choice. Prompted by Herodias, who was outraged by John the Baptist's condemnation of her marriage, Salome asked for the head of the Baptist on a platter. Because he did not want to go back on his word, Herod fulfilled her request. John was a cousin of Mary, the mother of Jesus. Accounts of his activities appear in the Bible in the gospels of Matthew, Mark, Luke, and John and in the Acts of the Apostles.

215　**Footman**: Death as someone who helps a person into the afterlife.

216　**To... Ball**: This phrase is another allusion to Marvell's "To His Coy Mistress" (See Note 14). In the last stanza of that poem, the speaker says, "Let us roll all our strength and all / Our sweetness up into one ball. " In Eliot's poem, the speaker asks whether it would have been worth it to do the same thing with a woman of his choosing.

217　**Lazarus**: Name of two *New Testament* figures: 1) Lazarus of Bethany, brother of Martha and Mary. Jesus raised him from the dead (*Gospel of John*, 11: 18, 30, 32, 38); 2) Lazarus, a leprous beggar (*Gospel of Luke*, 16: 19-31). When Lazarus died, he was taken into heaven. When a rich man named Dives died, he went to hell. He requested that Lazarus be returned to earth to warn his brothers about the horror of hell, but his request was denied.

Come back to tell you all, I shall tell you all" —

If one, settling a pillow by her head,

Should say: "That is not what I meant at all.

That is not it, at all. "

100 And would it have been worth it, after all,

Would it have been worthwhile,

After the sunsets and the door-yards and the sprinkled streets[218],

After the novels, after the teacups, after the skirts that trail along the floor —

And this, and so much more? —

105 It is impossible to say just what I mean!

But as if a magic lantern[219] threw the nerves in patterns on a screen:

Would it have been worthwhile

If one, settling a pillow or throwing off a shawl,

And turning toward the window, should say:

110 "That is not it at all,

That is not what I meant, at all. "

...

No! I am not Prince Hamlet[220], nor was meant to be;

Am an attendant lord[221], one that will do

To swell a progress, start a scene or two,

115 Advise the prince; no doubt, an easy tool,

Deferential, glad to be of use,

Politic, cautious, and meticulous;

Full of high sentence, but a bit obtuse;

At times, indeed, almost ridiculous—

120 Almost, at times, the Fool.

I grow old... I grow old...

---

218   **sprinkled streets**: refers to the practice of wetting dirt streets with oil or water to control dust.

219   **magic lantern**: early type of slide projector. The magic lantern (also called sciopticon) projected an image from a glass plate.

220   **Hamlet**: The protagonist of Shakespeare's *Hamlet, Prince of Denmark*, famous for his hesitancy and indecision while plotting to avenge the murder of his father, King Hamlet, by the king's brother, Claudius. Prufrock is like young Hamlet in that the latter is also indecisive. However, Prufrock decides not to compare himself with Hamlet, who is charismatic and even majestic in spite of his shortcomings, but with an attendant lord.

221   **an attendant lord**: a minor figure. It's an allusion to Polonius, the lord chamberlain in *Hamlet, Prince of Denmark*. Polonius, a bootlicking advisor to the new king, Claudius, sometimes uses a whole paragraph of important-sounding words to say what most other people could say in a simple declarative sentence. His pedantry makes him look foolish at times.

I shall wear the bottoms of my trousers rolled. [222]

Shall I part my hair behind? Do I dare to eat a peach?

I shall wear white flannel trousers, and walk upon the peach. [223]

125 I have heard the mermaids[224] singing, each to each.

I do not think that they will sing to me. [225]

I have seen them riding seaward on the waves,

Combing the white hair of the waves blown back

When the wind blows the water white and black.

130 We have lingered in the chambers of the sea

By sea-girls wreathed with seaweed red and brown

Till human voices wake us, and we drown. [226]

■ Study Questions

1. According to Lines 1-14, What are "you and I" going out to "make"? What do the streets lead to? For what does Prufrock say there will be time in Line 27? In Lines 32-34?

2. According to Lines 37-46, what would Prufrock "disturb" if he dared to ask his question? Why "in short" doesn't Prufrock "force the moment to its crisis" (lines 75-86)? What remark by someone "settling a pillow" would make asking the question not worthwhile (Lines 87-98)?

3. After he fails to ask his question, who does Prufrock say he is and is not (Lines 111-119)?

4. Whom has Prufrock heard singing, according to Lines 124-131? What does he think these creatures will not do?

5. What do the opening quotation from Dante, the descriptions of the fog, and the simile in Line 3 suggest about Prufrock's mood or feelings?

6. Reread Lines 10-11, 45-46, 80, and 93-94. What do these lines suggest about Prufrock's opinion of the question he considers asking? What does the title suggest about the question? What is Prufrock trying to avoid when he keeps saying "there will be time" in Lines 23-48?

7. Why would Prufrock think of himself as "you and I," or "we"? What do the following lines reveal about Prufrock's view of his life and his self-image: the opening quotation, Lines 51, 73-74, 82, and 85?

---

[222] **wear... rolled**: roll up the bottom of the trousers (as one become shorter when he grows old).

[223] The speaker realizes that time is passing and that he is growing old. However, like other men going through a middle-age crisis, he considers changing his hairstyle and clothes.

[224] **mermaids**: probably an allusion to the sirens in Homer's *Odyssey*.

[225] Like Odysseus in the *Odyssey*, he has heard the song of the sirens. However, they are not singing to him. In other words, he is not confident enough to be lured by the mermaids.

[226] In Western legends, the sirens had the power to lure men to visit them in caves beneath the sea; but when their singing stopped the spell was broken, and the men would drown. Therefore, when "human voices wake us", the singing of the mermaids is stopped and "we drown".

8. How would Prufrock be like Lazarus if he asked the question? In not asking the question, why is he unlike Hamlet?

9. What do the images in Lines 121-123 suggest about the future Prufrock foresees for himself? Is this future different from his past?

10. How are the mermaids unlike the women Prufrock visits? Why is it significant that Prufrock hears the mermaids? Why does Prufrock think that they will not sing for him?

11. In what ways are we all like Prufrock some of the time? Why might a middle-aged person in particular identify with him?

12. Tell how this poem helps explain why the young Eliot called the modern world a "waste land" and why Gertrude Stein called the young generation who had fought in World War I a "lost generation".

William Carlos Williams (1883—1963)

Dr. William Carlos Williams (sometimes known as WCW), an American poet and practicing pediatrician, delivered over 2,000 babies and wrote poems on his prescription pads. A classmate of Ezra Pound, WCW in his early poetry reveals the influence of imagism. He later went on to champion the use of colloquial speech; his ear for the natural rhythms of American English helped free American poetry from the iambic meter that dominated English verse since the Renaissance. His sympathy for ordinary working people,  children, and everyday events in modem urban settings make his poetry attractive and accessible.

Williams was born in Rutherford, New Jersey. From 1897 to 1899 he was schooled in Switzerland, with some time in Paris. In 1902 he graduated from high school in New York and was accepted into the dental school of the University of Pennsylvania, but soon transferred to the medical school. There began his long-lived friendships with Ezra Pound, H. D. (Hilda Doolittle), and artist Charles Demuth, which did much to intensify an interest in writing poetry. Because his mother was an artist, Williams tried painting. After his study in Germany, Williams took up the job of doctor. Almost all his life he remained in Rutherford where he continued his medical practice until poor health forced him to retire.

For Williams, poetry writing is of primary importance while medical practice is a must for survival. In 1909, Williams published his first poetry collection, *Poems*; in 1913, Elkin Mathews, Pound's publisher, published a second collection, *The Tempers*, in London. These early poems were Romantic verses in style of traditional 19th century English poetry. When Williams sent Pound a copy of an early book of his verse, Pound wrote back from London with kindly but severe criticism: "Your book," he said, "would not attract even passing attention here. There are fine lines in it, but nowhere I think do you add anything to the poets you have used as models."

Within a few years, however, Williams developed his own style and achieved his own voice. Never again was he an imitator. He became a Modernist and initially an Imagist. Similar to Ezra Pound, Williams endeavored to "make it new" from the very beginning. In 1914, some of his poems were collected in *Des Imagistes* which was the first anthology of Imagism. Though the influence of Imagism stayed throughout William's career, he felt dissatisfied with these poetic principles and turned to objectivism soon. He regarded poetry as a thing like a cubist painting or a symphony which dealt with concrete particulars and let the ideas take care of themselves. His purpose was not to point a moral or teach a lesson; rather, he wanted his readers to see through his eyes the beauty of the real as he said, "No ideas but in things". In his best work he makes us think that a poem is just right—neither a word too few nor a word too much. His poem is to capture an instant of time like an imposed snapshot—a concept he derived

from photographers and artists he met at galleries. Like photographs, his poems often hint at hidden possibilities or attractions.

A great lover of everyday American life, Williams was deeply influenced by Whitman's literary theory. He believed that American poetry must be rooted in America as its source of subject matter. Unlike Pound and Eliot, Williams celebrated the world before his eyes and scorned allusions to history, religion, and ancient literature. He often wrote of his patients and neighbors, working-class men and women in the industrialized section of New Jersey near the town of Paterson. As a whole, his poetry reflected America in the process of urbanization and industrialization, a disapproval of Pound and Eliot's internationalism. His observations are contained in *Paterson* (1946—1958), a poem of epic length filled with delightful glimpses of urban American life. Another major work, *In the American Grain* (1925), explores the mythic greatness of famous Americans.

Williams lived long in the shadow of Pound and Eliot. However, his lifelong endeavor to be different finally brought about recognition. His reputation as a poet has risen dramatically since World War II when a younger generation of poets testified to the influence of his work on their career. His works were mainly collected in *Sour Grapes* (1921), *Spring and All* (1923), *The Desert Music* (1954), *The Journey of Love* (1955), *Collected Poems* (1921—1931), *Complete Poems* (1906—1938, 1938), *Collected Later Poems* (1950), and *Pictures from Brueghel* (1962). And now he is judged to be among the best and most important poets writing between the wars.

■ Selected Readings

"The Red Wheelbarrow" *is one of the masterpieces of William Carlos Williams. It is a simplest poem composed of one sentence broken up at various intervals. It is truthful to say that "so much depends upon" each line of the poem as the form of the poem is also its meaning.*

The poem presents a single image—a rain-glazed wheelbarrow and some chickens beside. It is a bright colored picture of everyday life: The contrast of the white chicken beside the red wheelbarrow is a testament to the colors of the world we live in and that fall within the spectrum of our site. In keeping with Imagist principles, it does not explain the picture. Yet, when a picture is composed of words, it is presented as if seeing a film, one frame after another, with few differences to each but changes distinguish themselves gradually from solemnity to liveliness. In his statement that the objects themselves are important, the poet implies that the observing and imaginative experience of the objects is of equal importance. Williams, then as a representative imagists, through the "fresh daily" image, convey to the reader his poetic preference to "No idea but in things".

The Red Wheelbarrow

so much
depends upon

a red wheel
barrow

5   glazed with rain
water

beside the white

chickens.

■ Study Questions

1. What three items are mentioned in the poem? What does the first line tell us about them?

2. Why might the objects in the poem be very important? Can we be sure? Explain.

3. What elements of Imagism does this poem exhibit? What elements of Modernist literature in general does the poem display?

*About "**The Great Figure**", Williams in his Autobiography writes: "Once on a hot July day coming back exhausted from the Post Graduate Clinic, I dropped in as I sometimes did at Marsden [Hartley]'s studio on Fifteenth Street for a talk, a little drink maybe and to see what he was doing. As I approached his number, I heard a great clatter of bells and the roar of a fire engine passing the end of the street down Ninth Avenue. I turned just in time to see a golden figure 5 on a red background flash by. The impression was so sudden and forceful that I took a piece of paper out of my pocket and wrote a short poem about it." By describing the experience of seeing a fire truck passing on a rainy night, the poet reveals that life offers sudden moments when a shape and a color strike us as unforgettable.*

The Great Figure

The Figure 5 in Gold By Charles Demuth (1883—1935)

Among the rain

and lights

I saw the figure 5

in gold

5　on a red

firetruck

moving

tense

unheeded

10　to gong clangs

siren howls

and wheels rumbling

through the dark city.

■ Study Questions

1. According to the title, what sort of figure is the figure 5?

2. On what is the figure 5 printed? What color is it?

3. How is the figure 5 moving? Through what is it moving?

4. Explain how the figure 5 can literally be "moving tense".

5. Why is it significant that the figure 5 is "in gold"? And why is it significant that the city is "dark"?

6. By whom is the figure 5 "unheeded"? Is it really unheeded? Why?

7. What does this poem suggest about beauty? About modern life?

8. Based on the poems by Williams that you have read, what generalization would you make about his subject matter? Do you find his poems "poetic"? Why or why not?

Pieter Brueghel: *Kermess*

(1567—1568)

"*The Dance*" consists of 12 *lines of rhythmic verse written in response to a painting by Pieter Brueghel the Elder (1525—1569). The painting, "Kermess" ("Peasant Dance"), depicts sturdy, well-fed peasants on holiday — dancing, drinking, making music, venting the sexual impulse, and abandoning themselves to the spirit of carnival. Williams' poem, through concrete visual and auditory images and through the strong, measured rhythm, captures the hearty vitality that the painting evokes.*

The Dance

In Breughel's[227] great picture, The Kermess[228],

the dancers go round, they go round and

around, the squeal and the blare and the

tweedle of bagpipes, a bugle and fiddles

5   tipping their bellies, (round as the thick-

sided glasses whose wash they impound[229])

their hips and their bellies off balance

to turn them. Kicking and rolling about

the Fair Grounds, swinging their butts, those

10   shanks must be sound to bear up under such

rollicking[230] measures, prance as they dance

in Breughel's great picture, The Kermess

■ Study Questions

1. What is the scene the poem portrays?

2. This poem depicts some motions, sounds, and shapes. Which words present sounds? Which describes motions? Which are for shapes?

3. Is the music to which the people dance professional and melodious? Is their dancing professional? How do we know?

4. Identify six poetic devices that help the poet capture the dancing or its musical accompaniment.

5. What does the poet seem to admire about Breughel's painting?

6. The poem is certainly free verse. How does the form show Williams' idea of speaking as a common America?

7. Compare the painting by Breughel with the description in "The Dance". What visual details has the poet captured in words?

---

[227] **Breughel**: Pieter Breughel, Flemish painter. He is an expert at revealing farmer's life.

[228] **The Kermess**: Refers to the painting *The Wedding Dance* by Breughel; kermess: bazaar in the open air.

[229] **wash they impound**: Liquid they drink.

[230] **rollicking**: Carefree and high-spirited; boisterous.

Robert Frost (1874—1963)

Robert Lee Frost, a poet of dignity, simplicity, and ambiguity, has proved to be one of the most popular American poets of the 20th century. A four-time winner of the Pulitzer Prize, in 1960 Frost received from Congress a gold medal for his contribution to American culture and the following January, at age 86, had the honor of reciting at President John F. Kennedy's inauguration. [231] Actually, during his life time, Frost won almost all the great honors a poet can receive in this world, except the Nobel Prize. His works have been translated into most foreign languages and are being continually enjoyed all over the world.

Born in San Francisco, Frost returned in early youth with his family to the country area which he is closely associated—New England. There he stayed for most of his life time and made its experience the subject matter of most of his poems, earning himself the name Poet of New England. Frost's mother, who wrote poetry herself, introduced him to the works of the English Romantic writers, the New England Transcendentalists, and the poets of her native Scotland. After briefly attending Dartmouth and Harvard colleges and working as a journalist and a schoolteacher, Frost purchased a farm in New Hampshire. Here, between farm chores, he began his career as a poet.

Frost wrote not only of the natural world but also of his snuggle to raise a family against a backdrop of financial hardship and of the bleak bouts of depression that would assail him all his life. In 1912, unable to get his poems published in America, he sold his farm and took his family to England.

In London Frost became acquainted with Ezra Pound and his associates, and he was able to publish his first volume, *A Boy's Will*, in 1913. Another volume, *North of Boston*, followed soon after. Through the influence of Pound and other critics, Frost became known on this side of the Atlantic, so that, by the time he returned to America in 1915, he was well on the road to fame.

Despite the debt of gratitude he owed Pound and the Modernists, Frost never subscribed to all the tenets of Modernism. To be sure, he was familiar with the ideas of William James and other modern psychologists, but he was equally familiar with the works of Bryant, Emerson, and other 19th century masters. In Frost's work we find traces of the Romantic love of nature that marked the literature of the 19th century coupled with a modern sense of irony. We find in Frost's poems some of Thoreau's love of isolation, Hawthorne's dark vision, Longfellow's traditional craftsmanship, Dickinson's dry humor, and Robinson's realistic characterization.

Eclectic in many ways, Frost is nevertheless able to achieve a quiet, reflective New England voice all his own. He speaks a common speech, unaffected, a modern Plain Style. His voice rings in poems that puzzle over many of the same thought-provoking questions that American poets have always explored, but Frost's poems display a 20th century poet's uncertainty about what the answers to those questions maybe.

■ Selected Readings

*"**Stopping by Woods on a Snowy Evening**" presents a picture of tranquility: On a winter evening, a sleigh driver stopped by a wood while everything is covered with snow. The traveler is enjoying a momentary relaxation on the onerous journey of life. The woods, appearing in peace and harmony, are lovely, but "dark and deep" — they also present the temptation of death. The traveler, probably the poet as well, was for a while attracted by this mixed*

231   What he recited was "The Gift Outright".

scene. Fortunately, his former promises reminded him of his responsibility in the world and he was thus detached from the scene. Implying an analogy between the traveler's actions in the poem and a person's journey through life, the poet reveals that, in the hard struggle of life, people would feel tired and desire to have a momentary relief from the obligations of the world.

Stopping by Woods on a Snowy Evening

Whose woods[232] these are I think I know.
His house is in the village though;
He will not see me stopping here
To watch his woods fill up with snow[233].

5   My little horse must think it queer
To stop without a farmhouse near
Between the woods and frozen lake
The darkest evening of the year.

He gives his harness bells a shake
10   To ask if there is some mistake.
The only other sound's the sweep
Of easy wind and downy flake[234].

The woods are lovely, dark and deep[235].
But I have promises to keep,
15   And miles to go before I sleep,
And miles to go before I sleep.

■ Study Questions

1. What causes the speaker to stop?
2. What do the owner of the woods and the horse have in common? How do they differ from the speaker?
3. It is extremely important to select the right word, with the most appropriate connotation, to present a thought or an image. Why do you suppose Frost chose to use *woods* instead of *the forest*? Why did he choose *easy* instead of *gentle* in Stanza 3?
4. Why does the speaker leave the woods? Does he regret leaving?
5. What might the incident in the woods represent? What might Lines 15-16, especially "miles to go" and "before I sleep" mean?

---

232   **woods**: An image frequently appears in Frost's poems, symbolizing the mystery of nature, death or catastrophe.
233   **snow**: Another frequent image in Frost's poems, symbolizing something of purity and loftiness.
234   **downy flake**: The soft and finely patterned snow flakes.
235   **dark and deep**: An alliterated phrase that enhances the mysterious atmosphere of woods in darkness.

6. Describe the rhyme scheme of the poem. How is the poem "knit" to a close?

*As we have seen, Robert Frost is a master of pulling a thread out of what looks like quite a simple theme. "**The Road Not Taken**" begins with the observation of nature. Yet by the end, all the simple words condense into a serious, philosophical proposition: anyone in life confronted with making a choice has to give up something desirable in order to get another. Then, whatever follows, he must accept the consequence of his choice for it is not possible for him to return to the beginning and have another chance to choose differently. Frost is asserting that nature is fair and honest to everyone. Thus all the varieties of human destiny result from each person's spontaneous capability of making choices.*

Some also view it as a symbolic poem. The "yellow wood" may symbolize sophisticated society, in which most people are likely to follow a profitable and easier way; each "road" symbolizes a possibility in life; the "traveler" is the embodiment of every individual in the human world; the road which is "grassy and wanted wear" refers to a solitary life style; while "way leads to way" implies the complicated circumstances of the human world. Through the description of "The Road Not Taken", the poet presents to the reader his experience of making a choice. With simple words and profound connotation, Robert Frost teaches delightfully in the form of a natural poem.

The Road Not Taken

Two roads diverged[236] in a yellow wood[237],
And sorry I could not travel both
And be one traveler, long I stood
And looked down one as far as I could
5 To where it bent[238] in the undergrowth.

Then took the other, as just as fair[239],
And having perhaps the better claim[240],
Because it was grassy and wanted wear[241];
Though as for that the passing there
10 Had worn them really about the same. [242]

And both that morning equally lay
In leaves no step had trodden black.

---

236 **diverged**: went out in different directions.
237 **yellow wood**: an implication of the season of autumn.
238 **bent**: turned away; disappeared.
239 **as just as fair**: (the second road looks) in the same condition as the first one. My choice of the second road is as reasonable as the choice of the first.
240 **the better claim**: a better reason.
241 **wanted wear**: (the other road is) not quite worn out; (it appears) isolated, less trodden.
242 **Though as for that... the same**: For this reason (being wanted wear), however, many people have also chosen to take the second road so that the two roads have been trodden in almost the same degree, neither is better than the other.

Oh, I kept the first for another day!

Yet knowing how way leads on to way[243],

15　I doubted if I should ever come back.

I shall be telling this with a sigh

Somewhere ages and ages hence:

Two roads diverged in a wood, and I—

I took the one less traveled by,

20　And that has made all the difference.

■ Study Questions

1. What diverged in the yellow wood? About what was the speaker sorry in the first stanza? Where does the speaker stand and look?

2. For what did the speaker "keep" the first road? What did he doubt?

3. How does the speaker think he will be telling this story "ages and ages hence"? What has "made all the differences"?

4. Considering Lines 9-10 and 11-12, how different were the two roads? What is Frost therefore saying?

5. What might the roads represent? What does his choice indicate about the speaker?

6. Does the speaker think he made the wrong choice? Why or why not? How is his attitude related to the title?

7. This poem is usually interpreted as an assertion of individualism, but critic Lawrence Thompson has argued that it is a slightly mocking satire on a perennially hesitant walking partner of Frost's who always wondered what would have happened if he had chosen their path differently. What evidence can you find in the poem to support each of these views?

"*Mending Wall*," *like most of Frost's poems, describes a chore about New England country life: two neighbors meet every spring to mend the wall between the lands of the two families. While "I" believe "There where it is we do not need the wall", "he" insists "Good fences make good neighbors". Again, like his other poems, "Mending Wall" is highly philosophical. Yet the meaning of the poem seems quite ambiguous—people argue against each other on whether the poet agrees on the Neighbor's reply as they are not certain about the symbolic meaning of the Wall. Now it is generally accepted that the Wall is a symbol of the many barriers between people. By this symbol, the poet means to show that people need to be separate individuals as well as members of a community. The establishment of these barriers is usually for the maintenance of normal social order, but too many barriers may also break the natural between individuals. Thus people frequently have a mixed impulse to break down the Wall they are mending, as is the common experience of human beings.*

243　**way leads on to way**: one road may branch into several minor ways.

Mending Wall

Something there is that doesn't love a wall,

That sends[244] the frozen-ground-swell[245] under it

And spills the upper boulders in the sun,

And makes gaps even two can pass abreast

5　The work of hunters is another thing:

I have come after them and made repair

Where they have left not one stone on a stone,

But they would have the rabbit out of hiding,

To please the yelping dogs. The gaps I mean,

10　No one has seen them made or heard them made,

But at spring mending-time we find them there.

I let my neighbor know beyond the hill;

And on a day we meet to walk the line[246]

And set the wall between us as we go.

15　We keep the wall between us once again.

To each the boulders that have fallen to each. [247]

And some are loaves and some so nearly balls

We have to use a spell[248] to make them balance:

"Stay where you are until our backs are turned!"

20　We wear our fingers rough with handling them.

Oh, just another kind of outdoor game,

One on a side. [249] It comes to little more;

There where it is we do not need the wall:

He is all pine and I am apple orchard.

25　My apple trees will never get across

And eat the cones under his pines, I tell him

He only says, "Good fences make good neighbors. "

Spring is the mischief in me[250], and I wonder

244　**sends**: causes to become.

245　**frozen-ground-swell**: Freezing expands the damp earth. It shoves the earth up in a "ground-swell", which causes the stone wall to crumble.

246　**walk the line**: walk along the fence together, repairing it as they go.

247　**To each... each**: Each takes up the boulders that have fallen on his side of the wall.

248　**spell**: word supposed to have some magic power.

249　**Oh, just... One on a side**: Oh, (mending wall is) just like another kind of outdoor game (so it isn't like a job that we really need to do). One works on each side of the wall (as in playing tennis or other court games).

250　**Spring is the mischief in me**: The springtime causes the speaker to be playful.

If I could put a notion in his head[251]:

30 "Why do they make good neighbors? Isn't it

Where there are cows? But here there are no cows

Before I built a wall I'd ask to know

What I was walling in or walling out[252],

And to whom I was like[253] to give offense[254].

35 Something there is that doesn't love a wall,

That wants it down. " I could say "Elves" to him[255],

But it's not elves exactly, and I'd rather

He said it for himself. I see him there,

Bringing a stone grasped firmly by the top

40 In each hand, like an old-stone savage armed.

He moves in darkness as it seems to me,

Not of woods only and the shade of trees.

He will not go behind his father's saying.

And he likes having thought of it so well

45 He says again "Good fences make good neighbors".

Study Questions

1. According to Lines 1-9, what happens because "Something there is that doesn't love a wall"? What other kind of destruction to the wall (Lines 5-9) is not as significant to the speaker?

2. Describe how the speaker and his neighbor go about fixing the wall at spring mending-time.

3. According to the speaker in Lines 24-36, why do he and his neighbor not need a wall? What does the neighbor say?

4. What universal trait in human beings is the speaker referring to when he says, "Something there is that doesn't love a wall"? What is that something?

5. Describe the character of the neighbor as seen by the speaker.

6. Does the speaker definitely want the wall torn down? How do you know?

Sherwood Anderson (1876—1941)

Sherwood Anderson, a very peculiar writer in modern American literary history, was a controversial figure throughout his creative life. While people used to consider him a minor writer or even a "one-book writer", critics today tend to accept him as a historical landmark and an influence upon other American Modernist writers.

Anderson grew up in Camden and Clyde, small Ohio towns much like the one he invented as the setting of his

---

251 **put a notion in his head**: have him enlightened; make him understand.

252 **walling in or walling out**: protecting or defending against.

253 **like**: likely.

254 **give offense**: attack or insult somebody.

255 **I could say "Elves" to him**: The speaker could tell his neighbor the fairies knocked down the wall.

most famous work, *Winesburg*, *Ohio* (1919). He lived there until late in his teens when he went to Chicago. He joined the army and served in the Spanish-American War. Then he got a family and moved to Cleveland and later returned to Chicago, where he pursued an unsatisfying career in advertising. In 1912, he made a dramatic change in his life with his decision to write, choosing to be, in Maxwell Ceismar's words, "among the fools of life, rather than the fools of material power".

In Chicago Anderson was influenced by Carl Sandburg, Theodore Dreiser, Edgar Lee Masters, and other Chicago writers. Enlightened by the poems of Masters' *Spoon River Anthology*, Anderson began to record, in prose, his own feelings about life in small-town America. All his collections of short stories—*Winesburg*, *Ohio*, *Triumph of the Egg* (1921), *Horses and Men* (1923), and *Death in the Woods* (1933)—are explorations of small-town life.

Like Masters, Anderson did not believe that country town life was the rose-colored picture that so many other writers painted. His characters are often lonely and isolated, dissatisfied with their world and frustrated in their attempts to find something better. Anderson treated them realistically, in the simple language that Gertrude Stein did much to encourage and that would in turn influence the styles of Ernest Hemingway, William Faulkner, Thomas Woolf, John Updike, and many other modern and contemporary American writers.

Like many other great American writers, Anderson is prolific. Beginning his career of letters in his late thirties, Anderson altogether published four collections of short stories, eight novels (*Windy McPherson's Son*, 1916; *Marching Men*, 1917; *Poor White*, 1920; *Many Marriages*, 1923; *Dark Laughter*, 1925; *Perhaps Women*, 1931; *Beyond Desire*, 1932; and *Kit Brandon*, 1936), three books of poems and plays, more than three hundred articles, reviews, and essays, and three volumes of autobiography.

Yet anderson was primarily a short story writer, or, as he called himself, a storyteller. Unwilling to accept the direction of the American short story, Anderson developed what we now recognize as its modern incarnation by making revolutionary contributions to its form and content. He was the first American writer who broke determinedly away from the tradition of gentility that had dominated the writing of fiction in the United States; and who had the courage to explore new materials. He influenced the development of the American short story more strongly than anyone else except, possibly, Edgar Allan Poe did. It is through Anderson's achievements that the contemporary American short story has become a major form of literature.

■ Selected Reading

Anderson was not interested in telling "plot stories" that filled the magazines at his time. In the center of a plot story is usually a man of mystery with secret information locked in vault-like places. The man has keys to drawers or cabinets that contain other keys to secret places, and the plot almost always turns on the disclosure of documents that lie hidden. Anderson strongly opposed to the plot stories because they rely too heavily on information as the propeller.

Anderson broke the pattern and never held back any information to create suspense. The narrator, through his usually disorderly narration, shares with the reader everything he knows. The things he tells are not very strange. Actually the story is often very common—a common person doing his everyday job on a common day. Yet when it comes to a certain point, it becomes clear that there is something extremely significant in the commonplace the narrator tells about. As a result, the tales from Anderson's Midwestern drawl are not incidents or episodes, but moments of revelation, each complete in itself.

Looking into Anderson's short stories, the reader will find that they are but the work of the Moment that has nothing to do with plot or conflict. It is simply related to the character. Actually not much happens in the story, but everything in the story has worked together to bring about this Moment at which a sudden significant perception is achieved. Everything in the story seems plain and meaningless until that brief moment, in which Anderson revealed, with his sincere compassion, the deepest secret of each character's being, the fear, the frustration, or the love or hope that the character kept within and was often afraid to reveal. This moment of sudden aliveness, the epiphany, is a moment of revelation, or, in David D. Anderson's words, a Moment of Insight. At this point the surface of things is removed and the essence is exposed. Anderson's aim to see through the external into the inward of the character is then fulfilled.

The Egg

　　My father was, I am sure, intended by nature to be a cheerful, kindly man. Until he was thirty-four years old he worked as a farm hand for a man named Thomas Butterworth whose place lay near the town of Bidwell, Ohio. He had then a horse of his own and on Saturday evenings drove into town to spend a few hours in social intercourse with other farm hands. In town he drank several glasses of beer and stood about in Ben Head's saloon—crowded on Saturday evenings with visiting farm hands. Songs were sung and glasses thumped on the bar. At ten o'clock father drove home along a lonely country road, made his horse comfortable for the night and himself went to bed, quite happy in his position in life. He had at that time no notion of trying to rise in the world.

　　It was in the spring of his thirty-fifth year that father married my mother, then a country school teacher, and in the following spring I came wriggling and crying into the world. Something happened to the two people. They became ambitious. The American passion for getting up in the world took possession of them.

　　It may have been that mother was responsible. Being a school teacher she had no doubt read books and magazines. She had, I presume, read of how Garfield, Lincoln, and other Americans rose from poverty to fame and greatness and as I lay beside her—in the days of her lying-in—she may have dreamed that I would some day rule men and cities. At any rate she induced father to give up his place as a farm hand, sell his horse and embark on an independent enterprise of his own. She was a tall silent woman with a long nose and troubled gray eyes. For herself she wanted nothing. For father and myself she was incurably ambitious.

　　The first venture into which the two people went turned out badly. They rented ten acres of poor stony land on Griggs's Road, eight miles from Bidwell, and launched into chicken raising. I grew into boyhood on the place and got my first impressions of life there. From the beginning they were impression disaster and if, in my turn, I am a gloomy man inclined to see the darker side of life, I attribute it to the fact that what should have been for me the happy joyous days of childhood were spent on a chicken farm.

　　One unversed in such matters can have no notion of the many and tragic things that can happen to a chicken. It is born out of an egg, lives for a few weeks as a tiny fluffy thing such as you will see pictured on Easter cards, then becomes hideously naked, eats quantities of corn and meal bought by the sweat of your father's brow, gets diseases called pip, cholera, and other names, stands looking with stupid eyes at the sun, becomes sick and dies. A few hens and now and then a rooster, intended to serve God's mysterious ends, struggle through to maturity. The hens lay eggs out of which come other chickens and the dreadful cycle is thus made complete. It is all unbelievably complex. Most philosophers must have been raised on chicken farms. One hopes for so much from a chicken and is so dreadfully disillusioned. Small chickens, just setting out on the journey of life, look so bright and alert and they are in fact so dreadfully stupid. They are so much like people they mix one up in one's judgments of life. If disease does not kill them they wait until your expectations are thoroughly aroused and then walk under the wheels of a wagon—to go squashed and dead back to their maker. Vermin infest their youth, and fortunes must be spent for curative powders. In later life I have seen how a literature has been built up on the subject of fortunes to be made out of the raising of chickens. It is intended to be read by the gods who have just eaten of the tree of the knowledge of good and evil. It is a hopeful literature and declares that much may be done by simple ambitious people who own a few hens. Do not be led astray by it. It was not written for you. Go hunt for gold on the frozen hills of Alaska, put your faith in the honesty of a politician, believe if you will that the world is daily growing better of good and evil. It is a hopeful literature and declares that much may be done by simple ambitious people who own a few hens. Do not be led astray by it. It was not written for you. Go hunt for gold on the frozen hills of Alaska, put your faith in the honesty of a politician, believe if you will that the world is daily growing better and that good will triumph over evil, but do not read and believe the literature that is written concerning the hen. It was not written for you.

I, however, digress. My tale does not primarily concern itself with the hen. If correctly told it will center on the egg. For ten years my father and mother struggled to make our chicken farm pay and then they gave up that struggle and began another. They moved into the town of Bidwell, Ohio, and embarked in the restaurant business. After ten years of worry with incubators that did not hatch, and with tiny—and in their own way lovely—balls of fluff that passed on into semi-naked pullet hood and from that into dead hen-hood, we threw all aside and packing our belongings on a wagon drove down Griggs's Road toward Bidwell, a tiny caravan of hope looking for a new place from which to start on our upward journey through life.

We must have been a sad looking lot, not, I fancy, unlike refugees fleeing from a battlefield. Mother and I walked in the road. The wagon that contained our goods had been borrowed for the day from Mr. Albert Griggs, a neighbor. Out of its sides stuck the legs of cheap chairs and at the back of the pile of beds, tables, and boxes filled with kitchen utensils was a crate of live chickens, and on top of that the baby carriage in which I had been wheeled about in my infancy.

Why we stuck to the baby carriage I don't know. It was unlikely other children would be born and the wheels were broken. People who have few possessions cling tightly to those they have. That is one of the facts that make life so discouraging.

Father rode on top of the wagon. He was then a bald-headed man of forty-five, a little fat and from long association with mother and the chickens he had become habitually silent and discouraged. All during our ten years on the chicken farm he had worked as a laborer on neighboring farms and most of the money he had earned had been spent for remedies to cure chicken diseases, on Wilmer's White Wonder Cholera Cure or Professor Bidlow's Egg Producer or some other preparations that mother found advertised in the poultry papers. There were two little patches of hair on father's head just above his ears. I remember that as a child I used to sit looking at him when he had gone to sleep in a chair before the stove on Sunday afternoons in the winter. I had at that time already begun to read books and have notions of my own and the bald path that led over the top of his head was, I fancied, something like a broad road, such a road as Caesar might have made on which to lead his legions out of Rome and into the wonders of an unknown world. The tufts of hair that grew above father's ears were, I thought, like forests. I fell into a half-sleeping, half-waking state and dreamed I was a tiny thing going along the road into a far beautiful place where there were no chicken farms and where life was a happy eggless affair.

One might write a book concerning our flight from the chicken farm into town. Mother and I walked the entire eight miles—she to be sure that nothing fell from the wagon and I to see the wonders of the world. On the seat of the wagon beside father was his greatest treasure. I will tell you of that.

On a chicken farm where hundreds and even thousands of chickens come out of eggs surprising things sometimes happen. Grotesques are born out of eggs as out of people. The accident does not often occur—perhaps once in a thousand births. A chicken is, you see, born that has four legs, two pairs of wings, two heads or what not. The things do not live. They go quickly back to the hand of their maker that has for a moment trembled. The fact that the poor little things could not live was one of the tragedies of life to father. He had some sort of notion that if he could but bring into hen hood or rooster hood a five-legged hen or a two-headed rooster his fortune would be made. He dreamed of taking the wonder about to county fairs' and growing rich by exhibiting it to other farm hands.

At any rate he saved all the little monstrous things that had been born on our chicken farm. They were preserved in alcohol and put each in its own glass bottle. These he had carefully put into a box and on our journey into town it was carried on the wagon seat beside him. He drove the horses with one hand and with the other clung to the box. When we got to our destination the box was taken down at once and the bottles removed. All during our days as keepers of a restaurant in the town of Bidwell, Ohio, the grotesques in their little glass bottles sat on a shelf back of the counter. Mother sometimes protested but father was a rock on the subject of his treasure. The grotesques were, he declared, valuable. People, he said, liked to look at strange and wonderful things.

Did I say that we embarked in the restaurant business in the town of Bidwell, Ohio? I exaggerated a little. The town itself lay at the foot of a low hill and on the shore of a small river. The railroad did not run through the town and the station was a mile away to the north at a place called Fickle-Ville. There had been a cider mill and pickle factory at the station, but before the time of our coming they had both gone out of business. In the morning and in the evening busses came down to the station along a road called Turner's Pike from the hotel on the main street of Bidwell. Our going to the out-of-the-way place to embark in the restaurant business was mother's idea. She talked of it for a year and then one day went off and rented an empty store building opposite the railroad station. It was her idea that the restaurant would be profitable. Traveling men, she said, would be always waiting around to take trains out of town and town people would come to the station to await incoming trains. They would come to the restaurant to buy pieces of pie and drink coffee. Now that I am older I know that she had another motive in going. She was ambitious for me. She wanted me to rise in the world, to get into a town school and become a man of the towns.

At Pickleville father and mother worked hard as they always had done. At first there was the necessity of putting our place into shape to be a restaurant. That took a month. Father built a shelf on which he put tins of vegetables. He painted a sign on which he put his name in large red letters. Below his name was the sharp command— "EAT HERE" —that was so seldom obeyed. A showcase was bought and filled with cigars and tobacco. Mother scrubbed the floor and the walls of the room. I went to school in the town and was glad to be away from the farm and from the presence of the discouraged, sad-looking chickens. Still I was not very joyous. In the evening I walked home from school along Turner's Pike and remembered the children I had seen playing in the town school yard. A troop of little girls had gone hopping about and singing. I tried that. Down along the frozen road I went hopping solemnly on one leg. "Hippity hop to the barber shop," I sang shrilly. Then I stopped and looked doubtfully about. I was afraid of being seen in my gay mood. It must have seemed to me that I was doing a thing that should not be done by one who, like myself, had been raised on a chicken farm where death was a daily visitor.

Mother decided that our restaurant should remain open at night. At ten in the evening a passenger train went north past our door followed by a local freight. The freight crew had switching to do in Pickleville and when the work was done they came to our restaurant for hot coffee and food. Sometimes one of them ordered a fried egg. In the morning at four they returned north-bound and again visited us. A little trade began to grow up. Mother slept at night and during the day tended the restaurant and fed our boarders while father slept. He slept in the same bed mother had occupied during the night and I went off to the town of Bidwell and to school. During the long nights, while mother and I slept, father cooked meats that were to go into sandwiches for the lunch baskets of our boarders. Then an idea in regard to getting up in the world came into his head. The American spirit took hold of him. He also became ambitious.

In the long nights when there was little to do father had time to think. That was his undoing. He decided that he had in the past been an unsuccessful man because he had not been cheerful enough and that in the future he would adopt a cheerful outlook on life. In the early morning he came upstairs and got into bed with mother. She woke and the two talked. From my bed in the comer I listened.

It was father's idea that both he and mother should try to entertain the people who came to eat at our restaurant. I cannot now remember his words, but he gave the impression of one about to become in some obscure way a kind of public entertainer. When people, particularly young people from the town of Bidwell, came into our place, as on very rare occasions they did, bright entertaining conversation was to be made. From father's words I gathered that something of the jolly innkeeper effect was to be sought. Mother must have been doubtful from the first, but she said nothing discouraging. It was father's notion that a passion for the company of himself and mother would spring up in the breasts of the younger people of the town of Bidwell. In the evening bright happy groups would come singing down Turner's Pike. They would troop shouting with joy and laughter into our place. There would be song and festivity. I do not mean to give the impression that father spoke so elaborately of the matter. He was as I have said an uncommunicative man. "They want some place to go. I tell you they want some place to go," he said over and over. That was as far as he got. My own imagination has filled in the blanks.

For two or three weeks this notion of father's invaded our house. We did not talk much, but in our daily lives tried earnestly to make smiles take the place of glum looks. Mother smiled at the boarders and I, catching the infection, smiled at our cat. Father became a little feverish in his anxiety to please. There was no doubt, lurking somewhere in him, a touch of the spirit of the showman. He did not waste much of his ammunition on the railroad men he served at night but seemed to be waiting for a young man or woman from Bidwell to come in to show what he could do. On the counter in the restaurant there was a wire basket kept always filled with eggs, and it must have been before his eyes when the idea of being entertaining was born in his brain. There was something pre-natal about the way eggs kept themselves connected with the development of his idea. At any rate an egg ruined his new impulse in life. Late one night I was awakened by a roar of anger coming from father's throat. Both mother and I sat upright in our beds. With trembling hands she lighted a lamp that stood on a table by her head. Downstairs the front door of our restaurant went shut with a bang and in a few minutes father tramped up the stairs. He held an egg in his hand and his hand trembled as though he were having a chill. There was a half-insane light in his eyes. As he stood glaring at us I was sure he intended throwing the egg at either mother or me. Then he laid it gently on the table beside the lamp and dropped on his knees beside mother's bed. He began to cry like a boy and I, carried away by his grief, cried with him. The two of us filled the little upstairs room with our wailing voices. It is ridiculous, but of the picture we made I can remember only the fact that mother's hand continually stroked the bald path that ran across the top of his head. I have forgotten what mother said to him and how she induced him to tell her of what had happened downstairs. His explanation also has gone out of my mind. I remember only my own grief and fright and the shiny path over my father's head glowing in the lamp light as he knelt by the bed.

As to what happened downstairs. For some unexplainable reason I know the story as well as though I had been a witness to my father's discomfiture. One in time gets to know many unexplainable things. On that evening young Joe Kane, son of a merchant of Bidwell, came to Pickleville to meet his father, who was expected on the ten o'clock evening train from the South. The train was three hours late and Joe came into our place to loaf about and to wait for its arrival. The local freight train came in and the freight crew were fed. Joe was left alone in the restaurant with father.

From the moment he came into our place the Bidwell young man must have been puzzled by my father's actions. It was his notion that father was angry at him for hanging around. He noticed that the restaurant keeper was apparently disturbed by his presence and he thought of going out. However, it began to rain and he did not fancy the long walk to town and back. He bought a five-cent cigar and ordered a cup of coffee. He had a newspaper in his pocket and took it out and began to read. "I'm waiting for the evening train. It's late," he said apologetically.

For a long time father, whom Joe Kane had never seen before, remained silently gazing at his visitor. He was no doubt suffering from an attack of stage fright. As so often happens in life he had thought so much and so often of the situation that now confronted him that he was somewhat nervous in its presence.

For one thing, he did not know what to do with his hands. He thrust one of them nervously over the counter and shook hands with Joe Kane. "How-de-do," he said. Joe Kane put his newspaper down and stared at him. Father's eye lighted on the basket of eggs that sat on the counter and he began to talk. "Well," he began hesitatingly, "well, you have heard of Christopher Columbus, eh?" He seemed to be angry. "That Christopher Columbus was a cheat," he declared emphatically. "He talked of making an egg stand on its end. He talked, he did, and then he went and broke the end of the egg."

My father seemed to his visitor to be beside himself at the duplicity of Christopher Columbus. He muttered and swore. He declared it was wrong to teach children that Christopher Columbus was a great man when, after all, he cheated at the critical moment. He had declared he would make an egg stand on end and then when his bluff had been called he had done a trick. Still grumbling at Columbus, father took an egg from the basket on the counter and began to walk up and down. He rolled the egg between the palms of his hands. He smiled genially. He began to mumble words regarding the effect to be produced on an egg by the electricity that comes out of the human body. He declared that without breaking its shell and by virtue of rolling it back and forth in his hands he could stand the egg on its end. He explained that the warmth of his hands and the gentle rolling movement he gave the egg created a new center of gravity, and Joe Kane was mildly interested. "I have handled thousands of eggs," father said. "No one knows more about eggs than I do."

He stood the egg on the counter and it fell on its side. He tried the trick again and again, each time rolling the egg between the palms of his hands and saying the words regarding the wonders of electricity and the laws of gravity. When after a half hour's effort he did succeed in making the egg stand for a moment he looked up to find that his visitor was no longer watching. By the time he had succeeded in calling Joe Kane's attention to the success of his effort the egg had again rolled over and lay on its side.

Afire with the showman's passion and at the same time a good deal disconcerted by the failure of his first effort, father now took the bottles containing the poultry monstrosities down from their place on the shelf and began to show them to his visitor. "How would you like to have seven legs and two heads like this fellow?" he asked, exhibiting the most remarkable of his treasures. A cheerful smile played over his face. He reached over the counter and tried to slap Joe Kane on the shoulder as he had seen men do in Ben Head's saloon when he was a young farm hand and drove to town on Saturday evenings. His visitor was made a little ill by the sight of the body of the terribly deformed bird floating in the alcohol in the bottle and got up to go. Coming from behind the counter father took hold of the young man's arm and led him back to his seat. He grew a little angry and for a moment had to turn his face away and force himself to smile. Then he put the bottles back on the shelf. In an outburst of generosity he fairly compelled Joe Kane to have a fresh cup of coffee and another cigar at his expense. Then he took a pan and filling it with vinegar, taken from a Jug that sat beneath the counter, he declared himself about to do a new trick. "I will heat this egg in this pan of vinegar," he said. "Then I will put it through the neck of a bottle without breaking the shell. When the egg is inside the bottle it will resume its normal shape and the shell will become hard again. Then I will give the bottle with the egg in it to you. You can take it about with you wherever you go. People will want to know how you got the egg in the bottle. Don't tell them. Keep them guessing. That is the way to have fun with this trick."

Father grinned and winked at his visitor. Joe Kane decided that the man who confronted him was mildly insane but harmless. He drank the cup of coffee that had been given him and began to read his paper again. When the egg had been heated in vinegar father carried it on a spoon to the counter and going into a back room got an empty bottle. He was angry because his visitor did not watch him as he began to do his trick, but nevertheless went cheerfully to work. For a long time he struggled, trying to get the egg to go through the neck of the bottle. He put the pan of vinegar back on the stove, intending to reheat the egg, then picked it up and burned his fingers. After a second bath in the hot vinegar the shell of the egg had been softened a little but not enough for his purpose. He worked and worked and a spirit of desperate determination took possession of him. When he thought that at last the trick was about to be consummated the delayed train came in at the station and Joe Kane started to go nonchalantly out at the door. Father made a last desperate effort to conquer the egg and make it do the thing that would establish his reputation as one who knew how to entertain guests who came into his restaurant. He worried the egg. He attempted to be somewhat rough with it. He swore and the sweat stood out on his forehead. The egg broke under his hand. When the contents spurted over his clothes, Joe Kane, who had stopped at the door, turned and laughed.

A roar of anger rose from my father's throat. He danced and shouted a string of inarticulate words. Grabbing another egg from the basket on the counter, he threw it, just missing the head of the young man as he dodged through the door and escaped.

Father came upstairs to mother and me with an egg in his hand. I do not know what he intended to do. I imagine he had some idea of destroying it, of destroying all eggs, and that he intended to let mother and me see him begin. When, however, he got into the presence of mother something happened to him. He laid the egg gently on the table and dropped on his knees by the bed as I have already explained. He later decided to close the restaurant for the night and to come upstairs and get into bed. When he did so he blew out the light and after much muttered conversation both he and mother went to sleep. I suppose I went to sleep also, but my sleep was troubled. I awoke at dawn and for a long time looked at the egg that lay on the table. I wondered why eggs had to be and why from the egg came the hen who again laid the egg. The question got into my blood. It has stayed there, I imagine, because I am the son of my father. At any rate, the problem remains unsolved in my mind. And that, I conclude, is but another evidence of the complete and final triumph of the egg—at least as far as my family is concerned.

■ Study Questions

1. What kind of man was the boy narrator's father before he married? What changes did he undergo after marriage? What was the reason according to the narrator? What was the first venture that the couple went into? What was the result?

2. How does the narrator feel about and view chickens? Why does the narrator claim to have had trouble, even as a child, being happy?

3. What was the father's attitude towards his collection of "grotesques"? What did he say about them?

4. After he opens his restaurant, how does the "American spirit" take hold of the father? What is the immediate result?

5. Who was Joe Kane? Why did he enter the restaurant? How did the father treat him? Why did the father get angry at last? What did the father do then? What was the mother's and the boy's reaction to it?

6. Anderson says his story "If correctly told... will center on the egg". How does the egg link the two parts of the story?

7. "In leaving the country for the town and the... upward Journey through life", why does Anderson describe the family as a sad-looking lot? Why is the figure "... not, I fancy, unlike refugees fleeing from a battlefield" used? To carry the figure further, to what do refugees flee? Do they have a well-defined objective ahead of them?

8. Could Anderson's picture of an almost hysterical father true to life? What makes you believe or disbelieve it? How do you account for the apparent change in the father when he comes "into the presence of mother"?

9. Why did the boy wonder "why eggs had to be and why from the egg came the hen who again laid the egg"? What question odes Anderson intend to raise in the reader's mind?

10. What sardonic humor do you find in the story?

Ernest Hemingway (1899—1961)

Ernest Hemingway, an American Nobel Prize winner in literature, is arguably the most popular American novelist of the 20th century. He was famous for his novels and short stories written in his spare, laconic, yet intense prose with short sentences and very specific details. Almost all his stories deal with the theme of courage in face of tragedy. They reveal man's impotence and despairing courage to assert himself against overwhelming odds.

Born in Illinois, Hemingway spent childhood vacations in Michigan on hunting and fishing trips. He volunteered for an ambulance unit in France during World War Ⅰ, but was wounded and hospitalized for six months. After the war as a war correspondent based in Paris, he met expatriate American writers Sherwood Andersen, Ezra Pound, F. Scott Fitzgerald, and Gertrude stein. Stein, in particular, influenced his spare style.

After his novel *The Sun Also Rises* (1926) brought him fame, he covered the Spanish civil War, World War Ⅱ, and the fighting in China in the 1940s. On a safari in Africa, he was badly injured when his small plane crashed; still, he continued to enjoy hunting and sport fishing, activities that inspired some of his best work. *The Old Man and the Sea* (1952), a short poetic novel about a poor, old fisherman who heroically catches a huge fish devoured by sharks, won him the Pulitzer Prize in 1953; the next year he received the Nobel Prize. Discouraged by a troubled family background, illness, and the belief that he was losing his gift for writing, Hemingway shot himself to death in 1961.

Hemingway is generally regarded as spokesman for the Lost Generation. He wrote of war, death, and the "lost generation" of cynical survivor. A believer in the "cult of experience", Hemingway often involved his characters in dangerous situations in order to reveal their inner natures; in his later works, the danger sometimes becomes an occasion for masculine assertion. So His characters are not dreamers but tough bullfighters, soldiers, and athletes. His characters represent a certain type, alienated and painful, but not evil and ugly, courageous and dignified, but deeply scarred and disillusioned. There is a particular term, "the code hero", for his character. The code hero with courage lives by a pattern which gives life meaning and value.

Hemingway's hallmark is a clean style devoid of unnecessary words. Often he uses understatement. He once compared his writing to icebergs: "There is seven-eighths of it under water for every part that shows." It is true, his sentences only give one small bit of the meaning and the rest is implied. The reader must go very deep beneath the surface to understand the full meaning of his writing. So his writing, though simple in diction, terse in sentence and colloquial in style, carries emotion. Hemingway is good at using the dramatic point of view. He does not tell us how the characters feel, what they look like and everything is presented by showing instead of telling, but we can infer the state of mind from their conversation or actions. Hemingway is also a master of pause in narration. There is momentary narrative pause, but the action continues between silences, and sometimes the characters say nothing, but emotion contains.

Quite a few of Hemingway's novels: *The Sun also Rises*, *A Farewell to Arms* (1929), *To Have and Have Not* (1937), *For Whom the Bell Tolls* (1940), *The Old Man and the Sea*, *Islands in the Stream* (1970), and short stories: "The Killers", "The Snows of Kilimanjaro", and "The Breaking Point" have been adapted by US and UK film makers.

■ Selected Reading

*In Ernest Hemingway's "**A Clean, Well-Lighted Place**", two characters converse about another, interpreting his character and behavior and in the process revealing a good deal about themselves—their way of seeing the world and responding to it.*

A Clean, Well-Lighted Place

It was late and every one had left the cafe except an old man who sat in the shadow the leaves of the tree made against the electric light. In the day time the street was dusty, but at night the dew settled the dust and the old man liked to sit late because he was deaf and now at night it was quiet and he felt the difference. The two waiters inside the cafe knew that the old man was a little drunk, and while he was a good client they knew that if he became too drunk he would leave without paying, so they kept watch on him.

"Last week he tried to commit suicide," one waiter said.

"Why?"

"He was in despair. "

"What about?"

"Nothing. "

"How do you know it was nothing?"

"He has plenty of money. "

They sat together at a table that was close against the wall near the door of the cafe and looked at the terrace where the tables were all empty except where the old man sat in the shadow of the leaves of the tree that moved slightly in the wind. A girl and a soldier went by in the street. The street light shone on the brass number on his collar. The girl wore no head covering and hurried beside him.

"The guard will pick him up," one waiter said.

"What does it matter if he gets what he's after?"

"He had better get off the street now. The guard will get him. They went by five minutes ago. "

The old man sitting in the shadow rapped on his saucer with his glass. The younger waiter went over to him.

"What do you want?"

The old man looked at him. "Another brandy," he said.

"You'll be drunk," the waiter said. The old man looked at him. The waiter went away.

"He'll stay all night," he said to his colleague. "I'm sleepy now. I never get into bed before three o'clock. He should have killed himself last week. "

The waiter took the brandy bottle and another saucer from the counter inside the cafe and marched out to the old man's table. He put down the saucer and poured the glass full of brandy.

"You should have killed yourself last week," he said to the deaf man. The old man motioned with his finger. "A little more," he said. The waiter poured on into the glass so that the brandy slopped over and ran down the stem into the top saucer of the pile. "Thank you," the old man said. The waiter took the bottle back inside the cafe. He sat down at the table with his colleague again.

"He's drunk now," he said.

"He's drunk every night. "

"What did he want to kill himself for?"

"How should I know. "

"How did he do it?"

"He hung himself with a rope."

"Who cut him down?"

"His niece."

"Why did they do it?"

"Fear for his soul."

"How much money has he got?"

"He's got plenty."

"He must be eighty years old."

"Anyway I should say he was eighty."

"I wish he would go home. I never get to bed before three o'clock. What kind of hour is that to go to bed?"

"He stays up because he likes it."

"He's lonely. I'm not lonely. I have a wife waiting in bed for me."

"He had a wife once too."

"A wife would be no good to him now."

"You can't tell. He might be better with a wife."

"His niece looks after him."

"I know. You said she cut him down."

"I wouldn't want to be that old. An old man is a nasty thing."

"Not always. This old man is clean. He drinks without spilling. Even now, drunk. Look at him."

"I don't want to look at him. I wish he would go home. He has no regard for those who must work."

The old man looked from his glass across the square[256], then over at the waiters.

"Another brandy," he said, pointing to his glass. The waiter who was in a hurry came over.

"Finished," he said, speaking with that omission of syntax stupid people employ when talking to drunken people or foreigners. "No more tonight. Close now[257]."

"Another," said the old man.

"No. Finished." The waiter wiped the edge of the table with a towel and shook his head.

The old man stood up, slowly counted the saucers[258], took a leather coin purse from his pocket and paid for the drinks, leaving half a peseta tip.

The waiter watched him go down the street, a very old man walking unsteadily but with dignity.

---

256 **across the square**: Here "square" refers to the plaza. The cafe is on the sidewalk.

257 **Close now**: We are closing now.

258 The saucers record the number of drinks he must pay for.

"Why didn't you let him stay and drink?" the unhurried waiter asked. They were putting up the shutters. "It is not half-past two. "

"I want to go home to bed. "

"What is an hour?"

"More to me than to him. "

"An hour is the same. "

"You talk like an old man yourself. He can buy a bottle and drink at home. "

"It's not the same. "

"No, it is not, " agreed the waiter with a wife. He did not wish to be unjust. He was only in a hurry.

"And you? You have no fear of going home before your usual hour?"

"Are you trying to insult me?"

"No, hombre[259], only to make a joke. "

"No, " the waiter who was in a hurry said, rising from pulling down the metal shutters. "I have confidence. I am all confidence. "

"You have youth, confidence, and a job, " the older waiter said. "You have everything. "

"And what do you lack?"

"Everything but work. "

"You have everything I have. "

"No. I have never had confidence and I am not young. "

"Come on. Stop talking nonsense and lock up. "

"I am of those who like to stay late at the cafe, " the older waiter said. "With all those who do not want to go to bed. With all those who need a light for the night. "

"I want to go home and into bed. "

"We are of two different kinds, " the older waiter said. He was now dressed to go home. "It is not only a question of youth and confidence although those things are very beautiful. Each night I am reluctant to close up because there may be some one who needs the cafe. "

"Hombre, there are bodegas[260] open all night long. "

"You do not understand. This is a clean and pleasant cafe. It is well lighted. The light is very good and also, now, there are shadows of the leaves. "

"Good night, " said the younger waiter.

"Good night, " the other said. Turning off the electric light he continued the conversation with himself. It is the light of course but it is necessary that the place be clean and pleasant. You do not want music. Certainly you do not want music. Nor can you stand before a bar with dignity although that is all that is provided for these hours. What did he fear? It was not fear or dread. It

---

259   **hombre**: Spanish for "man". This is a friendly form of address.
260   **Bodegas**: Spanish for "wine cellars".

was a nothing that he knew too well. It was all a nothing and a man was nothing too. It was only that and light was all it needed and a certain cleanness and order. Some lived in it and never felt it but he knew it all was nada y pues nada[261] y nada y pues nada. Our nada who art in nada, nada be thy name thy kingdom nada thy will be nada in nada as it is in nada. Give us this nada our daily nada and nada us our nada as we nada our nadas and nada us not into nada but deliver us from nada; pues nada. Hail nothing full of nothing, nothing is with thee. He smiled and stood before a bar with a shining steam pressure coffee machine.

"What's yours?" asked the barman.

"Nada."

"Otro loco was[262]," said the barman and turned away.

"A little cup," said the waiter.

The barman poured it for him.

"The light is very bright and pleasant but the bar is unpolished," the waiter said.

The barman looked at him but did not answer. It was too late at night for conversation.

"You want another capita[263]?" the barman asked.

"No, thank you," said the waiter and went out. He disliked bars and bodegas. A clean, well-lighted cafe was a very different thing. Now, without thinking further, he would go home to his room. He would lie in the bed and finally, with daylight, he would go to sleep. After all, he said to himself, it is probably only insomnia. Many must have it.

■ Study Questions

1. Who begins the conversation in the story?

2. Why did the old man try to commit suicide?

3. What differences are there between the two waiters' attitude towards the old man?

4. What is the significance of the appearance of the soldier and the girl in the story?

5. What do you think is the significance of the title of the story?

6. What is the significance of the garbled Lord Prayer?

7. What is the feature of the narrative style?

"*Hills Like White Elephants*" *is a perfect example of Hemingway's dramatic narration. The concrete, factual details are introduced without comment; and the action and the characters are allowed to present themselves directly to the reader without benefit of an intervening narrator. What we are shown are two Americans, a man and a woman, sitting at a table next to a railroad station, waiting for the train from Barcelona. The weather is hot, they order two beers, and they begin a casual, listless conversation that gradually reveals the situation, the tension that exists between them, and the underlying differences in attitudes and sensibilities that threaten their entire relationship. The differences in sensibilities are first clearly signaled by her imaginative observation that the hills in the distance "look*

---

261 **nada ypues nada**: Spanish for "nothing and then nothing".

262 **Otm loco was**: Spanish for "another crazy one".

263 **capita**: Spanish for "little cup".

like white elephants", his indifferent response, and the cynicism of her curt reply. This story, telescoped into the forty minutes it takes for the train to arrive, unfolds slowly, inexorably, almost artlessly, through the medium of flat, unemotional dialogue. The story we witness and assembly largely by ourselves is one of two unhappy people caught up in a conflict which given the differences in their respective characters and personalities will not yield a clear-cut or satisfactory resolution.

Hills Like White Elephants

The hills across the valley of the Ebro were long and white. On this side there was no shade and no trees and the station was between two lines of rails in the sun. Close against the side of the station there was the warm shadow of the building and a curtain, made of strings of bamboo beads, hung across the open door into the bar, to keep out flies. The American and the girl with him sat at a table in the shade, outside the building. It was very hot and the express from Barcelona would come in forty minutes. It stopped at this junction for two minutes and went on to Madrid.

"What should we drink?" the girl asked. She had taken off her hatband put it on the table.

"It's pretty hot," the man said.

"Let's drink beer."

"*Dos cervezas,*" the man said into the curtain.

"Big ones?" a woman asked from the doorway.

"Yes. Two big ones."

The woman brought two glasses of beer and two felt pads. She put the felt pads and the beer glasses on the table and looked at the man and the girl. The girl was looking off at the line of hills. They were white in them and the country was brown and dry.

"They look like white elephants," she said.

"I've never seen one," the man drank his beer.

"No, you wouldn't have."

"I might have," the man said. "Just because you say I wouldn't have doesn't prove anything."

The girl looked at the bead curtain. "They've painted something on it," she said. "What does it say?"

"Anis del Tom. It's a drink."

"Could we try it?"

The man called "Listen" through the curtain. The woman came out from the bar.

"Four reales."

"*We want two Anis del Torn.*"

"With water?"

"Do you want it with water?"

"I don't know," the girl said. "Is it good with water?"

"It's all right."

"You want them with water?" asked the woman.

"Yes, with water."

"It tastes like licorice," the girl said and put the glass down.

"That's the way with everything."

"Yes," said the girl. "Everything tastes of licorice. Especially all the things you've waited so long for, like absinthe."

"Oh, cut it out."

"You started it," the girl said. "I was being amused. I was having a fine time."

"Well, let's try and have a fine time."

"All right I was trying. I said the mountains looked like white elephants. Wasn't that bright?"

"That was bright."

"I wanted to try this new drink: That's all we do, isn't it—look at things and try new drinks?"

"I guess so."

The girl looked across at the hills.

"They're lovely hills," she said. "They don't really look like white elephants. I just meant the coloring of their skin through the trees."

"Should we have another drink?"

"All right."

The warm wind blew the bead curtain against the table.

"The beer's nice and cool," the man said.

"It's lovely," the girl said.

"It's really an awfully simple operation. Jig," the man said. "It's not really an operation at all."

The girl looked at the ground the table legs rested on.

"I know you wouldn't mind it. Jig. It's really not anything. It's just to let the air in."

The girl did not say anything.

"I'll go with you and to stay with you all the time. They just let the air in and then it's all perfectly natural."

"Then what will we do afterward?"

"We'll be fine afterward. Just like we were before."

"What makes you think so?"

"That's the only thing that bothers us. It's the only thing that's made us unhappy."

The girl looked at the bead curtain, put her hand out and took hold of two of the strings of beads.

"And you think then we'll be all right and be happy."

"I know we will. You don't have to be afraid. I've known lots of people that have done it."

"So have I," said the girl. "And afterward they were all so happy."

"Well," the man said, "if you don't want to you don't have to. I wouldn't have you do it if you didn't want to. But I know it's perfectly simple."

"And you really want to?"

"I think it's the best thing to do. But I don't want you to do it if you don't really want to."

"And if I do it you'll be happy and things will be like they were and you'll love me?"

"I love you now. You know I love you."

"I know. But if I do it, then it will be nice again if I say things are like white elephants, and you'll like it?"

"I'll love it I love it now but I just can't think about it. You know how I get when I worry."

"If I do it you won't ever worry?"

"I won't worry about that because it's perfectly simple."

"Then I'll do it. Because I don't care about me."

"What do you mean?"

"I don't care about me."

"Well, I care about you."

"Oh, yes. But I don't care about me. And I'll do it and then everything will be fine."

"I don't want you to do it if you feel that way."

The girl stood up and walked to the end of the station. Across, on the other side, were fields of grain and trees along the banks of the Ebro. Far away, beyond the river, were mountains. The shadow of a cloud moved across the field of grain and she saw the river through the trees.

"And we could have all this," she said. "And we could have everything and every day we make it more impossible."

"What did you say?"

"I said we could have everything."

"We can have everything."

"No, we can't."

"We can have the whole world."

"No, we can't."

"We can go everywhere."

"No, we can't. It isn't ours any more."

"It's ours."

"No, it isn't. And once they take it away, you never get it back."

"But they haven't taken it away."

"Well wait and see."

"Come on back in the shade," he said. "You mustn't feel that way."

"I don't feel any way," the girl said. "I just know things."

"I don't want you to do anything that you don't want to do—"

"Nor that isn't good for me," she said. "I know. Could we have another beer?"

"All right. But you've got to realize—"

"I realize," the girl said. "Can't we maybe stop talking?"

They sat down at the table and the girl looked across at the hills on the dry side of the valley and the man looked at her and at the table.

"You've got to realize," he said. "that I don't want you to do it if you don't want to. I'm perfectly willing to go through with it if it means anything to you."

"Doesn't it mean anything to you? We could get along."

"Of course it does. But I don't want anybody but you. I don't want any one else. And I know it's perfectly simple."

"Yes, you know it's perfectly simple."

"It's all right for you to say that, but I do know it."

"Would you do something for me now?"

"I'd do anything for you."

"Would you please please please please please please please stop talking?"

He did not say anything but looked at the bags against the wall of the station. There were labels on them from all the hotels where they had spent nights.

"But I don't want you to," he said, "I don't care anything about it."

"I'll scream," the girl said.

The woman came out through the curtains with two glasses of beer and put them down on the damp felt pads. "The train comes in five minutes," she said.

"What did she say?" asked the girl.

"That the train is coming in five minutes."

The girl smiled brightly at the woman, to thank her.

"I'd better take the bags over to the other side of the station," the man said. She smiled at him.

"All right. Then come back and we'll finish the beer."

He picked up the two heavy bags and carried them around the station to the other tracks. He looked up the tracks but could not see the train. Coming back, he walked through the barroom, where people waiting for the train were drinking. He drank an Anis at the bar arid looked at the people. They were all waiting reasonably for the train. He went out through the bead curtain. She was sitting at the table and smiled at him.

"Do you feel better?" he asked.

"I feel fine," she said. "There's nothing wrong with me. I feel fine."

■ Study Questions

1. When and where does the story take place? Where are the girl and the man living?

2. What does the girl think about the hills? What's the man's reaction?

3. What does the girl say about "all the things you've waited so long for"?

4. What are the girl and the man arguing about? Hills like white elephants? New drinks? Or something else?

5. Does the man seriously try to understand the girl? Does the girl misunderstand the man's concern?

6. Is the man's reassurance of the other side of things convincing?

7. Why does Hemingway provide so little information about his characters? What's the significance of the setting?

8. What's your general impression of the man and the woman?

9. Has the quarrel been resolved when the story ends? Why did they smile at each other? Will there be love and happiness afterwards? Why?

10. Why does the author choose the title as it is?

11. Does this story help explain the attitude of the "lost generation" after World War I ? Do you think that the characters could be found around you as well? Why or why not?

LITERARY FOCUS

The American Novel

Unlike poetry and drama, novels are a relatively modern invention. A **novel** can best be defined as a book-length prose fiction. Early novels in English fall into three categories: the **picaresque novel**, a loose series of episodes recounting the adventures of wanderers and lovable rogues, often with a satiric aim; the **novel of sentiment**, a highly emotional tale of romance and tears that ends with a moral message; and the **gothic novel**, a tale of mystery and fear that includes elements of the supernatural as well as the romantic.

The earliest American novels also fall into these categories. Hugh Henry Brackenridge's *Modern Chivalry* (1792) is a picaresque adventure story that pokes fun at political problems during George Washington's presidency; Susanna Rowson's *Charlotte Temple* (1790) is a sentimental moral tale; and Charles Brockden Brown's *Wieland* (1798) and *Ormond* (1799) are tales of gothic horror that incidentally explore the psychological motivations of their characters.

The 19th century witnesses that America begins to produce major novelists who are still widely read today. James Fenimore Cooper's Leatherstocking Tales (the first being published in 1823) are romantic adventures chronicling the exploits of Natty Bumppo, a noble frontiersman who becomes the model for the classic American hero. At about the same time William Gilmore Simms of South Carolina was writing similar Romantic adventure tales, earning for himself the nickname "the southern Cooper."

Another major novelist of the pre-Civil War period is Nathaniel Hawthorne, who is best known for his masterpiece, *The Scarlet Letter* (1850). *The Scarlet Letter* is a tightly woven tale that explores the nature of sin; it is a work of complex symbolism and profound insights into its characters' minds and hearts. The nature of good and evil is also probed in *Moby-Dick* (1851), a tale of whales and whalers by Herman Melville. *Moby-Dick*'s profound philosophical questioning and its almost Shakespearean language place it among the outstanding novels of the 19th century.

After confronting the realities of the Civil War, American novelists turn more and more toward Realistic fiction. In the works of Mark Twain, local color makes for true-to-life adventure, and Twain as a satirist never shirks from depicting the real world in all its folly. Twain's use of dialect and colloquial language has a strong impact on almost all American writers following him; novels with adolescent heroes like Twain's *Huckleberry Finn* (1884) appear again and again in American fiction.

William Dean Howells sets forth the principles of Realism in the 1890s, and if his *Rise of Silas Lapham* (1885) only partially reflects his theories, his ideas are masterfully realized in the novels of his friend Henry James. James explores the realities of society and the nature of the human mind in such works as *The American* (1877), *The Portrait of a Lady* (1881), and *The Turn of the Screw* (1898). His novel *The Ambassadors* (1903) is considered to be a masterpiece of psychological realism, writing that probes deeply into the complexities of characters' thoughts and motivations.

Realism is carried one step further in the Naturalistic novels of Stephen Crane, Theodore Dreiser, and Frank Norris. In the grim world of Dreiser's *Sister Carrie* (1900) and *An American Tragedy* (1925), characters are trapped by overwhelming forces that they cannot control or even understand. Norris' *McTeague* (1899) is a brutally frank portrait of greed, while *The Octopus* (1901) tells of the grim life of western ranchers battling the railroads.

Regionalism and Realism work hand in hand in the novels of Edith Wharton, which include *The Hous of Mirth* (1905), *Ethan Frame* (1911), and *The Age of Innocence* (1920). Ole Rolvaag's *Giants in the Earth* (1927) describes the life of Norwegian immigrants in South Dakota, while Willa Gather offers a poetical portrait of the Nebraska frontier in *My Antonia* (1918) and celebrates America's past in the equally lyrical *Death Comes for the Archbishop* (1927). Lyricism is also an element of Thomas Wolfe's autobiographical novel *Look Homeward, Angel* (1929) while Ellen Glasgow offers powerful pictures of the changing South in *Barren Ground* (1925) and *Vein of Iron* (1935). Sinclair Lewis, the first American to win the Nobel Prize for Literature, was a sharp social critic, writing about small town America in *Main Street* (1920), businessmen in *Babbitt* (1922), and the medical profession in *Arrowsmith* (1925). American social values between the two world wars are also explored by F. Scott Fitzgerald in *The Great Gatsby* (1925), by John dos Passes in his trilogy *U. S. A.*, and by Nathanael West in *Day of the Locust* (1939).

Probably the three most outstanding novelists of America before World War Ⅱ are Ernest Hemingway, William Faulkner, and John Steinbeck. Hemingway further develops the American hero in such works as *A Farewell to Arms* (1929), a tale of love during World War Ⅰ, and *For Whom the Bell Tolls* (1940), a story of an American who fights in the Spanish Civil War. Hemingway's detached, journalistic prose style has been much imitated. Faulkner writes lyrical "stream-of-consciousness" novels set in his native South, including *The Sound and the Fury*

(1929), a portrait of a once aristocratic family, and *Light in August* (1932). Steinbeck draws warm, human portraits in such novels as *Of Mice and Men* (1937) and *The Grapes of Wrath* (1939), a saga of a dust-bowl family driven to find a new life in California. Other important writers of fiction before World War Ⅱ include Katherine Anne Porter, Eudora Welty, William Saroyan, and Thornton Wilder.

Novelists writing since World War Ⅱ have turned more and more toward experimental fiction. Ralph Ellison's powerful novel *Invisible Man* (1952) is complex in its symbolism and its structure, while Joseph Heller explores World War Ⅱ itself in his fragmenty dark comedy *Catch-22* (1961). Other postwar American novelists to achieve international recognition include Carson McCullers, Bernard Malamud, John Updike, Truman Capote, and Saul Bellow, the most recent American winner of the Nobel Prize for Literature.

READING FOR APPRECIATION

Making Inferences

The words *imply* and *infer* are sometimes confused. To imply something is to suggest without stating it directly. For example, a person who asks, "Are you going to be using the car tonight?" is usually implying "I'd like to use the car." To infer is to "draw out" a meaning or a suggestion that is not stated directly; the person who is asked if he or she is going to be using the car infers that the person asking wants to use it.

A speaker or an author can imply; a listener or a reader can infer. Both of these processes are at work, or should be at work, in much modern literature. When a writer and a reader are both participating in these actions with attention and imagination, the experience of literature can be its most creative and satisfying.

Of course not everything in literature demands that we make inferences. Often things are what they are, and statements can be taken for just what they say. When someone once asked Ezra Pound what the frogs "meant" in one of his poems, Pound replied that sometimes "frogs is frogs."

Yet the selections in this unit often do demand that we make inferences. In "*The Road Not Taken*" we soon infer that the poem is about more than a walk Robert Frost once took in the woods. The poet implies that the roads in the wood are in some sense "the roads of life" when he tells us that he will be "telling this with a sigh" at some time in the future and says that his choice of road has made "all the difference." The clues are so strong that we know we must make some inferences about these "roads."

Making inferences is a vital part of reading literature. An author can imply a great deal in a story or a poem, but if we do not infer from what is there and participate as we read, we leave the experience of literature incomplete.

VOICE OF THE AGE

"Make It New"

When Ezra Pound said, "Make it new," he expressed what so many American artists felt. The 20th century, so vastly different from what had come before it, presented a whole world that had to be re-seen, re-evaluated, and re-imagined. The writers in this unit built into their poems and stories the surprise of the new, the shock of the new. It inspired some to celebrate; it left some with confusion and a sense of loss. Their works contained unusual images, desperate questions, and experiments in reordering the world. "What now would make sense?" they asked. "How should we face the future?" These artists reshaped literature toward new relationships between people and the *new* New World.

Eliot: *Do I dare / Disturb the universe? ...*

Williams: *so much / depends upon // a red wheel / barrow // glazed with rain / water // beside the white / chickens.*

Anderson: *On a chicken farm where hundreds and even thousands of chickens come out of eggs surprising things sometimes happen. Grotesques are born out of eggs as out of people.*

Hemingway: *Some lived in it and never felt it but he knew it all was nada y pues nada y nada y pues nada. Our nada who art in nada, nada be thy name thy kingdom nada thy will be nada in nada as it is in nada. Give us this nada our daily nada and nada us our nada as we nada our nadas and nada us not into nada but deliver us from nada; pues nada. Hail nothing full of nothing, nothing is with thee.*

Whether the modern age inspired them or dispirited them, the writers grouped here affirmed the power of the imagination. The act of writing itself was a way of ordering a disordered time and place, an authentic source of delight. Through literature life still offered meaning, beauty, and a measure of joy.

Chapter 8

MID-CENTURY VOICES 1930—1960

INTRODUCTION

The Great Depression

The Great Depression—beginning with the great stock market crash—came as a bang to the vibrant, experimental, and roaring 1920s. Started after October 29, 1929, known as Black Tuesday, it first struck the Wall Street and quickly spread to Europe and every part of the world, with devastating effects in both the industrialized countries and those which exported raw materials. International trade declined sharply, as did personal incomes, tax revenues, prices and profits. Cities all around the world were hit hard, especially those dependent on heavy industry. Construction was virtually halted in many countries. Farming and rural areas suffered as crop prices fell by 40 to 60 percent. Mining and logging areas had perhaps the most striking blow because the demand fell sharply and there were few employment alternatives.

In the Great Depression the American dream had become a nightmare. What was once the land of opportunity was now the land of desperation. What was once the land of hope and optimism had become the land of despair. The American people were questioning all the maxims—democracy, capitalism, and individualism—on which they had based their lives. As the Great Depression deepened, the cities of America could no longer be celebrated as Carl Sandburg had celebrated Chicago—laughing as a "fighter laughs who has never lost a battle." The best hope for a better life was California. Many Dust Bowl farmers packed their families into cars, tied their few possessions on the back, and sought work in the agricultural fields or cities of the West—their role as independent land owners gone forever. Instead of advancement, survival became the keyword.

The poverty and despair of the 1930s brought forth a new attitude toward government and society. President Franklin Roosevelt called for a "New Deal" for the American people, and his administrations began many programs of direct and indirect assistance to those who had lost not only their jobs but faith in their own future.

Americans confronted a decade of self-doubt that was all the more shocking because of the vivid decade that had preceded it.

The Literature of Crisis

The 1920s was defined by three major designations: the Jazz Age, the Lost Generation, and the Wasteland—all with significant literary associations. Of them all the Jazz Age, as represented best in F. Scott Fitzgerald's fiction, was most clearly cut off by the stock market collapse and the ensuing depression. It is the period of the 1920s alone. But the Lost Generation continued to be lost in the 1930s. The third term, the Wasteland, established by Eliot in his 1922 poem, had perhaps an even longer life; it has come to represent an age extending from the 1920s to 1945 and may indeed suggest the central features of the landscape of this larger period. The Wasteland poets continued to develop and sharpen both their verse and their ideas into the 1930s and 1940s. [264] As a matter of fact, many of the great artists of the early 20th century had years to live and some of their greatest works still to produce. Yet these artists had done their shocking work, their influential work, in the first decades of the century.

The next generation (though all of them were not necessarily younger than the generation of the 1920s), the writers in this unit, absorbed the lessons of the Modernists: They grew up in an atmosphere of Modernism and incorporated into their own work the discoveries and experiments, the new styles and forms, of Modernism. Yet they also witnessed the hard lessons of a nation's poverty and suffering. These writers—striving for both artistic excellence and social commitment—produced what critic Alfred Kazin has called the literature of crisis.

In this era of social crisis, the writers were reconsidering both the possibilities of realism as an artistic mode and the place of art in society. The artists were engaged in a variety of ways in dealing with the phenomenon of modernity: the advent of mass culture, rapid changes in technology and social order, a growing faith in science and progress combined with the pervasive sense that in the 1930s modernity was in a state of collapse.

This was an era of nostalgia and a fascination with myth as a principle for ordering both art and society. It was also the time in which film overtook print as the dominant medium in American culture, a development about which both writers and filmmakers were acutely conscious.

Literature of the Depression Era came in many different forms. There were stage plays, comics, poetry, and, of course, novels. Many of these works were brought about through President Franklin D. Roosevelt's New Deal programs that encouraged those without work to write. Some works from this mass production of literature went on to become great works that the country would read for years to come while other faded slowly in to the shadows.

The major fiction writers of the time produced novels closely tied to the lives of ordinary people, literature in which style and experiment stepped aside in favor of human stories told with emotion and social commitment. These were the kind of books produced by John Steinbeck, John Dos Passos, and James T. Farrell. Dos Passos' trilogy *U. S. A* (completed 1936) used journalistic techniques and a style imitating newsreels to tell an episodic story of social unrest and the decline of individuality. The undoubted masterpiece of this type of novel is Steinbeck's *Grapes of Wrath* (1939).

The 1930s is also an era of nostalgia. In contrast to the Realist writers of the time, two American novelists combined a feeling for the people with a continued reliance on the American Romantic tradition. Thomas Wolfe's novels—including *Of Time and the River* (1935) and *You Can't Go Home Again* (1940)—are highly

---

264　The Wasteland then runs into and disappears in the Age of Anxiety.

autobiographical, lyrical journeys into the artist's own self. William Faulkner's large, complex novels are Romantic in another sense. They create a whole world of their own. *The Sound and the Fury* (1929), *Absalom, Absalom*! (1936), and *The Hamlet* (1940) are among the Faulkner novels that detail the decline of southern aristocratic families and the rise of the opportunistic people who replace them. In a style often demanding, often a kind of modern gothic, Faulkner's novels raise his characters to mythic proportions. Modern and Romantic, both Wolfe and Faulkner reflect a profound understanding of the common people and of their time and place. In a time of social crisis, they emphasized the individual.

Postwar America

During the 1930s Americans watched the rise of Fascism in Europe, as Mussolini came to power in Italy, Hitler in Germany, and Franco in Spain. In 1939, they watched World War II break out and Europe once again become an enormous battleground.

The 1940s are pretty well defined by World War II. US isolationism was shattered by the Japanese bombing of Pearl Harbor. As President Franklin D. Roosevelt guided the country on the homefront, Dwight D. Eisenhower commanded the troops in Europe. Gen. Douglas MacArthur and Adm. Chester Nimitz led them in the Pacific. The successful use of penicillin by 1941 revolutionized medicine. Developed first to help the military personnel survive war wounds, it also helped increase survival rates for surgery. The first eye bank was established at New York Hospital in 1944. Unemployment almost disappeared, as most men were drafted and sent off to war. The government reclassified 55 percent of their jobs, allowing women and blacks to fill them. First, single women were actively recruited to the workforce. In 1943, with virtually all the single women employed, married women were allowed to work.

After the war, the men returned, having seen the rest of the world. No longer was the family farm an ideal; no longer would blacks accept lesser status. The GI Bill allowed more men than ever before to get a college education. Women had to give up their jobs to the returning men, but they had tasted independence.

The effect of World War II on American culture and literature, in spite of general prosperity, was quite different from that of World War I (even rock music, in some ways a derivative of Jazz, produced quite different effects). The American public did not enter the war in 1941 with the same naïve idealism they had shown in 1917, and as a result they were less affected by a postwar disillusionment. They were affected eventually, however, by postwar fears, by living with the threat of the bomb after it became generally available, by scientific "progress" that soon made the atom bomb the H-bomb and annihilation a daily possibility. There was also an almost imperceptible sliding into the Korean War or Police Action, which made peace time curiously resemble the war years. In America, however, there was a political swing to the right, from McCarthyism (U. S. Senator 1946—1957) and anti-intellectualism which swept the nation during his career to the victory of moderate Republicanism under Eisenhower. The growth of the military-industrial complex against which President Eisenhower issued his warning at the close of his administration in 1960 assured economic prosperity at the cost of some of our previous social gains and freedom.

Postwar Literature

Literature experienced something of a closing in, a withdrawal, during the postwar period. Of course writers of the stature of Faulkner, Hemingway, and Eliot (expatriated in England) continued to produce major work and developed what came to be seen as a mythological symbolism in their total structure. All three were awarded the Nobel Prize for Literature during this time. But the younger generation for the most part was content to imitate the past. In both fiction and poetry, the age of technical innovation was over, only in drama did new things get tried like the "memory" play of Tennessee Williams and new combinations of realism and expressionism in his plays and those of Arthur Miller (Albee comes late in the fifties, to be sure, but seems to belong to the next age). Wallace Stevens emerged to be a place of honor during these years, but he had been writing his poetry steadily since 1916 and only put the capstone on his career in this period. Eudora Welty was almost the only fiction writer to develop an original and distinctive style between 1945 and 1960 and to arrive at major stature. American writers, having discovered their true national idiom in an earlier time, now set about perfecting and refining the literary techniques invented by the generations before them.

So far as the subject is concerned, some postwar literature directly confronts the events of the time. W. H. Auden's "Unknown Citizen", for example, portrays an individual dwarfed by the State. Yet much of the literature seems to respond indirectly to its own time, turning away as if in self-protection.

However, the literature of 1930—1960 is so varied that it is difficult to make generalizations about it. Indeed, generalizations about periods of literature are always dangerous and must be taken only as indications of tendencies. Yet we do notice in postwar writing a trend toward poems and stories that celebrate private experiences, memories of childhood, or moments of private happiness. Literature reflects the world in which it is created even if that reflection is a withdrawal from public concerns into private experience.

W. H. Auden (1907—1973)

Wystan Hugh Auden (who signed his works **W. H. Auden**), an Anglo-American writer, was one of the master craftsmen of English verse. In many ways he wrote against the grain of Modernism, basing his poems upon a wide knowledge of traditional meters and forms. His poems are not afraid of sentiment or nostalgia, but they characteristically surprise us with reminders of realities. His work is noted for its stylistic and technical achievements, its engagement with moral and political issues, and its variety of tone, form, and content.

Throughout his career he was both controversial and influential. After his death, some of his poems, notably "Funeral Blues" ("Stop all the clocks") and "September 1, 1939", became widely known through films, broadcasts, and popular media.

Auden was born an Englishman, and it was as an English poet that he made a dazzling, youthful reputation. After 1939, however, he lived mostly in America, becoming an American citizen in 1946. As the titles of two collections of his verse suggest, there is *The English Auden* and *The American Auden*.

The English Auden made a reputation for himself while still an undergraduate at Oxford University. His first volume, *Poems*, appeared in 1930. Throughout the thirties he continued to amaze the reading public with his brash verses that reflected an interest in science, industrial landscapes, and modern psychology. He even plunged into politics. He saw Nazi Germany at first hand, and he worked with the Republican side against the Fascists in Spain. Some of Auden's fine early poems are marred by a heavy insistence on his political ideas.

In 1939 he began a new life and freed himself from the restrictions of Europe. He came to New York, where he produced some of his finest works. In America he felt a revival of his Christianity, which grew stronger as he grew older. He taught at Swarthmore College during World War Ⅱ, and in 1948 he won the Pulitzer Prize for *The*

Age of Anxiety, a long poem that uses Old English alliterations as it follows the lives of four people through a postwar world of uncertainty and isolation. His other major volumes are *Nones* (1951), *The Shield of Achilles* (1955), and *Homage to Clio* (1960). A prolific and versatile writer, Auden also collaborated with the great modern composer Igor Stravinsky on an opera, *The Rake's Progress*, in addition to producing lively literary criticism.

In his later years Auden lived in a house he bought in Kirchstetten, Austria. He died in Vienna in 1973 and was buried near his beloved house. On his memorial plaque in London's Westminster Abbey are words from the poem he wrote in memory of the Irish poet W. B. Yeats— "In the prison of his days / Teach the free man how to praise" — words that sum up his own life as well.

■ Selected Readings

Auden's poems are marked by exquisite craft, wise observation of history, and trust in the value of art. Like **"The Unknown Citizen"** *they can sharply describe the relationships between people and the governments they create. Like* **"If I Could Tell You"** *they can brim with a deeply moving human sympathy.*

If I Could Tell You

Time will say nothing but I told you so,
Time only knows the price we have to pay;
If I could tell you I would let you know.

If we should weep when clowns put on their show,
5   If we should stumble when musicians play,
Time will say nothing but I told you so.

There are no fortunes to be told, although,
Because I love you more than I can say,
If I could tell you I would let you know.

10   The winds must come from somewhere when they blow,
There must be reasons why the leaves decay;
Time will say nothing but I told you so.

Perhaps the roses really want to grow,
The vision seriously intends to stay;
15   If I could tell you I would let you know.

Suppose the lions all get up and go,
And all the brooks and soldiers run away;
Will Time say nothing but I told you so?
If I could tell you I would let you know.

■ Study Questions

1. According to the poem, what is the only thing that time will say? What would the speaker do if he could? Why would he do this, according to the third stanza?

2. What does the fourth stanza say about the winds and the leaves? What does the fifth stanza say about the roses and the vision?

3. What seems to be the relationship between the speaker and the person he addressed? Which images in the poem suggest this relationship?

4. What does the speaker fear will happen to the roses and the vision? What does he therefore fear will happen to his relationship with the person he addresses? Is he certain about the future?

5. Might this poem be about more than the relationship between the speaker and the person addressed? Explain.

6. In what ways is this poem reminiscent of poetry of previous centuries? (Consider both the form and content of the poem.) In what way is it a "modern" poem? (Consider the tone, or attitude, of the poet.)

The Unknown Citizen

(To JS/07/M/378
This Marble Monument
Is Erected by the State)

He was found by the Bureau of Statistics to be

One against whom there was no official complaint,

And all the reports on his conduct agree

That, in the modern sense of an old-fashioned word, he was a saint,

5   For in everything he did he served the Greater Community.

Except for the War till the day he retired

He worked in a factory and never got fired,

But satisfied his employers, Fudge Motors Inc.

Yet he wasn't a scab[265] or odd in his views,

10   For his Union reports that he paid his dues,

(Our report on his Union shows it was sound)

And our Social Psychology workers found

That he was popular with his mates and liked a drink.

The Press are convinced that he bought a paper every day

15   And that his reactions to advertisements were normal in every way.

Policies taken out in his name prove that he was fully insured,

And his Health-card shows he was once in hospital but left it cured.

Both Producers Research and High-Grade Living declare

---

265 **scab**: worker who refuses to strike or replaces a striker.

He was fully sensible to the advantages of the Installment Plan

20 And had everything necessary to the Modern Man,

A phonograph, a radio, a car and a frigidaire.

Our researchers into Public Opinion are content

That he held the proper opinions for the time of year;

When there was peace, he was for peace; when there was war, he went.

25 He was married and added five children to the population,

Which our Eugenist[266] says was the right number for a parent of his generation,

And our teachers report that he never interfered with their education.

Was he free? Was he happy? The question is absurd:

Had anything been wrong, we should certainly have heard.

■ Study Questions

1. According to the inscription under the title, on what does this poem appear? Who has erected it?

2. According to Lines 1-5, in what sense was the unknown citizen a "saint"? Identify at least four organizations or groups of people who have passed positive judgments on the unknown citizen. Except for the war, where did the unknown citizen work until he retired (Line 7)?

3. What questions are asked in the last two lines of the poem? According to the poem, why are these questions absurd?

4. What kind of "State", or government, has erected this monument? Why would a government erect a public monument to an "unknown citizen"?

5. Describe at least four ways in which the unknown citizen was found to be "ideal". Does the *poet* find such behavior ideal?

6. What is ironic about the last two lines of the poem?

7. Basically, what is this poem criticizing?

8. What aspects of the modern world does this poem make you think about? Do you agree with the poet's opinion of everything he criticizes? Why or why not?

Theodore Roethke (1908—1963)

Theodore Roethke, winner of the Pulitzer Prize, the National Book Award, and the Bollingen Prize, was one of the most important American poets during the middle decades of the 20th century. Many of his poems have received a higher honor than any official prize can bestow: They have become favorite poems with many readers.

Roethke fashioned his poems from intense memories of his childhood and boyhood in Michigan. His father and grandfather were florists, and Roethke grew up in a world of flowers, plants, and large commercial greenhouses. Roethke was a genius in writing

---

266 **Eugenist**: specialist in eugenics, the movement to improve inherited traits in humans.

poetry, but a reserved person in manner. His talent was first inspired by the beauty of his father's greenhouse, where every leaf and petal appeared significant to the boy as the embodiment of life, and meanwhile, as the symbol for something delicate and pleasant in this world. Nevertheless, outside the greenhouse, he found himself in torturing conflict with the ingrained values of conventional society. He had to make himself occupied in teaching and reading voraciously the books of the masters he admired: William Blake, William Butler Yeats, Walt Whitman, and Emerson. His first book of poetry, *Open House*, appeared in public in 1941 with controversial comments. However, he did not give up until his accidental drowning in a friend's swimming pool in 1963 when he had already been a popular poet among the readers and the critics as well.

Roethke's poems are closely observed lyrics. He details the processes of the natural world and, like Emerson and Whitman, almost mystically identifies with nature: "In my veins, in my bones I feel it." Images of growth and decay can be found in all of his books, including *Open House*, *The Lost Son* (1948), *The Waking* (1953), and *Words for the Wind* (1958). In his poems, metaphysical tension expresses itself in varied metaphors and fractured syntax, but he was, unlike most poets of his time, always optimistic in discussing such themes as life and death. He worked diligently to write poems in simple words and easy structure. As everyone can see, his early poems were written in a traditional style, while in the latter ones, some modern experimental skills can be largely traced.

■ Selected Reading

"*My Papa's Waltz*" *is selected from* The Lost Son, *a collection of the autobiographical poems about the poet's childhood days with his father. The poem tells how the father was dancing with his little son after a whole day's labor and drinking of some whisky. Although the father's steps were clumsy and the son was too short to dance on the floor, they both enjoyed the crazy waltz in spite of the mother's frowning. The poem presents a living scene of a happy family of the laboring class.*

My Papa's Waltz

The whiskey on your breath
Could make a small boy dizzy;
But I hung on like death:
Such waltzing was not easy.

5　We romped until the pans
Slid from the kitchen shelf;
My mother's countenance
Could not unfrown itself.

The hand that held my wrist
10　Was battered[267] on one knuckle;
At every step you missed
My right ear scraped a buckle.

267　**battered**: damaged to lose shape.

You beat time on my head[268]

With a palm caked hard by dirt[269],

15 Then waltzed me off to bed

Still clinging to your shirt.

■ Study Questions

1. What had the father probably done before the dance?

2. Where was the mother? What did she do?

3. Did the father dance well? The son? In what way did the father and the son dance?

4. What did the son do in the end?

5. What did the son feel about his Papa's waltz?

6. What is the rhyme scheme of the poem? Could you find out any modern poetic traces in this poem? What are they?

Langston Hughes (1902—1967)

Langston Hughes, American poet, novelist, playwright, short story writer, and columnist, is best known for his work during the Harlem Renaissance.

Hughes was born in a black family in Joplin, Missouri. From a very young age, he was not without racial pride and dignity; being proud of the music, history, and legend of black culture. In 1921, Hughes enrolled at Columbia University and published his first poem "The Negro Speaks of Rivers". Nevertheless, bored by formal education, Hughes left the university one year later for Africa and Europe, first as a sailor, then as a cook and busboy.

The story is always told that one day in 1926, when Hughes, who'd returned to the States years before, was waiting a table in a restaurant, he served a guest, instead of the menu, with several poems, for he had recognized the man to be a very popular poet of the time, Vachel Lindsay[270]. As a result, encouragement fell on his prepared head and Hughes got the good fortune to collect his poems into a book, *The Wearing Blues*, and had it published in the same year. Good fortune was continued in the next year when another book, *Fine Clothes to the Jew*, followed suit. After finishing college education in 1929, Hughes began to support himself by his pen. He worked diligently and tried nearly every literary form and style: poetry, fiction, drama, and essays for newspapers.

Langston Hughes was the first prominent Black writer in American literary history. He contributed to the treasure house of literature over 60 books; out of them 12 are collections of poems. Besides, he was also a master in fiction writing and composer of plays for children. Besides what are mentioned above, the other collections of

---

268 **beat time on my head**: lightly knocked at my head to produce or to keep with the rhythm of the music.

269 **a palm caked hard by dirt**: a palm covered thickly with dirt (due to the hard toil for years).

270 **Vachel Lindsay** (1879—1931) was born Nicholas Vachel Lindsay in Springfield, Illinois. During the 1920's he was one of America's most popular poets. He was especially known for his beautiful art work that accompanied many of his poems and for his unique way of performing his poetry instead of just reading it. Because of his use of American Midwest themes he also became known as the "Prairie Troubador". People also admired the "tramps" or walking tours he took throughout America, exchanging poetry for room and board. Young people today seem to appreciate many of Lindsay's themes: his love for individualism, nature, and simplicity; and his hatred for hypocrisy and pettiness.

Hughes include *Dear Lovely Death* （1931）, *The Negro Mother* （1931）, *Dream Keeper* （1932）, *The New Song* （1938）, *Shakespeare in Harlem* （1942）, and *Ask Your Mama*. （1961）.

Hughes was the first writer who brought the stories of Black people in the Harlem area into American literature and initiated a new trend in Black literature. This resulted in the later famous literary and artistic movement known as the "Harlem Renaissance" and Hughes became the spokesman of Black writers.

As a Black lyric poet, Hughes took great advantage of the rhythms of jazz and the blues and, in addition, developed subjects from Black life and racial themes. In his poems readers of the first half of the 20th century were satisfied to find primitivism combined with classical technique. Hughes reached the summit of his achievements when he was honored with the informal title of "Poet Laureate of Harlem".

Hughes' poems were characterized by short lines and simple stanza patterns, but with strong rhythms of jazz and strict rhyme schemes derived from blues songs. Two principal themes of the poetry are constantly passionate presentation of Black life by applying rhythms and refrains from jazz and blues, and poems of racial protest.

Langston Hughes was also an accomplished writer of fiction, with a novel and several collections of stories to his credit. Largely autobiographical, and set in locations around the world （but most frequently in the United States）, many of Hughes' stories revolve around the same themes: the ultimately demeaning patronage of whites; the challenges of realizing dreams in a world of limited opportunity; and the timeless tensions between the sexes. By turns poignant and indignant, these stories achieve power by revealing small moments that betray more universal truths.

■ Selected Readings

*In the long line of human history, each civilization flourishes along a river. In "**The Negro Speaks of Rivers**", "I" is the symbol of human beings, who have shared very much with the development of the four great river valleys. By mentioning his involvement with rivers, the poet expresses his passionate love for world civilization.*

The Negro Speaks of Rivers

I've known rivers:
I've known rivers ancient as the world and older than
　　the flow of human blood in human veins.

My soul has grown deep like the rivers.
I bathed in the Euphrates[271] when dawns were young[272].
5　I built my hut near the Congo[273] and it lulled me to sleep.
I looked upon the Nile[274] and raised the pyramids above it.

271　**the Euphrates**: the river runs through Turkey, Syria and Iraq to the Persian Gulf; the Euphrates is often believed to be on the cradles of world civilization.

272　**when dawns were young**: at the dawn, the very early stage of world civilization.

273　**the Congo**: the second longest river in Africa. It runs through west central Africa into the Atlantic and is believed to be original area of Black culture.

274　**the Nile**: the longest river in Africa, often considered as one of the cradles of human civilization.

I heard the singing of the Mississippi[275] when Abe Lincoln[276] went

    down to New Orleans, and I've seen its

    muddy bosom turn all golden in the sunset.

I've known rivers:

Ancient, dusky rivers.

10   My soul has grown deep like the rivers.

■ Study Questions

1. How old are the rivers (Line 2)?
2. Where did the speaker bath? Where did he build the hut and what did it cause him to do?
3. What did "I" do above the Nile?
4. What was the bosom of the Mississippi like? What did it do to everything around?
5. Why should "I" choose to compare the running of the ancient rivers with "the flow of human blood in human veins"? What if he changes it to "the flow of the water in pipes"?
6. Why is Lincoln the only person mentioned in the poem? What did Lincoln do in New Orleans? Is it relevant to the Mississippi?

*Langston Hughes was a master of many literary forms, but it is as a short-story writer that his talents are combined in an especially vibrant way: his gift for humor and irony, his love of the vernacular, his brilliance in depicting character, and his profound perceptions about American life are all logged as one. "**Early Autumn**" showcases Hughes' literary blossoming as well as the development of his personal and artistic concerns. The poignant, witty, angry, and deeply poetic story demonstrate Hughes' uncanny gift for elucidating the most vexing questions of human nature. The story of doomed passions set against the gloomy background of the bleak Washington Square is one of its most noticeable characteristics.*

Early Autumn

When Bill was very young, they had been in love. Many nights they had spent walking, talking together. Then something not very important had come between them, and they didn't speak. Impulsively, she had married a man she thought she loved. Bill went away, bitter about women.

Yesterday, walking across Washington Square, she saw him for the first time in years.

"Bill Walker," she said.

He stopped. At first he did not recognize her, to him she looked so old.

---

275 **the Mississippi**: the longest river in the North American continent. It flows from its northern source in Minnesota to the Gulf of Mexico, and used to be the most important artery of transportation in the United States and the one that nourished the American nation.

276 **Abe Lincoln**: Abraham Lincoln, who is always remembered as one who issued the Emancipation Proclamation which liberate some four million Black slaves in the South.

"Mary! Where did you come from?"

Unconsciously, she lifted her face as though wanting a kiss, but he held out his hand. She took it.

"I live in New York now," she said.

"Oh" —smiling politely, then a little frown came quickly between his eyes.

"Always wondered what happened to you, Bill. "

"I'm a lawyer. Nice firm, way downtown. "

"Married yet?"

"Sure. Two kids. "

"Oh," she said.

A great many people went past them through the park. People they didn't know. It was late afternoon. Nearly sunset. Cold.

"And your husband?" he asked her.

"We have three children. I work in the bursar's office at Columbia. "

"You're looking very... " (he wanted to say old) "... well," he said.

She understood. Under the trees in Washington Square, she found herself desperately reaching back into the past. She had been older than he then in Ohio. Now she was not young at all. Bill was still young.

"We live on Central Park West," she said. "Come and see us sometime. "

"Sure," he replied. "You and your husband must have dinner with my family some night. Any night. Lucille and I'd love to have you. "

The leaves fell slowly from the trees in the Square. Fell without wind. Autumn dusk. She felt a little sick.

"We'd love it," she answered.

"You ought to see my kids. " He grinned.

Suddenly the lights came on up the whole length of Fifth Avenue, chains of misty brilliance in the blue air.

"There's my bus," she said.

He held out his hand, "Good-bye. "

"When... " she wanted to say, but the bus was ready to pull off. The lights on the avenue blurred, twinkled, blurred. And she was afraid to open her mouth as she entered the bus. Afraid it would be impossible to utter a word.

Suddenly she shrieked very loudly, "Good-bye!" But the bus door had closed.

The bus started. People came between them outside, people crossing the street, people they didn't know. Space and people. She lost sight of Bill. Then she remembered she had forgotten to give him her address—or to ask him for his—or tell him that her youngest boy was named Bill, too.

■ Study Questions

1. Why did Mary and Bill separate? What did Mary do then? And Bill?

2. How long had it been since that? Where did they meet again? Who first recognized the other? What did Mary do unconsciously? What was Bill's reaction? What did Mary do then?

3. Did they invite each other to a family meeting? Was Bill's invitation genuine?

4. For what reason did the lights on the avenue blur, twinkle, and then blur?

5. What did Mary realize that she had forgotten to do at the end of the story?

6. What significance does the sentence "Then a little frown came quickly between his eyes" have to the development of this story?

7. The tone of the story is revealed by the characters' conversations, is it strained or humorous? Explain.

8. Very often the way in which a character perceives the setting, and the way he or she reacts to it, will tell the reader more about the character and his or her state of mind than it will about the setting itself. This is particularly true of works in which the author carefully controls the point of view. From what point of view is this story told? Find out the modifiers such as "cold" and "blue air" and explain how the setting helps reveal the state of the character's mind.

William Faulkner (1897—1962)

William Cuthbert Faulkner, one of the most influential American writers of the 20th century, is considered to be one of the most important "Southern writers". He was relatively unknown before receiving the Nobel Prize for Literature in 1949, but his work is now favored by the general public and critics.

Faulkner was born William Falkner in New Albany, Mississippi, and raised in and heavily influenced by that state, as well as by the history and culture of the South. Faulkner attended the University of Mississippi in oxford before and after his service in the Royal Canadian Air Force in World War I. Thereafter he lived in Oxford most of his

life, though he spent much time in Hollywood as a screenwriter and it was in New Orleans that his literary career began. There he met Sherwood Anderson, who encouraged him to turn from poetry to fiction and helped him get his first novel published. The work that won him a Nobel Prize in 1950 is the depiction of life in his fictional Yoknapatawpha County—a cosmos of his own, an entire world apart. Yoknapatawpha County was the name of his imagined landscape, and he proudly claimed to be its "Sole Owner and Proprietor". He populated it with a broad spectrum of remarkable characters—fanners, hunters, aristocrats, businessmen, former black slaves, dispossessed Indians, and several generations of whole families moving on different levels of southern society. He set his characters in a country he knew well and against a background of history he profoundly understood. In this way, he created a kind of mythical kingdom that exists simultaneously in the past and in the present.

Faulkner's most celebrated novels were mostly the product of a prodigious decade of creative effort. They include *The Sound and the Fury* (1929), *As 1 Lay Dying* (1930), *Sanctuary* (1931), *Light in August* (1932), *Absalom, Absalom* (1936), *The Wild Palms* (1939), and *The Hamlet* (1940). Faulkner was a prolific writer of short stories: his first short story collection, *These* 13 (1932), includes many of his most acclaimed (and most frequently anthologized) stories, including "A Rose for Emily", "Barn Burning", "Red Leaves", "That Evening Sun", and "Dry September". Other widely read short stories can be found in *Go Down, Moses* (1942), and his *Collected Stories*（1950）.

In his fiction, Faulkner depicts the bitterness of southern history with poetic expression. His important subjects are childhood, families, sex, obsessions, the past and the modern southern memory, myth and reality, race, and alienation. As a regionalist, he was very critical of southern society. His theme is essentially an analysis of the underlying cause for the failure and decay of the South before the Civil War. His fiction carries a strong sense of fragmentation in social community and within the individual himself due to loss of love and lack of emotional response.

Faulkner's writing has often been criticized as being dense, meandering and difficult to understand due to his heavy use of such literary techniques as symbolism, allegory, multiple narrators and points of view, non-linear narrative, and especially stream of consciousness. Faulkner was known for an experimental style with meticulous attention to diction and cadence, in contrast to the minimalist understatement of his peer Ernest Hemingway. "Requiem for a Nun", the only play that Faulkner had ever published, includes an introduction that is actually one sentence spanning more than a page.

It is true that Faulkner's writing style is complex. His works are full of repetition, inconsistent punctuation, long and puzzling sentences, flashbacks, and multiple points of view. His works are often wrote in the stream-of-consciousness mode. To farther complicate matters, the consciousness he presented was sometimes that of a child, an idiot, or a person on the edge of madness. But as readers gradually understand, the difficulty of the style was in keeping with the complexity of the subject. For it was part of Faulkner's aim to represent in the consciousness of his characters the tangled interrelationships between the modern American present and the historical past. The complexity of Faulkner's style also shows in the way he presented the setting and interpreted characters. He seldom put emphasis on reality, but on symbolic approach to literature in order to discover the truth of the human heart.

■ Selected Reading

"A Rose for Emily" is one of the representatives of Faulkner's most successful works. Emily, the heroine in the story had been a proud and aloof girl born into a noble family. Her father was very fastidious about her marriage and drove away every man who paid court to her. After her father's death, Emily got to know a Yankee, a foreman who came to the town to pave the sidewalk. Just when the neighbors were guessing whether Emily would marry the Yankee, this man disappeared. Before the man's disappearance, Emily had gone to the druggist to buy some arsenic and people guessed that Emily was probably deserted by her lover and wanted to commit suicide. But Emily did not die, only became more eccentric and inaccessible. Twenty years later when Emily died, people had the chance to enter her mysterious house. In one bedroom upstairs, people found her white marriage dress, and the dry and rotten body of the Yankee on the bed. On the pillow next to that of the dead man, people discovered the indention of a head. It seemed that someone had just slept on the pillow, on which there was a long strand of iron-gray hair.

The story is compact in structure, ingenious-conceived in plot, concise in language, and clear-cut in characterization. There are some symbolic meanings in the representation of the characters: Emily is an embodiment of the South and the Yankee is an incarnation of the North, and the absurd murder symbolizes the conflict between the South and the North of America. Yet what Faulkner intends to say through this story is far more than that.

A Rose for Emily

I

When Miss Emily Grierson died, our whole town went to her funeral: the men through a sort of respectful affection for a fallen monument, the women mostly out of curiosity to see the inside of her house, which no one save an old manservant—a combined gardener and cook—had seen in at least ten years.

It was a big, squarish frame house that had once been white, decorated with cupolas and spires and scrolled balconies in the heavily lightsome style of the seventies, set on what had once been our most select street. But garages and cotton gins had encroached and obliterated even the august names of that neighborhood; only Miss Emily's house was left, lining its stubborn and coquettish decay above the cotton wagons and the gasoline pumps—an eyesore among eyesores. And now Miss Emily had gone to join the representatives of those august names where they lay in the cedar-bemused cemetery among the ranked and anonymous graves of Union and Confederate soldiers who fell at the battle of Jefferson.

Alive, Miss Emily had been a tradition, a duty, and a care; a sort of hereditary obligation upon the town, dating from that day in 1894 when Colonel Sartoris, the mayor—he who fathered the edict that no Negro woman should appear on the streets without an apron—remitted her taxes, the dispensation dating from the death of her father on into perpetuity. Not that Miss Emily would have accepted charity. Colonel Sartoris invented an involved tale to the effect that Miss Emily's father had loaned money to the town, which the town, as a matter of business, preferred this way of repaying. Only a man of Colonel Sartoris' generation and thought could have invented it, and only a woman could have believed it.

When the next generation, with its more modern ideas, became mayors and aldermen, this arrangement created some little dissatisfaction. On the first of the year they mailed her a tax notice. February came, and there was no reply. They wrote her a formal letter, asking her to call at the sheriff's office at her convenience. A week later the mayor wrote her himself, offering to call or to send his car for her, and received in reply a note on paper of an archaic shape, in a thin, flowing calligraphy in faded ink, to the effect that she no longer went out at all. The tax notice was also enclosed, without comment.

They called a special meeting of the Board of Aldermen. A deputation waited upon her, knocked at the door through which no visitor had passed since she ceased giving china-painting lessons eight or ten years earlier. They were admitted by the old Negro into a dim hall from which a stairway mounted into still more shadow. It smelled of dust and disuse—a close, dank smell. The Negro led them into the parlor. It was furnished in heavy, leather-covered furniture. When the Negro opened the blinds of one window, a faint dust rose sluggishly about their thighs, spinning with slow motes in the single sun-ray. On a tarnished gilt easel before the fireplace stood a crayon portrait of Miss Emily's father.

They rose when she entered—a small, fat woman in black, with a thin gold chain descending to her waist and vanishing into her belt, leaning on an ebony cane with a tarnished gold head. Her skeleton was small and spare; perhaps that was why what would have been merely plumpness in another was obesity in her. She looked bloated, like a body long submerged in motionless water, and of that pallid hue. Her eyes, lost in the fatty ridges of her face, looked like two small pieces of coal pressed into a lump of dough as they moved from one face to another while the visitors stated their errand.

She did not ask them to sit. She just stood in the door and listened quietly until the spokesman came to a stumbling halt. Then they could hear the invisible watch ticking at the end of the gold chain.

Her voice was dry and cold, "I have no taxes in Jefferson. Colonel Sartoris explained it to me. Perhaps one of you can gain access to the city records and satisfy yourselves."

"But we have. We are the city authorities. Miss Emily. Didn't you get a notice from the sheriff, signed by him?"

"I received a paper, yes," Miss Emily said. "Perhaps he considers himself the sheriff... I have no taxes in Jefferson."

"But there is nothing on the books to show that, you see. We must go by the—"

"See Colonel Sartoris. I have no taxes in Jefferson."

"But, Miss Emily—"

"See Colonel Sartoris." (Colonel Sartoris had been dead almost ten years.) "I have no taxes in Jefferson. Tobe!" The Negro appeared. "Show these gentlemen out."

II

So she vanquished them, horse and foot, just as she had vanquished their fathers thirty years before about the smell. That was two years after her father's death and a short time after her sweetheart—the one we believed would marry her—had deserted her. After her father's death she went out very little; after her sweetheart went away, people hardly saw her at all. A few of the ladies had the temerity to call, but were not received, and the only sign of life about the place was the Negro man—a young man then—going in and out with a market basket.

"Just as if a man—any man—could keep a kitchen properly," the ladies said; so they were not surprised when the smell developed. It was another link between the gross, teeming world and the high and mighty Griersons.

A neighbor, a woman, complained to the mayor. Judge Stevens, eighty years old.

"But what will you have me do about it, madam?" he said.

"Why, send her word to stop it," the woman said. "Isn't there a law?"

"I'm sure that won't be necessary," Judge Stevens said. "It's probably just a snake or a rat that nigger of hers killed in the yard. I'll speak to him about it."

The next day he received two more complaints, one from a man who came in diffident deprecation. "We really must do something about it, Judge. I'd be the last one in the world to bother Miss Emily, but we've got to do something." That night the Board of Aldermen met—three gray-beards and one younger man, a member of the rising generation.

"It's simple enough," he said. "Send her word to have her place cleaned up. Give her a certain time to do it in, and if she don't..."

"Dammit, sir," Judge Stevens said, "will you accuse a lady to her face of smelling bad?"

So the next night, after midnight, four men crossed Miss Emily's lawn and slunk about the house like burglars, sniffing along the base of the brickwork and at the cellar openings while one of them performed a regular sowing motion with his hand out of a sack slung from his shoulder. They broke open the cellar door and sprinkled lime there, and in all the outbuildings. As they recrossed the lawn, a window that had been dark was lighted and Miss Emily sat in it, the light behind her, and her upright torso motionless as that of an idol. They crept quietly across the lawn and into the shadow of the locusts that lined the street. After a week or two the smell went away.

That was when people had begun to feel really sorry for her. People in our town, remembering how old lady Wyatt, her great-aunt, had gone completely crazy at last, believed that the Griersons held themselves a little too high for what they really were. None of the young men were quite good enough for Miss Emily and such. We had long thought of them as a tableau; Miss Emily a slender figure in white in the background, her father a spraddled silhouette in the foreground, his back to her and clutching a horsewhip, the two of them framed by the back-flung front door. So when she got to be thirty and was still single, we were not pleased exactly, but vindicated; even with insanity in the family she wouldn't have turned down all of her chances if they had really materialized.

When her father died, it got about that the house was all that was left to her; and in a way, people were glad. At last they could pity Miss Emily. Being left alone, and a pauper, she had become humanized. Now she too would know the old thrill and the old despair of a penny more or less.

The day after his death all the ladies prepared to call at the house and offer condolence and aid, as is our custom. Miss Emily met them at the door, dressed as usual and with no trace of grief on her face. She told them that her father was not dead. She did that for three days, with the ministers calling on her, and the doctors, trying to persuade her to let them dispose of the body. Just as they were about to resort to law and force, she broke down, and they buried her father quickly.

We did not say she was crazy then. We believed she had to do that. We remembered all the young men her father had driven away, and we knew that with nothing left, she would have to cling to that which had robbed her, as people will.

III

She was sick for a long time. When we saw her again, her hair was cut short, making her look like a girl, with a vague resemblance to those angels in colored church windows—sort of tragic and serene.

The town had just let the contracts for paving the sidewalks, and in the summer after her father's death they began to work. The construction company came with niggers and mules and machinery, and a foreman named Homer Barren, a Yankee—a big, dark, ready man, with a big voice and eyes lighter than his face. The little boys would follow in groups to hear him cuss the niggers, and the niggers singing in time to the rise and fall of picks. Pretty soon he knew everybody in town. Whenever you heard a lot of laughing anywhere about the square, Homer Barron would be in the center of the group. Presently we began to see him and Miss Emily on Sunday afternoons driving in the yellow-wheeled buggy and the matched team of bays from the livery stable.

At first we were glad that Miss Emily would have an interest, because the ladies all said, "Of course a Grierson would not think seriously of a Northerner, a day laborer." But there were still others, older people, who said that even grief could not cause a real lady to forget *noblesse oblige*—without calling it *noblesse oblige*. They just said, "Poor Emily. Her kinsfolk should come to her." She had some kin in Alabama; but years ago her father had fallen out with them over the estate of old lady Wyatt, the crazy woman, and there was no communication between the two families. They had not even been represented at the funeral.

And as soon as the old people said, "Poor Emily," the whispering began. "Do you suppose it's really so?" they said to one another. "Of course it is. What else could..." This behind their hands; rustling of craned silk and satin behind jalousies closed upon the sun of Sunday afternoon as the thin, swift clop-clop-clop of the matched team passed: "Poor Emily."

She carried her head high enough—even when we believed that she was fallen. It was as if she demanded more than ever the recognition of her dignity as the last Grierson; as if it had wanted that touch of earthiness to reaffirm her imperviousness. Like when she bought the rat poison, the arsenic. That was over a year after they had begun to say "Poor Emily", and while the two female cousins were visiting her.

"I want some poison," she said to the druggist. She was over thirty then, still a slight woman, though thinner than usual, with cold, haughty black eyes in a face the flesh of which was strained across the temples and about the eye-sockets as you imagine a lighthouse-keeper's face ought to look.

"I want some poison," she said.

"Yes, Miss Emily. What kind? For rats and such? I'd recom—"

"I want the best you have. I don't care what kind."

The druggist named several. "They'll kill anything up to an elephant. But what you want is—"

"Arsenic," Miss Emily said. "Is that a good one?"

"Is... arsenic? Yes ma'am. But what you want—"

"I want arsenic."

The druggist looked down at her. She looked back at him, erect, her face like a strained flag. "Why, of course," the druggist said. "If that's what you want. But the law requires you to tell what you are going to use it for."

Miss Emily just stared at him, her head tilled back in order to look him eye for eye, until he looked away and went and got the arsenic and wrapped it up. The Negro delivery boy brought her the package; the druggist didn't come back. When she opened the package at home there was written on the box, under the skull and bones: "For rats. "

IV

So the next day we all said, "She will kill herself" ; and we said it would be the best thing. When she had first begun to be seen with Homer Barren, we had said, "She will marry him. " Then we said, "She will persuade him yet", because Homer himself had remarked—he liked men, and it was known that he drank with the younger men in the Elk's Club—that he was not a marrying man. Later we said, "Poor Emily", behind the jalousies as they passed on Sunday afternoon in the glittering buggy. Miss Emily with her head high and Homer Barren with his hat cocked and a cigar in his teeth, reins and whip in a yellow glove.

Then some of the ladies began to say that it was a disgrace to the town and a bad example to the young people. The men did not want to interfere, but at last the ladies forced the Baptist minister—Miss Emily's people were Episcopal—to call upon her. He would never divulge what happened during that interview, but he refused to go back again. The next Sunday they again drove about the streets, and the following day the minister's wife wrote to Miss Emily's relations in Alabama.

So she had blood-kin under her roof again and we sat back to watch developments. At first nothing happened. Then we were sure that they were to be married. We learned that Miss Emily had been to the jeweler's and ordered a man's toilet set in silver, with the letters H. B. on each piece. Two days later we learned that she had bought a complete outfit of men's clothing, including a nightshirt, and we said, "They are married. " We were really glad. We were glad because the two female cousins were even more Grierson than Miss Emily had ever been.

So we were not surprised when Homer Barren—the streets had been finished some time since—was gone. We were a little disappointed that there was not a public blowing-off, but we believed that he had gone on to prepare for Miss Emily's coming, or to give her a chance to get rid of the cousins. (By that time it was a cabal, and we were all Miss Emily's allies to help circumvent the cousins.) Sure enough, after another week they departed. And, as we had expected all along, within three days Homer Barren was back in town. A neighbor saw the Negro man admit him at the kitchen door at dusk one evening.

And that was the last we saw of Homer Barron. And of Miss Emily for some time. The Negro man went in and out with the market basket, but the front door remained closed. Now and then we would see her at a window for a moment, as the men did that night when they sprinkled the lime, but for almost six months she did not appear on the streets. Then we knew that this was to be expected too; as if that quality of her father which had thwarted her woman's life so many times had been too virulent and too furious to die.

When we next saw Miss Emily, she had grown fat and her hair was turning gray. During the next few years it grew grayer and grayer until it attained an even pepper-and-salt iron-gray, when it ceased turning. Up to the day of her death at seventy-four it was still that vigorous iron-gray, like the hair of an active man.

From that time on her front door remained closed, save for a period of six or seven years, when she was about forty, during which she gave lessons in china-painting. She fitted up a studio in one of the downstairs rooms, where the daughters and granddaughters of Colonel Sartoris' contemporaries were sent to her with the same regularity and in the same spirit that they were sent on Sundays with a twenty-five cent piece for the collection plate. Meanwhile her taxes had been remitted.

Then the newer generation became the backbone and the spirit of the town, and the painting pupils grew up and fell away and did not send their children to her with boxes of color and tedious brushes and pictures cut from the ladies' magazines. The front door closed upon the last one and remained closed for good. When the town got free postal delivery Miss Emily alone refused to let them fasten the metal numbers above her door and attach a mailbox to it. She would not listen to them.

Daily, monthly, yearly we watched the Negro grow grayer and more stooped, going in and out with the market basket. Each December we sent her a tax notice, which would be returned by the post office a week later, unclaimed. Now and then we would see her in one of the downstairs windows—she had evidently shut up the top floor of the house—like the carven torso of an idol in a niche, looking or not looking at us, we could never tell which. Thus she passed from generation to generation—dear, inescapable, impervious, tranquil, and perverse.

And so she died. Fell ill in the house filled with dust and shadows, with only a doddering Negro man to wait on her. We did not even know she was sick; we had long since given up trying to get any information from the Negro. He talked to no one, probably not even to her, for his voice had grown harsh and rusty, as if from disuse.

She died in one of the downstairs rooms, in a heavy walnut bed with a curtain, her gray head propped on a pillow yellow and moldy with age and lack of sunlight.

V

The Negro met the first of the ladies at the front door and let them in, with their hushed, sibilant voices and their quick, curious glances, and then he disappeared. He walked right through the house and out the back and was not seen again.

The two female cousins came at once. They held the funeral on the second day, with the town coming to look at Miss Emily beneath a mass of bought flowers, with the crayon face of her father musing profoundly above the bier and the ladies sibilant and macabre; and the very old men— some in their brushed Confederate uniforms—on the porch and the lawn, talking of Miss Emily as if she had been a contemporary of theirs, believing that they had danced with her and courted her perhaps, confusing time with its mathematical progression, as the old do, to whom all the past is not a diminishing road, but, instead, a huge meadow which no winter ever quite touches, divided from them now by the narrow bottleneck of the most recent decade of years.

Already we knew that there was one room in that region above stairs which no one had seen in forty years, and which would have to be forced. They waited until Miss Emily was decently in the ground before they opened it.

The violence of breaking down the door seemed to fill this room with pervading dust. A thin, acrid pall as of the tomb seemed to lie everywhere upon this room decked and furnished as for a bridal: upon the valance curtains of faded rose color, upon the rose-shaded lights, upon the dressing table, upon the delicate array of crystal and the man's toilet things backed with tarnished silver, silver so tarnished that the monogram was obscured. Among them lay a collar and tie, as if they had just been removed, which, lifted, left upon the surface a pale crescent in the dust. Upon a chair hung the suit, carefully folded; beneath it the two mute shoes and the discarded socks.

The man himself lay in the bed.

For a long while we just stood there, looking down at the profound and fleshless grin. The body had apparently once lain in the attitude of an embrace, but now the long sleep that outlasts love, that conquers even the grimace of love, had cuckolded him. What was left of him, rotted beneath what was left of the nightshirt, had become inextricable from the bed in which he lay; and upon him and upon the pillow beside him lay that even coating of the patient and biding dust.

Then we noticed that in the second pillow was the indentation of a head. One of us lifted something from it, and leaning forward, that faint and invisible dust dry and acrid in the nostrils, we saw a long strand of iron-gray hair.

■ Study Questions

1. According to the first paragraph, what did people go to Miss Emily's funeral for?

2. What did Miss Emily mean to the townspeople when she was alive? Why was she "a sort of hereditary obligation upon the town"? How did the "next generation" think about this "obligation"? What did they do about it? What was the result?

3. In Part Ⅱ, What troubled the neighbors? Whom did they complain to? What was the reply? How was the problem solved?

4. What had been the attitude of Emily's father towards her love and marriage? How did Emily react when her father died?

5. What was Homer Barron? Where was he from? How did the townspeople respond to his love affairs with Emily?

6. How did Emily get the poison? What did people think she would do with it?

7. What kind of goods did Emily buy and sent to the townspeople the wrong message that she was going to get married?

8. In the eyes of the townspeople, what did Emily do after her lover "disappeared"? What did they find in the room in which "no one had seen in forty years"? What did Emily actually do about her lover? What did she actually do with the poison? What was the actual cause of the terrible smell that once upset the neighborhood?

9. What's the effect of the use of the pronoun "we" by the narrator?

10. How is Faulkner's handling of chronology expressive of the nature of memory?

11. What does Emily represent to her town and her region? What attitudes toward social classes figure in the action and how do these change?

12. What is the relation between comic elements and the melancholy or shocking ingredients of the story?

13. What does Homer Barron represent?

14. What motives can you attribute to Emily for her killing of Homer Barron? How are these motives related to the theme?

Arthur Miller (1915—2005)

Arthur Miller, along with Tennessee Williams, led the postwar new drama. While his position in the history of American (and indeed world) drama is assured, it may be many years before there is general agreement about the nature of his contribution and the order in which his plays should be ranked, for there is at the heart of his work something which seems to perplex and divide his critics. Some dismiss him as little more than a disciple of Ibsen; others cite him as a penetrating critic of American society and an important innovator in the theatre. Some critics call his work "bloodless", while others admire the subtlety of his characterization. There is disagreement, too, about whether Miller's dramatic vision is profound or superficial, clear-eyed or sentimental.

Arthur Miller was born in the Harlem district of New York. His father was a Jewish clothing manufacturer who was to lose all his business in 1929 during the Depression. The "crash" of 1929 and the Depression were the major influences on the playwright's view of life. Miller became convinced that there was an invisible world behind the apparent one, and he began to search for the hidden laws that would explain this catastrophe. In the same year the family moved to a small house in Brooklyn.

After leaving high school, Miller started a series of jobs until he settled down as a shipping clerk in an automobile-parts warehouse in Manhattan at $15 a week. It was there that he discovered serious literature. In this year at the warehouse he read more than he had in the rest of his life. He was drawn to the great Russian novelists, especially Dostoyevsky, and he began to dream of becoming a writer.

In 1934 Miller applied to the University of Michigan, enrolling in journalism and becoming a night editor on the student paper. At university he began to widen his political perspectives. He became interested in the Spanish Civil War, and found himself increasingly attached to the socialist ideals of the time.

He won several prizes for drama when he was a student in the University. In the March break of his second year at Michigan, Miller tried for one of the annual Hopwood literary prizes and spent six days writing *No Villain*. Some three days later he was awarded the first prize of $250 and his playwriting career had began. Then, Miller revised *No Villain* which, under the title *They Too Arise*, was awarded a $1,250 award by the Theatre Guild's Bureau of New Plays and was produced in Ann Arbor and Detroit. He also wrote his second play, *Honor at Dawn*, which in June won him his second Hopwood Award. In his final year Miller completed a third play, *The Great Disobedience*, but it failed to win the Hopwood Award.

In 1938 he graduated from the University of Michigan. Six years later he had his first Broadway production *The Man Who Had All the Luck*, but closed after four days.

By the time his first commercial success, *All My Sons* (1947), was produced, he had already written eight or nine plays. In 1949 he won a Pulitzer Prize with *Death of a Salesman* (1947) and achieved an international reputation. Among his further works are an adaptation of Ibsen's *Enemy of the people* and *The Crucible* (both containing political implications, the latter of which is actually a thinly veiled indictment of the fanatic McCarthyism in the US in the early 1950s), *After the Fall*, *Incident at Vichy* (1964), and *The Price* (1968).

A typical theme of Arthur Miller's plays concerns the dilemma of modern man in relation to his family and work. What occurs often in a Miller play is that the hero finds himself under a pressure from his society and his ethics, tries in vain to extricate himself from the physical and spiritual quandary into which he has fallen and finds release only in death, often in the form of actual or virtual suicide. The world is harsh. There is little or no choice for the hero. Either he submits to the impossible demands of society, or he rejects them. He dies in either case. Miller is, however, not completely pessimistic. Reading his plays, one feels a faith in man and in life, however vague it may be, though very often gloom overweighs hope.

Miller has also published a number of books of non-fiction accompanied by his wife Inge Morath's photographs: *In Russia*, *In the Country*, *Chinese Encounters*, and *Salesman in Beijing*, the last of which was based on his experience in rehearsing *Death of a Salesman* with Beijing People's Art Theatre in 1983.

Arthur Miller's latest works include: *The Last Yankee* (1991), *The Ride Down Mt. Morgan* (1991), *The American Clock* (1993) and *Broken Glass* (1994).

■ Selected Reading

Death of a Salesman, *a sad version of the American dream, stands apart from almost all of Arthur Miller's other works. It's Miller's most successful attempt at creating individual characters with universal significance. Its plot revolves around the last twenty-four hours in the life of Willy Loman, the hard-working sixty-three-year-old traveling salesman whose ideas of professional, public success jar with the realities of his private desires and modest accomplishments.*

Act II of the play opens happily with Willy making plans to ask his boss for a desk job and then meet his sons for dinner. However, when Willy sees his boss he will not give him a different job and finally tells Willy he is fired. This triggers memories of his brother Ben offering him a job, which he turned down. Willy then goes to Charley's office to borrow money and meets Charley's son Bernard, whom Willy had ridiculed as a boy but who is now a successful lawyer. Charley again offers him a job and Willy is again furious at the "insult".

In the restaurant that evening, Biff tells Happy that Oliver did not remember him—he realized he had been lying to himself about his importance in the company. As he was leaving the office he stole a fountain pen. Willy enters and Biff tries to tell him what has happened but Willy won't listen. Biff and Happy leave Willy alone in the restroom. Willy remembers an incident in Boston where Biff discovers him with a woman which had devastated Biff.

On the boys' return to the house, Linda is furious. Willy is talking to his brother Ben (in his mind) about his plan to commit suicide so his family can have the insurance money. Biff and Willy argue again and Biff tells his family that he has lost every job he ever had through stealing and that he has been in jail. However, Willy sees Biff's admission as a sign that Biff likes him and decides that if he leaves him the money he will be "magnificent". As the others go to bed, Willy leaves the house and crashes his car.

from *The Death of a Salesman*

ACT II

* * * * * *   * * * * * *

Charley stares after him a moment and follows. All light blacks out. Suddenly raucous music is heard, and a red glow rises behind the screen at right. Stanley, a young waiter, appears, carrying a table, followed by Happy, who is carrying two chairs.

STANLEY (*Pitting the table down*): That's all right, Mr. Loman, I can handle it myself. He turns and takes the chairs from Happy and places them at the table.

HAPPY (*Glancing around*): Oh, this is better.

STANLEY: Sure, in the front there you're in the middle of all kinds a noise. Whenever you got a party, Mr. Loman, you just tell me and I'll put you back here. Y'know, there's a lotta people they don't like it private, because when they go out they like to see a lotta action around them because they're sick and tired to stay in the house by theirself. But I know you, you ain't from Hackensack. You know what I mean?

HAPPY (*Sitting down*): So how's it coming, Stanley?

STANLEY: Ah, it's a dog's life. I only wish during the war they'd a took me in the Army—I could been dead by now.

HAPPY: My brother's back, Stanley.

STANLEY: Oh, he come back, heh? From the Far West.

HAPPY: Yeah, big cattle man, my brother, so treat him right. And my father's coining too.

STANLEY: Oh, your father too!

HAPPY: You got a couple of nice lobsters?

STANLEY: Hundred per cent, big.

HAPPY: I want them with the claws.

STANLEY: Don't worry, I don't give you no mice. (*Happy laughs.*) How about some wine? It'll put a head on the meal.

HAPPY: No. You remember, Stanley, that recipe I brought you from overseas? With the champagne in it?

STANLEY: Oh, yeah, sure. I still got it tacked up yet in the kitchen. But that'll have to cost a buck apiece anyways.

HAPPY: That's all right.

STANLEY: What'd you, hit a number or somethin'?

HAPPY: No, it's a little celebration. My brother is—think he pulled off a big deal today. I think we're going into business together.

STANLEY: Great! That's the best for you. Because a family business, you know what I mean? —that's the best.

HAPPY: That's what I think.

STANLEY: 'Cause what's the difference? Somebody steals? It's in the family. Know what I mean? (*Soft voice*) Like this bartender here. The boss is goin' crazy what kinda leak he's got in the cash register. You put it in but it don't come out.

HAPPY (*Raising his head*): Sh!

STANLEY: What?

HAPPY: You notice I wasn't lookin' right or left, was I?

STANLEY: No.

HAPPY: And my eyes are closed.

STANLEY: So what's the—

HAPPY: Strudel's comin'.

STANLEY (*Catching on, looks around*): Ah, no, there's no—

(*He breaks off as a furred, lavishly dressed girl enters and sits at the next table. Both fallow her with their eyes.*)

STANLEY: Geez, how'd ya know?

HAPPY: I got radar or something. (*Staring directly at her profile.*) Oooooooo... Stanley.

STANLEY: I think that's for you. Mr. Loman.

HAPPY: Look at that mouth. Oh, God. And the binoculars.

STANLEY: Geez, you got a life, Mr. Loman.

HAPPY: Wait on her.

STANLEY (*Going to the girl's table*): Would you like a menu, ma'am?

GIRL: I'm expecting someone, but I'd like a—

HAPPY: Why don't you bring her—excuse me, miss, do you mind? I sell champagne, and I'd like you to try my brand. Bring her a champagne, Stanley.

GIRL: That's awfully nice of you.

HAPPY: Don't mention it. It's all company money. (*He laughs.*)

GIRL: That's a charming product to be selling, isn't it?

HAPPY: Oh, gets to be like everything else. Selling is selling, y'know.

GIRL: I suppose.

HAPPY: You don't happen to sell, do you?

GIRL: No, I don't sell.

HAPPY: Would you object to a compliment from a stranger? You ought to be on a magazine cover.

GIRL (*Looking at him a little archly*): I have been.

(*Stanley comes in with a glass of champagne.*)

HAPPY: What'd I say before, Stanley? You see? She's a cover girl.

STANLEY: Oh, I could see. I could see.

HAPPY (*To the Girl*): What magazine?

GIRL: Oh, a lot of them. (*She takes the drink.*) Thank you.

HAPPY: You know what they say in France, don't you? "Champagne is the drink of the complexion" —Hya, Biff!

(*Biff has entered and sits with Happy.*)

BIFF：Hello, kid. Sorry, I'm late.

HAPPY：I just got here. Uh, Miss?

GIRL：Forsythe.

HAPPY：Miss Forsythe, this is my brother.

BIFF：Is Dad here?

HAPPY：His name is Biff. You might've heard of him. Great football player.

GIRL：Really? What team?

HAPPY：Are you familiar with football?

GIRL：No, I'm afraid I'm not.

HAPPY：Biff is quarterback[277] with the New York Giants.

GIRL：Well, that is nice, isn't it? (*She drinks.*)

HAPPY：Good health.

GIRL：I'm happy to meet you.

HAPPY：That's my name. Hap. It's really Harold, but at West Point they called me Happy.

GIRL (*Now really impressed*)：Oh, I see. How do you do? She turns her profile.

BIFF：Isn't Dad coming?

HAPPY：You want her?

BIFF：Oh, I could never make that.

HAPPY：I remember the time that idea would never come into your head. Where's the old confidence, Biff?

BIFF：I just saw Oliver—

HAPPY：Wait a minute. I've got to see that old confidence again. Do you want her? She's on call.

BIFF：Oh, no. (*He turns to look at the Girl.*)

HAPPY：I'm telling you. Watch this. (*Turning to the Girl.*) Honey? (*She turns to him.*) Are you busy?

GIRL：Well, I am… but I could make a phone call.

HAPPY：Do that, will you, honey? And see if you can get a friend. We'll be here for a while. Biff is one of the greatest football players in the country.

GIRL (*Standing up*)：Well, I'm certainly happy to meet you.

HAPPY：Come back soon.

GIRL：I'll try.

HAPPY：Don't try, honey, try hard.

277　**quarterback**：a position in American and Canadian football. Quarterbacks are members of the offensive team and line up directly behind the center, in the middle of the offensive line. A quarterback is usually the leader of the offensive team, and initiates most plays. In addition, the quarterback is responsible for calling the signals before most plays.

(*The Girl exits. Stanley follows*, *shaking his head in bewildered admiration.*)

HAPPY: Isn't that a shame now? A beautiful girl like that? That's why I can't get married. There's not a good woman in a thousand. New York is loaded with them, kid!

BIFF: Hap, look—

HAPPY: I told you she was on call!

BIFF (*Strangely unnerved*): Cut it out, will ya? I want to say something to you.

HAPPY: Did you see Oliver?

BIFF: I saw him all right. Now look, I want to tell Dad a couple of things and I want you to help me.

HAPPY: What? Is he going to back you?

BIFF: Are you crazy? You're out of your goddam head, you know that?

HAPPY: Why? What happened?

BIFF (*Breathlessly*): I did a terrible thing today, Hap, It's been the strangest day I ever went through. I'm all numb, I swear.

HAPPY: You mean he wouldn't see you?

BIFF: Well, I waited six hours for him, see? All day. Kept sending my name in. Even tried to date his secretary so she'd get me to him, but no soap.

HAPPY: Because you're not showin' the old confidence, Biff. He remembered you, didn't he?

BIFF (*Stopping Happy with a gesture*): Finally, about five o'clock, he comes out. Didn't remember who I was or anything. I felt like such an idiot, Hap.

HAPPY: Did you tell him my Florida idea?

BIFF: He walked away. I saw him for one minute. I got so mad I could've torn the walls down! How the hell did I ever get the idea I was a salesman there? I even believed myself that I'd been a salesman for him! And then he gave me one look and—I realized what a ridiculous lie my whole life has been! We've been talking in a dream for fifteen years. I was a shipping clerk.

HAPPY: What'd you do?

BIFF (*With great tension and wonder*): Well, he left, see. And the secretary went out. I was all alone in the waiting-room. I don't know what came over me, Hap. The next thing I know I'm in his office—paneled walls, everything. I can't explain it. I—Hap, I took his fountain pen.

HAPPY: Geez, did he catch you?

BIFF: I ran out. I ran down all eleven flights. I ran and ran and ran.

HAPPY: That was an awful dumb—what'd you do that for?

BIFF (*Agonized*): I don't know. I just—wanted to take something. I don't know. You gotta help me, Hap. I'm gonna tell Pop.

HAPPY: You crazy? What for?

BIFF: Hap, he's got to understand that I'm not the man somebody lends that kind of money to.

He thinks I've been spiting him all these years and it's eating him up.

HAPPY: That's just it. You tell him something nice.

BIFF: I can't.

HAPPY: Say you got a lunch date with Oliver tomorrow.

BIFF: So what do I do tomorrow?

HAPPY: You leave the house tomorrow and come back at night and say Oliver is thinking it over. And he thinks it over for a couple of weeks, and gradually it fades away and nobody's the worse.

BIFF: But it'll go on forever!

HAPPY: Dad is never so happy as when he's looking forward to something!

(*Willy enters.*)

HAPPY: Hello, scout!

WILLY: Gee, I haven't been here in years!

(*Stanley has followed Willy in and sets a chair for him. Stanley starts off but Happy stops him.*)

HAPPY: Stanley!

(*Stanley stands by, waiting for an order.*)

BIFF (*Going to Willy with guilt, as to an invalid*): Sit down, Pop. You want a drink?

WILLY: Sure, I don't mind.

BIFF: Let's get a load on.

WILLY: You look worried.

BIFF: N-no. (*To Stanley.*) Scotch all around. Make it doubles.

STANLEY: Doubles, right. (*He goes.*)

WILLY: You had a couple already, didn't you?

BIFF: Just a couple, yeah.

WILLY: Well, what happened, boy? (*Nodding affirmatively, with a smile.*) Everything go all right?

BIFF (*Takes a breath, then reaches wit and grasps Willy's hand*): Pal... (*He is smiling bravely, and Willy is smiling too.*) I had an experience today.

HAPPY: Terrific, Pop.

WILLY: That so? What happened?

BIFF (*High, slightly alcoholic, above the earth*): I'm going to tell you everything from first to last. It's been a strange day. *Silence.* (*He looks around, composes himself as best he can, but his breath keeps breaking the rhythm of his voice.*) I had to wait quite a while for him, and—

BIFF: Yeah, Oliver. All day, as a matter of cold fact. And a lot of—instance—facts, Pop, facts about my life came back to me. Who was it, Pop? Who ever said I was a salesman with Oliver?

WILLY: Well, you were.

BIFF: No, Dad, I was a shipping clerk.

WILLY: But you were practically—

BIFF (*With determination*): Dad, I don't know who said it first, but I was never a salesman for Bill Oliver.

WILLY: What're you talking about?

BIFF: Let's hold on to the facts tonight, Pop. We're not going to get anywhere bullin' around. I was a shipping clerk.

WILLY (*Angrily*): All right, now listen to me—

BIFF: Why don't you let me finish?

WILLY: I'm not interested in stories about the past or any crap of that kind because the woods are burning, boys, you understand? There's a big blaze going on all around. I was fired today.

BIFF (*Shocked*): How could you be?

WILLY: I was fired, I'm looking for a little good news to tell your mother, because the woman has waited and the woman has suffered. The gist of it is that I haven't got a story left in my head, Biff. So don't give me a lecture about facts and aspects. I am not interested. Now what've you got to say to me?

(*Stanley enters with three drinks. They wait until he leaves.*)

WILLY: Did you see Oliver?

BIFF: Jesus, Dad!

WILLY: You mean you didn't go up there?

HAPPY: Sure, he went up there.

BIFF: I did. I—saw him. How could they fire you?

WILLY (*On the edge of his chair*): What kind of a welcome did he give you?

BIFF: He won't even let you work on commission?

WILLY: I'm out! (*Driving.*) So tell me, he gave you a warm welcome?

HAPPY: Sure, Pop, sure!

BIFF (*Driven*): Well, it was kind of—

WILLY: I was wondering if he'd remember you. (*To Happy.*) Imagine, man doesn't see him for ten, twelve years and gives him that kind of welcome!

HAPPY: Damn right!

BIFF(*Trying to return to the offensive*): Pop, look—

WILLY: You know why he remembered you, don't you? Because you impressed him in those days.

BIFF: Let's talk quietly and get this down to the facts, huh?

WILLY (*As though Biff had been interrupting*): Well, what happened? It's great news, Biff. Did he take you into his office or'd you talk in the waiting-room?

BIFF：Well, he came in, see, and—

WILLY(*with a big smile*)：What'd he say? Betcha he threw his arm around you.

BIFF：Well, he kinda—

WILLY (*To Biff*)：He's a fine man. (*To Happy.*) Very hard man to see, y'know.

HAPPY (*agreeing*)：Oh, I know.

WILLY (*To Biff*)：Is that where you had the drinks?

BIFF：Yeah, he gave me a couple of—no, no!

HAPPY (*Cutting in*)：He told him my Florida idea.

WILLY：Don't interrupt. (*To Biff.*) How'd he react to the Florida idea?

BIFF：Dad, will you give me a minute to explain?

WILLY：I've been waiting for you to explain since I sat down here! What happened? He took you into his office and what?

BIFF：Well—I talked. And—and he listened, see.

WILLY：Famous for the way he listens, y'know. What was his answer?

BIFF：His answer was—(*He breaks off, suddenly angry.*) Dad, you're not letting me tell you what I want to tell you!

WILLY (*Accusing, angered*)：You didn't see him, did you?

BIFF：I did see him!

WILLY：What'd you insult him or something? You insulted him, didn't you?

BIFF：Listen, will you let me out of it, will you just let me out of it!

HAPPY：What the hell!

WILLY：Tell me what happened!

BIFF (*To Happy*)：I can't talk to him!

(*A single trumpet note jars the ear. The light of green leaves stains the house, which holds the air of night and a dream. Young Bernard enters and knocks on the door of the house.*)

YOUNG BERNARD (*Frantically*)：Mrs. Loman, Mrs. Loman!

HAPPY：Tell him what happened!

BIFF (*To Happy*)：Shut up and leave me alone!

WILLY：No, no! You had to go and flunk math!

BIFF：What math? What're you talking about?

YOUNG BERNARD：Mrs. Loman, Mrs. Loman!

(*Linda appears in the house, as of old.*)

WILLY (*Wildly*)：Math, math, math!

BIFF：Take it easy, Pop!

YOUNG BERNARD：Mrs. Loman!

WILLY (*Furiously*)：If you hadn't flunked you'd've been set by now!

BIFF：Now, look. I'm gonna tell you what happened, and you're going to listen to me.

YOUNG BERNARD：Mrs. Loman!

BIFF: I waited six hours—

HAPPY: What the hell are you saying?

BIFF: I kept sending in my name but he wouldn't see me. So finally he... (*He continues unheard as light fades low on the restaurant.*)

YOUNG BERNARD: Biff flunked math!

LINDA: No!

YOUNG BERNARD: Birnbaum flunked him! They won't graduate him!

LINDA: But they have to. He's gotta go to the university. Where is he? Biff! Biff!

YOUNG BERNARD: No, he left. He went to Grand Central.

LINDA: Grand—You mean he went to Boston!

YOUNG BERNARD: Is Uncle Willy in Boston?

LINDA: Oh, maybe Willy can talk to the teacher. Oh, the poor, poor boy!

(*Light on house area snaps out.*)

BIFF (*At the table, now audible, holding up a gold fountain pen*): ... so I'm washed up with Oliver, you understand? Are you listening to me?

WILLY (*At a loss*): Yeah, sure. If you hadn't flunked—

BIFF: Flunked what? What're you talking about?

WILLY: Don't blame everything on me! I didn't flunk math—you did! What pen?

HAPPY: That was awful dumb, Biff, a pen like that is worth—

WILLY (*Seeing the pen for the first time*): You took Oliver's pen?

BIFF (*Weakening*): Dad, I just explained it to you.

WILLY: You stole Bill Oliver's fountain pen!

BIFF: I didn't exactly steal it! That's just what I've been explaining to you!

HAPPY: He had it in his hand and just then Oliver walked in, so he got nervous and stuck it in his pocket!

WILLY: My God, Biff!

BIFF: I never intended to do it, Dad!

■ Study Questions

1. Willy and Biff have different explanations for Biff's failure to succeed in the business world. How are their explanations different?

2. What evidence shows that Willy may have chosen a profession that is at odds with his natural inclinations?

3. Analyze the role of seeds in Act Ⅱ's final segment. What do they stand for?

4. *Death of a Salesman* is one of the foundational texts describing the American dream. How does Miller's play differ from the more traditional model? Is Miller overwhelmingly cynical on the topic?

5. Describe the significance of names in this play. How do Happy and Biff's names contrast with or support their characters? Interpret the name "Loman".

6. Discuss the gender relationships in this play. Are there any positive models for a harmonious relationship? Does Miller find this concept plausible?

LITERARY FOCUS

Psychological Analysis

Psychological analysis of literary works evolved as modern psychology itself began to take form during the early 20th century. Although this type of critique employs the concepts expressed by many noted sociologists, including Carl Jung, Alfred Adler and Otto Rank, none have contributed as heavily to this field of study as Sigmund Freud has. While many aspects of his theories have been discounted by contemporary psychologists, the fundamental ideas he expressed have withstood the test of time. Five of these, in particular, form the basis of the psychological analysis of authors and the books they write.

1. The Primacy of the Unconscious: Freud believed that every individual has a conscious and an unconscious mind. Moreover, he believed that it was the unconscious mind that plays the largest role in shaping one's personality. He maintained that the vast differences between real and apparent motives are a result of this delineation between the two aspects of the soul.

2. The Iceberg Theory of the Psyche: Freud believed that the psyche, or "soul", of an individual was shaped like an iceberg. The small part that remained above the surface for all to see was the ego, the individual's self image that he projected to the world. Below the surface, much larger, the pleasure-principle, the id, remained away from public view. Lining this iceberg was the superego, representing parental influences. Between the conscious mind (the ego) and the unconscious mind (the id), at the "waterline" of the iceberg, was a line separating the two parts of the individual. Occasionally, the id would poke through that line, but, in most psychologically well-adjusted people, this barrier was a strong one.

3. Dreams are an expression of our unconscious mind: One of Freud's best-known theories states that the conflict between the ego and the id is continued while we sleep. He believed that these two aspects of our psyche expressed themselves while we sleep, using a language of symbolism and hidden meanings. He believed that id-driven dreams were outbursts of instinct and repression and that realistic dreams were an example of our ego's iron control over our soul even while we sleep.

4. Infantile behavior is essentially sexual: Freud believed that during an individual's formative years, he or she was entirely governed by his developing id. This developing unconscious often takes sexual and/or hostile mannerisms, as in the case of the Oedipus complex, in which a young boy falls in love with his mother and is jealous of and hateful towards his father for the attentions he receives from her. Freud also believed that any repression or neurosis formed during this time period would later surface as damaging outbursts in the mature adult.

5. The relationship between neurosis and creativity: Freud's last theory applies more to the author than the characters in his works. Freud believed that those who create (artists, poets, etc.) are using their creativity as a sort of therapy. He believed that an individual relieved his or her own neurotic tension through their creative work. In addition, these individuals give us insights into the nature of reality and the people who inhabit it. Thus, psychoanalyzing a work of literature can give us great insight into the unconscious of the author.

These five concepts can be employed in the study of characters and their actions in a literary forum, as well as giving us insight into the nature of man in general.

■ Thinking About Psychological Analysis

Select a character that you believe to be suitable for "psychological analysis" from any of the works in this course book. Analyze the possible subconscious causes for the character's words and actions to deepen our understanding or explore a new perspective of the character's disposition or destiny.

READING FOR APPRECIATION

Beyond the Surface

We sometimes hear people say that when they read literature they look for "hidden meanings". Yet no writer wants to hide his or her meanings from us. Writers want to reveal their meanings. Nevertheless, they seldom tell us directly what a poem or a story means.

Literature is an art of implication. It wants to surprise us, to make us participate in the experience it offers. Often it deals with the questions, the enigmas, the mysteries of our existence. No, writers do not want to hide anything from us, yet they do expect our cooperation. They expect us to go beyond the surface.

Look again at the poems by W. H. Auden that open this unit. In both of them, Auden expects us to go beyond the surface, to open ourselves to suggestions. In one of the poems the refrain, "If I could tell you I would let you know", may make us think: Life is filled with mysteries and wonders, experiences we cannot fully explain. The poet suggests that he is in love but wondering about, worrying about, what will become of this love. The poem is about uncertainty, and it asks us to share its mixture of delight and sorrow.

In "The Unknown Citizen" we look beyond the surface to see that Auden is not the speaker of the poem. He is not part of the government that seems so "concerned" for the citizen, nor does he like a government that judges people by statistics and reports. By the end of the poem, we know that the government would never have heard whether or not the Unknown Citizen felt free or happy. But what has happened to us as readers? We have joined the poet in his experience. How much less powerful these poems would be if Auden had merely stated his meanings!

Prose, too, asks us to look beyond the surface. In Katherine Anne Porter's "Jilting of Granny Weatherall", the point of the story is that Granny has never forgotten or forgiven the man who jilted her many years before. Her long and seemingly successful life has always been troubled by that memory. Porter's story is more moving because she allows us to watch that thought troubling Granny's mind, rising, receding, and rising to the surface again. The real action of the story is just a bit beyond Granny's consciousness. As readers beyond the surface, we gain a finer experience by not having the point spelled out for us.

Throughout *Death of a Salesman* the Lomans in general cannot distinguish between reality and illusion. This is a major theme and source of conflict in the play. Willy cannot see who he and his sons are. He believes that they are great men who have what it takes to be successful and beat the business world. Unfortunately, he is mistaken. In reality, Willy and his sons are not, and cannot, be successful. This reality versus illusion problem eventually brings about Willy's downfall. Willy is unable to see change. He is man lost in the modern era of technology. He says, "How can they whip cheese?" and is constantly "In a race with the junkyard." Willy has lost at trying to live the American Dream and the play can be viewed as commentary about society. Willy was a man who had worked all his life by the machinery of Democracy and Free Enterprise and was then spit mercilessly out, spent like a "piece of fruit". Arthur Miller has no intention to tell the reader his purpose of composing this modern tragedy directly. In fact, he does not mention the term American dream at all. A careful analysis of the illusion on the surface, however, adds greatly to the attraction of the play.

As readers we do not always see the full implications of a work of literature. That is why we study literature, discuss it, and write about it: to discover what is beyond the surface. Our discussions, whether spoken or written, are attempts to share our enthusiasms and puzzlements. For literature is not only communication between writer and reader; it is communication within a community of readers, too. Each member of that community may see or feel slightly different possibilities in a story or play or poem. By sharing our thoughts, each of us comes to have a larger experience of literature and of life.

VOICE OF THE AGE

A Usable Past

One critic has said that Americans have spent much of their time and imagination on a quest for a usable past. The years from 1930 to 1960 seem to have been spent largely in that search. The shock of the Depression and the cataclysm of World War II forced many Americans to think twice about what part of the American tradition was still meaningful to them. Many of the authors mentioned in this unit reveal a desire to look back at the past—whether in its personal or public aspects—and draw strength, ideas, or at least some kind of lesson from it.

W. H. Auden: *Time will say nothing but I told you so, / Time only knows the price we have to pay; / If I could tell you I would let you know.*

Theodore Roethke: *The whiskey on your breath / Could make a small boy dizzy; / But I hung on like death: / Such waltzing was not easy.*

Langston Hughes: *I've known rivers: / I've known rivers ancient as the world and older than / the flow of human blood in human veins.*

Faulkner: *Alive, Miss Emily had been a tradition, a duty, and a care; a sort of hereditary obligation upon the town, dating from that day in 1894 when Colonel Sartoris, the mayor—he who fathered the edict that no Negro woman should appear on the streets without an apron—remitted her taxes, the dispensation dating from the death of her father on into perpetuity. Not that Miss Emily would have accepted charity. Colonel Sartoris invented an involved tale to the effect that Miss Emily's father had loaned money to the town, which the town, as a matter of business, preferred this way of repaying. Only a man of Colonel Sartoris' generation and thought could have invented it, and only a woman could have believed it.*

The writers mentioned in this unit stepped back into the past to see what they could retrieve. Some found inspiring models for living. Others discovered that the past can never be exactly repeated, that in a new time new heroes and new definitions of heroism must be created.

Chapter 9

IN OUR TIME 1960—PRESENT

INTRODUCTION

The Contemporary Experience

The 1960s were the age of youth, as 70 million children from the post-war baby boom became teenagers and young adults. The movement away from the conservative 1950s continued and eventually resulted in revolutionary ways of thinking and real change in the cultural fabric of American life. Once again Americans seemed to be face to face with a New World.

The 1960s were also a turbulent time in America. The Civil Rights movement made great changes in society. The hippie movement endorsed drugs, rock music, mystic religions and sexual freedom. While the Space Race continued between the two Super Powers, in 1962, the Cuba Missile Crisis broke out. President John F. Kennedy readied troops to invade Cuba, and the Soviet Union prepared to fire at US cities if they made a move. Then came the assassination of John F. Kennedy in 1963. Vice President Lyndon B. Johnson became the President and was reelected the following year. Soon he involved the whole nation into the Vietnam War. The anti-war sentiment grew in the US. Johnson, blamed by many for the war and the racial unrest in the country, did not run for reelection in 1968. John Kennedy's brother, Robert campaigned for the nomination for President and he, too was killed. This decade also saw the assassination of two leaders of the Civil Rights movement—Malcolm X in 1965 and Martin Luther King in 1968.

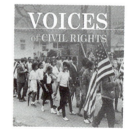

The chaotic events of the 60s, including war and social change, seemed destined to continue in the 70s. Major trends included a growing disillusionment of government, advances in civil rights, increased influence of the women's movement, a heightened concern for the environment, and increased space exploration. Many of the "radical" ideas of the 60s gained wider acceptance in the new decade, and were mainstreamed into American life and culture.

The 1980s became the Me! Me! Me! generation of status seekers. Adrienne Rich[278] once wrote: "In Those Years / In those years, people will say, we lost track / of the meaning of we, of you / we found ourselves / reduced to *I* / and the whole thing? / became silly, ironic, terrible: / we were trying to live a personal life / and yes, that was the only life / we could bear witness to // But the great dark birds of history screamed and plunged / into our personal weather / They were headed somewhere else but their beaks and pinions drove / along the shore, through the rags of fog / where we stood, saying I. " Published in 1991, the poem surely speaks to the 1980s generation. During this decade, hostile takeovers, leveraged buyouts, and mega-mergers spawned a new breed of billionaire. Donald Trump, Leona Helmsley, and Ivan Boesky iconed the meteoric rise and fall of the rich and famous. "If you've got it, flaunt it and you can have it all!" were watchwords. Forbes' list of 400 richest people became more important than its 500 largest companies. Binge buying and credit became a way of life and "Shop Til you Drop" was the watchword. Labels were everything, even (or especially) for the children. Video games, aerobics, minivans, camcorders, and talk shows became part of the American lives. The decade began with double-digit inflation; Reagan declared a war on drugs; Kermit didn't find it easy to be green; hospital costs rose; the country lost many, many of its finest talents to AIDS; unemployment rose. At the turn of the decade, many were happy to leave the spendthrift 80s for the 90s, although some thought the 80s totally awesome.

Since the 1990s, people all over the world have been experiencing an electronic age. The World Wide Web was born in 1992, changing the way we communicate (e-mail), spend our money (online gambling, stores), and do business (e-commerce). By 1994, 3 million people were online. And by 1998, this figure increased to 100 million people. Today, billions of people have been connected. Internet lingo like plug-ins, BTW (by the way), GOK (God only knows), IMHO (in my humble  opinion), FAQS, SPAM, FTP, ISP, and phrases like "See you online" or "The server's down" or "Bill Gates" became part of our everyday vocabulary.

What is it that makes the contemporary experience different from the past? Many historians feel that the time people now live through is the most difficult to describe. Nevertheless, hundreds of books are produced each year trying to explain what it means to be a contemporary American. One thing is sure: Americans are continuing as ever to balance their ideas and realities, to look closely at their goals and their impressive national achievements. Americans seem to have created a new sense of the possible without giving up the American dream.

Literature in the 60s and 70s

The tension, horror, and meaninglessness of contemporary American life became a major theme of novelists during the 1960s and 70s. While authors such as Saul Bellow, Bernard Malamud, Hortense Calisher, and Philip Roth presented the varied responses of urban intellectuals, usually Jews, and John Updike and John Cheever treated the largely Protestant middle class, William Burroughs, Joyce Carol Oates, and Raymond Carver unsparingly depicted the conflict and violence inherent in American life at all levels of society.

Irony and so-called black humor were the weapons of authors like Roth, Joseph Heller, and Jules Feiffer. However, other writers, notably Donald Barthelme, Jerzy Kosinski, Thomas Pynchon, and Kurt Vonnegut, Jr. , expressed their view of the world as unreal, as mad, by writing fantasies that were by turns charming, obscure,

---

278   Adrienne Rich (1929—   ) is an American feminist, poet, teacher, and writer. She was the winner of the National Book Award for Poetry in 1974 and the National Medal of Arts in 1997, both of which she refused.

exciting, profound, and terrifying. Many of these writers have been called postmodern, but the term encompasses a number of chrematistics, including multiculturalism, self-reflection, and attention to new means of communication.

Although the poets Allen Ginsberg, Gregory Corso, and Lawrence Ferlinghetti gained initial recognition as part of the "beat generation," their individual reputations were soon firmly established. Writers of "perceptual verse" such as Charles Olson, Robert Creeley, Denise Levertov, and Robert Duncan became widely recognized during the 1960s. One of the most provocative and active poets of the decade was Robert Lowell, who often wrote of the anguish and corruption in modern life. His practice of revelation about his personal life evolved into so-called confessional poetry, which was also written by such poets as Anne Sexton, Sylvia Plath, and, in a sense, John Berryman. Accomplished poets with idiosyncratic styles were Elizabeth Bishop and James Dickey. To some degree, poetry has also become polarized along ideological lines, as shown in the work of feminist poet Adrienne Rich. Meanwhile, the bittersweet lyrics of James Merrill expressed the concerns of a generation.

The Beat Generation

Jan Gregory Allen Lawrence Herbert Ann
Kerouac Corso Ginsberg Ferlinghetti Huncke Charters

Contemporary Literature

The pressure and fascination of actual events during the 1960s intrigued many writers of fiction, and Truman Capote,[279] John Hersey, James Michener, and Norman Mailer wrote with perception and style about political conventions, murders, demonstrations, and presidential elections. Post-Vietnam War American literature has called into question many previously unchallenged assumptions about life. In addition, writing in many prose styles, such novelists as Don DeLillo, Peter Taylor, William Kennedy, Richard Ford, Robert Stone, E. Annie Proulx, and T. Coraghessen Boyle have explored a wide variety of experiences and attitudes in contemporary American society. The literature of the 1980s and 90s also encompasses the work of African-American (e. g., Nobel Prize-winner Toni Morrison, Alice Walker, and Gloria Naylor), Latino (e. g., Oscar Hijuelos, Rudolfo Anaya, and Sandra Cisneros), Native American (e. g., Louise Erdrich and N. Scott Momaday), Asian-American (e. g., Maxine Hong Kingston and Amy Tan), and homosexual (e. g., Edmund Wilson, David Leavitt, and Rita Mae Brown) writers, who previously were often excluded or ignored in mainstream literature.

Surprisingly, the contemporary American literature is fundamentally traditional, but the traditions it follows are the traditions of Modernism. Modernism, the extraordinary efforts and accomplishments of the writers and artists of the early decades of the 20th century, has become heritage. There have been no major movements in literature since that time, only refinements, restatements, all building on the shoulders of those literary giants of the country—Pound, Eliot, Frost, Stevens, Hemingway, Faulkner, etc.

Modernism has given us forms and techniques that we have not yet exhausted. Even literature that calls itself postmodern is dependent upon the Modernist tradition. Modern free verse with its irregular rhythms, its use of association instead of direct statement, and its breakdown of standard forms still intrigues contemporary poets. The stream-of-consciousness technique in prose, the creation of prose poems, the imitation of storytelling techniques

---

[279] **Truman Capote** (1924—1984) was an American writer whose non-fiction, stories, novels and plays are recognized literary classics, including the novella *Breakfast at Tiffany's* (1958) and *In Cold Blood* (1965), which he labeled a "non-fiction novel." At least 20 films and TV dramas have been produced from Capote novels, stories and screenplays.

taken from movies, continue to be exciting when used by today's American novelists.

Some of American writers still seem experimental; some try to incorporate Modernist techniques into more conventional forms. However, to a certain extent, we have become so used to the "modern" style of writing and expression that we often hardly notice it. Literature is following the path taken by modern music: The "outrageous" harmonies that seemed so new in early 20th-century music are now a part of the everyday sounds on television, in movies, and in popular songs.

Technology has greatly affected this age, of course. The paperback revolution has made more books available to more people than ever before in history. Television, computers, and word processors have changed the ways people absorb information, the way writers write, the way people read and organize their thoughts. Although our time appears to many people to be an age of images—pictures on screens—many others realize that for the subtleties of communication we are still vitally dependent upon words.

The selections in this unit can only begin to display the great variety of writing taking place in contemporary American literature. American poets are still consolidating the treasures of Modernism; many of the poems written today seem as if they could have been written in the 1920s. American prose writers are trying to find ways of telling stories that will be both "new" and accessible to most people. The invention, for example, of the form called the nonfiction novel tries to do just that.

Earlier in this century, people talked about the "death of the novel", but the talk was premature. In addition to those writers represented in the following sections, there are many other American novelists who have created and are creating exciting fiction.

Robert Penn Warren (1905—1989)

Robert Penn Warren, American poet, novelist, and literary critic, was one of the founders of the New Criticism. He was also a charter member of the Fellowship of Southern Writers. While most famous from the success of his novel *All the King's Men* (1946), Warren also won two Pulitzer Prizes for his poetry. In addition, he collaborated with critic Cleanth Brooks on two of the most influential textbooks for teaching literature, *Understanding Poetry* and *Understanding Fiction*.

Warren was born in Kentucky. He graduated from Clarksville High School (TN), Vanderbilt University in 1925, and the University of California, Berkeley in 1926. While still an undergraduate at Vanderbilt, Warren became associated with the group of poets there known as the Fugitives, and somewhat later, during the early 1930s, Warren and some of the same writers formed a group known as the Southern Agrarians. He contributed "The Briar Patch" to the Agrarian manifesto *I'll Take My Stand* along with 11 other Southern writers and poets (including fellow Vanderbilt poets/critics John Crowe Ransom, Allen Tate, and Donald Davidson). In "The Briar Patch" the young Warren defends racial segregation, in line with the traditionalist conservative political leanings of the Agrarian group, although Davidson deemed Warren's stances in the essay so progressive that he argued for excluding it from the collection. However, Warren recanted these views in the 1950s by writing an article in *Life* magazine on the Civil Rights Movement and adopted a high profile as a supporter of racial integration. He also published *Who Speaks for the Negro*, a collection of interviews with black civil rights leaders including Malcolm X, in 1965, further distinguishing his political leanings from the more conservative philosophies associated with fellow Agrarians such as Tate, Cleanth Brooks, and particularly Davidson.

Warren served as the Consultant in Poetry to the Library of Congress, Poet Laureate, 1944—1945 and went on to win the Pulitzer Prize in 1947, for his best known work, the novel *All the King's Men*, whose main character, Willie Stark, resembles the radical populist governor of Louisiana, Huey Pierce Long (1893—1935), whom Warren was able to observe closely while teaching at Louisiana State University in Baton Rouge from 1933—1942. Warren won Pulitzer Prizes in poetry in 1958 for *Promises: Poems* 1954—1956, and in 1979 for *Now and Then*. He is the only writer ever to win the Pulitzer in both fiction and poetry. *All the King's Men*, starring Broderick Crawford, became a highly successful film, winning the Academy Award for Best Picture in 1949. A 2006 film adaptation by writer/director Steven Zaillian featured Sean Penn as Willie Stark and Jude Law as Jack Burden.

In 1981, Warren was selected as a MacArthur Fellow and later was named as the first U.S. Poet Laureate Consultant in Poetry on February 26, 1986. In April 2005, the United States Postal Service issued a commemorative stamp to mark the 100th anniversary of Penn Warren's birth. Introduced at the Post Office in his native Guthrie, it depicts the author as he appeared in a 1948 photograph, with a background scene of a political rally designed to evoke the setting of *All the King's Men*.

■ Selected Reading

Warren's Audubon: A Vision illustrates a style of modern writing that began with Ezra Pound's Cantos, *poetry that includes fragments of actual historical documents. Warren's poem is a tribute to John James Audubon (1785—1851), the great American naturalist and painter, who traveled through America studying and painting the birds and other animals native to this continent. Audubon's masterpiece is the huge volume of colored engravings called* Birds of America *(1827—1838). Warren's tribute moves back and forth between a re-creation of Audubon's life and vision (the subtitle of the poem is "A Vision") and quotations from Audubon's own writing.*

from *Audubon: A Vision*

He walked in the world. Knew the lust of the eye.

Wrote: "Ever since a Boy I have had an astonishing desire
　　　　to see Much of the World and particularly
　　　　to acquire a true knowledge of the Birds of North America."

5　　He dreamed of hunting with Boone[280], from imagination painted his portrait.
　　　He proved that the buzzard does not scent its repast, but sights it.
　　　He looked in the eye of the wounded white-headed eagle.

---

[280] **Boone**: Daniel Boone (1734—1820), U.S. frontiersman.

Wrote: "… the Noble Fellow looked at his Enemies
         with a Contemptible Eye. "

10   At dusk he stood on a bluff, and the bellowing of buffalo
     Was like distant ocean. He saw
     Bones whiten the plain in the hot daylight.

     He saw the Indian, and felt the splendor of God.

     Wrote: "… for there I see the Man Naked from his
15   hand and yet free from acquired Sorrow. "

     Below the salt[281], in rich houses, he sat, and knew insult.
     In the lobbies and couloirs[282] of greatness he dangled,
     And was not unacquainted with contumely[283].

     Wrote: "My Lovely Miss Pirrie of Oackley Passed by Me
20   this Morning, but did not remember how beautiful
           I had rendered her face once by Painting it
           at her Request with Pastelles. "

     Wrote: "… but thanks to My humble talents I can run
           the gantlet[284] throu this World without her help. "

25   And ran it, and ran undistracted by promise of ease,
     Nor even the kind condescension of Daniel Webster. [285]

     Wrote: "… would give me a fat place was I willing to
           have one; but I love indepenn and piece more
           than humbug and money. "

---

[281] **Below the salt**: in a less honored position. Guests were once seated at the upper or lower part of the table with a bowl of salt in the middle; honored guests were above the salt.

[282] **couloirs**: corridors.

[283] **contumely**: rudeness.

[284] **run the gantlet**: here, to carry on while being criticized or opposed from all sides.

[285] **Daniel Webster**: U. S. orator and statesman (1792—1852) who served in the House of Representatives, in the Senate, and as Secretary of State.

30   And proved same, but in the end, entered

On honor. Far, over the ocean, in the silken salons,[286]

With hair worn long like a hunter's, eyes shining,

He whistled the birdcalls of his distant forest.

Wrote: "... in my sleep I continually dream of birds. "

35   And in the end, entered into his earned house,

And slept in a bed, and with Lucy.[287]

                   But the fiddle

Soon lay on the shelf untouched, the mouthpiece

Of the flute was dry, and his brushes.

40   his mind

Was darkened, and his last joy

Was in the lullaby they sang him, in Spanish, at sunset.

He died, and was mourned, who had loved the world.

Who had written: "... a world which though wicked

45   enough in all conscience is *perhaps* as

good as worlds unknown. "

■ Study Questions

1. According to Line 1, what did Audubon know? According to Line 4, what did he wish " particularly to acquire"? With whom did Audubon dream of hunting (Lines 5-7)? What did he prove about the buzzard? In what eye did he look?

2. What did Audubon hear at dusk as he stood on the bluff? What did he see in the hot day-light? What did he feel when he saw the Indian (Line 13)? According to Line 16, what did Audubon know when he sat below the salt in " rich houses" ? What is Miss Pirrie's behavior an example of, according to Line 18?

3. Why, according to Lines 27-29, did Audubon refuse Daniel Webster's offer of a " fat place" to live? What happened to Audubon soon after he settled in his " earned house" ? At the end of the poem, what words does Audubon use to describe the world?

4. What does " lust of the eye" suggest about Audubon's interest in nature? What do the allusions to Boone and the Indian suggest?

---

[286] **Far... salons**: referring to Audubon's art exhibitions in Great Britain.

[287] **Lucy**: Lucy Bakewell, Audubon's wife.

5. Was Audubon well-educated? Did he contribute to the science of ornithology?

6. What does the image of the bones whitening on the plain imply about the buffalo, and what does "wounded" imply about the bald eagle? What does the poem suggest Audubon had in common with these animals?

7. What does Audubon seem to represent for the poet? What would insults and rudeness to Audubon therefore represent? What would Audubon's death signify?

8. What other heroes whom you have read about in this book have qualities in common with those of Audubon as Warren portrays him? What other works of literature are concerned with themes similar to those of this poem?

John Updike (1932—   )

John Updike, American novelist, short story writer and poet, is internationally known for his Rabbit series: *Rabbit, Run* (1960), *Rabbit Redux* (1971), *Rabbit Is Rich* (1981), *Rabbit At Rest* (1990), and *Rabbit Remembered* (2001). Among them the third and the fourth one both won Pulitzer Prizes for Updike. The series follow the life of Harry "Rabbit" Angstrom, a star athlete, from his youth through the social and sexual upheavals of the 1960s, to later periods of his life, and to final decline. Describing his subject as "the American small town, Protestant middle class," Updike is well known for his careful craftsmanship and prolific writing. Updike's oeuvre has been large, consisting of novels, collections of poems, short stories, and essays.

John Updike was born in Reading in Pennsylvania, but until he was 13 he lived in Shillington, a smaller city near Reading. Updike's childhood was shadowed by psoriasis and stammering, but his mother encouraged him to write. Later Updike entered Harvard University on a full scholarship. In 1959 he published a well-regarded collection of short stories, *The Same Door*, which included both "Who Made Yellow Roses Yellow?" and "A Trillion Feet of Gas." Besides the Rabbit Series, he has published a few other novels, including *The Centaur* (1963, National Book Award), *The Coup* (1978, about a fictional Cold-War-era African dictatorship), *The Witches of Eastwick* (1984, later made into a movie of the same name), *Roger's Version* (1986), and *Gertrude and Claudius* (2000, a post-modern novel serving as the prelude to the story of *Hamlet*).

Updike favors realism and naturalism in his writing. For instance, the opening of *Rabbit, Run* spans several pages describing a pick-up basketball game in intricate detail. His writing typically focuses on relationships among people: friends, married couples, or those in extramarital affairs. *Couples* and the Rabbit series, in particular, follow this pattern. In the Rabbit books, the changing social, political, and economic history of America forms the background to the Angstroms' marriage and acts occasionally as a commentary on it—and vice versa.

Updike is also a well-known and practicing critic (*Assorted Prose*, 1965; *Picked-Up Pieces*, 1975; *Hugging the Shore*, 1983; *Odd Jobs*, 1991; *More Matter*, 1999), and is often in the center of critical wars of words. Among the writers whose works he has reviewed are such names as Philip Roth, Saul Bellow, Kurt Vonnegut, Joyce Carol Oates, Iris Murdoch, and Isabel Allende. The majority of Updike's non-fiction, however, has been occasional, and he considers the opportunity to produce reviews educational for himself. In his reviews Updike measures writing with traditional maxims: felicity in style, accuracy in presenting one's subject, precision in describing the external and inner world, and humanistic values.

In his autobiographical piece, "The Dogwood Tree: A Boyhood," Updike called sex, art, and religion "the three great secret things" in human experience. James Yerkes has defined in his introduction to *John Updike and Religion* (2002), a collection of essays dealing with the religious vision of the author, "the religious consciousness in Updike may best be characterized as our sense of an unavoidable, unbearable, and unbelievable Sacred Presence." Existential questions have been in the center of Updike's work from the beginning of his career. He has also read theologians for guidance and regularly attended church for worship.

Updike has received almost all kinds of awards in the United States (except for the *international* Nobel Prize). In 1976, at the age of 32, he became a member of the American Academy of Arts and Letters, the youngest person ever elected, and was invited by the State Department to tour Eastern Europe as part of a cultural exchange program between the United States and the Soviet Union. In November 2003 Updike received the National Medal for Humanities at the White House, joining a very small group of notables who have been honored with both the National Medal of Art and the National Medal for the Humanities.

While Updike has continued to publish at the rate of about a book a year, critical opinion on his work since the early 1990s has been generally muted, and sometimes damning. Nevertheless, his novelistic scope in recent years has been wide. After Updike laid Rabbit Angstrom to rest, his alter ego, Jewish American novelist Harry Bech, is still on the literary scene. In *Seek My Face* (2002) he explored the post-war art scene; in *Villages* (2004), Updike returns to the familiar territory of infidelities in New England. His twenty-second novel, *Terrorist*, the story of a fervent, eighteen-year-old Muslim in New Jersey, was published in June 2006. The same year Updike was awarded the Rea Award for the Short Story for his outstanding achievement in that genre.

■ Selected Reading

Apart from his great achievement in novels, John Updike has also contributed actively to the revitalization of the short story writing at that time through formal experimentation and stylistic excellence. Few authors of short fiction have been so widely anthologized and featured with such frequency in Best American Short Stories and Prize Stories: The O. Henry Awards. Like his New England forebear Hawthorne, Updike has exhibited a sustained mastery of the short story form throughout his career, shaping a canon of short fiction that merits our attention. Among his hundreds of short stories, "A Gift from the City", "Pigeon Feathers", "A&P", "Bech Takes Potluck", "The Happiest I've Been", "Separating", "The Music School", "Gesturing", and "A Sandstone Farmhouse" are the most brilliant ones.

Making its first appearance in The New Yorker in 1961, "A&P" has been Updike's best known, most anthologized and most frequently taught short story. However, the seemingly simple story assumes a reader with considerable literary and cultural knowledge.

John Updike's penchant for appropriating great works of literature and giving them contemporary restatement in his own fiction is abundantly documented—as is the fact that, among his favorite sources, James Joyce looms large. In the story, the protagonist Sammy impulsively asserts principles in a cultural climate that has put the supermarket in place of the church, which strongly resembles Joyce's acclaimed "Araby".

A & P

In walks these three girls in nothing but bathing suits. I'm in the third check-out slot, with my back to the door, so I don't see them until they're over by the bread. The one that caught my  eye first was the one in the plaid green two-piece. She was a chunky kid, with a good tan and a sweet broad soft-looking can with those two crescents of white just under it, where the sun never seems to hit, at the top of the backs of her legs. I stood there with my hand on a box of HiHo crackers trying to remember if I rang it up or not. I ring it up again and the customer starts giving me hell. She's one of these cash-register-watchers, a witch about fifty with rouge on her cheekbones and no eyebrows, and I know it made her day to trip me up. She'd been watching cash registers forty years and probably never seen a mistake before.

By the time I got her feathers smoothed and her goodies into a bag—she gives me a little snort in passing, if she'd been born at the right time they would have burned her over in Salem—by the time I get her on her way the girls had circled around the bread and were coming back, without a pushcart, back my way along the counters, in the aisle between the check-outs and the Special bins. They didn't even have shoes on. There was this chunky one, with the two-piece—it was bright green and the seams on the bra were still sharp and her belly was still pretty pale so I guessed she just got it (the suit)—there was this one, with one of those chubby berry-faces, the lips all bunched together under her nose, this one, and a tall one, with black hair that hadn't quite frizzed right, and one of these sunburns right across under the eyes, and a chin that was too long—you know, the kind of girl other girls think is very "striking" and "attractive" but never quite makes it, as they very well know, which is why they like her so much—and then the third one, that wasn't quite so tall. She was the queen. She kind of led them, the other two peeking around and making their shoulders round. She didn't look around, not this queen, she just walked straight on slowly, on these long white prima donna legs. She came down a little hard on her heels, as if she didn't walk in her bare feet that much, putting down her heels and then letting the weight move along to her toes as if she was testing the floor with every step, putting a little deliberate extra action into it. You never know for sure how girls' minds work (do you really think it's a mind in there or just a little buzz like a bee in a glass jar?) but you got the idea she had talked the other two into coming in here with her, and now she was showing them how to do it, walk slow and hold yourself straight.

She had on a kind of dirty-pink—beige maybe, I don't know—bathing suit with a little nubble all over it and, what got me, the straps were down. They were off her shoulders looped loose around the cool tops of her arms, and I guess as a result the suit had slipped a little on her, so all around the top of the cloth there was this shining rim. If it hadn't been there you wouldn't have known there could have been anything whiter than those shoulders. With the straps pushed off, there was nothing between the top of the suit and the top of her head except just her, this clean bare plane of the top of her chest down from the shoulder bones like a dented sheet of metal tilted in the light. I mean, it was more than pretty.

She had sort of oaky hair that the sun and salt had bleached, done up in a bun that was unravelling, and a kind of prim face. Walking into the A & P with your straps down, I suppose it's the only kind of face you can have. She held her head so high her neck, coming up out of those white shoulders, looked kind of stretched, but I didn't mind. The longer her neck was, the more of her there was.

She must have felt in the corner of her eye me and over my shoulder Stokesie in the second slot watching, but she didn't tip. Not this queen. She kept her eyes moving across the racks, and stopped, and turned so slow it made my stomach rub the inside of my apron, and buzzed to the other two, who kind of huddled against her for relief, and they all three of them went up the cat-and-dog-food-breakfast-cereal-macaroni-rice-raisins-seasonings-spreads-spaghetti-soft-drinks-rackers-and-cookies aisle. From the third slot I look straight up this aisle to the meat counter, and I watched them all the way. The fat one with the tan sort of fumbled with the cookies, but on second thought she put the packages back. The sheep pushing their carts down the aisle—the girls were walking against the usual traffic (not that we have one-way signs or anything)—were pretty hilarious. You could see them, when Queenie's white shoulders dawned on them, kind of jerk, or hop, or hiccup, but their eyes snapped back to their own baskets and on they pushed. I bet you could set off dynamite in an A & P and the people would by and large keep reaching and checking oatmeal off their lists and muttering "Let me see, there was a third thing, began with A, asparagus, no, ah, yes, applesauce!" or whatever it is they do mutter. But there was no doubt, this jiggled them. A few house-slaves in pin curlers even looked around after pushing their carts past to make sure what they had seen was correct.

You know, it's one thing to have a girl in a bathing suit down on the beach, where what with the glare nobody can look at each other much anyway, and another thing in the cool of the A & P, under the fluorescent lights, against all those stacked packages, with her feet paddling along naked over our checkerboard green-and-cream rubber-tile floor.

"Oh Daddy," Stokesie said beside me. "I feel so faint."

"Darling," I said. "Hold me tight." Stokesie's married, with two babies chalked up on his fuselage already, but as far as I can tell that's the only difference. He's twenty-two, and I was nineteen this April.

"Is it done?" he asks, the responsible married man finding his voice. I forgot to say he thinks he's going to be manager some sunny day, maybe in 1990 when it's called the Great Alexandrov and Petrooshki Tea Company or something.

What he meant was, our town is five miles from a beach, with a big summer colony out on the Point, but we're right in the middle of town, and the women generally put on a shirt or shorts or something before they get out of the car into the street. And anyway these are usually women with six children and varicose veins mapping their legs and nobody, including them, could care less. As I say, we're right in the middle of town, and if you stand at our front doors you can see two banks and the Congregational church and the newspaper store and three real-estate offices and about twenty-seven old free-loaders tearing up Central Street because the sewer broke again. It's not as if we're on the Cape; we're north of Boston and there's people in this town haven't seen the ocean for twenty years.

The girls had reached the meat counter and were asking McMahon something. He pointed, they pointed, and they shuffled out of sight behind a pyramid of Diet Delight peaches. All that was left for us to see was old McMahon patting his mouth and looking after them sizing up their joints.

Poor kids, I began to feel sorry for them, they couldn't help it.

...

Now here comes the sad part of the story, at least my family says it's sad but I don't think it's sad myself. The store's pretty empty, it being Thursday afternoon, so there was nothing much to do except lean on the register and wait for the girls to show up again. The whole store was like a pinball machine and I didn't know which tunnel they'd come out of. After a while they come around out of the far aisle, around the light bulbs, records at discount of the Caribbean Six or Tony Martin Sings or some such gunk you wonder they waste the wax on, six packs of candy bars, and plastic toys done up in cellophane that fall apart when a kid looks at them anyway. Around they come, Queenie still leading the way, and holding a little gray jar in her hand. Slots Three through Seven are unmanned and I could see her wondering between Stokes and me, but Stokesie with his usual luck draws an old party in baggy gray pants who stumbles up with four giant cans of pineapple juice ('what do these bums do with all that pineapple juice' I've often asked myself) so the girls come to me. Queenie puts down the jar and I take it into my fingers icy cold. Kingfish Fancy Herring Snacks in Pure Sour Cream: 49 ¢. Now her hands are empty, not a ring or a bracelet, bare as God made them, and I wonder where the money's coming from. Still with that prim look she lifts a folded dollar bill out of the hollow at the center of her nubbled pink top. The jar went heavy in my hand. Really, I thought that was so cute.

Then everybody's luck begins to run out. Lengel comes in from haggling with a truck full of cabbages on the lot and is about to scuttle into that door marked MANAGER behind which he hides all day when the girls touch his eye. Lengel's pretty dreary, teaches Sunday school and the rest, but he doesn't miss that much. He comes over and says, "Girls, this isn't the beach."

Queenie blushes, though maybe it's just a brush of sunburn I was noticing for the first time, now that she was so close. "My mother asked me to pick up a jar of herring snacks." Her voice kind of startled me, the way voices do when you see the people first, coming out so flat and dumb yet kind of tony, too, the way it ticked over "pick up" and "snacks". All of a sudden I slid right down her voice into her living room. Her father and the other men were standing around in ice-cream coats and bow ties and the women were in sandals picking up herring snacks on toothpicks off a big plate and they were all holding drinks the color of water with olives and sprigs of mint in them. When my parents have somebody over they get lemonade and if it's a real racy affair Schlitz in tall glasses with "They'll Do It Every Time" cartoons stencilled on.

"That's all right," Lengel said. "But this isn't the beach." His repeating this struck me as funny, as if it had just occurred to him, and he had been thinking all these years the A & P was a great big dune and he was the head lifeguard. He didn't like my smiling—as I say he doesn't miss much—but he concentrates on giving the girls that sad Sunday-school-superintendent stare.

Queenie's blush is no sunburn now, and the plump one in plaid, that I liked better from the back—a really sweet can—pipes up, "We weren't doing any shopping. We just came in for the one thing."

"That makes no difference," Lengel tells her, and I could see from the way his eyes went that he hadn't noticed she was wearing a two-piece before. "We want you decently dressed when you come in here."

"We are decent," Queenie says suddenly, her lower lip pushing, getting sore now that she remembers her place, a place from which the crowd that runs the A & P must look pretty crummy. Fancy Herring Snacks flashed in her very blue eyes.

"Girls, I don't want to argue with you. After this come in here with your shoulders covered. It's our policy." He turns his back. That's policy for you. Policy is what the kingpins want. What the others want is juvenile delinquency.

All this while, the customers had been showing up with their carts but, you know, sheep, seeing a scene, they had all bunched up on Stokesie, who shook open a paper bag as gently as peeling a peach, not wanting to miss a word. I could feel in the silence everybody getting nervous, most of all Lengel, who asks me, "Sammy, have you rung up this purchase?"

I thought and said "No" but it wasn't about that I was thinking. I go through the punches, 4, 9, GROC, TOT—it's more complicated than you think, and after you do it often enough, it begins to make a little song, that you hear words to, in my case "Hello (*bing*) there, you (*gung*) happy pee-pul (*splat*)" -the *splat* being the drawer flying out. I uncrease the bill, tenderly as you may imagine, it just having come from between the two smoothest scoops of vanilla I had ever known were there, and pass a half and a penny into her narrow pink palm, and nestle the herrings in a bag and twist its neck and hand it over, all the time thinking.

The girls, and who'd blame them, are in a hurry to get out, so I say "I quit" to Lengel quick enough for them to hear, hoping they'll stop and watch me, their unsuspected hero. They keep right on going, into the electric eye; the door flies open and they flicker across the lot to their car, Queenie and Plaid and Big Tall Goony-Goony (not that as raw material she was so bad), leaving me with Lengel and a kink in his eyebrow.

"Did you say something, Sammy?"

"I said I quit."

"I thought you did."

"You didn't have to embarrass them."

"It was they who were embarrassing us."

I started to say something that came out "Fiddle-de-doo". It's a saying of my grand-mother's, and I know she would have been pleased.

"I don't think you know what you're saying," Lengel said.

"I know you don't," I said. "But I do." I pull the bow at the back of my apron and start shrugging it off my shoulders. A couple customers that had been heading for my slot begin to knock against each other, like scared pigs in a chute.

Lengel sighs and begins to look very patient and old and gray. He's been a friend of my parents for years. "Sammy, you don't want to do this to your Mom and Dad," he tells me. It's true, I don't. But it seems to me that once you begin a gesture it's fatal not to go through with it. I fold the apron, "Sammy" stitched in red on the pocket, and put it on the counter, and drop the bow tie on top of it. The bow tie is theirs, if you've ever wondered. "You'll feel this for the rest of your life," Lengel says, and I know that's true, too, but remembering how he made that pretty girl blush makes me so scrunchy inside I punch the No Sale tab and the machine whirs "pee-pul" and the drawer splats out. One advantage to this scene taking place in summer, I can follow this up with a clean exit, there's no fumbling around getting your coat and galoshes, I just saunter into the electric eye in my white shirt that my mother ironed the night before, and the door heaves itself open, and outside the sunshine is skating around on the asphalt.

I look around for my girls, but they're gone, of course. There wasn't anybody but some young married screaming with her children about some candy they didn't get by the door of a powder-blue Falcon station wagon. Looking back in the big windows, over the bags of peat moss and aluminum lawn furniture stacked on the pavement, I could see Lengel in my place in the slot, checking the sheep through. His face was dark gray and his back stiff, as if he'd just had an injection of iron, and my stomach kind of fell as I felt how hard the world was going to be to me hereafter.

■ Study Questions

1. Where does the story happen? What kind of place is it? What kind of life people are living there, how they are dressed, how they behave?

2. Who is the protagonist of the short story? Can you describe his life in a few words?

3. What is "the sad part of the story"? Is it the clash between the manager of the grocery and the girls, or "my" quitting of the job, or the girls' un-appreciation of my heroic action?

4. What are the possible themes of the short story?

5. The story is written in the first person. What's the effect of doing that?

6. Updike has been considered a gentle satirist, poking fun at American life and customs. Can you find any traces in the story to support thin view?

7. There are several symbols in the story, can you identify them and try to find out how these symbols add meaning to the events in the story.

8. Is there anything that Updike's "A&P" shares with Nathaniel Hawthorne's "Young Goodman Brown"? Support your answer with details.

9. Compare and contrast Sammy's epiphany in "A&P" with that experienced by the narrator in "The Egg" by Sherwood Anderson.

Saul Bellow (1915—2005)

Saul Bellow, born **Solomon Bellows**, was an acclaimed Canadian-born American writer. He won the Nobel Prize for Literature in 1976 and the National Medal of Arts in 1988. Bellow is best known for writing novels that investigate isolation, spiritual dissociation, and the possibilities of human awakening. Bellow drew inspiration from Chicago, his adopted city, and he set much of his fiction there. His works exhibit a mix of high and low culture, and his fictional characters are also a potent mix of intellectual dreamers and street-smart confidence men.

Saul Bellow was born in Lachine, Quebec, Canada. Both his parents had emigrated there from Russia, where his father had been an importer of Egyptian onions. Growing up, Bellow learned four languages—English, Hebrew, Yiddish, and French. When he was nine, his family moved to Chicago, where, Bellow recalls, he spent most of his time in libraries. He attended the University of Chicago and then Northwestern University, from which he graduated in 1937 with honors in sociology and anthropology.

With a scholarship to the University of Wisconsin, Bellow was on his way toward an academic career in anthropology when he discovered a more urgent calling—literature. "Every time I worked on my thesis, it turned out to be a story," he told one interviewer. "I disappeared for the Christmas holidays and I never came back."

Bellow's first two novels, *Dangling Man* (1944) and *The Victim* (1947), won him a small following. *The Adventures of Augie March* (1953) won not only greater attention but the National Book Award as well, as did *Herzog* (1964) and *Mr. Sammler's Planet* (1970). His 1975 novel *Humboldt's Gift* was awarded the Pulitzer Prize. Propelled by its success, Bellow won the Nobel Prize in literature next year. His recent novels include *The Deans December* (1982), *More Die of Heartbreak* (1987), *A Theft* (1989), *The Bellarosa Connection* (1989), *The Actual* (1997), and *Ravelstein* (2000).

When leading authors and critics were asked to name the twenty best books written since World War Ⅱ, four of Saul Bellow's novels—*Herzog*, *Henderson the Rain King* (1959), *Seize the Day* (1956), and *The Adventures of Augie March*-made the list. Bellow is often referred to as the most important American writer of his generation. He is, as the critic Leslie Fiedler said, "of all our novelists the one we need most to understand."

■ Selected Reading

In his "Nobel Prize Acceptance Speech", Bellow explores the power and value of literature in our time. In stirring language he calls on writers—and on readers—to return to "the center", to the human concerns that are "simple and true".

from *Nobel Prize Acceptance Speech*

Every year we see scores of books and articles by writers who tell Americans what a state they are in. All reflect the current crises; all tell us what we must do about them—these analysts are produced by the very disorder and confusion they prescribe for. It is as a novelist that I am considering the extreme moral sensitivity of our contemporaries, their desire for perfection, their intolerance of the defects of society, the touching, the comical boundlessness of their demands, their anxiety, their irritability, their sensitivity, their tender-mindedness, their goodness, their convulsiveness, the recklessness with which they experiment with drugs and touch-therapies[288] and bombs...

And art and literature—what of them? Well, there is a violent uproar but we are not absolutely dominated by it. We are still able to think, to discriminate, and to feel. The purer, subtler, higher activities have not succumbed to fury or to nonsense. Not yet. Books continue to be written and read. It may be more difficult to cut through the whirling mind of a modern reader

---

[288] **touch-therapies**: any of various group psychotherapies in which patients touch one another as part of the treatment.

but it is still possible to reach the quiet zone. In the quiet zone we novelists may find that he is devoutly waiting for us. When complications increase, the desire for essentials increases too. The unending cycle of crises that began with the First World War has formed a kind of person, one who has lived through strange and terrible things, and in whom there is an observable shrinkage of prejudices, a casting off of disappointing ideologies, an ability to live with many kinds of madness, and an immense desire for certain durable human goods—truth, for instance; freedom; wisdom. I don't think I am exaggerating; there is plenty of evidence for this. Disintegration? Well, yes. Much is disintegrating but we are experiencing also an odd kind of refining process.

Hegel[289] long ago observed that art no longer engaged the central energies of man. These energies were now engaged by science—a "relentless spirit of rational inquiry." Art had moved to the margins. There it formed "a wide and splendidly varied horizon". ...

There were European writers in the Nineteenth Century who would not give up the connection of literature with the main human enterprise. The very suggestion would have shocked Tolstoi and Dostoevski,[290] But in the West a separation between great artists and the general public took place. Artists developed a marked contempt for the average reader and the bourgeois[291] mass. The best of them saw clearly enough what sort of civilization Europe had produced, brilliant but unstable, vulnerable, fated to be overtaken by catastrophe.

Despite a show of radicalism and innovation our contemporaries are really very conservative, They follow their Nineteenth Century leaders and hold to the old standards, interpreting history and society much as they were interpreted in the last century. What would writers do today if it occurred to them that literature might once again engage those "central energies," if they were to recognize that an immense desire had arisen for a return from the periphery, for what is simple and true?

Of course we can't come back to the center simply because we wish to, though the realization that we are wanted might electrify us. The force of the crisis is so great that it might summon us back. But prescriptions are futile. One can't tell writers what to do. The imagination must find its own path. But one can fervently wish that they—that we—would come back from the periphery. We writers do not represent mankind adequately. What account do Americans give of themselves, what accounts of them are given by psychologists, sociologists, historians, journalists, and writers? In a kind of contractual daylight they see themselves in the ways with which we are desperately familiar. These images of contractual daylight, so boring to Robbe-Grillet[292] and to me, originate in the contemporary world view: We put into our books the consumer, civil servant,

---

289   **Hegel**: Georg Wilhelm Friedrich Hegel (1770—1831), German philosopher.

290   **Tolstoi... Dostoevski**: Leo Tolstoi (1828—1910) and Feodor Dostoevski (1821—1881), Russian novelists.

291   **bourgeois**: materialistic, conventional, middle-class.

292   **Robbe-Grillet**: Alain Robbe-Grillet (born 1922), French novelist.

football fan, lover, television viewer. And in the contractual daylight version their life is a kind of death. There is another life coming from an insistent sense of what we are which denies these daylight formulations and the false life—the death-in-life—they make for us. For it is false, and we know it, and our secret and incoherent resistance to it cannot stop—that resistance arises from persistent intuitions. Perhaps humankind cannot hear too much reality, hut neither can it bear too much unreality, too much abuse of the truth...

What is at the center now? At the moment, neither art nor science but mankind determining, in confusion and obscurity, whether it will endure or go under. The whole species—everybody—has gotten into the act. At such a time it is essential to lighten ourselves, to dump encumbrances, including the encumbrances of education and all organized platitudes, to make judgments of our own, to perform acts of our own, Conrad[293] was right to appeal to that part of our being which is a gift.

We must look for that gift under the wreckage of many systems. The collapse of those systems may bring a blessed and necessary release from formulations, from misleading conceptions of being and consciousness. With increasing frequency I dismiss as "merely respectable" opinions I have long held—or thought I held—and try to discern what I have really lived by, and what others really live by. As for Hegel's art freed from "seriousness" and glowing on the margins, raising the soul above painful involvement in the limitations of reality through the serenity of form, that can exist nowhere now, during this struggle for survival. However, it is not as though the people who engaged in this struggle had only a rudimentary humanity, without culture, and knew nothing of art. Our very vices, our mutilations, show how rich we are in thought and culture. How much we know. How much we can feel. The struggles that convulse us make us want to simplify, to reconsider, to eliminate the tragic weakness which prevented writers—and readers—from being at once simple and true.

Writers are greatly respected. The intelligent public is wonderfully patient with them, continues to read them and endures disappointment after disappointment, waiting to hear from art what it does not hear from theology, philosophy, social theory, and what it cannot hear from pure science. Out of the struggle at the center has come an immense, painful longing for a broader, more flexible, fuller, more coherent, more comprehensive account of what we human beings are, who we are, and what this life is for. At the center humankind struggles with collective powers for its freedom, the individual struggles with dehumanization for the possession of his soul. If writers do not come again into the center it will not be because the center is pre-empted. It is not. They are free to enter. If they so wish.

The essence of our real condition, the complexity, the confusion, the pain of it is shown to us

---

[293] **Conrad**: Joseph Conrad (1857—1924), English novelist of Polish birth, whose books often deal with honor, morality, alienation, and guilt.

in glimpses, in what Proust[294] and Tolstoi thought of as "true impressions". This essence reveals, and then conceals itself. When it goes away it leaves us again in doubt. But our connection remains with the depths from which these glimpses come. The sense of our real powers, powers we seem to derive from the universe itself, also comes and goes. We are reluctant to talk about this because there is nothing we can prove, because our language is inadequate, and because few people are willing to risk the embarrassment. They would have to say, "There is a spirit" and that is taboo. So almost everyone keeps quiet about it, although almost everyone is aware of it.

The value of literature lies in these intermittent "true impressions". A novel moves back and forth between the world of objects, of actions, of appearances, and that other world from which these "true impressions" come and which moves us to believe that the good we hang onto so tenaciously—in the face of evil, so obstinately—is no illusion.

No one who has spent years in the writing of novels can be unaware of this. The novel can't be compared to the epic, or to the monuments of poetic drama. But it is the best we can do just now. It is a sort of latter-day lean-to, a hovel in which the spirit takes shelter. A novel is balanced between a few true impresssions and the multitude of false ones that make up most of what we call life. It tells us that for every human being there is a diversity of existences, that the single existence is itself an illusion in part, that these many existences signify something, tend to something, fulfill something; it promises us meaning, harmony and even Justice. What Conrad said was true, art attempts to find in the universe, in matter as well as in the facts of life, what is fundamental, enduring, essential.

■ Study Questions

1. What does Bellow say he is considering as a novelist (Paragraph 1)? What does he say happens "when complications increase" (Paragraph 2)? What sort of person does he say has been produced by the cycle of crises that began with World War I?

2. What did Hegel observe about art? What was Hegel's opinion about art "on the margin"?

3. According to Page 601, what is at the center now, and what sort of people are involved in it? With what and for what does Bellow say humankind struggles "at the center"? With what and for what does he say the individual struggles?

4. What does Bellow say is shown to us "in glimpses"? What does he say literature can do in this regard? With which of Conrad's ideas about art does Bellow agree in his final sentence?

5. What kind of literature is Hegel's literature "on the periphery"? To what sort of audience does it appeal? Does Bellow approve of such literature?

6. Summarize Bellow's opinion of modern human beings. What does he believe that all of us understand, at least "in glimpses"?

7. For what kind of literature does Bellow argue?

8. Which 20th-century American writers that you have read do you think are "on the periphery"? Which do you think address "the center"? Support your answers.

---

[294] **Proust**: Marcel Proust (1871—1922), French novelist.

Edward Albee (1928—   )

Edward Albee is an American playwright best known for his plays of the Theatre of the Absurd, including *The Zoo Story* (1958), *The Sandbox* (1959), *Who's Afraid of Virginia Woolf?* (1962), and a rewrite of the book for the unsuccessful musical version of Truman Capote's *Breakfast at Tiffany's* (1966). His works are considered well-crafted and often unsympathetic examinations of the modern condition. His early plays repudiate the values of the post-war American society, and he seems likely to stay in history alongside Eugene O'Neill, Tennessee Williams, and Arthur Miller. However, Albee's dedication to continuing to evolve his voice—as evidenced in later productions such as *The Goat or Who is Sylvia* (2002)—also routinely marks him as distinct from other American playwrights of his era.

If Albee has hints that he alone is the heir of the great traditions of O'Neill and Williams, he has probably told a truth. Albee first began writing when he was still in school, and learned substantially from his social experience as office boy, restaurant counterman, and Western Union messenger. His first play, *The Zoo Story*, was first staged in Berlin in 1959 and then in Greenwich Village in 1960. It won Vernon Rice Memorial Award. Dealing with human encounter and the search for communion, the play shows Albee's dramatic structure: normal opening, increasing tangle, peak of intensity and quick drop-off. Its style is "absurdist", but the message of the play is in fact very positive. It tells people that they can and must break out of their aloneness.

The Zoo Story marked the beginning of his literary career, though he wrote plays for a decade earlier. Then he turned out *The Sandbox*, *The Death Of Bessie Smith* (1962), *The Ballad of the Sad Café* (1963), *Tiny Alice* (1964), *The Delicate Balance* (1966, *Pulitzer Prize*), *Everything in Garden* (1967), *Box* (1968), *Listening* (1975), *Quotations from Chairman Mao Tse-tung* (1987), and *Finding the Sun* (1993). From the late 1960s, Albee stressed formal elegance rather than emotional intensity. He also made several stage adaptations from the books of other authors. In all these plays, he had written serious criticisms of American society and explored the capacity of the people in modern society for self-delusion and self-destruction.

Several of his plays are studies of families where a strong-willed wife dominates a weak husband. Such a play is *Who's Afraid of Virginia Woolf?*, dealing with martial conflict and reconciliation. It is generally regarded as his masterpiece. The play tells of George, who is a history professor at a small New England college. His wife, Martha is the daughter of the college president. When George and Martha bring a young colleague Nick and his nervous wife Honey back from a party, the elder couple involve Nick and Honey in the verbal abuse that seems to be a nightly ritual with them. Honey drinks too much and becomes ill. Martha tries to seduce Nick. The sexuality of all four characters is denounced. In the end when George and Martha's imaginary son, created by them as some kind of sustenance, is declared dead by Martha, thereby acknowledging their illusions and allowing compassionate feelings to surface.

Albee once explained that the title of this play means "who's afraid of living a life without false illusion", and that it is "an examination of whether or not we, as a society, have failed the principles of the American Revolution". This play has brought him fame and critical recognition.

Albee's early plays were evidently influenced by European experimental movements of the 1950s such as "Theater of the Absurd" and "Theater of Cruelty", but he developed his own powerful style, neither as sociological as Miller nor as psychological as Williams. His plays "reveal a talent for wit and penetrating dialogue, and they offer compelling portrayals of psychological and physical violence and of what Albee sees as the complacency and emptiness of contemporary life". Albee's plays are mainly appreciated for "the oblique of its expression, its theme of emotional commitment, its shifting linguistic rhythms, (and) its dynamic colloquial lexicon".

■ Selected Reading

The Zoo Story is a one-act, two-character piece with an economical construction. Jerry and Peter meet in Central Park, New York. Out of loneliness, Jerry desires to connect with someone outside of himself, but Peter wants to dismiss him as obstreperous. Jerry has to goad Peter into a fight and kills himself upon the knife he has given Peter. No matter what the cost, authentic contact has been achieved.

This play represents the alienation of the individual from his fellow men, the terrible loneliness of every living human being. It exhibits certain characteristics of Existentialism. Jerry is a highly individualistic, nonconformist character. Being incompatible with the conformist society, he feels isolation, while Peter, a representative of that society, is satisfied with the reality of life. Jerry's life is a struggle for existence—in the jungle of the city. The conflict of values, the attack on the bourgeois code, is acted out on a park bench and is surely one of the basic situations of human existence that Sartre talks of as constituting dramatizable material. Moreover, Jerry qualifies as an Existentialist hero: he makes his choices freely. His decision to impale himself on the knife Peter is holding is a deliberate act. His death is an act of protest against the wrongs of the city, the injustice of the system, the bourgeois values and the isolation of man. The play suggests that the price of survival under these conditions may be the murder of our fellow man, even when accomplished accidentally or unwillingly. Albee represents that the cannibalism of the human condition is completely absurd. At the end Jerry taunts Peter: "Hurry away, your parakeets are making the dinner... the cats...are setting the table..." Through this we can see that man's condition is not only absurd but also subhuman, which is perhaps what Albee means by the title, The Zoo Story.

The Zoo Story

THE PAYERS:

PETER: *A man in his early forties, neither fat nor gaunt, neither handsome nor homely. He wears tweeds, smokes a pipe, carries horn-rimmed glasses. Although he is moving into middle age, his dress and his manner would suggest a man younger.*

JERRY: *A man in his late thirties, not poorly dressed, but carelessly. What was once a trim and lightly muscled body has begun to go to fat; and while he is no longer handsome, it is evident that he once was. His fall from physical grace should not suggest debauchery; he has, to come closest to it, a great weariness.*

THE SCENE:

It is Central Park; a Sunday afternoon in summer; the present. There are two park benches, one toward either side of the stage; they both face the audience. Behind them: foliage, trees, sky. At the beginning, Peter is seated on one of the benches.

Stage Directions:

As the curtain rises, PETER is seated on the bench stage-right. He is reading a book. He stops reading, cleans his glasses, goes back to reading. JERRY enters.

JERRY: I've been to the zoo. (PETER *doesn't notice*) I said, I've been to the zoo. MISTER, I'VE BEEN TO THE ZOO!

PETER: Hm? … What? … I'm sorry, were you talking to me?

JERRY: I went to the zoo, and then I walked until I came here. Have I been walking north?

PETER: (*Puzzled*) North? Why… I … I think so. Let me see.

JERRY: (*Pointing past the audience*) Is that Fifth Avenue?

PETER: Why yes; yes, it is.

JERRY: And what is that cross street there; that one, to the right?

PETER: That? Oh, That's Seventy-fourth Street.

JERRY: And the zoo is around Sixty-fifth Street; so, I've been walking north.

PETER: (*Anxious to get back to his reading*) Yes; it would seem so.

JERRY: Good old north. [295]

PETER: (*Lightly, by reflex*) Ha, ha.

JERRY: (*After a slight pause*) But not due north.

PETER: I… well, no, not due north; but, we… call it north. It's northerly.

JERRY: (*Watches as* PETER, *anxious to dismiss him, prepares his pipe*) Well, boy; you're not going to get lung cancer, are you?

PETER: (*Looks up, a little annoyed, then smiles*) No, sir. Not from this.

JERRY: No, sir. What you'll probably get is cancer of the mouth, and then you'll have to wear one of those things Freud word after they took one whole side of his jaw away. What do they call those things?

PETER: (*Uncomfortable*) A prosthesis? [296]

JERRY: The very thing! A prosthesis. You're an educated man, aren't you? Are you a doctor?

PETER: Oh, no; no. I read about it somewhere; *Time* magazine, I think. (*He turns to his book*)

JERRY: Well, *Time* magazine isn't for blockheads. [297]

PETER: No, I suppose not.

JERRY: (*After a pause*) Boy, I'm glad that's Fifth Avenue there.

PETER: (*Vaguely*) Yes.

JERRY: I don't like the west side of the park much.

PETER: Oh? (*Then, slightly wary, but interested*) Why?

JERRY: (*Off hand*) I don't know.

PETER: Oh. (*He returns to his book*)

---

[295] **Good old north:** Complete north. Good: Complete; old: (Slang) used as an intensive.

[296] **prosthesis:** the addition of an artificial part to supply a defect of the body.

[297] **blockheads:** fools.

JERRY: (*He stands for a few seconds, looking at PETER, who finally looks up again, puzzled*) Do you mind if we talk?

PETER: (*Obviously minding*) Why... no, no.

JERRY: Yes you do; you do.

PETER: (*Puts his book down, his pipe out and away, smiling*) No, really; I don't mind at all, really.

JERRY: It's... it's a nice day.

PETER: (*Stares unnecessarily at the sky*) Yes, it is lovely.

JERRY: I've been to the zoo.

PETER: Yes, I think you said so... didn't you?

JERRY: You'll read about it in the papers tomorrow, if you don't see it on your TV tonight. You have TV, haven't you?

PETER: Why yes, we have two; one for the children.

JERRY: You're married!

PETER: (*With pleased emphasis*) Why, certainly.

JERRY: It isn't a law, for God's sake.

PETER: No... no, of course not.

JERRY: And you have a wife.

PETER: (*Bewildered by the seeming lack of communication*) Yes!

JERRY: And you have children.

PETER: Yes; two.

JERRY: Boys?

PETER: No, girls... both girls.

JERRY: But you wanted boys.

PETER: Well... Naturally, every man wants a son, but...

JERRY: (*Lightly mocking*) But that's the way the cookie crumbles?[298]

PETER: (*Annoyed*) I wasn't going to say that.

JERRY: And you're not going to have any more kids, are you?

PETER: (*A Bit distantly*) No. No more. (*Then back, and irksome*) Why did you say that? How would you know about that?

JERRY: The way you cross your legs, perhaps; something in the voice. Or maybe I'm just guessing. Is it your wife?[299]

PETER: (*Furious*) That's none of your business! (*A silence*) Do you understand? (*JERRY nods. PETER is quiet now*) Well, you're right. We'll have no more children.

JERRY: (*Softly*) That is the way the cookie crumbles.

---

298 **the cookie crumbles**: (here) things happen.

299 **Is it your wife?**: Is it the idea of your wife?

PETER：(*Forgiving*) Yes... I guess so.

JERRY：Well, now; what else?

PETER：What were you saying about the zoo... that I'd read about it, or see...?

JERRY：I'll tell you about it, soon. Do you mind if I ask you questions?

PETER：Oh, not really.

JERRY：I'll tell you why I do it; I don't talk to many people except to say like: give me a beer, or where's the john,[300] or what time does the feature go on, or keep your hands to yourself, buddy.[301] You know-things like that.

PETER：I must say I don't...

JERRY：But every once in a while I like to talk to somebody, really talk; like to get to know somebody, know all about him.

PETER：(*Lightly laughing, still a little uncomfortable*) And am I the guinea pig[302] for today?

JERRY：On a sun-drenched afternoon like this? Who better than a nice married man with two daughters and... uh... a dog? (PETER *shakes his head*) No? Two dogs. (PETER *shakes his head again*) Hm. No dogs? (PETER *shakes his head, sadly*) Oh, that's a shame. But you look like an animal man. CATS? (PETER *nods his head, ruefully*) Cats! But, that can't be your idea. No, sir. Your wife and daughters? (PETER *nods his head*) Is there anything else I should know?

PETER：(*He has to clear his throat*) There are... there are two parakeets. One... one for each of my daughters.

JERRY：Birds.

PETER：My daughters keep them in a cage in their bedroom.

JERRY：Do they carry disease? The birds.

PETER：I don't believe so.

JERRY：That's too bad. If they did you could set them loose in the house and the cats could eat them and die, maybe. (PETER *looks blank for a moment, then laughs*) And what else? What do you do to support your enormous household?

PETER：I... uh... I have an executive position with a... a small publishing house. We... uh... we publish textbooks.

JERRY：That sounds nice; very nice. What do you make?

PETER：(*Still cheerful*) Now look here!

JERRY：Oh, come on.

PETER：Well, I make around eighteen thousand a year, but I don't carry more than forty dollars at any one time... in case you're a... a holdup man... ha,ha, ha.

---

300 **john**：(slang) water-closet.

301 **buddy**：(slang, as a familiar form of address) chum, mate.

302 **guinea pig**：(informal) the subject of any experiment.

JERRY: (*Ignoring the above*) Where do you live? (PETER *is reluctant*) Oh, look; I'm not going to rob you, and I'm not going to kidnap your parakeets, your cats, or your daughters.

PETER: (*Too loud*) I live between Lexington and Third Avenue, on Seventy-fourth Street.

JERRY: That wasn't so hard, was it?

PETER: I didn't mean to seem... ah... it's that you don't really carry on a conversation; you just ask questions. And I'm... I'm normally... uh... reticent. Why do you just stand there?

JERRY: I'll start walking around in a little while, and eventually I'll sit down. (*Recalling*) Wait until you see the expression on his face.

PETER: What? Whose face? Look here; is this something about the zoo?

JERRY: (*Distantly*) The what?

PETER: The zoo; the zoo. Something about the zoo.

JERRY: The zoo.

PETER: You mentioned it several times.

JERRY: (*Still distant, but returning abruptly*) The zoo? Oh, yes; the zoo. I was there before I came here. I told you that. Say, what's the dividing line between upper-middle-class and lower-upper-middle class?

PETER: My dear fellow, I...

JERRY: Don't my dear fellow me. [303]

PETER: (*Unhappily*) Was I patronizing? I believe I was; I'm sorry. But, you see, your question about the classes bewildered me.

JERRY: And when you're bewildered you become patronizing.

PETER: I... I don't express myself too well, sometimes. (*He attempts a joke on himself*) I'm in publishing, not writing.

JERRY: (*Amused, but not at the humor*) So be it. The truth is; I was being patronizing.

PETER: Oh, now; you needn't say that. (*It is at this point that JERRY may begin to move about the stage with slowly increasing determination and authority, but pacing himself, so that the long speech about the dog comes at the high point of the arc.*)

JERRY: All right. Who are your favorite writers? Baudelaire[304] and J. P. Marquand?[305]

PETER: (*Wary*) Well, I like a great many writers; I have a considerable... catholicity of taste, if I may say so. Those two men are fine, each in his way. (*Warming up*) Baudelaire, of course... uh... is by far the finer of the two, but Marquand has a place... in our... uh... national...

JERRY: Skip it.

PETER: I... sorry.

---

303 **Don't my dear fellow me:** Don't call me "my dear fellow".

304 **Baudelaire:** Charles Pierre Baudelaire (1821—1867), French poet and critic.

305 **J. P. Marquand:** (1893—1960), American popular novelist.

JERRY: Do you know what I did before I went to the zoo today? I walked all the way up Fifth Avenue from Washington Square; all the way.

PETER: Oh, you live in the Village![306]   (*This seems to enlighten* PETER)

JERRY: No, I don't took the subway down to the Village so I could walk all the way Fifth Avenue to the zoo. It's one of those things a person has to do; sometimes a person has to go a very long distance out of his way to came back a short distance correctly.

PETER: (*Almost pouting*) Oh, I thought you lived in the Village.

JERRY: What were you trying to do? Make sense out of things? Bring order? The old pigeonhole bit? Well, that's easy; I'll tell you. I live in a four-story brownstone rooming-house[307] on the upper West side between Columbus Avenue and Central Park West. I live on the top floor; rear; west. It's a laughably small room, and one of my walls is made of beaverboard; this beaverboard separates my room from another laughably small room, so I assume that the two rooms were once one room, a small room, but not necessarily laughable. The room beyond my beaverboard wall is occupied by a colored queen who always keeps his door pen; well, not always but always when he's plucking his eyebrows, which he does with Buddhist concentration. This colored queen has rotten teeth, which is rare, and he has a Japanese kimono, which is also pretty rare; and he wears this kimono to and from the john in the hall, which is pretty frequent. I mean, he goes to the john a lot. He never bothers me, and he never brings anyone up to his room. All the does is pluck his eyebrows, wear his kimono and go to the john. Now, the two front rooms on my floor are a little large, I guess; but they're pretty small, too. There's Puerto Rican family in one of them, a husband, a wife, and some kids; I don't know how many. These people entertain a lot. And in the other front room, there's somebody living there, but I don't know who it is. I've never seen who it is. Never. Never ever.

PETER: (*Embarrassed*) Why... why do you live there?

JERRY: (*From a distance again*) I don't know.

PETER: It doesn't sound like a very nice place... where you live.

JERRY: Well, no; it isn't an apartment in the East Seventies. But, then again, I don't have one wife, two daughters, two cats and two parakeets. What I do have, I have toilet articles,[308] a few clothes, a hot plate that I'm not supposed to have, a can opener, one that works with a key, you know; a knife, two forks, and two spoons, one small, one larger; three plates, a cup, a saucer, a drinking glass, two picture frames, both empty, eight or nine books, a pack of pornographic playing cards[309], regular deck, an old Western Union typewriter that

---

306 **Oh, you live in the Village**: Peter tries to praise Jerry for a Bohemian life in the village (Greenwich Village).

307 **rooming-house**: (U. S.) building where a number of independent rooms can be rented.

308 **toilet articles**: such things as a hair-brush, comb, hand mirror, etc.

309 **pornographic playing cards**: playing cards in which obscene subjects are treated.

prints nothing but capital letters, and a small strongbox without a lock which has in it... what? Rocks! Some rocks... sea-rounded rocks I picked up on the beach when I was a kid. Under which... weighed down... are some letters... please letters[310]... please why don't you do this, and please when will you do that letters. And when will you do that letters. And when letters,[311] too. When will you write? When? These letters are form more recent years.

PETER: (*Stares glumly at his shoes, then*) About those two empty picture frames...?

JERRY: I don't see why they need any explanation at all, Isn't it clear? I don't have pictures of anyone to put in them.

PETER: Your parents... perhaps... a girl friend...

JERRY: You're a very sweet man, and you're possessed of a truly enviable innocence. But good old Mom and good old Pop are dead... you know? ... I'm broken up about it, too... I mean really. BUT. That particular vaudeville act[312] is playing the cloud circuit now. So I don't see how I can look at them, all neat and framed. Besides, or, rather, to be pointed about it, good old Mom walked out on good old Pop[313] when I was ten and a half years old; she embarked on an adulterous turn of our southern states... a journey of a year's duration... and her most constant companion... among others, among many others... was a Mr. Barleycorn. At least, that's what good old Pop told me after he went down... came back... brought her body north. We'd received the news between Christmas and New Year's, you see, that good old Mom had parted with the ghost in some dump in Alabama. And, without the ghost... she was less welcome, I mean, what was she? A stiff... a northern stiff. At any rate, good old Pop celebrated the New Year for an even two weeks and then slapped into the front of a somewhat moving city omnibus, which sort of cleaned things out family-wise.[314] Well no; then there was Mom's sister, who was given neither to sin nor the consolations of the bottle. I moved in on her,[315] and my memory of her is slight excepting I remember still that she did all things dourly: sleeping, eating, working, praying, she dropped dead on the stairs to her apartment, my apartment then, to, on the afternoon of my high school graduation. A terribly middle-European joke, if you ask me.

PETER: Oh, my; oh, my...

JERRY: Oh, your what? But that was a long time ago, and I have no feeling about any of it that I care to admit to myself. Perhaps you can see, though, why good old Mom and good old Pop are frameless. What's your name? Your first name?

PETER: I'm Peter.

---

310   **please letters:** letters full of "please".

311   **when letters:** letters full of "when".

312   **That particular vaudeville act:** That particular vaudeville front of "a somewhat moving city omnibus".

313   **walk out on good old Pop:** (slang) abandon or desert good old Pop.

314   **family-wise:** family way.

315   **moved in on her:** moved to her place without her permission.

JERRY: I'd forgotten to ask you. I'm Jerry.

PETER: (*With a slight, nervous laugh*) Hello, Jerry.

JERRY: (*Nods his hello*) And let's see now; what's the point of having a girl's picture, especially in two frames? I have two picture frames, you remember. I never see the pretty little ladies more than once, you remember. I never see the pretty little ladies more than once, and most of them wouldn't be caught in the same room with a camera. It's odd, and I wonder if it's sad.

PETER: The girls?

JERRY: No. I wonder if it's sad that I never see the little ladies more than once. I've never been able to have sex with, or, how is it put? ... make love to anybody more than once. Once; that's it... oh, wait; for a week and a half, when I was fifteen... and I hang my head in shame that puberty was late... I was a h-o-m-o-s-x-u-a-l. I mean, I was queer... (*Very fast*) ... queer, queer, queer...with bells ringing, banners snapping in the wind. And for those eleven days, I met at least twice a day with the park superintendent's son... a Greek boy, whose birthday was the same as mine, except he was a year older. I think I was very much in love... maybe just with sex. But that was the jazz for a very special hotel, wasn't it? And now; oh, do I love the little ladies; really, I love them. For about an hour.

PETER: Well, it seems perfectly simple to me...

JERRY: (*Angry*) Look! Are you going to tell me to get married and have parakeets?

PETER: (*Angry himself*) Forget the parakeets! And stay single if you want to. It's no business of mine. I didn't start this conversation in the...

JERRY: All right, all right. I'm sorry. All right? You're not angry?

PETER: (*Laughing*) No, I'm not angry.

JERRY: (*Relieved*) Good. (*Now back to his previous tone*) Interesting that you asked me about the picture frames. I would have thought that you would have asked me about the pornographic playing cards.

PETER: (*With a knowing smile*) Oh, I've seen those cards.

JERRY: That's not the point. (*Laughs*) I suppose when you were a kid you and your pals passed them around, or you had a pack of your own.

PETER: Well, I guess a lot of us did.

JERRY: and you threw them away just before you got married.

PETER: Oh, now; look here. I didn't need anything like that when I got older.

JERRY: No?

PETER: (*Embarrassed*) I'd rather not talk about these things.

JERRY: So? Don't. Besides, I wasn't trying to plumb your post adolescent sexual life and hard times; what I wanted to get at is you're a kid, and pornographic playing cards when you're older. It's that when you're a kid you use the cards as a substitute for a real experience, and when you're older you use real experience as a substitute for the fantasy. But I imagine you'd rather bear about what happened at the zoo.

PETER: (*Enthusiastic*) Oh, yes; the zoo. (*Then, awkward*) That is... if you...

JERRY: Let me tell you about why I went... well, let me tell you some things. I've told you about the fourth floor of the rooming house where I live. I think the rooms are better as you go down, floor by floor. I guess they are; I don't know. I don't know any of the people on the third and second floors. Oh, wait! I do know that there's a lady living on the third floor, in the front. I know because she cries all the time. Whenever I go out or come back in, whenever I pass her door, I always hear her crying, muffled, but... very determined. Very determined indeed. But the one I'm getting to, and too harsh in describing people. I don't like to. But the landlady is a fat, ugly, mean, stupid, unwashed, misanthropic, cheap, drunken bag of garbage. And you may have noticed that I very seldom use profanity, so I can't describe her as well as I might.

PETER: You describe her... vividly.

JERRY: Well, thanks. Anyway, she has a dog, and I will tell you about the dog, and she and her dog are the gatekeepers of my dwelling. The woman is bad enough, she leans around in the entrance hall, spying to see that I don't bring in things or people, and when she's had her midafternoon pint of lemon-flavored gin she always stops me in the hall, and grabs ahold of my coat or my arm, and she presses her disgusting body up against me to keep me in a corner so she can talk to me. The smell of her body and her breath... you can't imagine it... and somewhere, some where in the back of that pea-sized brain of hers, an organ developed just enough to let her eat, drink, and emit, she has some foul parody of sexual desire. And I, Peter, I am the object of her sweaty lust.

PETER: That's disgusting. That's... horrible.

JERRY: But I have found a way to keep her off. When she talks to me, when she presses herself to my body and mumbles about her room and how I should come there, I merely say: but, Love; wasn't yesterday enough for you, and the day before? Then she puzzles, she makes slits of her tiny eyes, she sways a little, and then, Peter... and it is at this moment that I think I might be doing some good in that tormented house... a simple-minded smile begins to form on her unthinkable face, and she giggles and groans as she thinks about yesterday and the day before; as she believes and relives what never happened. Then, she motions to that black monster of a dog she has, and she goes back to her room. And I am safe until our next meeting.

PETER: It's so... unthinkable. I find it hard to believe that people such as that really are.

JERRY: (*Lightly mocking*) It's for reading about, isn't it?

PETER: (*Seriously*) Yes.

JERRY: And fact is better left to fiction, you're right, Peter. Well, what I have been meaning to tell you about is the dog; I shall, now.

PETER: (*Nervously*) Oh, yes; the dog.

JERRY: Don't go. You're not thinking of going, are you?

PETER: Well... no, I don't think so.

JERRY: (*As if to a child*) Because after I tell you about the dog, do you know what then? Then ... then I'll tell you about what happened at the zoo.

PETER: (*Laughing faintly*) You're... you're full of stories, aren't you?

JERRY: You don't have to listen. Nobody is holding you here; remember that. Keep that in your mind.

PETER: (*Irritably*) I know that.

JERRY: You do? Good. (*The following long speech, it seems to me, should be done with a great deal of action, to achieve a hypnotic effect on* PETER, *and on the audience, too. Some specific actions have been suggested, but the director and the actor playing* JERRY *might best work it out for themselves*) ALL RIGHT. (*As if reading from a huge billboard*) THE STORY OF JERRY AND THE DOG! (*Natural again*) What I am going to tell you has something to do with how sometimes it's necessary to go a long distance out of the way in order to come back a short distance correctly; or, maybe I only think that it has something to do with that. But, it's why I went to the zoo today, and why I walked north... northerly, rather... until I came here. All right. The dog, I think I told you, is a black monster of a best: an oversized head, tiny, tiny ears, and eyes... bloodshot, infected, maybe; and a body you can see the ribs through the skin. The dog is black, all black except for the bloodshot eyes, and... yes... and an open sore on its... right forepaw; that is red, too. And, oh yes; the poor monster, most always has an erection... of sorts. That's red, too. And... what else? ... oh, yes; there's a gray-yellow-white color, too, when he bares his fangs. Like this: Grrrrrrr! Which is what he did when he saw me for the first time... the day I moved in. I worried about that animal the very first minute I met him. Now, animals don't take to me like Saint Francis had birds hanging off him all the time. What I mean is: animals are indifferent to me... like people (*He smiles slightly*) ... most of the time. But this dog wasn't indifferent. From the very beginning he'd snarl and then go for me, to get one of my legs. Not like he was rabid, you know; he was sort of a stubbly dog, but he wasn't half-assed, either. It was a good, stumbly run; but I always got away, he got a piece of my trouser leg, look, you can see right here, where it's mended; he got that the second day I lived there; but, I kicked free and got upstairs fast, so that was that. (*Puzzles*) I still don't know to this day how the other roomers manage it, but you know what I think: I think it had to do only with me. Cozy. So. Anyway, this went on for over a week, whenever I came in; but never when I went out. That's funny. Or, it was funny, I could pack up and live in the street for all the dog cared. Well, I thought about it up in my room one day, one of the times after I'd bolted upstairs, and I made up my mind. I decided: First, I'll kill the dog with kindness,[316] and if that doesn't work... I'll just

---

316　**kill the dog with kindness**: harm the dog by being excessively kind.

kill him. (PETER *winces*) Don't react, Peter; just listen. So, the next day I went out and bought a bag of hamburgers, medium rare, no catsup, no onion; and on the way home I threw away all the rolls and kept just the meat. (*Action for the following*, *perhaps*) when I got back to the rooming-house the dog was waiting for me. I half opened the door that led into the entrance hall, and there he was; waiting for me. It figured. I went in, very cautiously, and I had the hamburgers, you remember; I opened the bag, and I set the meat down about twelve feet from where the dog was snarling at me. Like so! He snarled; stopped snarling; sniffed; moved slowly; then faster; then faster toward the meat. Well, when he got to it he stopped, and he looked at me. I smiled; but tentatively, you understand, he turned his face back to the hamburgers, smelled, sniffed some more, and then ... RRRAAAAGGGGG HHHH, like that... he tore into them. It was as if he had never eaten anything in his life before, except like garbage. Which might very well have been the truth. I don't think the landlady ever eats anything but garbage. But. he ate all the hamburgers, almost all at once, making sounds in his throat like a woman. Then, when he'd finished the meat, the hamburger, and tried to eat the paper, too, he sat down and smiled. I think he smiled; I know cats do. It was a very gratifying few moments, then, BAM, he snarled and made for me again. He didn't get me this time, either. So, I got upstairs, and I lay down on my bed and started to think about the dog again. To be truthful, I was offended, and I was damn mad, too. It was six perfectly good hamburgers with not enough pork in them to make it disgusting. I was of fended. But after a while, I decided try it for a few more days. If you think about it, this dog had what amounted to an antipathy toward me; really. And, I wondered if I mightn't overcome this antipathy. So, I tried it for five more days, but it was always the same: snarl, sniff: move; faster; stare; gobble; RAAGGGHHH; smile; snarl; BAM. Well, now; by this time Columbus Avenue was strewn with hamburger rolls and I was less offended than disgusted. So, I decided to kill the dog. (PETER *raises a hand in protest*) Oh, don't be so alarmed, peter; I didn't succeed. The day I tried to kill the dog I bought only one hamburger and what I thought was a murderous portion of rat poison. When I bought the hamburger I asked the man not to bother with the roll, all I wanted was the meat. I expected some reaction from him, like: we don't sell no hamburgers without rolls; or, wha'd'ya wanna do, eat it out'a ya han's?[317] But no; he smiled benignly, wrapped up the hamburger in waxed paper, and said: a bite for ya pussy-cat? I wanted to say: No, not really; it's part of a plan to poison a dog I know. But, you can't say "a dog I know" without sounding funny; so I said, a little too loud, I'm afraid, and too formally; YES, A BITE FOR MY PUSSY-CAT. People looked up. It always happens when I try to simplify things; people look up. But that's neither hither nor thither. So. On my way back to the rooming-house, I kneaded the hamburger and the rat poison together between my hands, at point feeling as much sadness as

---

317 **eat it out'a ya han's**: eat it out of your hands.

disgust. I opened the door to the entrance hall, and there the monster was, waiting to take the moment he took to smile before he went for me gave me time enough to get out of range. BUT, there he was; malevolence with an erection, waiting. I put the poison patty down, moved toward the stairs and watched. The poor animal gobbled the food down as usual, smiled, which made me almost sick, and then, BAM. But, I sprinted up the stairs, as usual, and the dog didn't get me, as usual. AND IT CAME TO PASS THAT THE BEAST WAS DEATHLY ILL. I knew this because he no longer attended me, and because the landlady sobered up. She stopped me in the hall the same evening of the attempted murder and confided the information that God had struck her puppy-dog a surely fatal blow. She had forgotten her bewildered lust, and her eyes were wide open for the first time. They looked like the dog's eyes. She sniveled and implored me to pray for the animal. I wanted to say to her: Madam, I have myself to pray for, the colored queen, the Puerto Rican family, the person in the front room whom I've never seen, the woman who cries deliberately behind her closed door, and the rest of the people in all rooming-houses, everywhere; besides, Madam, I don't understand how to pray. But... to simplify things... I told her I would pray. She looked up. She said that I was a liar, and that I probably wanted the dog to die. I told her, and there was so much truth here, that I didn't want the dog to die. I didn't, and not just because I'd poisoned him. I'm afraid that I must tell you I wanted the dog to live so that I could see what our new relationship might come to. (PETER *indicates his increasing displeasure and slowly growing antagonism*) Please understand, peter; that sort of thing is important. You must believe me; it is important. We have to know the effect of our actions. (*Another deep sigh*) Well, anyway; the dog recovered. I have no idea why, unless he was a descendant of the puppy that guarded the gates of hell or some such resort. I'm not up on my mythology. (*He pronounces the word myth-o-logy*) Are you? (PETER *sets to thinking, but* JERRY *goes on*) At any rate, and you've missed the eight-thousand-dollar question, peter; at any rate, the dog recovered his health and the landlady recovered her thirst, in no way altered by the bow-wow's deliverance. When I came home from a movie that was playing on Forty-second Street, a movie I'd seen, or one that was very much like one or several I'd seen, after the landlady told me pumpkins[318] was better, I was so hoping for the dog to be waiting for me. I was... well, how would you put it... enticed? ... fascinated? ... no, I don't think so... heart-shatteringly anxious, that's it; I was heart-shatteringly anxious to confront my friend again. (PETER *reacts scoffing*) Yes, Peter; friend. That's the only word for it. I was heart-shatteringly et cetera to confront my doggy friend again. I came in the door and advanced, unafraid, to the center of the entrance hall. The beast was there... looking at me. And, you know, he looked better for his scrape with the nevermind. I stopped; I looked at him; he looked at me. I think... I think we stayed a long time that way... still, stone-statue

[318] **pumpkins**: puppy kin; young dog.

... just looking at one another. I looked more into his face than he looked into mine. I mean, I can concentrate longer at looking into a dog's face than a dog can concentrate at looking into mine, or into anybody else's face, for that matter. But during that twenty seconds or two hours that we looked into each other's face, we made the dog now, and I wanted him to love me. I had tried to love, and I had tried to kill, and both had been unsuccessful by themselves. I hoped ... and I don't really know why I expected the dog to understand anything, much less my motivations... I hoped that the dog would understand. (PETER seems to be hypnotized) It's just... it's just that...(JERRY *is abnormally tense, now*)... it's just that if you can't deal with people, you have to make a start somewhere. WITH ANIMALS! (*Much faster now, and like a conspirator*) Don't you see? A person has to have some way of dealing with SOMETHING. If not with people... if not with people... SOMETHING... with a bed, with a cockroach, with a mirror... no, that's too hard, that's one of the last steps. With a cockroach, with a... with a... with a carper, a roll of toilet paper... no, not that, either... that's a mirror, too; always check bleeding. You see how hard it is to find things? With a street corner, and too many lights, all colors reflecting on he oily-wet streets... with a wisp of smoke, a wisp... of smoke... with... with pornographic playing cards, with a strongbox... WITHOUT A LOCK... with vomiting, with crying, with fury because the pretty little ladies aren't pretty little ladies, with making money with your body which is an act of love and I could prove it, with howling because you're alive; with God. How about that? WITH GOD WHO IS A COLORED QUEEN WHO WEARS A KIMONO AND PLUCKS HIS EYEBROWS, WHO IS A WOMAN WHO CRIES WITH DETERMINATION BEHIND HER CLOSED DOOR... with God who, I'm told, turned his back on the whole thing some time ago... with... some day, with people. (JERRY *sighs the next word heavily*) People. With an idea; a concept. And where better, where ever better in this humiliating excuse for a jail, where better to communicate one single, simple-minded idea than in an entrance hall? Where? It would be A START! Where better to make a beginning... to understand and just possibly be understood... a beginning of an understanding, than with... (*Here* JERRY *seems to fall into almost grotesque fatigue*)... than with A DOG. Just that; a dog. (*Here there is a silence that might be prolonged for a moment or so* ; *then* JERRY *wearily finishes his story*) A dog. It seemed like a perfectly sensible idea. Man is a dog's best friend, remember. So; the dog and I looked at each other. I longer than the dog. And what I saw then has been the same ever since. When ever the dog and I see each other we both stop where we are. We regard each other with a mixture of sadness and suspicion, and then we feign indifference. We walk past each other safely; we have an understanding. It's very sad, but you'll have to admit that it is an understanding. We had made many attempts at contact, and we had failed. The dog has returned to garbage, and I to solitary but free passage. I have not returned. I mean to say, I have gained solitary free passage, if that much further loss can be said to be gain. I have learned that neither kindness nor cruelty by themselves; independent of each other, creates any effect beyond themselves; and I have learned that the two combined, together, at the same time, are the teaching emotion. And what is gained is loss. And what has been the result: the dog and I have attained a compromise; more of bargain, really. We neither love nor hurt because we do not try to reach each other. And, was trying to feed the dog an act of love? If we can so misunderstand, well then, why have we invented the word love in the first place? (*There is silence.* JERRY *moves to* PETER's *bench and sits down beside him. This is the first time* JERRY *has sat down during the play*) the story of Jerry and the Dog; the end. (PETER *is silent*) Well, Peter? (JERRY *is suddenly cheerful*) Well, Peter? Do you think I could sell that story to the *Reader's Digest* and make a couple of hundred bucks for The Most Unforgettable Character I've Ever Met? Huh? (JERRY *is animated, but* PETER *is disturbed*) Oh, come on now, peter; tell me what you think.

PETER: (*Numb*) I... don't understand what... I don't think I...(*Now, almost tearfully*) why did you tell me all of this?...

JERRY: Why not?

PETER: I DON'T UNDERSTAND!

JERRY: (*Furious, but whispering*) That's a lie.

PETER: No. No, it's not.

JERRY: (*Quietly*) I tried to explain it to you as I went along. I went slowly; it all has to do with ...

PETER: I DON'T WANT TO HEAR ANY MORE. I don't understand you, or your landlady, or her dog...

JERRY: Her dog! I thought it was my... No. No, you're right. It is her dog! (*Looks at* PETER *intently, shaking his head*) I don't know what I was thinking about; of course you don't understand. (*In a monotone, wearily*) I don't live in your block; I'm not married to two parakeets, or whatever your setup is. I am a permanent transient, and my home is the sickening rooming houses on the West Side of New York City, which is the greatest city in the world. Amen.

PETER: I'm... I'm sorry; I didn't mean to...

JERRY: Forget it. I suppose you don't quite know what to make of me, eh?

PETER: (*A joke*) We get all kinds in publishing. (*Chuckles*)

JERRY: You're a funny man. (*He forces a laugh*) You know that? You're a very... a richly comic person...

PETER: (*Modestly, but amused*) Oh, now, not really. (*Still chuckling*)

JERRY: Peter, do I annoy you, or confuse you?

PETER: (*Lightly*) Well, I must confess that this wasn't the kind of afternoon I'd anticipated.

JERRY: You mean, I'm not the gentleman you were expecting.

PETER: I wasn't expecting anybody.

JERRY: No, I don't imagine you were. But I'm here, and I'm not leaving.

PETER: (*Consulting his watch*) Well, you may not be, but I must be getting home soon.

JERRY: Oh, come on; stay a while longer.

PETER: I really should get home; you see...

JERRY: (*Tickles* PETER'S *ribs with his fingers*) Oh, come on.

PETER: (*He is very ticklish*; as JERRY *continues to tickle him his voice becomes falsetto*) No, I... OHHHHH! Don't do that. Stop, Stop. Ohhh, no, no.

JERRY: Oh, come on.

PETER: (*As* JERRY *tickles*) Oh, hee, hee. I must go. I... hee, hee, hee. After all, stop stop, hee, hee, hee, after all, the parakeets will be getting dinner ready soon. Hee, hee. And the cats are setting the table. Stop, stop, and, and... (PETER *is beside himself now*) ... and we're having... hee, hee... uh... ho, ho, ho. (JERRY *stops tickling* PETER, *but the combination of the tickling and his own mad whimsy has* PETER *laughing almost hysterically. As his laughter continues, then subsides,* JERRY *watches him, with a curious fixed smile*)

JERRY: Peter?

PETER: Oh, ha, ha, ha, ha. What? What?

JERRY: Listen, now.

PETER: Oh, ho, ho. What... what is it, Jerry? Oh, my.

JERRY: (*Mysteriously*) Peter, do you want to know what happened at the zoo?

PETER: Ah, ha, ha. The what? Oh, yes; the zoo, Oh, ho, ho. Well, I had my own zoo there for a moment with... hee, hee, the parakeets getting dinner ready, and the... ha, ha, whatever it was, the...

JERRY: (*Calmly*) Yes, that was very funny, Peter. I wouldn't have expected it. But do you want to hear about what happened at the zoo, or not?

PETER: Yes. Yes, by all means; tell me what happened at the zoo. Oh, my. I don't know what happened to me.

JERRY: Now I'll let you in on what happened at the zoo; but first, I should tell you why I went to the zoo. I went to the zoo to find out more about the way people exist with animals, and the way animals exist with each other, and with people too. It probably wasn't a fair test, what with everyone separated by bars from everyone else, the animals for the most part from each other, and always the people from the animals. But, if it's a zoo, that's the way it is. (*He pokes* PETER *on the arm*) Move over.

PETER: (*Friendly*) I'm sorry, haven't you enough room? (*He shifts a little*)

JERRY: (*Smiling slightly*) Well, all the animals are there, and all the people are there, and it's Sunday and all the children are there. (*He pokes* PETER *again*) Move over.

PETER: (*Patiently, still friendly*) All right. (*He moves some more, and* JERRY *has all the room he might need*)

JERRY: And it's a hot day, so all the stench is there, too, and all the balloon sellers, and all the ice cream sellers, and all the seals are barking, and all the birds are screaming. (*Pokes*

PETER *harder*) Move over!

PETER：(*Beginning to be annoyed*) look here, you have more than enough room! (*But he moves more, and is now fairly cramped at one end of the bench*)

JERRY：And I am there, and it's feeding time at the lions' house, and the lion keeper comes into the lion cage, one of the lion cages, to feed one of the lions. (*Punches* PETER *on the arm, hard*) MOVE OVER!

PETER：(*Very annoyed*) I can't move over any more, and stop hitting me. What's the matter with you?

JERRY：Do you want to hear the story? (*Punches* PETER'S *arm again*)

PETER：(*Flabbergasted*) I'm not so sure! I certainly don't want to be punched in the arm.

JERRY：(*Punches* PETER'S *arm again*) Like that?

PETER：Stop it! What's the matter with you?

JERRY：I'm crazy, you bastard.

PETER：that isn't funny.

JERRY：Listen to me, Peter. I want this bench. You go sit on the bench over there, and if you're good I'll tell you are rest of the story.

PETER：(*Flustered*) But... whatever for? What is the matter with you? Besides, I see no reason why I should give up this bench. I sit on this bench almost every Sunday afternoon, in good weather. It's secluded here; there's never anyone sitting here, so I have it all to myself.

JERRY：(*Softly*) Get off this bench, Peter; I want it.

PETER：(*Almost whining*) No.

JERRY：I said I want this bench, and I'm going to have it. Now get over there.

PETER：People can't have everything they want. You should know that; it's a rule; people can have some of the things they want, but they can't have everything.

JERRY：(*Laughs*) Imbecile! You're slow-witted!

PETER：Stop that!

JERRY：You're a vegetable! Go lie down on the ground.

PETER：(*Intense*) Now you listen to me. I've put up with you all afternoon.

JERRY：Not really.

PETER：LONG ENOUGH. I've put up with you long enough. I've listened to you because you seemed... well, because I thought you wanted to talk to somebody.

JERRY：You put things well; economically, and, yet... oh, what is the word I want to put justice to your... JESUS, you make me sick... get off here and give me my bench.

PETER：MY BENCH!

JERRY：(*Pushes* PETER *almost, but not quite, off the bench*) Get out of my sight.

PETER：(*Regaining his position*) God da... mn you. That's enough! I've had enough of you. I will not give up this bench; you can't nave it, and that's that. Now, god away. (JERRY *snorts but does not move*) GO away, I said. (JERRY *does not move*) Get away from here. If you don't move on... you're a bum... that's what you are... If you don't move on, I'll get a policeman here and make you go. (JERRY *laughs*, *stays*) I warn you, I'll call a policeman.

JERRY: (*Softly*) You won't find a policeman around here; they're all over on the west side of the park chasing fairies down from trees or out of the bushes. That's all they do. That's their function. So scream your head off; it won't do you any good.

PETER: You look ridiculous: a grown man screaming for the police on a bright Sunday afternoon in the park with nobody harming you. If a policeman did fill his quota and come sledging over this way he'd probably take you in as a nut.

PETER: (*With disgust and impotence*) Great God, I just came here to read, and now you want me to give up the bench. You're mad.

JERRY: Hey, I got news for you, as they say. I'm on your precious bench, and you're never going to have it for yourself again.

PETER: (*Furious*) Look, you; get off my bench. I don't care if it makes any sense or not. I want this bench to myself; I want you OFF IT!

JERRY: (*Mocking*) Aw... look who's mad.

PETER: GET OUT!

JERRY: No.

PETER: I WARN YOU!

JERRY: Do you know how ridiculous you look now?

PETER: (*His fury and self-consciousness have possessed him*) It doesn't matter. (*He is almost crying*) GET AWAY FROM MY BENCH!

JERRY: Why? You have everything in the world you want; you've told me about your home, and your family, and your own little zoo. You have everything, and now you want this bench. Are these the things men fight for? Tell me, Peter, is this bench, this iron and this wood, is this your honor? Is this the thing in the world you'd fight for? Can you think of anything more absurd?

PETER: Absurd? Look, I'm not going to talk to you about honor, or even try to explain it to you. Besides, it isn't a question of honor; but even if it were, you wouldn't understand.

JERRY: (*Contemptuously*) You don't even know what you're saying, do you? This is probably the first time in your life you've had anything more trying to face than changing your cats' toilet box. Stupid! Don't you have any idea, not even the slightest, what other people need?

PETER: Oh, boy, listen to you; well, you don't need this bench. That's sure.

JERRY: Yes; yes, I do.

PETER: (*Quivering*) I've come here for years; I have hours of great pleasure, great satisfaction, right here. And that's important to a man. I'm a responsible person, and I'm a GROWNUP. This is my bench, and you have no right to take it away from me.

JERRY: Fight for it, then. Defend yourself; defend your bench.

PETER: You've pushed me to it. Get up and fight.

JERRY: Like a man?

PETER: (*Still angry*) Yes, like a man, if you insist on mocking me even further.

JERRY: I'll have to give you credit for one thing; you are a vegetable, and a slightly nearsighted one, I think...

PETER: THAT'S ENOUGH...

JERRY: ... but, you know, as they say on TV all the time you know and I mean this, Peter, you have a certain dignity; it surprises me...

PETER: STOP!

JERRY: (*Rises lazily*) Very well, Peter, we'll battle for the bench, but we're not evenly matched. (*He takes out and clicks open an ugly looking knife*)

PETER: (*Suddenly awakening to the reality of the situation*) You are mad! You're stark raving mad! YOU'RE GOING TO KILL ME! (*But before* PETER *has time to think what to do,* JERRY *tosses the knife at* PETER'S *feet*)

JERRY: There you go. Pick it up. You have the knife and we'll be more evenly matched.

PETER: (*Horrified*) No!

JERRY: (*Rushes over to* PETER, *grabs him by the collar*; PETER *rises*; *their faces almost touch*) Now you pick up that knife and you fight with me. You fight for your self-respect; you fight for that goddamned bench.

PETER: (*Struggling*) No! Let... let go of me! He... Help!

JERRY: (*Slaps* PETER *on each "fight"*) You fight, you miserable bastard; fight for that bench; fight for your parakeets; fight for your cats; fight for your two daughters; fight for your wife; fight for your manhood, you pathetic little vegetable. (*Spits in* PETER'S *face*) You couldn't even get your wife with a male child.

PETER: (*Breaks away, enraged*) It's a matter of genetics, not manhood, you... you monster. (*He darts down, picks up the knife and backs off a little*; *he is breathing heavily*) I'll give you one last chance; get out of here and leave me alone! (*He holds the knife with a firm arm, but far in front of him, not to attack, but to defend*)

JERRY: (*Sighs heavily*) So be it! (*With a rush he charges* Peter *and impales himself on the knife. Tableau*: *For just a moment, complete silence,* JERRY *impaled on the knife at the end of* PETER's *still firm arm. Then* PETER *screams, pulls away, leaving the knife in* JERRY. JERRY *is motionless, on point. Then he too, screams, and it must be the sound of an if furcated and fatally wounded animal. With the knife in him, he stumbles back to the bench that* PETER *had vacated. He crumbles there, sitting, facing* PETER, *his eyes wide in agony, his mouth open*)

PETER: (*Whispering*) Oh my God, oh my God, oh my God...(*He repeats these words many times, very rapidly*)

JERRY: (JERRY *is dying*; *but now his expression seems to change. His features relax, and while* *his voice varies, sometimes wrenched with pain, for the most part he seems removed from his dying. He smiles*) Thank you, Peter. I mean that, now; thank you very much. (PETER's *mouth drops open. He cannot move; he is transfixed*) Oh, Peter, I was so afraid I'd drive you away. (*He laughs as best he can*) You don't know how afraid I was you'd go away and leave me. And now I'll tell you what happened at the zoo. I think... I think this is what happened at the zoo... I think. I think that while I was at the zoo I decided that I would walk north... northerly, rather... until I found you... or somebody... and I decided that I would talk to you ... I would tell you things... and things that I would tell you would... Well, here we are. You see? Here we are. But... I don't know... could I have planned all this? No... no, I couldn't have. But I think I did. And now I've told you what you wanted to know, haven't I? And now you know all about what happened at the zoo. And now you know what you'll see in your TV, and the face I told you about... you remember... the face I told you about... my face, the face you see right now. Peter... Peter? ... Peter... thank you. I came unto you (*He laughs, so faintly*) and you have comforted me. Dear Peter.

PETER: (*Almost fainting*) Oh my God!

JERRY: You'd better go now. Somebody might come by, and you don't want to be here when anyone comes.

PETER: (*Does not move, but begins to weep*) Oh my God, on my God.

JERRY: (*Most faintly, now; he is very near death*) You won't be coming back here any more, Peter; you've been dispossessed. You've lost your bench, but you've not really a vegetable; it's all right, you're an animal. You're an animal, too. But you'd better hurry now, Peter. Hurry, you'd better go... see? (JERRY *takes a handkerchief finger prints*) Hurry away, Peter. (PETER *begins to stagger away*) Wait... wait, Peter. Take your book... book. Right here... beside me...on your bench... my bench, rather. Come... take your book. (PETER *starts for the book, but retreats*) Hurry... Peter. (PETER *rushes to the bench, grabs the book, retreats*) Very good, Peter... very good. Now... hurry away. (PETER *hesitates for a moment, then flees, stage-left*) Hurry away... (*His eyes are closed now*) Hurry away, your parakeets are making the dinner... the cats... are setting the table...

PETER: (*Off stage*) (*A pitiful howl*) OH MY GOD!

JERRY: (*His eyes still closed, he shakes his head and speaks; a combination of scornful mimicry and supplication*) Oh... my... God. (*He is dead.*)

CURTAIN

■ Study Questions

1. What does Jerry's story about the dog mean?

2. Why does Jerry usurp Peter's bench?

3. What do Jerry's comments on his family background, and his dead parents in particular, reveal about his character?

4. What is the significance of the props associated with each character: Harry's knife and Peter's book?

5. What is your reaction to the end of the play? Does Peter release Jerry from his hell at the end?

6. What is the significance of the title of this play? Does the play suggest that human beings are like caged and isolated animals in any way? Can Peter be said to live in a metaphorical zoo?

7. What are the parodies of sexuality associated with Jerry and how do they compare with the sexual and domestic realities of Peter's life?

8. Can Jerry and Peter be seen as two sides of the same coin, representing different manifestations of sterility in modern society?

9. How does the play suggest that animalistic violence lies beneath a thin veneer of civilization in modern society?

10. How does the blend of realism and symbolism in this play compare with "*The Glass Menagerie*" and "*The School*"? Look carefully for symbolic details throughout the play.

11. What mythological and Biblical parallels are suggested by Jerry's language as he describes his life (and by Peter's name)? Several critics have viewed Jerry as a Christ figure, a Christ parody, and a Jeremiah who denounces false gods. What do you think of these interpretations?

LITERARY FOCUS

Theatre of the Absurd

The Theatre of the Absurd is a designation for particular plays of absurdist fiction written by a number of primarily European playwrights in the late 1960s, as well as one for the style of theatre which has evolved from their work. Their work express the belief that human existence has no meaning or purpose and therefore all communication breaks down. Logical construction and argument gives way to irrational and illogical speech and to its ultimate conclusion, silence.

Critic Martin Esslin coins the term "Theatre of the Absurd" in his 1960 essay and, later, book of the same name. He relates these plays based on a broad theme of the Absurd, similar to the way Albert Camus uses the term in his 1942 essay, *The Myth of Sisyphus*. The Absurd in these plays takes the form of man's reaction to a world apparently without meaning, and/or man as a puppet controlled or menaced by invisible outside forces. Though the term is applied to a wide range of plays, some characteristics coincide in many of the plays: broad comedy mixed with horrific or tragic images; characters caught in hopeless situations forced to do repetitive or meaningless actions; dialogue full of clichés, wordplay, and nonsense; plots that are cyclical or absurdly expansive; either a parody or dismissal of realism and the concept of the "well-made play".

The Theatre of the Absurd is commonly associated with Existentialism, and Existentialism was an influential philosophy in Paris during the rise of the Theatre of the Absurd; however, to call it Existentialist theatre is problematic for many reasons. It gained this association partly because it was named (by Esslin) after the concept of "absurdism" advocated by Albert Camus, a philosopher commonly called Existentialist though he frequently resisted that label. Absurdism is most accurately called Existentialist in the way Franz Kafka's work is labeled Existentialist : it embodies an aspect of the philosophy though the writer may not be a committed follower.

Many of the Absurdists were contemporaries with Jean-Paul Sartre, the philosophical spokesman for Existentialism in Paris, but few Absurdists actually committed to Sartre's own Existentialist philosophy, as expressed in *Being and Nothingness*, and many of the Absurdists had a complicated relationship with him. In comparison to Sartre's concepts of the function of literature, for example, the primary focus of the best-known absurdist Samuel Beckett was on the *failure* of man to overcome "absurdity"; as James Knowlson asserts, Beckett's work focuses "on poverty, failure, exile and loss— as he put it, on man as a 'non-knower' and as a 'non-can-er'." Beckett himself once said, though he liked *Nausea*, he generally found the writing style of Sartre and Heidegger to be "too philosophical" and he considered himself "not a philosopher".

The absurdist plays are absurd in that they focus not on logical acts, realistic occurrences, or traditional character development; they, instead, focus on human beings trapped in an incomprehensible world subject to any occurrence, no matter how illogical. The theme of incomprehensibility is coupled with the inadequacy of language to form meaningful human connections. According to Martin Esslin, Absurdism is "the inevitable devaluation of ideals, purity, and purpose". Absurdist drama asks its viewer to "draw his own conclusions, make his own errors". Though Theatre of the Absurd may be seen as nonsense, "they have something to say and can be understood". Esslin makes a distinction between the dictionary definition of absurd ("out of harmony" in the musical sense) and drama's understanding of the Absurd, "Absurd is that which is devoid of purpose... Cut off from his religious, metaphysical, and transcendental roots, man is lost; all his actions become senseless, absurd, (and) useless."

The characters in Absurdist drama are lost and floating in an incomprehensible universe and they abandon rational devices and discursive thought because these approaches are inadequate. Many characters appear as automatons stuck in routines speaking only in cliché. Characters are frequently stereotypical, archetypal, or flat character types. The more complex characters are in crisis because the world around them is incomprehensible.

The plots of many Absurdist plays feature characters in interdependent pairs, commonly either two males or a male and a female. Some Beckett scholars call this the "pseudocouple". The two characters may be roughly equal or have a begrudging interdependence (like Vladamir and Estragon in *Waiting for Godot*); one character may be clearly dominant and may torture the passive character (like Pozzo and Lucky in *Waiting for Godot*); the relationship of the characters may shift dramatically throughout the play (as in many of Albee's plays).

Despite its reputation for nonsense language, much of the dialogue in Absurdist plays is naturalistic. The moments when characters resort to nonsense language or clichés—when words appear to have lost their denotative function, thus creating misunderstanding among the characters, making the Theatre of the Absurd distinctive. Language frequently gains a certain phonetic, rhythmical, almost musical quality, opening up a wide range of often comedic playfulness. Much of the dialogue in Absurdist drama (especially in Beckett's and Albee's plays, for example) reflects a kind of evasiveness and inability to make a connection. When language that is apparently nonsensical appears, it also demonstrates this disconnection.

■ Thinking about Theatre of the Absurd

- What is the meaning of a play of the Absurd in which "man is lost; all his actions become senseless, absurd, and useless"? What characteristics have made "The Zoo Story" a play of the Theatre of the Absurd? Please take into consideration its theoretical basis, theme, characterization, plot, and language.

READING FOR APPRECIATION

The Aural Imagination

Literature begins with a human voice speaking. Earlier in this course book we talked about the sound of prose and the sound of poetry, to remind ourselves of the importance—and the pleasure—of hearing literature. The selections in this unit remind us once again how essential it is to hear not only the speakers of nonfiction and the songs of poets but also the variety of characters in fiction and drama.

Just as we heard the emotion in Abraham Lincoln's "Gettysburg Address", so we can hear the solemnness and anxiety in Soul Bellow's "Nobel Prize Acceptance Speech". When we read the speech, can we hear the speech exactly as he once delivered it? No, because only a sound device like a tape recorder or a disc player would indicate his pauses and emphases. Still we can hear in our minds a reasonable version of the sound of that speech. We can hear the grave, formal, Jewish American way of talking. We can hear the starts and stops, the parenthetical explanations, the anxious thoughts, of a formal speech:

> It is as a novelist that I am considering the extreme moral sensitivity of our contemporaries, their desire
> for perfection, their intolerance of the defects of society, the touching, the comical boundlessness of their
> demands, their anxiety, their irritability, their sensitivity, their tender-mindedness, their goodness, their
> convulsiveness, the recklessness with which they experiment with drugs and touch-therapies and bombs...

In spite of its serious purpose, this colloquial writing—an essay actually used as a public speech—is still easy to hear. It comes alive because we read it with an aural imagination, imagining an actual person talking.

In poetry too, of course, we listen for the music of the poem or the special tone of the poet. In Robert Penn Warren's "Audubon: A Vision" we give a poetic sound to a historical figure's self-assertion because of the poet's deliberate rearrangement of the original words:

> He walked in the world. Knew the lust of the eye.
> Wrote: "Ever since a Boy I have had an astonishing desire

> to see Much of the World and particularly
>
> to acquire a true knowledge of the Birds of North America. "

The poem is serious; it sounds bitter and grief at the destruction brought by human beings to the nature, yet it sounds soft and tender when it points to the unspoiled natural scenes (At dusk he stood on a bluff, and the bellowing of buffalo / Was like distant ocean. He saw/Bones whiten the plain in the hot daylight). Through our aural imaginations, we become, for a few moments, "the Noble Fellow looked at his Enemies / with a Contemptible Eye. "

Fiction writing makes a different kind of demand on our aural imagination. In fiction we want to hear the voice of imaginary characters, sometimes a great number of them, talking at once, having conversations, responding to each other. In John Updike's "A & P," for example, the dialogue of the characters asks us to imagine the emotions and feelings underlying the tone. We want to hear the dispute in the voices during the following dramatic exchange between the narrator who intends to be kind to his customers (and some beautiful young ladies in particular) and Lengel who has been disturbed by the young ladies who are not dressing "decently" :

"Did you say something, Sammy?"

"I said I quit. "

"I thought you did. "

"You didn't have to embarrass them. "

"It was they who were embarrassing us. "

How would you sound Peter's and Jerry's final words in Edward Albee's *The Zoo Story*? Their final words are the same, but the sound and the tone are totally different. Peter's "OH MY GOD" makes a "pitiful howl"; Jerry's "Oh... my... God" sounds extremely weak as he has been stabbed and is dying, but it is much more complicated and meaningful as the expression carries more implications.

Each of these works of fiction and drama—in fact, any story or play you will ever read—calls your aural imagination into action. It is through this use of your imagination that you, along with the writers you read, create the characters of fiction and drama.

VOICE OF THE AGE

Questions

The writers of our time are questioners. In the poetry, fiction, and nonfiction they ask who we are and who we are becoming. They ask what we should be doing and why we should do it. They wonder how we can become the heroes of our own lives.

The writers of our time ask questions about our identity, about our relationships with one another and with the natural world, about how we are trying to express ourselves. They know that only by asking questions can people begin to answer them.

Robert Hayden: *What did I know, what did I know / Of love's austere and lonely offices*! ("Those Winter Sundays")

John Ashbery: *What's a plain level? It is that and other things, / Bringing a system of them into play. Play?* ("Paradoxes and Oxymorons")

Olga Cabral: *Does the Twentieth Century make sense at all?* ("Help")

Bellow: *What is at the center now?*

Albee: *Are these the things men fight for? Tell me, Peter, is this bench, this iron and this wood, is this your honor? Is this the thing in the world you'd fight for? Can you think of anything more absurd?*

Throughout American literature the great artists have asked the most serious questions, and the greatest have achieved some answers. For the Puritans, the answer lay in a profound religious vision. For Emerson, the answer was a transcendental oneness with the universe. For Whitman, only a constant celebration of life was an adequate response. For Dickinson, intense personal commitment tempered with a cool sense of irony provided the greatest satisfaction. For Faulkner, a mythological world threw a light on reality. For Stevens, the power of the human imagination held the key.

There is no doubt that the American writers will continue to ask questions and continue to offer answers about living. It is for this reason that we will continue to read them, need them, and love them.

BIBLIOGRAPHY

Baym, Nina, et al. *The Norton Anthology of American Literature.* New York & London: W. W. Norton & Company, 1995.

Brooks, Cleanth, and Robert Penn Warren. *Understanding Fiction.* Beijing: Foreign Language Teaching and Research Press & Pearson Education, 2004.

Brooks, Cleanth, and Robert Penn Warren. *Understanding Poetry.* Beijing: Foreign Language Teaching and Research Press & Pearson Education, 2004.

Brooks, Cleanth, R. W. B. Lewis, and Robert Penn Warren. *American Literature: The Makers and the Making.* New York: St. Martin's Press, 1974.

Cunliffe, Marcus. *The Literature of the United States.* Brighton: Penguin Books, 1970.

Elliott, Emory, general ed. *The Columbia History of the American Novel.* Beijing: Foreign Language Teaching and Research Press & Columbia University Press, 2005.

Hawthorn, Jeremy. *Studying the Novel.* London: Hoddor Arnold, 2005.

Kearns, George. *American Literature.* Mission Hills, California: Glencoe Publishing Company, 1984.

Leitch, Vincent B. , general ed. *The Norton Anthology of Theory and Criticism.* New York & London: W. W. Norton & Company, 2001.

Lentricchia, Frank, and Andrew DuBois. *Close Reading*: A Reader. Durham and London: Duke University Press, 2003.

McDonald, Gail. *American Literature and Culture* 1900—1960. Oxford: Blackwell Publishing Ltd. , 2007.

Parini, Jay, and Brett C. Millier. *The Columbia History of the American Poetry.* Beijing: Foreign Language Teaching and Research Press & Columbia University Press, 2005.

Pizer, Donald. *The Cambridge Companion to American Realism and Naturalism.* Cambridge: Cambridge UP, 1995.

Rivkin, Julie, and Michael Ryan. Literary Theory: An Anthology. Oxford: Blackwell Publishing Ltd. , 2004.

Toff, Nancy, editor-in-chief. *Modern Critical Views* (series). Philadelphia: Chelsea House Publishers, 1999.

Wallis, Mick, and Simon Shepherd. *Studying Plays.* London: Hoddor Arnold, 1998.

Ward, Geoff. *The Writing of America: Literature and Cultural Identity from the Puritans to the Present.* Cambridge: Polity, 2002.

Weinstein, Philip M. *The Cambridge Companion to William Faulkner.* Cambridge: Cambridge UP, 1995. [1]

---

[1] *The Cambridge Companion* is a series of essay-collections concerning various aspects and writers of American and English literature. Among the collections, all those on American literature (only two are listed above) are important references to this course book.